LAST OF THE FREE

BY THE SAME AUTHOR

The Making of the Crofting Community

Skye: The Island

For the People's Cause: From the Writings of John Murdoch

The Claim of Crofting: The Scottish Highlands and Islands, 1930–90

Scottish Highlanders: A People and their Place

A Dance Called America: The Scottish Highlands, the United States and Canada

On the Other Side of Sorrow: Nature and People in the Scottish Highlands

Glencoe and the Indians

LAST OF THE FREE

A Millennial History of the Highlands and Islands of Scotland

JAMES HUNTER

EDINBURGH AND LONDON

First published in Great Britain in 1999 by
MAINSTREAM PUBLISHING COMPANY (EDINBURGH) LTD
7 Albany Street
Edinburgh EH1 3UG

ISBN 1 84018 376 4

This edition 2000

A catalogue record for this book is available from the British Library

Maps by Wendy Price Cartographic Services
Typeset in Stone Serif
Printed and bound in Great Britain by
Creative Print and Design Wales

Contents

For Evelyn again

Foreword

The Highlands and Islands comprise half of Scotland and one-sixth of Britain. Clearly, such an area should not be accepted as a drain on the nation's economy and social vitality, but rather encouraged to realise its potential as a worthwhile contributor to our nation's economic, social and environmental wellbeing.

It was in early 1997 that Highlands and Islands Enterprise decided to help mark the new millennium by assisting Mainstream Publishing to commission from James Hunter a history of the area. As a development agency, HIE's key concerns are with the present and the future. However, examination of the past also reveals events and influences that have shaped this most fascinating and beautiful region.

HIE exercised no editorial control of Jim's work in producing this uniquely comprehensive and stimulating account. But we asked him to ensure that his book dealt, as far as possible and in a way that no previous history has done, with all the different parts of the Highlands and Islands. If Jim's conclusions served to provoke debate about the area's experience and its future, we added, that would be no bad thing. Jim has, I think, met this remit in full.

When, in October 1998, the Secretary of State for Scotland appointed Jim Hunter to head the board of HIE, we gained a chairman with immense knowledge of the Highlands and Islands. Jim's appointment, of course, also resulted in this history becoming more of an 'in-house' production than anyone had envisaged the year before.

However, having read the results of Jim Hunter's extensive research, I am glad there was nothing which prevented us from being involved in this project. Jim's book, I believe, is a momentous contribution to the chronicling of the Highlands and Islands. All of us at HIE are proud to be associated with it, and I take pleasure in commending it.

Iain A. Robertson CBE, Chief Executive,
Highlands and Islands Enterprise

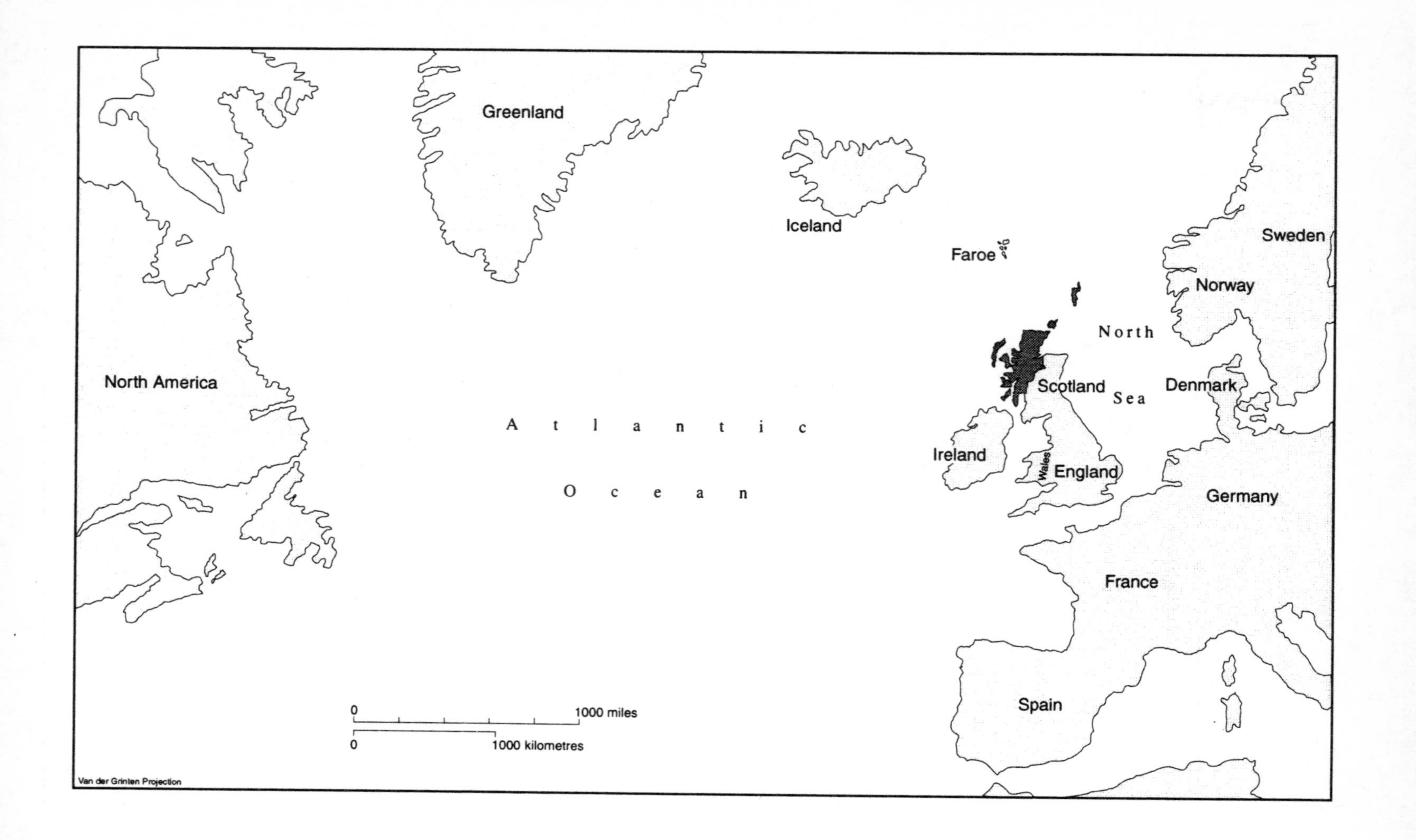
Greenland
Iceland
Faroe
Sweden
Norway
North
Sea
North America
Scotland
Denmark
Atlantic
Ocean
Ireland
Wales
England
Germany
France
Spain
0
1000 miles
0
1000 kilometres
Van der Grinten Projection

Unst
Yell
Sullom Voe
Shetland Islands
Mainland
Scalloway
Lerwick
Mousa
Sumburgh
Fair Isle
Westray
Egilsay
Gairsay
Orkney Islands
Skara Brae
Mainland
Stromness
Kirkwall
Dounreay
Thurso
Reay
Halkirk
Wick
Caithness
Strathnaver
Strath of Kildonan
Sutherland
Helmsdale
Dunrobin
Dornoch
Dornoch Firth
Moray Firth
Assynt
Ullapool
Western Isles
Carloway
Calanais
Lewis
Harris
Stornoway
North Uist
Benbecula
South Uist
Barra
Strathrusdale
Easter Ross
Nigg
Alness
Invergordon
Dingwall
Black Isle
Nairn
Forres
Elgin
Fort George
Wester Ross
INVERNESS
Culloden
Lochindorb
Grantown on Spey
Harlaw
ABERDEEN
Glendale
Dunvegan
Orbost
Portree
Raasay
Braes
Skye
Kyle of Lochalsh
Glenelg
Great Glen
Aviemore
Rothiemurchus
Badenoch
Sabhal Mor Ostaig
Armadale
Knoydart
Glengarry
Rum
Eigg
Lochaber
Achnacarry
Inverlochy
Fort William
Moidart
Hebrides
Strontian
Ballachulish
Glencoe
Killiecrankie
Tobermory
Morvern
Duror
Dunkeld
Ardtornish
Scone
PERTH
Crieff
Tiree
Mull
Oban
Iona
Argyll
Inveraray
Dunadd
Colonsay
Lochgilphead
Falkirk
EDINBURGH
GLASGOW
Finlagan
Islay
Largs
Kintyre
Arran
Campbeltown
Historic, or other, site
Battle site
0 30mls
0 40 kms

Introduction

A couple of months into 1979, the newspaper then paying my wages sent me to Sutherland. There, while looking into the story that had brought me north, I met an elderly crofter with whom, after disposing of the business in hand, I began to speak of more general matters. Our talk turned to plans, shortly afterwards voted on, to devolve political power from London to Edinburgh. I favoured such devolution. And because my new acquaintance had made several suggestions as to how Highlands and Islands prospects could be improved, I took it for granted – thinking the cause of the Highlands and Islands could only benefit from a measure of Scottish home rule – that he shared my devolutionary enthusiasms. But no. The Highlands and Islands, I was informed sternly, would gain little from Scotland's projected legislature.

'Why?' I asked.

'In London,' came the reply, 'they might not give a damn about folk up here. But in Edinburgh they've always hated us.'

In the event, no Edinburgh parliament was forthcoming in 1979. Twenty years on, however, not long before this book's publication, just such a parliament, the first since 1707, at last took shape. What members of this parliament will do for residents of the Highlands and Islands remains, at the time of writing, to be seen. But they will, I trust, view us more positively than our ancestors were viewed by their pre-1707 forerunners – whose treatment of the Highlands and Islands was such as to explain why my Sutherland informant, a man who knew his history, thought the way he did.

My own pro-devolutionary sentiments, I should make clear, have not altered. For what it is worth, I have backed, for as long as I have been politically aware, a greater degree of self-government for Scotland. I still do. But what I nowadays question more than I did – which is why I began with my Sutherland encounter of all those years ago –

is the notion that such self-government will, of itself, enhance the prospects of those of us living in the Highlands and Islands. Back in 1979, on being told that a possibly neglectful London was preferable – from a Highlands and Islands perspective – to an allegedly antagonistic Edinburgh, I came unhesitatingly to Edinburgh's defence. Today, if asked to choose between the two, I would be tempted to opt, as it were, for neither. Perhaps, I would be inclined to suggest, the people of the Highlands and Islands should be looking rather less to both Edinburgh and London. Maybe, I might want to add, we should be seeking to exercise more control, from within our own area, over matters of Highlands and Islands significance. Our predecessors, after all, once exercised exactly that type of control. And when they did, as this book shows, our corner of the world performed, in relation to comparable localities, rather more impressively than it has done since.

When, in 83AD, the Roman Empire's legions approached the area we know as the Highlands and Islands, Rome's forces were opposed, as ensuing pages explain, by a warrior chieftain named Calgacus. Words attributed to that chieftain, by one of his contemporaries, supply this book's title. The Romans, Calgacus is supposed to have said, were tyrants, pillagers, oppressors:

> A rich enemy excites their cupidity; a poor one, their lust for power. East and West alike have failed to satisfy them. They are the only people on earth to whose covetousness both riches and poverty are equally tempting. To robbery, butchery and rapine, they give the lying name of 'government'; they create a desolation and call it peace.[1]

In all of Britain, Calgacus reportedly told his followers, only they had managed to evade Rome's grip:

> We, the most distant dwellers upon earth, the last of the free, have been shielded till today by our very remoteness and by the obscurity in which it has shrouded our name.[2]

The liberty of which Calgacus spoke, of course, was not liberty in the twenty-first-century sense of the term. Both democracy and its associated human rights were every bit as lacking among Calgacus's folk as they were lacking among the generality of Rome's subjects. But the first-century Highlands and Islands were nevertheless free to the extent that the region, before 83AD, had not been subject to external domination. Nor was the Roman Empire's incursion into the area – an incursion which lasted only for a year or two – to change this situation fundamentally. Much was to alter in the Highlands and Islands in the course of the Christian era's first millennium. The society of which Calgacus was part evolved into the various kingdoms of the Picts. Entirely new groupings – first the Gaels, then the Vikings – put in an appearance. One set of political structures, as a result, more than once gave way to others. But every such structure – irrespective of who controlled it – was rooted, or quickly became rooted, in the Highlands and Islands. The region continued to possess, as it had probably possessed for thousands of years, its own power centres. It remained, in Calgacus's sense, free.

During the opening centuries of the second millennium, however, this freedom was gradually, but inexorably, lost. That happened because of the expansion into the Highlands and Islands of the medieval Scottish state – a state whose rulers were committed to eradicating both Highlands and Islands autonomy and all those other features, whether social, cultural or linguistic, which differentiated the region from localities closer to Scotland's Edinburgh-centred heartland. The Highlands and Islands casualties of this assimilationist policy included, in succession, the Kingdom of Moray, the Earldom of Orkney, the Lordship of the Isles and the various clans in which, even when they were formally part of Scotland, our area's inhabitants – or a large proportion of them – vested much of what remained of their previous distinctiveness. Clanship, admittedly, was not finally destroyed until London, to revert to the terminology of my opening paragraphs, replaced Edinburgh; until, in other words, Scotland itself merged with England to form, in 1707, the United Kingdom. Hence my reluctance to assent, in 1979, to the proposition that British rule, in a Highlands and Islands context, has proved itself superior to the Scottish rule it replaced. Prior to the closing decades of the nineteenth century, it seems to me, United Kingdom governments treated the Highlands and Islands in much the same way as those governments' Edinburgh precursors had done. Indeed the integration of the Highlands and Islands into the wider area to the south was never more total than in the late eighteenth and early nineteenth centuries. Nor were the people of the Highlands and Islands ever more vulnerable to externally directed manipulation than was the case at that time – a time which witnessed, among other tragedies, the Highland Clearances.

There is nothing accidental, this book maintains, about the clearances – the absolute nadir of the entire Highlands and Islands experience – having occurred when inhabitants of the Highlands and Islands were more bereft than at any other point in their history of the means to shape their own destiny. Nor is there anything fortuitous, this book also maintains, about the more recent upturn in Highlands and Islands prospects – an upturn evident in economic and other gains – having coincided with a period, commencing towards the nineteenth century's close, when United Kingdom politicians have at last conceded that the Highlands and Islands are sufficiently unique to require institutions, and even laws, of their own.

This book's central thesis, then, is to be found in the linkage it makes between Highlands and Islands autonomy and Highlands and Islands success. When our autonomy was complete, we were capable – through centres like Iona's seventh-century monastery and through institutions like Orkney's eleventh-century earldom – of exercising influence on a Europe-wide basis. Even when our autonomy was only partial, as in the time of the late-medieval Lordship of the Isles, our society's performance continued to be, by that era's standards, relatively confident and self-assured. But when, between the sixteenth century and the eighteenth, the last remnants of our earlier independence ceased to exist, the Highlands and Islands were plunged into a series of crises and catastrophes from which the region's people – aided, I repeat, by our having regained a significant, if still comparatively small, say in our own affairs – are only now beginning to recover.

This is to condense what is set out at greater length, and with a little more subtlety, on the pages which follow. But those pages, of course, have a job to do beyond making the case I have just summarised. Their task, above all, is to provide an impression of the overall nature of humanity's presence – lasting for some ten thousand years so far – in the Highlands and Islands. That presence has been singularly eventful. And if this book does not convey some sense of the drama that has unfolded here, over the last hundred centuries, then the fault lies entirely with my having failed to do justice to the raw material – sometimes exciting, sometimes moving, sometimes provoking, always, I think, fascinating – on which the ensuing narrative is based.

It is typical of the Highlands and Islands that the issue of what exactly they consist of geographically is – like so much else about the region – a matter of dispute. And one, at least, of my good friends will be offended by the borders I have chosen. For better or worse, however, this book's boundaries are, in essence, those which are today considered to delimit the Highlands and Islands administratively. On occasion, I stray across those boundaries – into Perthshire, for example. On occasion, too, I take due cognisance of developments in one or other of the more distant localities – Ireland, Norway, Faroe, Iceland and North America, for instance – with which, from time to time, the Highlands and Islands have interacted. But mostly I stick with Shetland, Orkney, the Hebrides and those parts of the mainland to the west and north of a line drawn from Loch Fyne, by way of the Drumochter Pass, to Forres.

Much has been published about this region's past, and I am grateful to the many authors, listed in my bibliography, on whose work I have drawn. It is one of my criticisms of much historical writing, however, that it is too library-bound, too document-driven. This book, therefore, relies more heavily than most historical accounts of the Highlands and Islands on what an American-based historian has called 'the archive of the feet' – that feeling for location which is only to be obtained by spending time in, and responding to, the places about which one writes.[3]

In this connection, it has been my great good fortune to have had lots of opportunities to get to know the Highlands and Islands. I grew up and went to school in this area. My home is here. And for much of my life – whether as a journalist, a broadcaster, an employee of the Scottish Crofters Union or, today, chairman of Highlands and Islands Enterprise – I have been grappling with Highlands and Islands issues. Over the years, then, I have visited hundreds of Highlands and Islands communities. I have been able to talk, as a result, to many Highlands and Islands people. What I have heard, and learned, from them has hugely influenced my approach to Highlands and Islands history. This approach, I believe, is none the worse for that.

CHAPTER ONE

The most distant dwellers upon Earth

8000BC–87AD

At Inchtuthil, about ten miles upstream from Perth, the Tay, one of Scotland's larger rivers, flows swiftly eastwards between wide shoals of gravel left by winter floods. Along the river's northern bank there runs a rutted track used by the anglers who are this secluded locality's most frequent visitors. Beyond the track is a narrow field, overlooked by a rampart-like escarpment. Trees grow thickly on the escarpment's slopes. At its crest, however, woodland gives way to a wide tract of gently undulating pasture which, towards its eastern and southern boundaries, contains a number of elongated mounds flanked by equally elongated trenches. These features, every bit as grass-grown as their surroundings, are by no means impressive. They indicate the site, for all that, of one of the most extensive fortresses ever built in the northern part of Britain.

This fortress's builders were Roman soldiers. Most of what they erected here – some sixty barrack blocks, six granaries, a hospital and much more besides – went up in the couple of years the Inchtuthil garrison knew as 819 and 820 *ab urbe condita*. That Latin phrase, 'from the city's founding', was integral to a dating system which harked back to Rome's origins. This system was to last for several more centuries. But it yielded eventually to a wholly new method of calculating time's advance – a calendar which took as its starting point the birth of an itinerant Jewish preacher whose execution in Jerusalem was watched, about fifty years before Rome's army installed itself beside the Tay, by soldiers of the sort stationed at Inchtuthil. This calendar is employed today in most parts of the world. When its mode of computation is applied to the mounds and trenches which are all that remain of the Inchtuthil fortress's perimeter defences, those mounds and trenches are reckoned to date from the ninth decade of the Christian era's opening century.

That century, like so many others, belonged to Rome and to the

Roman Empire. Politically, economically and – above all – militarily, Rome controlled not just the bulk of Europe but northern Africa and western Asia as well. Inchtuthil was located on what was the empire's most northerly frontier. To reach that frontier's southern equivalent, it would have been necessary to travel – by way of present-day England, France, Spain and Morocco – to the Atlas Mountains on the edge of the Sahara Desert. Rome's eastern borders were even more distant. The direct route to them from Inchtuthil – a route traversing only Roman territory – lay through modern Belgium, Germany, Austria, the Balkans and Turkey. Leaving Turkey and heading into what is nowadays Iraq, a first-century traveller – several thousand miles distant from Inchtuthil and in the vicinity of the Euphrates rather than the Tay – would have passed, at last, beyond the limits of Roman jurisdiction.

At the Inchtuthil garrison's back, then, there was one of the largest states ever to have existed. Facing that garrison, and delineated by the long line of hills to be seen by anyone looking northwards from the Inchtuthil fortress's site, was a region which, in relation to the Roman Empire's vast expanse, seems positively diminutive. The Highlands and Islands could readily have been hidden away, as it were, in any one of a dozen Roman provinces. And yet there was clearly something about this area which intrigued a number of the Roman military men who, around the time of the Inchtuthil fortress's construction, had the chance to explore at least a part of it. Here, one first-century Roman commander is said to have observed of the Highlands and Islands, 'the world and all created things come to an end'. That opinion, according at least to Tacitus, the first-century author who reported the commander's remarks, was shared by the people then living here. Those people thought themselves, or so Tacitus has one of them say in the course of the passage from which this book's title was extracted, 'the most distant dwellers upon earth'.[1]

These words are among the earliest to have been written about the Highlands and Islands. Given Tacitus's Mediterranean-centred perspective, it is not surprising that they characterise both the region and its inhabitants as isolated and unusual. What is possibly more remarkable – or would be if it were not for the sheer familiarity of this sort of approach to the area – is the fact that Tacitus anticipated the way in which the Highlands and Islands were to be depicted by a whole host of much later writers. Seventeen or eighteen centuries after Tacitus's death, in a period dominated by Britain's empire rather than by Rome's, poets and novelists like James MacPherson, Walter Scott, William Wordsworth and Robert Louis Stevenson outdid any

Roman in depicting the Highlands and Islands as irredeemably strange and exotic. The romance with which the region was thus imbued is a romance which lingers still. It colours, in particular, external attitudes to the Highlands and Islands. And it serves – in combination with the undoubted attractiveness of the area's natural environment – to entice to the Highlands and Islands the millions of tourists who come annually in the hope of discovering here a special sort of place.

Although practically none of them visit the spot in question, many such tourists pass within three miles of the site once occupied by the Inchtuthil fortress. That is no accident. The fortress was deliberately located within easy striking distance of the point, at Dunkeld Gorge, where the River Tay, flowing out of the hill country to the north, makes a right-angled junction with the comparatively low-lying terrain to be found in the central part of Scotland. Because this junction constitutes something of a gap in the wall of hills beyond Inchtuthil, it was inevitable that the surveyors and engineers responsible for laying out modern Scotland's transport network should have selected the course of the Tay when trying to find the most convenient route into the Highlands and Islands. As a result, a main road and a railway now share Dunkeld Gorge with the Tay's rushing waters. Thanks to that road and railway, far more people come this way today than in Roman times. But not every other circumstance has altered in the interim. The factors which make the valley of the Tay a modern thoroughfare of some importance are identical to the factors which drew Rome's army here. The train and the motor car might then have been the better part of two thousand years in the future. But people who were obliged to get about on horseback or on their own two feet were just as interested as their modern counterparts – and maybe more so – in minimising the number of steep gradients to be confronted in the course of any journey. Hence the fact that anyone looking to enter or exit the Highlands and Islands, in earlier centuries as much as in later ones, was likely to make for the line of least resistance as provided by Dunkeld Gorge. Hence, too, the attraction to the Roman military of what was available at Inchtuthil: a piece of flat, but also elevated, ground where a fortress could readily be built and from which the fortress's occupants could monitor the approaches to the Highlands and Islands.

The patrolling Roman soldiers who doubtless probed into, and beyond, Dunkeld Gorge would have found themselves in territory much less modified by human activity than the same territory is today. This area, two millennia ago, contained few substantial buildings, no large-scale settlements and absolutely nothing in the way of the roads, hydro-electric dams, power lines and wire fences which – along with equally artificial plantations consisting mainly of Scandinavian and North American conifers – impact so generally on the modern Highlands and Islands scene. But the fundamentals of Highlands and Islands geography have not altered in twenty centuries. North and west of Dunkeld are range after range of mountains. Here and there, a river floodplain – as in Strathnaver, Strathconon or Strathspey – provides a reasonably sized stretch of potentially cultivable soil. Other pockets of fertility are to be found in coastal locations: around Sumburgh in Shetland; on Argyll's Kintyre peninsula; at the head of Loch Indaal in Islay; on those other Hebridean islands, such as Harris, the Uists and Tiree, where shellsand has mingled with peat to create the highly productive meadowland known as *machair*. But it is only in Orkney, in the north-eastern half of Caithness and around the Dornoch, Cromarty, Beauly and Moray Firths – four eastern estuaries or inlets – that one comes across anything approximating to good farming country.

Being joined to the rest of Britain only by the narrow isthmus separating the Firth of Forth from the Firth of Clyde, the northern two-thirds of Scotland were thought by Tacitus to be 'virtually another island'. As for this remote region's appearance, it was 'a huge and shapeless tract of country' where 'woods', 'ravines', 'marshes' and 'trackless wilds' culminated in 'coasts beaten by a wild and open sea'. This sea was the Atlantic – which Romans called simply *Oceanus*, the ocean. And Tacitus, though he never ventured across the English Channel, was well aware of the extent to which the distinctive appearance of Britain's northerly and north-westerly periphery – in effect, the Highlands and Islands – is very much the outcome of Oceanus's complex interaction, in this quarter, with the adjacent landmass. Clearly drawing on the first-hand accounts of men who had sailed among the Hebrides and steered their ships into the fjord-like sea lochs which everywhere indent the West Highland coastline, Tacitus commented: 'Nowhere does the sea hold wider sway . . . In its ebb and flow it . . . penetrates deep inland and winds about, pushing its way even among . . . mountains, as if in its own domain.'[2]

The way that hills and water, sea and land, have been kaleidoscopically mixed with one another; the way the whole is overlaid by endlessly shifting patterns of light and shade as weather system follows weather system off the Atlantic: these are prominent among the elements which make our Highlands and Islands scenery so appealing. Underpinning that scenery, and contributing to its immense variety, is an intricate geology. Some of the region's rocks – the gneisses of Lewis and western Sutherland, for instance – are thousands of millions of years old. Others – the lavas of Mull and Skye, for example – are comparative juveniles, deriving from volcanic eruptions of fifty or sixty million years ago. But to anyone used, like me, to thinking of the past in historical – as opposed to geological – terms, even the latter epoch seems unimaginably remote. I find it mildly reassuring, therefore, that age, in a geological context, is by no means everything. The phenomenon which did most to give the Highlands and Islands their present form was one which culminated, not billions or millions of years back, but just a few thousand. That phenomenon was the ice age.

This most recent of the earth's repeated glaciations was at its most intense, in Scotland anyway, some 18,000 years ago – or, in present-day reckoning, about 16,000BC. Then the Highlands and Islands resembled modern Antarctica. An ice-cap so thick as to have buried even the highest peaks extended across the entire region; probably linking with its Norwegian equivalent in the area occupied today by the North Sea; certainly extending westwards, in the form of an ice-shelf, across the Hebrides and on into the Atlantic. Like its Antarctic equivalent, the Highlands and Islands ice-cap was subject to extreme cold, to violent storms, to repeated blizzards of windblown snow. But what mattered rather more – as a determinant of the future, at all events – was what was going on beneath the surface. Thousands of feet down, the underlying rock was being scoured, crushed and gouged out as Scotland's vast burden of ice – in the manner of a semi-petrified, slow-motion river – ground its way inexorably towards the sea.

The results of this abrasive process include the steep-sided glens and narrow lochs – many of them, as noted earlier, saltwater fjords rather than freshwater lakes – which are so typical of the present-day Highlands and Islands. Gradually revealed as the climate warmed and Scotland's glaciers shrank, all such features, by about 8000BC, were completely ice-free. The bones, so to say, of the modern Highlands and Islands landscape had come into existence. During the centuries which followed, those bones began to be fleshed over by an ever more variegated vegetation.

First came ground-hugging tundra plants of the kind still to be seen in the Canadian, Scandinavian or Russian north; then juniper and associated shrubs; then birch, hazel, willow, alder, oak, elm, scots pine and other trees. The leaves that now fell, through hundreds of successive autumns, had the effect of enriching with organic matter the gritty soils and gravels left by the retreating ice. Grasses and flowers, in consequence, proliferated. This proliferation was accompanied, inevitably, by the arrival of grazing animals such as reindeer, elk, red deer, fallow deer, wild horses and wild cattle. These, in turn, attracted the attention of carnivores – wolves, lynxes and bears among them. And to this rapidly expanding ecosystem – which also included insects, birds, fish and lots of smaller mammals – there was, at some stage, added the species which, several thousand years later, immodestly named itself *homo sapiens sapiens*, meaning wise, wise man.

The earliest human inhabitants of the post-glacial Highlands and Islands were folk who depended on hunting, on fishing, on gathering the eggs, nuts, berries, herbs and edible fungi to be found in the area's wildwoods. These people lived, therefore, in the way that most of our planet's men, women and children lived until relatively recently. And though their hunting-fishing-gathering existence could not have been without its hazards and uncertainties, it is unlikely, even by the standards of much later times, to have been particularly limiting or restrictive. Studies of its modern practitioners – such as Namibia's bushmen, Canada's Inuit and New Guinea's forest tribes – have shown that the hunting-gathering life, though never giving rise to much in the way of material goods, is seldom lacking in basic essentials. Successful hunters, just like successful seekers after forest products, certainly need to have an immensely detailed and sophisticated understanding of their natural surroundings. That is one reason why it is a mistake to think of hunter-gatherers as intellectually primitive and backward. But the food the hunter-gatherer family requires, as has been demonstrated by means of the most painstaking research, is generally obtained with less physical effort, and in much less time, than the food produced by families who grow crops or raise farm animals. Since the Highlands and Islands – in the era following the ice age – possessed a much more diverse and abundant environment than most of the places occupied by today's hunter-gatherers, the chances are, therefore, that the region's first humans lived more amply and more securely than, for instance, the half-starved and eviction-prone Highlanders and Islanders of just 150 years ago.

The Highlands and Islands of that much later period would produce a number of men who acquired fame as explorers – Alexander MacKenzie from Lewis and John Rae from Orkney, for example. But MacKenzie and Rae – for all the undoubted significance of what they achieved in localities like the Rocky Mountains and the Canadian

Arctic – seldom, if ever, looked out on hills, seas, rivers or forests which no human being had seen before. The places MacKenzie and Rae 'opened up' and 'discovered' were places long familiar to North America's native peoples – on whom, incidentally, both men relied heavily. In any list of Highlands and Islands explorers, then, pride of place ought not to go to Alexander MacKenzie, John Rae and their like but, rather, to those hunter-gatherers who first reconnoitred our own area. This area, to be sure, might have contained some humans in the millennia prior to its last ice age. But for thousands and thousands of years the Highlands and Islands had been rendered uninhabitable by the glaciers which had also reshaped the region's landscapes. The post-glacial explorers of the Highlands and Islands, it follows, were among the few women and men, in all the history of the world, to have known what it is like to enter truly virgin territory.

Where they came from, these men and women, is not known exactly. When they got here is not known exactly either. The hunter-gatherer travels light and leaves little for later archaeologists to investigate. But every now and then in the present-day Highlands and Islands – when a building's foundations are put in place, when a road is constructed, a drainage ditch dug, a hillside ploughed prior to afforestation – there are found the discoloured soils and the various other tell-tale traces which, to the trained eye, constitute evidence of hunter-gatherer encampments.

At the time of writing, the earliest such site to have been definitely dated in the Highlands and Islands – and, for that matter, in Scotland as a whole – is one located towards the head of Loch Scresort on the eastern coast of Rum. Here, in one of this mountainous and exposed island's more sheltered corners, there were erected, some seven thousand years before the Roman army reached Inchtuthil, several of the lightweight shelters – akin, perhaps, to Native American tipis – which served as home, for a period at least, to an itinerant hunter-gatherer group. This group and its successors were to occupy the same spot, on and off, through several centuries; leaving confirmation of their presence in the shape of stone arrowheads, stone skin-scrapers and other artefacts of that sort; leaving also, in a soil too acidic to preserve much else in the way of organic material, the shells of innumerable hazelnuts.

Today a largely treeless nature reserve where a conservation agency is making strenuous efforts to restore something approximating to natural woodland, Rum, when first occupied, was – as its ancient nutshells show – a very different sort of place. Even though the ice age had not long ended, Rum's climate, like the climate of the rest of the Highlands and Islands, was then warmer, drier and less stormy than is nowadays the case. Scrub, possibly even forest, covered island hillsides which are presently as bleak and barren as any in Europe. There would thus have been game to be stalked, birds to be snared, in Rum woods which no longer exist. And the island's encircling waters, still rich in fish and seals and seabirds, would then have been even richer – humanity, at the point when Rum acquired its first settlers, having hardly started on its long and continuing depletion of Scotland's marine resources.

For some four millennia – a period twice as long as the one which separates us from Inchtuthil's Roman garrison – the Highlands and Islands remained the preserve of a hunter-gatherer society similar to those other hunter-gatherer societies which emigrants from the area would long afterwards encounter in faraway continents and countries like North America, Australia, South Africa and New Zealand. Most such societies have been characterised by low population densities. In all probability, therefore, humanity's impact on the Highlands and Islands was, for a long time, minimal. Ten or twenty individuals may have had as much as several hundred square miles to themselves: moving from location to location as spring gave way to summer, summer to autumn, autumn to winter; hiking on foot through inland forest country; travelling by boat – in skin-covered, canoe-like craft, one surmises – from promontory to promontory, island to island.

On Oronsay, a tidal islet to the south of the larger Colonsay, there are still to be seen refuse mounds or middens – in effect, rubbish tips – created by hunter-gatherer bands and consisting of the remains of limpets, mussels, crabs, birds, seals, otter, red deer and wild boar. Elsewhere, what little survives of this distant era, which archaeologists call the mesolithic, survives below ground. But the last hundred years, and more especially the last two or three decades, have brought Rum-like discoveries of hunter-gatherer settlement from Islay, Jura, Oban, Ardnamurchan, Orkney, Caithness and Inverness. Further such discoveries will certainly be made; the starting date of settlement will be pushed back; our collections of mesolithic harpoons, fish-hooks, awls and other implements will gradually expand. But what we will never know for certain – archaeological evidence being of no great help in this regard – is how our remote ancestors felt about their way of life, about the other species on which they preyed, about the Highlands and Islands settings in which they found themselves.

For that reason, I commend two small experiments. The first involves nothing more strenuous than a stroll through one or other of the larger fragments of semi-natural forest which the Highlands and Islands still contain: the oakwoods near Loch Sunart, possibly; the pinewoods of Glen Affric or Strathspey, perhaps. For better or worse, wolf, bear, wild boar and beaver are long gone from such places. But birds still sing there as they sang six, seven, eight or nine thousand years back. The sun shines, on occasion, as it has always done. And the sound of water in hill burns is unchanged. So listen to such age-old noises as you walk. Look out for the effect of sunlight on foliage. Note the subtly different scents of each species of tree. Imagine that the forest stretches on and on – almost, as it were, forever. And consider yourself following, as you definitely will be, in some hunter-gatherer's footsteps.

My next proposed experiment will take rather more arranging. It requires a small boat, a fishing line, six brightly feathered hooks, a summer's evening, a West Highland sea loch, a mackerel shoal, a sharp knife, a fire and a frying pan. Hunting of the sort in which hunter-gatherers engaged is difficult now to undertake. But when a glinting, gleaming set of mackerel swarm frenziedly around your hooks; when you have hauled your half-dozen struggling, thrashing fish on board; and when, within the hour, you and your family have gutted, cleaned, cooked and eaten your catch; then, even if a little indirectly, you will have experienced something of what was experienced, all those millennia ago, by the first folk to take fish from Rum's Loch Scresort.

At about the time that hunter-gatherers were establishing themselves in the Highlands and Islands, other hunter-gatherers – inhabiting the crescent-shaped swathe of territory which starts in the Nile delta and stretches eastwards through present-day Israel and Jordan to the Persian Gulf – were embarking on what turned out to be one of the most decisive developments in human history. Instead of simply gathering the seeds of certain wild plants, they began to grow the same plants in plots of land which were set aside and cultivated for this purpose. Thus commenced arable farming. Alongside it there evolved the practice of herding and rearing some of the animal species which had earlier been hunted – such as sheep, goats, pigs and cattle. The cumulative result, attained only after a very gradual process of trial and error which went on over scores of generations, was the evolution of the agricultural systems which enabled human beings – of whom there had previously been no more than three or four million, it seems likely, in all the world – to multiply in a wholly unprecedented fashion.

The expansion of agriculture into regions other than the one in which it began was no straightforward matter. Europe, especially north-western Europe, is climatically very different from the Near and Middle East. Its people, even if they had wanted to, could not have become agriculturalists overnight. Farming practices had to be adapted to suit European conditions. New crop strains – new animal strains as well – had to be bred. And apart from the way in which agriculture enabled more people to live in a given area, there was, in any case, little that was self-evidently attractive about abandoning the hunter-gatherer existence for the farming life. The latter, as previously mentioned, involves far more toil, far more effort, than the former. Had it not been for humanity's enduring tendency to give the highest possible priority to its own expansion, therefore, agriculture might never have prevailed over what went before.

But prevail it eventually did. Again, precise dating is difficult. But by 3000BC, if not before, the Highlands and Islands had been largely given over, as the area has ever since been largely given over, to agriculture: to the cultivation of cereals where that was possible; to the raising of cattle, sheep and other animals in those numerous Highlands and Islands localities where, even in a period when the weather was a good deal better than it is today, stock-rearing was a much more practicable possibility than the growing of crops.

Aspects of the old order were to endure, of course. Hunting would continue to be an integral component of the Highlands and Islands economy for many millennia. Fishing – which, for all the extent to which it now relies on electronic and other technologies of the latest kind, remains dependent on the taking of wild creatures from the sea – is a key element in our economy still. But much was changed by agriculture all the same. Hunter-gatherers might have felled occasional trees with a view to obtaining timber. They might even have set fire to whole areas of woodland – in order, for example, to drive animals into traps. But farmers altered their surroundings much more fundamentally: engaging in wholesale clearance of forest, laying out fields, establishing boundaries.

That latter innovation – the one concerning boundaries – is indicative of the fundamental nature of the changes caused by farming. Hunter-gatherers wander from place to place, and they tend to regard the produce of the wild as a common resource. Farmers are necessarily tied to one location, and they – quite understandably – view crops and livestock as their personal possessions. By enclosing a piece of newly cleared land with a stone wall or with a turf embankment, then, a man was doing more than trying to protect his field from marauding animals. He was asserting the fact of his and his community's increasingly settled, as opposed to nomadic, way of life. He was demonstrating, too, that the new society, unlike its predecessor, was one in which it made sense to conceive of what we call property – this being, in origin, the revolutionary notion that both the territory on which agriculture was practised and the commodities in which agriculture resulted could legitimately be appropriated by particular groups, particular individuals.

A society in which people own things is very different from one in which nobody owns anything. Some of its members, generally those possessing the most property, acquire status and influence of a kind denied to others. With agriculture, then, came increased social differentiation. Such differentiation – accentuated, no doubt, by their adoption of farming having made people more numerous – resulted in the small and comparatively egalitarian groups of the hunter-gatherer epoch giving way to larger, more diverse, more stratified, communities. Just how these communities were organised in the Highlands and Islands is – and forever will be – an issue for debate. Probably they were given political direction by such rulers as gradually acquired the necessary wealth, authority and power. Probably they developed a priestly class whose task it would have been to supply answers to questions concerning life's purpose and meaning. The tombs which date from that time are certainly suggestive of religious conviction – while both those tombs and the other, more splendid, monuments which have survived from the same general era are eloquent testimony to the organising capacity of the societies responsible for their construction.

'It is left by traditione that these were a sort of men converted into stones by ane inchanter,' runs a seventeenth-century account of the great slabs of gnarled gneiss which, some five thousand years ago, were laboriously erected on a long, low ridge just to the south of the present-day crofting township of Calanais in Lewis. Calanais's standing stones are not thought today to have derived from an enchanter's spell. But modern accounts of how and why they were put in place seem sometimes to be scarcely less fanciful. Was this enormously impressive ring of vertically positioned rocks some sort of astronomical observatory? Was it a temple, a ceremonial centre, a triumphantly aggressive assertion of human dominance over the enormously extensive vista which the site commands – a vista comprising fields, moor, mountains, sea and sky?[3]

The honest answer is that we do not know. But one conclusion at least can fairly readily be reached by anyone who spends even a few minutes at Calanais; by anyone inspecting the scarcely less imposing and equally ancient cairns in Argyll's Kilmartin Glen; by anyone approaching the Stones of Stenness or the Ring of Brodgar in Orkney; by anyone prepared to venture into the interior of that other Orcadian example of early architectural prowess, the mound-like tomb known as Maes Howe. Calanais's tremendous scale; the feel for location that is so evident in the positioning of Brodgar's ring and Stenness's stones; the sheer extent of what was undertaken in Kilmartin Glen: the cumulative effect of all of this is to underline the point that the societies responsible for the planning and execution of such monuments were societies of considerable complexity.

They were societies of some skill and refinement, too. This, perhaps, is most evident at Maes Howe. On the occasions – usually in winter when I am more likely to have it to myself – I have entered Maes Howe's inner chamber, what has most impressed me about its intricately constructed stone walls is the manner in which they testify to the abilities of their builders. Little of what our modern world erects, I suspect, will last for more than a few decades. But so deftly was Maes Howe put together that it has endured for more than fifty centuries.

Head westwards from Maes Howe, by way of Stenness and Brodgar, and you come, after some seven or eight miles, to the dune-fringed Bay of Skaill on Orkney's Atlantic coast. Here there survive, at Skara Brae, houses dating from the period, the neolithic to archaeologists, when Maes Howe was planned and when the stones standing at Brodgar or at Stenness were placed in position.

There are eight or so homes in all at Skara Brae. And when compared to the smaller, more hovel-like, dwellings in which many Highlands and Islands families were living as recently as the start of the twentieth century, these homes are remarkably spacious. Their floor areas are large; their walls, still reaching a height of some ten feet, give plenty of scope for upright movement below rafters which have long since disappeared. The rafters in question possibly consisted of driftwood which had originated on the far side of the Atlantic – roof supports made from a type of tree then growing only in North America having featured in the construction of a house of similar vintage in Shetland. Certainly there could have been little local timber available to Skara Brae's neolithic inhabitants. Had there been, they would not have provided themselves with furnishings of a sort which enable visitors to the present-day Skara Brae to feel themselves in unusually direct contact with the distant past.

Orkney is blessed with a type of rock that is a builder's dream: a sandstone which splits readily into flat, even, straight-edged slabs. It was this sort of rock that was quarried by the folk who made Maes Howe. And it was this sort of rock, sliced as thinly as possible, which Skara Brae's residents, in the absence of any more convenient material, used to make the cupboards, closets, hearths, benches and box-shaped beds – beds filled originally, it is thought, with heather and rushes – still to be seen occupying the various spots where they were first placed about five thousand years ago.

Their exceptionally well-preserved domestic trappings give Skara Brae's neolithic residences a peculiarly lived-in look. It is relatively easy, therefore, when standing in sight of what would have been familiar objects to them, to imagine Skara Brae's neolithic occupants going about their daily business here beside the Bay of Skaill. As successive archaeological excavations have confirmed, they grew barley and wheat, those people; they kept cows, pigs, dogs, sheep, goats; and, as one would expect, they looked to the sea, as well as to the land, for their food requirements. Cod, saithe and other fish were eaten in Skara Brae. So were seals, gannets, fulmars, guillemots and the now-extinct great auk.

After centuries of occupation, Skara Brae's buildings were buried in sand which, at the height of a particularly severe Atlantic gale, was blown from Skaill Bay's dunes in such quantities as completely to overwhelm the village's site. This was to ensure Skara Brae's preservation – just as their more gradual disappearance under peat was to ensure the survival of the neolithic field systems which have recently been discovered in, for example, Shetland. The encroachment of sand and peat on previously fertile localities – whatever benefits it may have conferred on present-day archaeologists – was, of course, disastrous for the people who had previously been farming the localities in question. Those developments, moreover, turned out to signal a permanent deterioration in the Highlands and Islands climate. Never again was the region to enjoy such good weather as it must have enjoyed when wheat was harvested beside Skaill Bay and when, near Calanais, barley was grown in a spot where, when the Calanais Stones began to attract the attention of Victorian antiquaries, peat covered the ground to a depth of several feet.

Peat forms when high rainfall and cool temperatures combine to prevent the complete decomposition of organic matter. Vegetation which would otherwise decay completely is instead converted into a soft, spongy, super-saturated and ever-accumulating material. As Highlands and Islands households have long known, this material – on being cut into handily sized slabs which are then dried by wind and sun – burns readily in domestic fireplaces. But nothing other than the rankest of heathers and grasses grow on undrained peat bogs. As such bogs spread across more and more of the Highlands and Islands during the millennia following Skara Brae's abandonment, therefore, farmers – in addition to coping with an unwelcome shift to wetter, windier and more uncertain growing seasons – found themselves dealing with a situation in which good land was becoming steadily less plentiful. Nor was it only agriculture that was in retreat. Forest cover, too, was shrinking as trees – their roots and stumps still to be seen in many of the places where peat is excavated for fuel – gave way to open moorland. The Highlands and Islands of three and four thousand years ago, then, were beginning to acquire many of the physical characteristics that the area, nowadays associated much more with bogs and bare hills than with woodland, has retained into the present.

As time passed and their surroundings altered, people changed, adapted, looked for new ways to ensure their survival. Stone and bone implements gave way to others made from bronze. And bronze, in the course of the thousand years prior to the Roman army's arrival at Inchtuthil, gave way, in turn, to iron.

As well as making more effective tools, metal makes more efficient weapons. And weapons, in the closing centuries of that part of the Christian calendar which lies before the birth of Christ, were certainly deployed extensively in the Highlands and Islands. This was new. Examination of human skeletons dating from neolithic times – such as those excavated in recent years at Isbister in Orkney – show that, while many neolithic men and women incurred injuries of the kind caused by falls and heavy work, practically none suffered wounds in battle. Such wounds, it seems likely, became much commoner in the course of the bronze and iron ages – periods associated, in the Highlands and Islands as elsewhere in Europe, with a readier and readier recourse to the organised violence which, sadly, has ever since done so much to shape events in our part of the world.

Unlike its predecessors, the society occupying the Highlands and Islands during the iron age is one into which it is possible to obtain historical, as opposed to purely archaeological, insights. History depends, above all, on the written word. And writing – which the Sumerians, the Egyptians and other Middle and Near Eastern peoples had developed long before – was spreading, by the time the Highlands and Islands entered the iron age, to Greece. There, during the fourth, third and second centuries BC, men wrote extensively about the tribal groupings which then dominated a large part of central and western Europe. To the people constituting those groupings, Greek writers gave the name *Keltoi*, Celts. And since the Highlands and Islands are generally considered – with one or two cautions or provisos noted later – to have been predominantly Celtic in culture by this period, Greek accounts of Celts offer at least some pointers to what life was like in the iron-age Highlands and Islands.

When writing of Celts, Greek commentators, together with their Roman successors, described a type of society which historians have lately taken to calling heroic. By this is meant a society which consisted of frequently contending tribes; a society dominated by a warrior aristocracy; a society which valued daring, valour and fearlessness above all other things; a society organised, especially in its upper echelons, in such a way as to make it constantly ready for combat; a society which generally reckoned its wealth in terms of the cattle which constituted a particular prize in time of conflict; a society which typically set much store by jewellery and by other ostentatious ornamentation of that sort; a society given to feasting, to drinking, to music and to the publicly recited work of bards, or poets, whose function it was both to commemorate the great deeds of the society's leading men and to celebrate these men's – invariably prestigious – ancestry and lineage.

Although aspects of precisely this mode of life were to survive in the Highlands and Islands into the era of the factory, the steam engine and the American Revolution, it cannot be proved beyond doubt that the iron-age Highlands and Islands were organised in the way just outlined. The Greek and Roman writers on whose work the previous paragraph is based were inevitably more familiar with the continental Celts than with these folk's counterparts in the northernmost region of the British Isles. But both because of what is known about comparable populations elsewhere and because of what is known about the slightly later Highlands and Islands, it is, at the minimum, a reasonable inference that the people of the Highlands and Islands, when Jesus Christ was born in the then Roman province of Palestine, were organised on tribal – indeed, on what are nowadays labelled heroic – lines.

Those people, like their neolithic precursors of three thousand years earlier, ought not to be imagined – for all that Tacitus was shortly to make the Highlands and Islands appear so peripheral – as necessarily uncivilised. Tribalism, despite long-prevalent assumptions to the contrary, is not automatically to be equated with barbarity and backwardness. Two thousand years ago, admittedly, the inhabitants of the Highlands and Islands could neither read nor write. But they were capable, as the archaeological evidence shows, of producing pottery of high quality. They were capable, too, of designing and building structures still to be seen here and there across the Highlands and Islands – structures which, in their way, are every bit as impressive as the Calanais Stones, the Stones of Stenness or the Ring of Brodgar. These structures are the round towers known as brochs.

Although they had certain affinities with other buildings in other places, brochs, as such, were more or less confined to the Highlands and Islands. Here, however, they were very plentiful. Shetland alone, it has been calculated, contained over seventy. Caithness possessed more than a hundred. In Orkney, the Western Isles, Skye, and all along the north-western coastal fringe of the Highland mainland, they were almost as numerous.

To examine one or other of the better-preserved specimens – on the little island of Mousa to the east of the Shetland Mainland's Dunrossness peninsula, at Carloway on the western side of Lewis, in Gleann Beag to the south of Glenelg – is immediately to appreciate the competence of a broch's builders. Working with roughly dressed stone, and employing neither lime nor mortar, the people responsible for those edifices were capable of putting up walls which reached as high as forty feet and which – two thousand wet, wild, windy winters later – continue to resist the elements.

The broch known as Dun Telve in Gleann Beag – a narrow, east-west valley opening on to the Sound of Sleat – is like other brochs in having a circular perimeter wall. About fifteen feet thick at its base and tending gradually inwards on its outer side, this wall encloses an interior area more than thirty feet in diameter. Like its Mousa and Carloway equivalents, Dun Telve's perimeter wall is hollow – containing a series of rooms which are connected by still-usable stairways. When exploring these rooms, or when sitting on the grassy slopes above Dun Telve and looking down on this spectacular piece of iron-age architecture, brochs – not least because of the fact that Dun Telve's windowless walls are pierced only by a single, narrow and easily barred doorway – seem, to me at least, self-evidently defensive in intent. That particular assumption has been challenged by those who consider brochs, because of their comparatively limited storage space, to have been incapable of withstanding a protracted siege. This latter view, in turn, has been countered by the assertion that iron-age warfare consisted not of long sieges, but of hit-and-run raids. Universal agreement, in the absence of any way of accessing the iron-age mind, is unlikely to be attained. But it is nevertheless difficult, for this writer anyway, to resist the notion that brochs – whether as forts, as prestige residences or as a combination of the two – were once home to a status-obsessed and warlike tribal leadership of the kind the Greeks and Romans encountered elsewhere in the Celtic world.

Even today, the Carloway broch, perched on a rocky knoll within site of the Atlantic, looms imposingly over the croft houses in its immediate vicinity. Present-day Gleann Beag, as a result of nineteenth-century clearances, has far fewer modern homes than the western part of Lewis. But it is, by Highlands and Islands standards, a well-sheltered, fertile spot. It is easy, therefore, to imagine Dun Telve – together with a neighbouring broch called Dun Trodden – presiding, as it were, over an iron-age community of the sort that archaeological investigation is establishing as standard. Despite their being separated from the present by some twenty centuries, such communities, because they were the remote forerunner of modern crofting townships, would have had certain affinities with settlements of a type that still exist throughout the Highlands and Islands. Gleann Beag's iron-age homes would have clustered around the fields which nowadays extend westwards from Dun Telve. The first-rate hill pastures on the glen's northern flank would have been grazed, especially in summer, by the community's livestock. The way that iron-age Gleann Beag's inhabitants lived, in short, would not have differed, in its everyday fundamentals, from the way that many other people subsequently lived in much of the Highlands and Islands.

The name Gleann Beag – which means simply 'little valley' – is Gaelic; and, since Gaelic was not spoken here until several centuries after Dun Telve's construction, this place's iron-age occupants must have called it something else entirely. What that something else was cannot now be known, but that is not to say that the speech of the Highlands and Islands iron age is totally beyond reach. Not far from Gleann Beag is the ferry which connects Glenelg with a nearby island. In English, that island is the Isle of Skye. In Gaelic, it is *An t-Eilean Sgiathanach*. And in a geographical treatise compiled by Ptolemy, a second-century scholar resident in the Egyptian city of Alexandria, it is *Scetis Insula*. The words 'Skye', 'Sgiathanach' and 'Scetis' are obviously related. This means that anyone who talks today of the Isle of Skye, or of An t-Eilean Sgiathanach, is employing terms which, though their pronunciation will have altered substantially in the interim, can be traced ultimately to the iron age.

Such terms – and Ptolemy wrote also of *Malaius Insula*, meaning Mull, and *Orcades Insulae*, meaning Orkney – reached faraway Alexandria as a direct result of one of the first events in the history of the Highlands and Islands which can be dated. That event occurred in the late summer or early autumn of the year 83AD when, to the considerable alarm no doubt of the region's people, there could be seen – from many different locations on the Highlands and Islands coastline – the massed ships of the Roman navy.

✦

In 55BC, following his subjection of those continental Celtic realms the Romans knew as Gaul, Julius Caesar briefly undertook an armed reconnaissance of present-day Kent. Caesar came again the following year. But it was not until 43AD, almost a century later, that Rome, now ruled by the Emperor Claudius, embarked on the full-scale conquest of Britain. Subordinating Britain to Roman rule was to prove far from easy – the Celtic tribes then inhabiting the territories which afterwards came to be called England and Wales taking some three decades to master completely. By the early 80s, however, the more southerly part of Britain was under effective Roman control and Britain's Roman governor, Gnaeus Julius Agricola, was aiming forcibly to incorporate present-day Scotland, including the Highlands and Islands, into the Roman Empire.

The ensuing military campaign, of which Agricola took personal charge, was to be written up, some fifteen years later, by Cornelius Tacitus, the leading Roman historian whose words have already been quoted and whose wife was Agricola's daughter.

In the summer of 82, by which point he had consolidated his grip on those parts of Scotland to the south of the Forth-Clyde line, Agricola, according to Tacitus, pushed into Caledonia, the Roman name for northern Scotland. At the governor's disposal was one of the largest forces ever to be deployed anywhere near the Highlands and Islands. Consisting of many thousands of well-trained cavalrymen and foot-soldiers drawn from the legionary and auxiliary formations which made the Roman Empire so formidably powerful, and backed by naval ships carrying their own marine units, Agricola's invading army must have seemed, to those Caledonian tribespeople who caught sight of it, a truly terrifying spectacle.

'The war was pushed forward simultaneously by land and sea,' Tacitus wrote:

> And infantry, cavalry and marines, often meeting in the same camp, would mess and make merry together. They boasted, as

> soldiers will, of their several exploits and adventures, and matched the perilous depths of woods and ravines against the hazards of storms and waves, victories on land against the conquest of the ocean.[4]

But for all the apparent light-heartedness with which they went about their task, the Romans, as Tacitus acknowledged, discovered the Caledonians to be formidable opponents. At some point during 82, for example, one of Agricola's three army groups found itself in serious trouble when the Caledonians 'suddenly . . . massed for a night attack'. The detachment in question was presumably encamped in the regulation Roman manner, its tents pitched in orderly lines inside carefully laid-out earthworks which would have been constantly patrolled. But the Caledonians, Tacitus reported, 'cut down the sentries and broke in'. Soon the camp was in 'panic', with fighting 'raging' inside it. Had Agricola himself not arrived promptly with reinforcements – reinforcements whose appearance had the eventual effect of obliging the Caledonians to withdraw into nearby 'marshes and woods' – an entire Roman legion might well have been lost.[5]

The tried and tested Roman method of dealing with tribes like those of Caledonia was to manoeuvre such tribes – none of whom possessed anything approximating to a regular army – into a pitched battle of the sort calculated to give a huge tactical advantage to Rome's intensively drilled, highly disciplined and splendidly equipped troops. This was achieved in 83 when Agricola struck deeper and deeper into Caledonia – following much the same route as was to be taken by that other aspiring conqueror of the Highlands and Islands, the Duke of Cumberland, in 1746. Cumberland, also trying to bring about a decisive confrontation with his opponents, marched north in such a way as to keep to the east of the main mountain massif: advancing from Perth to Aberdeen by way of Dundee and Stonehaven; heading into the Highland heartland by way of the Aberdeenshire lowlands and the Moray coastal plain; coming finally to Culloden, just outside Inverness, where Cumberland famously crushed those Highlands and Islands clansmen who had risen in rebellion against his father, King George II. But for all that the still-discernible traces of Agricola's marching camps lie along the general line of Cumberland's advance, it is not known where exactly Agricola was when he at last encountered a Caledonian army 'posted on higher ground,' as Tacitus put it, 'in a manner calculated to impress and intimidate'.[6]

Tacitus called the place in question *Mons Graupius*. Since *mons* means 'mountain', the battle that now ensued, as is confirmed by Tacitus's description of it, clearly took place in hilly terrain: in the vicinity of Stonehaven, say some modern commentators; on the lower slopes of Bennachie in Aberdeenshire, assert others; near Inverness, in the judgement of a third contingent.

The Caledonians, according to Tacitus, brought 30,000 men to Mons Graupius. This implies that the army opposing Agricola was six times larger than the one which Cumberland confronted at Culloden more than sixteen centuries later. That may seem surprising, even unlikely. But account needs to be taken, in this context, of the fact that Agricola's forces, at somewhere in excess of 20,000, were themselves very sizeable – certainly more sizeable than Cumberland's. This shows that Agricola, a man of no small military ability, thought himself to be dealing with an enemy able to mobilise on a substantial scale. And Agricola, one might postulate, could well have had a firmer grasp of Caledonian realities than the modern historians who have queried his son-in-law's figures. Eighteenth-century British governments, after all, reckoned the Highland clans – most of them unrepresented at Culloden – to have had a total fighting strength of 30,000. There is no good reason to suppose that Caledonian capabilities would have been significantly less. The Caledonians, remember, were sufficiently well organised, and sufficiently well provided for, to have undertaken the construction of hundreds of brochs. They controlled, moreover, an area which – including, as it did, most of Scotland to the north of the Forth–Clyde isthmus – extended well beyond the relatively limited territories available to the clans of later times. Is it not perfectly conceivable, then, that the Caledonian tribes had the capacity to field at least as many men as those other tribes – the tribes we call clans – who were one day to take their place?

In overall charge of the Caledonians who mustered at Mons Graupius, Tacitus commented, was a man called Calgacus. This is a Latinised name of Celtic derivation. It can be translated as 'sword-wielder'. Together with what is known of the way other Celtic peoples – both in Gaul and in southern Britain – organised themselves in opposition to Rome, this fact is suggestive of how Calgacus might have acquired his military role. The Caledonian commander would certainly have been of elevated social position. Only a tribal leader of some standing would have been entrusted by other tribal leaders with generalship of the kind Calgacus evidently exercised. But Calgacus – whom it is tempting to imagine as having set out for Mons Graupius from a broch of the sort still standing in Gleann Beag – may not have been an especially prominent aristocrat. As had earlier been true of

Vercingetorix and Cassivellaunus, men who led Gauls and Britons against Julius Caesar, Calgacus could have been given command rank because, more than anyone else available, he had already demonstrated outstanding prowess in war.

Prior to battle commencing at Mons Graupius, Calgacus, according to Tacitus's account of proceedings, addressed his followers in the phrases quoted in this book's Introduction. Those phrases, of course, are Tacitus's, not Calgacus's. They were intended to give Romans pause for thought as to what their empire was about; they employ the well-worn techniques of Roman rhetoric; they are not to be taken – and were probably never meant to be taken – as an accurate rendering of such remarks as Calgacus may actually have made to his troops. But Calgacus, for all that, was the product of a Celtic society; and such societies, both in his time and much later, set enormous store by oratory. It is not at all improbable, then, that Calgacus spoke formally to his fighting men that day in 83AD. And it is not absolutely impossible – given the extent to which Tacitus obviously discussed Mons Graupius both with his father-in-law and with other veterans of the battle – that some small flavour of what the Caledonian commander had to say found its way into Latin sentences which would one day be cited approvingly by those American revolutionaries who saw in their quarrel with the eighteenth-century British Empire something analogous to Caledonian defiance of first-century Rome.

This defiance brought the Caledonians no joy at Mons Graupius. They fought bravely, Tacitus acknowledged of Calgacus's men. But they were overwhelmingly defeated all the same. Caledonian losses, by Tacitus's reckoning, amounted to around 10,000 – as against Roman casualties of just 360. These look, at first sight, to be almost unbelievable statistics. But when essentially tribal levies encounter professional armies, as British forces were long afterwards to demonstrate in Africa and elsewhere, such levies tend to suffer in the way the Caledonians were reported to have suffered at Mons Graupius. 'For the victors,' Tacitus wrote of the darkness which finally descended on that lost battlefield, 'it was a night of rejoicing over their triumph and their booty.' The surviving Caledonians, meanwhile, dispersed as best they could, 'men and women wailing together as they carried away their wounded'. Soon 'an awful silence reigned on every hand'.[7]

From a Highlands and Islands perspective, however, the long-term significance of Agricola's victory lies less in its scope than in its limits. The fleet sent, in Mons Graupius's immediate aftermath, into Highlands and Islands waters – where Roman sailors doubtless gathered the geographical data subsequently utilised by both Tacitus and Ptolemy – might have had an intimidatory effect. But no Roman army, in this instance, was to follow where the Roman navy led. Instead, Agricola withdrew to the present-day Lowlands where – possibly more conscious than some later writers that to account for 10,000 of Calgacus's fighters was to leave 20,000 at large – he ordered the construction of a whole series of fortifications. These appear to have had the object of bottling up the still unconquered Caledonians in their glens. And easily the largest of them was the fortress which took shape, during 84 and 85, at Inchtuthil.

Much the most striking thing which modern archaeologists have established about the Inchtuthil fortress is the fact that it was abandoned before it was completed. This abandonment, judging from evidence deriving from readily dateable Roman coins found on the site, took place in 86 or 87. Nor was there anything casual about it. On the contrary, the Inchtuthil garrison's withdrawal was extraordinarily absolute in character. Presumably with a view to denying all such assets to the Caledonians, Inchtuthil's buildings were systematically dismantled, its pottery was destroyed, its glassware was smashed and the better part of a million metal nails – potentially valuable to Caledonian weapon-makers – were buried carefully in a deep pit where they remained until discovered in the course of twentieth-century excavations.

Rome's other Central Scotland outposts were also vacated at this point. And since Tacitus – who would almost certainly have had something to say about such eventualities – made no mention of Calgacus having been killed or captured at Mons Graupius, it is by no means unlikely that the Caledonian war-leader survived to learn that Rome's army had, in effect, retreated from Caledonia's borders. That retreat was to result in Roman Britain's northern boundary being stabilised, in due course, on a line stretching across the present-day north of England from the Solway Firth to the mouth of the River Tyne. Along this line, starting in about 122, the Romans built the elaborate defensive complex known as Hadrian's Wall. Not long afterwards, admittedly, imperial forces were again in Central Scotland where, at this time, there was constructed, between Bridgeness on the Forth and Old Kilpatrick on the Clyde, a turf-built frontier dyke. But this, too, was quickly abandoned. And Roman interventions in present-day Scotland were afterwards temporary in nature – the most spectacular occurring at the start of the third century when the Emperor Septimus Severus personally led a very large expeditionary force into Caledonia.

Accident helped ensure that the Highlands and Islands were never ruled by Romans. Had Agricola – who seems to have set considerable store by the region's occupation – not been recalled to Rome in the immediate aftermath of Mons Graupius, and had the imperial authorities not been obliged simultaneously to cope with serious military setbacks in the vicinity of the Danube, it is perfectly possible that the Highlands and Islands would have been utterly subjugated. The area's hilly terrain, to be sure, would have made such subjugation difficult. But their mountain ranges – many of them far higher and more extensive than any in the Highlands and Islands – did not prevent the incorporation of present-day Spain, Switzerland and Turkey into the Roman Empire. What ensured the continuing autonomy of the Highlands and Islands, then, was not the region's geography. Neither was it the fighting skills of the Caledonian tribes – considerable, Mons Graupius notwithstanding, though these were. The people of the Highlands and Islands remained outside Rome's domain because their homeland, other than briefly in the early 80s, was never deemed worthy of the investment – in military manpower and resources – that would have been needed to bring about its conquest.

Those parts of Britain to the south of Hadrian's Wall were to remain under Rome's control until the opening decades of the fifth century. With the Highlands and Islands, however, Roman Britain – other than by way of occasional armed incursions – seems to have had few dealings. Furs and other items from the Highlands and Islands, such as the Caledonian bear which was shipped to Rome in Agricola's time, no doubt found their way into the empire. But many places much more distant from imperial borders than the Highlands and Islands – present-day Poland, for example – are a good deal richer in Roman artefacts than the northern part of Scotland. Because most such artefacts started life as trade goods, this suggests that commercial links between Caledonia and the Roman Empire were comparatively limited in scope. If that were indeed the case, the population of the Highlands and Islands would have had little to lose by aggravating the imperial authorities. And aggravating Roman Britain's rulers, as it happens, was something of a Highlands and Islands speciality. Among the numerous raiders who, in the course of the fourth century, did so much to undermine Roman rule in present-day England and Wales were many people whose homes were to be found in those territories lying beyond the former fortress of Inchtuthil. To those people, from the late third century onwards, the Romans gave the name of *Picti*, Picts.

CHAPTER TWO

Born of a noble lineage

88–793

On days when wind and weather conditions dictate such an approach, planes heading for Inverness's airport, some miles east of the town, follow a path which treats passengers to a panoramic view of the Great Glen. The product of a major weakness in the earth's crust, this most dramatic of geographical features – *Gleann Mor*, in Gaelic – is a deep and ruler-straight valley, much of it part-filled with water. At the Inverness end of the glen is the Moray Firth which opens into the North Sea. At the glen's other extremity is Loch Linnhe, an especially long Atlantic fjord. In between are three freshwater lochs – Loch Lochy, Loch Oich and Loch Ness. At the start of the nineteenth century, those three lochs were linked to Loch Linnhe, to the Moray Firth and to each other by the inland waterway known as the Caledonian Canal – a waterway which enables fishing boats and other craft to get safely and conveniently from the North Sea to the Atlantic. But for reasons which are obvious when one sees from the air the way in which it provides a direct and low-level route through otherwise intractable terrain, Gleann Mor was an important communications artery long before the Caledonian Canal was constructed. Through the Great Glen, for instance, there once travelled St Columba, the Gaelic-speaking churchman who founded on Iona, an island not far from Loch Linnhe's junction with the open ocean, a monastic community which was to play a key role in bringing Christianity to the Highlands and Islands.

Columba came this way with a view to visiting the Pictish king, Bridei, whose principal residence, in the shape of a well-guarded hillfort, was situated near Inverness. The saint's journey, made in the later part of the sixth century, was not without incident. That is clear from the account of Columba's life compiled, about a hundred years later, by a monk named Adomnan, one of the saint's successors as abbot of Iona.

Not far from Loch Ness – where tourists have long come in search of the loch's globally renowned, though nowadays elusive, monster – Columba, according to Adomnan, met with some 'local people' who were burying one of their neighbours. On the saint enquiring as to the circumstances of this man's death, the funeral-goers provided a blow-by-blow account – in which the Loch Ness Monster, or something very like it, featured prominently. 'They said,' Adomnan wrote, 'they had seen a water beast snatch him and maul him savagely as he was swimming . . . Although some men had put out in a little boat to rescue him, they were too late, but, reaching out with hooks, they had hauled in his wretched corpse.'[1]

The 'blessed man', as Adomnan habitually called Columba, was planning to cross the river – most probably the Ness – in which this incident had occurred. And not a bit intimidated by what he had been told, he prepared to do just that, 'sending one of his companions to swim across the river and sail back to him in a dinghy that was on the further side'. At Columba's bidding, the monk asked to fetch the dinghy slipped off his clothes and plunged into the water. 'But the beast was lying low on the riverbed,' Adomnan reported:

> It could sense that the water above was stirred by the swimmer, and suddenly swam up to the surface, rushing open-mouthed with a great roar towards the man as he was swimming mid-stream. All the bystanders . . . froze in terror, but the blessed man, looking on, raised his holy hand, made the sign of the cross in the air and, invoking the name of God, he commanded the fierce beast, saying: 'Go no further. Do not touch the man. Go back at once.'[2]

What next happened, Adomnan insisted, was a miracle: 'At the sound of the saint's voice, the beast fled in terror so fast one might have thought it was pulled back with ropes.'[3]

Equally miraculous were the circumstances surrounding Columba's arrival at Bridei's fortress. The king – 'puffed up with royal pride', as Adomnan put it – 'acted aloofly and would not have the gates opened at the first arrival of the blessed man'. Again, Columba was unruffled. Approaching the barred doors, 'he signed them with the sign of the Lord's cross' before raising his hand to knock. 'At once the bars were thrust back and the doors opened of themselves with all speed.'[4]

Although Craig Phadraig – a hill overlooking the northern end of the Caledonian Canal – is the favoured candidate, the precise location of King Bridei's residence is not known for certain. But within an hour or two's drive of modern Inverness, by far the largest urban centre in the twenty-first-century Highlands and Islands, it is possible to see – in Moray, on the Black Isle, in Easter Ross or in Sutherland – a representative sample of the so-called 'symbol stones' which constitute a tangible and definite survival from Bridei's time. Those memorials, also to be found in several other parts of the Highlands and Islands as well as in Aberdeenshire, Angus and Fife, cast no light on what may or may not have happened when Columba called on Bridei. But they attest to the Pictish realms – over which men of Bridei's sort presided – having been capable of producing craftsmanship of a high order.

The archetypal Pictish symbol stone is a vertical slab of rock on which there are incised a number of the intricate and subtly executed designs which give such monuments their name. Some designs are more or less naturalistic representations of eagles, geese, fish and the like. Others seem wholly abstract. And since nobody now can be sure as to the purpose and significance of their symbols, symbol stones have inevitably attracted much – often rather fevered – speculation of the type which also surrounds their neolithic counterparts. Such speculation, all the more so because of its having been accompanied by academic argument about the nature of the Pictish language and about the exact way in which Pictish kings succeeded one another, has had the effect of making Pictish society seem, in retrospect, somewhat strange, mysterious and problematic. This is unfortunate. While it is certainly the case that – as a result of there being few written records dealing directly with them – not a great deal is known about the Pictish people, what is known suggests they were far from untypical of their era.

The Latin word *Picti*, source of the term 'Pict', first surfaces in a text dating from 297 – a text in which the Picti in question are described as having raided Roman Britain. Perhaps *Picti* was no more than some Roman's stab at pronouncing the Picts' name for themselves. Perhaps, since the original Latin can be translated as 'painted ones', it was a mildly derogatory reference to Pictish body decoration – a possibility which has led, inevitably, to the suggestion that the Picts might have tattooed themselves with symbols of the sort they definitely carved in stone. Short of a peat-pickled Pict turning up in a Highland bog, this theory, like so many of the notions surrounding the Picts, is inherently unprovable. But what can be demonstrated from Roman sources of the 297 sort is that the Picts occupied territories which

Roman commentators of an earlier period had generally assigned to people they called *Caledonii* – in other words, to those tribes against whom Agricola had so determinedly waged war.

This does not mean that the Caledonians had somehow been displaced, or driven out, by the Picts. Rather it implies – and the implication is made all the stronger by one fourth-century Roman using *Caledonii* and *Picti* almost interchangeably – that the former had, as it were, evolved into the latter. Where there had once been a whole set of disparate tribes, it appears, there was beginning to be something approximating much more to a single, homogeneous, politically integrated people. To this people, irrespective of the label's origins, it evidently made sense – from a Roman perspective at any rate – to give the name of Picts.

The Picts, it should be stressed, were in no way engaged in the creation of a nation state. Such states, for the entire duration of the period under consideration in this chapter, remained far in the future. But when one recalls how Caledonian tribesmen – presumably drawn from a very wide area and from many different tribes – rallied to Calgacus at Mons Graupius, one can readily discern how Rome's long occupation of southern Britain could have acted as a spur to Caledonian unity. The military threat posed by Agricola and by his successors virtually demanded such unity if it was to be countered effectively. And despite their having vigorously resisted Rome's encroachments, the Caledonians could not have failed to be impressed by the smooth functioning, the enormous power, of the Roman state. Just as North American tribal peoples like the Cherokee would one day seek to resist white domination by deliberately adopting white ways of doing things, the Caledonians could well have sought to emulate, as far as possible, Roman methods of government. Hence, perhaps, the emergence of the situation prevailing when Columba met King Bridei – a situation in which such a ruler could look to exercise some degree of authority across a very wide area.

Pictland – the label attached long afterwards to those territories which were occupied by Picts in the post-Roman, or early-medieval, period – never possessed a centralised bureaucracy of the modern, or even later-medieval, type. Bridei and his equivalents, of whom Pictland might have possessed several at once, did not govern, therefore, in the way that later kings, in Edinburgh or London, were to govern. Even the most ambitious of early-medieval monarchs – and Bridei is unlikely to have been an exception to this rule – contented themselves with obtaining the allegiance of other, lesser, kings and chieftains. Instead of being concentrated in a single person, as was eventually – in principle, at any rate – to be the case, kingly power was thus dispersed among a number of individuals. Partly for that reason, partly because of an almost complete dearth of anything in the way of detailed information about Pictland's internal workings, it is difficult now to estimate the extent of the control wielded over the wider Highlands and Islands by a man like Bridei.

Bridei's influence – as is implied by the fact that Columba, himself a most prestigious figure, took the trouble to seek him out – was clearly considerable. That influence, however, was probably greatest in the immediate vicinity of the king's powerbase at the north-eastern end of the Great Glen. It may have been a good deal less significant in Caithness or on the west coast of the Highland mainland – localities which can now be reached in hours from Inverness but which, fourteen or fifteen centuries ago, were much harder to access from the south and from the east. As for Shetland, Orkney, Skye and the Western Isles, their inhabitants, most of whom appear to have been Pictish in culture and speech at this time, are likely to have regarded Bridei as a fairly distant presence. Such chiefs or minor kings as the various island groups possessed might have been subordinate, in some sense, to Bridei. His direct interventions in island life, however, are unlikely to have been other than occasional and sporadic.

Despite their apparent diffuseness, the Pictish realms – which, as already indicated, extended well beyond the Highlands and Islands – were of contemporary importance. Having first held off the Romans, the Picts – by means of the repeated attacks on Roman Britain in which they engaged throughout the fourth century – contributed to Rome's eventual abandonment, around 410, of its British possessions. This latter development was bound up with the gradual collapse of Roman rule right across western Europe. That collapse, in turn, was to result in whole sets of peoples becoming caught up in protracted disputes as to who was to control the territories, and exercise the overlordship, which the Roman Empire was finally giving up. Among the most formidable contenders for this type of authority, in the post-Roman British Isles at any rate, were the Picts. That is made apparent by the nature and outcome of Pictland's dealings with its neighbours.

Immediately prior to the Roman Empire's disintegration, the low-lying lands which stretch across the central part of Scotland were occupied, as they had been for a long period, by people of the sort Romans called Britons. Like those other Britons whom Romans encountered in present-day England, Scotland's Britons spoke the Celtic language which was eventually to evolve into modern Welsh.

This language has long been extinct in Scotland. Other than in Cornwall, where a variant of Welsh survived into modern times, it has long been extinct in England, too. There, in the course of the fifth, sixth and seventh centuries, invaders and settlers from continental Europe were to succeed in establishing themselves everywhere to the east of the Welsh mountains and the Cornish peninsula. Those incomers – principally Angles and Saxons – spoke the Germanic languages which have developed into modern English. And their influence on England, its very name owed to the Angles, was to be formative, crucial and enduring.

What might be called Welsh-speaking Scotland became centred, in post-Roman times, on the western kingdom of Strathclyde – its 'capital' being the hillfort which then occupied Dumbarton Rock and its territories marching, to the north, with those of the Picts. Strathclyde was to remain in being through several centuries. So was the kingdom – more Anglian than Saxon – which took the place of those other Welsh-speaking realms that had once occupied the present-day Lothians. This kingdom, which included the north-eastern part of modern England as well as the south-eastern part of modern Scotland, was Northumbria. Its originators may well have been German soldiers in the service of the Roman Empire – soldiers who were joined, in time, by further settlers drawn mostly from what is nowadays north-western Germany. The latter area, observed the eighth-century Northumbrian historian, Bede, in the course of his account of his people's departure from the continent, 'is said to have remained deserted from that day to this'. And though Bede – or, perhaps, his informants – exaggerated, there is no doubt that many people moved from mainland Europe to Northumbria. Nor is there any doubt as to this development's lasting significance. It is from Northumbria's Anglian language, for example, that there mainly derives the form of speech known today as Scots, Broad Scots or Lallans – still the vernacular in much of Lowland Scotland and the language in which many of Scotland's medieval and more recent poets, such as Gavin Dunbar and Robert Burns, were to write.[5]

Particularly in the seventh century, Northumbria's kings – men whose doings Bede was afterwards to chronicle – tried to extend their jurisdiction north of the Forth. But just as their Caledonian ancestors had managed to see off Rome's invading armies, so the Picts – who could mobilise significant naval, as well as land, forces when the occasion demanded – successfully resisted Northumbrian incursions. Pictland, as Bede acknowledged, consequently retained both its independence and its distinctive identity. That identity was given permanent expression, as noted earlier, in Pictland's symbol stones. It was given expression, too, in the Pictish language.

Considered by Bede to differ both from his own Anglian speech and from the Welsh-like language spoken in Strathclyde, the nature and origins of Pictish are topics which have sometimes been almost as contentious as the meaning of Pictland's famous symbols. Argument has raged all the more fiercely in the virtual absence of anything in the way of hard fact. Spoken Pictish has long been extinct. Written Pictish, if it ever existed, has not been preserved. As a result, only one or two syllables of Pictish can nowadays be reconstructed with any degree of confidence – the best-known of those syllables being the term *pett*, signifying a piece of land, which survives in Highlands and Islands placenames like Pitglassie, Pitcalnie, Pitfour and Pitgrudy. So scanty is our knowledge of Pictish, then, that any sweeping generalisation about the language is bound to be somewhat suspect. Today, however, there is a lot less support than once there was for the notion that Pictish – alone of all the languages spoken in the British Isles in the period preceding the arrival of Angles and Saxons – was non-Celtic in character. The Picts, it is maintained increasingly, spoke a Celtic language which was related to, though distinct from, the more southerly precursors of modern Welsh. It was this now-vanished language which Columba would have heard at the court of King Bridei. It was this now-vanished language, it seems likely, which was spoken by most folk living then in the Highlands and Islands. And it was this now-vanished language which was eventually to give way – across most of the Highlands and Islands – to the speech favoured by yet another of the many peoples who were on the move in the centuries following the fall of the Roman Empire. This particular people originated in Ireland. They spoke Gaelic and called themselves *Gaedil* or Gaels. But to the Romans, they were *Scoti*, Scots.

Overnighting in the Antrim coastal town of Ballycastle in the course of a 1997 summer holiday, I got into conversation with a barman about the many historical connections between that part of Ireland and Scotland. Throughout the nineteenth century and well into the twentieth, the barman said, Ballycastle's cattle sales attracted farmers from Argyll. And though this type of contact had diminished, the barman continued, new sorts of traffic were being promoted by the vehicle ferry which, that spring, had begun to make regular crossings of the North Channel – the name applied to the waters which divide Argyll's southward-pointing Kintyre peninsula from Ireland's north-easternmost promontories. Not that the new ferry was the only means of getting over to Scotland, the barman added. Just that evening, as it happened, a local fishing boat was taking 'a whole bunch of folk' to a party in the Hebridean island of Islay – some fifteen miles west of Kintyre and more than twenty miles north of Ballycastle.

Contact of this sort is a function of geography. Sit on a hilltop in Islay and observe how the Irish coast – from Malin Head in the west to Fair Head in the east – fills the southern horizon; stand on the deck of the Ballycastle–Campbeltown ferry and watch views of Islay give way, first, to views of Kintyre and, a little later, to views of Arran: do these things and is easy to understand why, over the millennia, there has been much coming and going across those narrow seas. The North Channel, it becomes clear on sailing over it, is no barrier to movement. Far from separating the Irish province of Ulster from the Highlands and Islands, the North Channel provides a most convenient means of getting from the one to the other.

It is by no means impossible that Rum's hunter-gatherers, or their ancestors, arrived in the Highlands and Islands by way of Ireland and the North Channel. It is certainly the case that there was contact between the two areas in neolithic, bronze-age and iron-age times. And it is equally certainly the case that such contact continued in the Roman period. Agricola was reported by Tacitus to have glimpsed Ireland from a viewpoint which was probably in present-day Ayrshire or Galloway but which may, just possibly, have been in Kintyre. 'I have often heard Agricola say that Ireland could be reduced and held by a single legion with a fair-sized force of auxiliaries,' Tacitus remarked. Agricola's claim, for better or worse, was never put to the test. But it is relevant to add that Tacitus made a good deal of the Roman commander having been accompanied, at this point, by 'an Irish prince' of whom Agricola, as Tacitus confessed, intended 'to make use' should he have had the chance of invading Ulster.[6]

The prince in question had apparently fled to Scotland as a result of a 'rebellion' in his own country. He is unlikely to have been the first, and he was definitely not the last, Irish person, or Gael, to make such a journey. There are grounds for thinking that Agricola's successors, as a means of countering Pictish pressure on Roman Britain's northern borders, may have encouraged Irish people to settle in central Scotland during the second century. Others from among the Irish were later to join the Picts in raiding Roman-ruled parts of the

British Isles. And on the Roman Empire's eventual withdrawal from the scene, Irish immigrants – utilising much the same sort of techniques as those which were helping Saxons and Angles to establish themselves further east – began to occupy mainland Britain's western fringes. Irish settlements thus came into existence, during the fifth century, in present-day Dyfed, Pembrokeshire and south-west England. By far the most important such settlement, however, was the one that took shape in the part of the Highlands and Islands which later became known as Argyll. This settlement was called Dalriada. And its long-term impact on the Highlands and Islands was to be profound.

Its own Gaelic traditions fixed Dalriada's beginnings in or around 500AD. It was then, according to those traditions, that Fergus Mor mac Eirc, together with others of the Dal Riata, a people whose lands had previously been confined to Antrim, came across the sea to settle in Argyll. Fergus, it is known or can be readily deduced, was a man of status and position: a ruler, an aristocrat, a son of his people's king. And although there is no absolute proof of his having done so, it is probable that Fergus did indeed leave Ulster for Argyll. It is probable, too, that he made this transition towards the end of the fifth century or at the beginning of the sixth. It is probable, finally, that Fergus was accompanied by a warrior band of the sort which commonly attached itself, during this period, to individuals of his class.

But if it is legitimate to imagine Fergus Mor mac Eirc stepping ashore in Argyll some fifteen hundred years ago, one should not necessarily envisage him as having, by that act, brought Dalriada into existence. Fergus and his followers ought not to be seen as occupying roles of the sort long afterwards taken on by the founders of Europe's overseas colonies. Fergus, after all, had travelled just a few miles. He had come, it is virtually certain, to a place which the Dal Riata had known intimately for a long time: a place they could see from their original homeland; a place which they could readily visit; a place where, it is more than likely, a substantial number of Irish people had already set up home. But for all that he might have been less of a pioneer than is sometimes suggested, Fergus Mor mac Eirc, by joining such Irish emigrants as may have preceded him to Argyll, did something significant all the same. He signalled that he, Fergus, a king's son and a person of consequence, was transferring his base of operations from one side of the North Channel to the other – from Ireland to the land Gaelic-speakers called, and still call, *Alba*. There could be no more striking indication of the extent to which, from this point forward, Argyll – its name meaning the country of the Gaels –

can be considered an integral part of the wider, Gaelic-speaking world over which men like Fergus Mor presided.

Sixth-century Gaelic differed substantially from Pictish – which is why the Gaelic-speaking Columba, when in the company of Bridei and other Picts, had to make use of interpreters. But other than by those few linguists and historians who argue that the Picts were not Celts, both languages are nowadays categorised as Celtic. The social institutions developed by the two languages' speakers are generally categorised as Celtic also. And as between Pictland on the one hand, and Ireland on the other, many such institutions – not altogether surprisingly if both the Picts and the Irish shared the same Celtic heritage – appear to have been similar. The means by which this came about – the means, in other words, by which Ireland and Pictland became Celtic in the first place – are far from clear. The processes in question, which might have involved earlier versions of the sort of migration afterwards undertaken by the Dal Riata, are likely to have occurred at least as far back as the opening phases of the iron age. Those processes, because of their sheer antiquity, are not susceptible to much in the way of meaningful historical analysis. And a great deal of what eventually resulted from iron age developments is equally obscure. So little is known about the overall composition of King Bridei's Pictland, for example, that no worthwhile account can be given of the many Highlands and Islands communities which were part of it. This makes all the more welcome the fact that it is possible to describe with some confidence – Dalriada's early-medieval society being relatively well documented – the nature of those other Highlands and Islands communities which Fergus Mor mac Eirc, and his immediate heirs, knew at first hand.

At the centre of Gaelic-speaking society, in Fergus's time and long afterwards, was the *tuath*, consisting of a tribe, clan or kindred (such as the Dal Riata) and presided over by a *ri* or king (such as Fergus's father). *Tuatha* were diminutive in scale – with Ireland as a whole containing some 150 – and with each *tuath* having a total population of just two or three thousand. Being small in size and being almost wholly dependent economically on agriculture, a *tuath* might be expected to have possessed an egalitarian, even democratic, social structure. In fact, *tuatha* were intensely hierarchical, their populations being divided into three broad groups. At the lowest level, with little or nothing in the way of standing, were slaves, serfs and the like. Presiding over this unfree class were people best depicted as farmers: people who enjoyed rather more in the way of status; people whose various rights and privileges were guaranteed by the customary law to which everyone in the *tuath* was subject. Above and beyond its farming families, finally, was the *tuath*'s ruling order – this order comprising the tightly knit and often interrelated aristocrats, or gentry, whose function it was to provide the *tuath* both with its warriors and with its king.

Nor did the workings of the hierarchical principle stop with the king or *ri* of each separate *tuath*. Just as a slave was subordinate to a farmer, a farmer subordinate to a warrior and a warrior subordinate to a king, so the king himself might be subordinate to a superior king. Hence the simultaneous existence in early-medieval Ireland of the *ri tuaithe* or king of a single *tuath*, the *ruiri* or overking (ruling over the kings of other *tuatha* as well as governing his own *tuath*), and the *ri ruirech* or high king (who was superior even to overkings).

Pictland – where Bridei, it can reasonably be postulated, held a position akin to that of either an overking or a high king – may have been organised in much the same manner as Ireland. Dalriada, unsurprisingly in view of its Ulster origins and links, certainly conformed to the Irish pattern.

Dalriada's internal mechanics are laid bare in the so-called *Senchus Fer nAlban*. This text's Gaelic title is usually translated as 'The History of the Men of Scotland'. But the Senchus's seventh-century authors were rather less concerned with history, as that term is now used, than they were concerned with compiling, for the benefit of some person in authority, a comprehensive account of Dalriada's military capabilities. Hence the extent to which the Senchus consists of facts and figures of the kind that are so irritatingly lacking in respect of Dalriada's Pictish neighbours – facts and figures which, although intended originally to do little more than summarise the fighting strength of different districts, can be reworked in such as way as to illuminate Dalriada's political and constitutional arrangements.

From the Senchus, then, it can be demonstrated that Dalriada, a hundred or so years on from the time of Fergus Mor, was divided, in effect, into at least three *tuatha*. These *tuatha*, in turn, can be identified with three tribes: the *Cenel Loairn*, holding Colonsay and the north-central part of Argyll still known as Lorne; the *Cenel nOengusa*, occupying principally Islay; and the *Cenel nGabrain*, whose lands included the mainland localities of Kintyre and Cowal as well as the islands of Gigha, Arran and Bute. *Cenel* here stands approximately for 'kindred'. And the proper names associated with each of the kindreds in question are those of their reputed, or actual, founders – Oengus, Loarn and Gabran. All three *tuatha* or kindreds, at any given moment, would have possessed a king. And one of those three kings, it might be expected in the light of what is known about Irish practice, is likely to have acted as overking in respect of the other two.

Although the picture is complicated by the eventual emergence of a fourth kindred, this was, indeed, how matters turned out – with the overkingship of Dalriada being held, for much of the sixth and seventh centuries, by the Cenel nGabrain. Nor is there any mystery as to why this should have been so. As compared with Dalriada's other kindreds, the Cenel nGabrain possessed more extensive territories and, as the Senchus shows, could raise the largest number of fighting men.

The main road north from Kintyre – a road initially offering, to the left, wide views of Gigha, Islay and Jura – heads for Oban by way of Tarbert, Ardrishaig and Lochgilphead. Just beyond Lochgilphead this road, which has previously kept close to the coast, heads inland. All around are highly productive fields – first worked, the better part of four thousand years before Fergus Mor mac Eirc left Antrim, by the people responsible for the erection of the standing stones and other structures still to be seen in nearby Kilmartin Glen. A little to the south of that particular locality, on a rocky hillock which looks steeper and higher than it actually is as a result of its being entirely surrounded by flat farmland, there stood, some thirteen or fourteen centuries ago, the hillfort of Dunadd, one of Dalriada's more important political and military centres.

The many hundreds of fertile acres which are visible from Dunadd's summit would have supported, in the hillfort's heyday, a substantial number of farming families. Those families would have been Gaelic-speaking but their background was probably more complex than this fact suggests – by no means the entire population of Dalriada consisting of people of Irish extraction. The men in charge of Dunadd and similar hillforts, such as Dunollie near Oban, were definitely of Irish descent. But many of Dalriada's lesser folk very probably belonged to families that had been resident in Argyll since long before Gaels began crossing the North Channel – families whose members would gradually have adopted the language of the immigrant group who, by one means or another, had made themselves Dalriada's rulers.

Some part of the land within sight of Dunadd may well have been tilled, on behalf of its owners, by men and women who were slaves – men and women who had been taken prisoner, perhaps, in the course of Dalriada's various wars with peoples such as the Picts and the Northumbrians. But much of Argyll's better-quality land would have been occupied, at this point, by free farmers who, as long as they supplied Dalriada's ruling nobility with such foodstuffs and services as the latter demanded, were entitled to occupy their land on a more or less permanent basis.

Something of the way in which these farmers lived can be deduced from the ancient Gaelic texts in which there are preserved early-medieval Ireland's laws. These laws, which would have operated also in Dalriada, deal – in immense detail – with the day-to-day functioning of the society which gave rise to them. This was a society without towns and without money; a society which depended for its survival, as had been the case since neolithic times, on the rearing of cattle and the growing of barley, oats, rye and other cereals; a society very vulnerable, therefore, to the vagaries of weather and climate; a society which could preserve perishable foodstuffs, such as meat and fish, only by salting them; a society which knew no sweetener other than the honey its beekeepers got from the bees to which Ireland's law texts, in recognition of the value attaching to such creatures, devote a quite extraordinary amount of space.

The generality of Dalriada's people were by no means affluent. But as its law texts show, the Gaelic-speaking world to which Dalriada belonged was, in theory at least, well regulated. Not just a *tuath*'s nobles, but every one of its freemen, possessed clearly defined rights. And for all that their legal standing was generally much inferior to that of males, a *tuath*'s female residents, too, could look to the law to safeguard their position in a way that was most unusual in the Europe of that time. Among the legal rights available to the people of every *tuath*, for example, were the clearly stipulated fourteen grounds – ranging from a husband's impotence to his physical abuse of his wife – on which a married woman could obtain a divorce.

But it was with the management both of a *tuath*'s land and of its other natural assets that the makers of early Gaelic law were most preoccupied. The law texts deal at length with topics such as ploughing, manuring and the control of stock. They deal equally carefully with people's rights in rivers, woodland and the like. Thus each family living in a tuath was entitled to take from the common resource represented by this *tuath*'s forests: 'the night's supply of kindling'; 'cooking material'; 'the framework of every vehicle, yoke and plough'; 'timber of a carriage for a corpse'; 'the shaft fit for a spear'; 'the makings of a churnstaff'.[7]

Rules and ordinances of this sort antedated the development of literacy. To begin with, therefore, they were transmitted from one generation to the next by men who, as well as passing judgement on particular cases, had to keep in their heads whole bodies of law. The few highly trained individuals who could perform these feats were, not surprisingly, much esteemed. Like bards or poets, who were of approximately equivalent status and who similarly functioned as repositories of their society's accumulated wisdom, lawmen were part of the retinue customarily surrounding a *tuath*'s king. Such individuals, therefore, would have been present when the leading men of Dalriada gathered, as they doubtless did from time to time, in places like Dunadd's hillfort.

Much the most tantalising of this hillfort's few surviving traces are the carvings which are to be seen in the weathered rock at Dunadd's summit. Among those carvings are the hollowed-out shapes of two human feet. Markings of this sort are discernible elsewhere – in the iron-age settlement of Clickhimin in Shetland, for example. And they appear to have played some role in the complex rituals which are known from later sources to have surrounded an early-medieval king's inauguration. There can, admittedly, be no certainty now as to what ceremonies took place in Dalriada when a king, or overking, took power. But it is by no means inconceivable that such ceremonies included one intended to symbolise a ruler's rootedness in his people's portion of the earth. Modern visitors to Dunadd who yield to the temptation, as I have done, to place their bare feet in the hillock's 'footprints', therefore, might well be doing what Dalriada's kings once did.

Apart from its carvings and the crumbled remnants of its defensive walls, Dunadd today is totally bereft of pointers to its former significance. But among the objects which archaeologists have uncovered here are spears, swords, knives, brooches, pottery and glassware. Not least because some of the items in question are of continental origin, those finds are indicative of Dunadd having been, as well as a military strongpoint, both a trading centre and a place – by contemporary standards anyway – of some considerable wealth. Here, by way of tribute to the ruler who presided over them, the generality of people living in the surrounding countryside were doubtless expected to bring the various commodities required for the maintenance of a king's entourage. Here Dalriada's warriors would have feasted; here Dalriada's poets would have declaimed their Gaelic verses; here Dalriada's musicians would have played. And here, one can safely guess, there would have been recited sagas such as the *Tain Bo Cuailgne* – an epic account of how the saga's supernaturally endowed hero, Cu

Chulainn, singlehandedly saved Ulster from defeat at the hands of an army led by the almost equally fearsome Queen Medb of Connaught.

Something of the *Tain*'s narrative and descriptive power is encapsulated in its account of its central figure preparing to confront his enemies:

> Cu Chulainn . . . stepped into his . . . war-chariot that bristled with points of iron and narrow blades, with hooks and hard prongs and heroic frontal spikes, with ripping instruments and tearing nails on its shafts and straps and loops and cords. The body of the chariot was spare and slight and erect, fitted for the feats of a champion, with space for a lordly warrior's eight weapons, speedy as the wind or as a swallow or a deer darting over the level plain. The chariot was settled down on two fast steeds, wild and wicked, neat-headed and narrow-bodied, with slender quarters and roan breast, firm in hoof and harness – a notable sight in the trim chariot-shafts. One horse was lithe and swift-leaping, high-arched and powerful, long-bodied and with great hooves. The other flowing-maned and shining, slight and slender in hoof and heel.[8]

Tales featuring Cu Chulainn and other legendary figures of similar vintage were to be told in the Gaelic-speaking Highlands and Islands for many hundreds of years. As reworked in the eighteenth century by the Badenoch-born writer, James MacPherson, such tales were to become Europe-wide bestsellers and to give the northern part of Scotland its enduring reputation – a reputation reflected, for instance, in many twentieth-century films – as a place uniquely redolent of great deeds, of daring, of romance. MacPherson, to be sure, altered and embellished his raw materials. But those materials existed independently of his utilisation of them: in the form of narratives collected in the Hebrides by pioneering nineteenth-century folklorists like John Francis Campbell and Alexander Carmichael; in the form of stories which, taken to North America by nineteenth-century emigrants, were still being told in Cape Breton Island farmhouses in the second half of the twentieth century.

There is something almost awe-inspiring in the sheer force of a spoken tradition which originated in Ireland, which reached the Highlands and Islands by way of Dalriada, which survived in the Highlands and Islands through one and a half millennia, which was carried across the Atlantic by victims of the Highland Clearances, and which – in an age moulded more by nuclear weapons than by mythic

Gaelic warriors – could be heard, and recorded, in modern Canada.

This oral tradition's staying power is all the more remarkable in light of the fact that it was already old when Dalriada took shape. The *Tain* extract reproduced above is the work of the modern Irish poet and translator, Thomas Kinsella, whose primary sources were the various versions of the saga recorded in medieval Gaelic manuscripts. But the world which the *Tain* describes, the world in which it was first imagined, was one in which neither manuscripts nor writing existed. That is evident from the *Tain*'s detailed description of Cu Chulainn's chariot. In Ireland, as elsewhere, such chariots had gone out of use long before Fergus Mor mac Eirc is said to have come to Argyll. Much earlier, however, they had been integral to the type of warfare waged by Celtic peoples – Julius Caesar having encountered chariots both in Gaul and in Britain, Agricola having met with them in Caledonia. And so the *Tain Bo Cuailgne*, it seems, is, in part at least, a reflection of the era preceding Dalriada's formation: the era of which, in the Highlands and Islands, the brochs are the most enduring product; the era which – appropriately enough in view of the *Tain*'s portrayal of it – has come to be dubbed heroic.

The *Tain Bo Cuailgne*, as its contents make clear, was the product of a Gaelic-speaking society which was still pagan. By the time Dalriada took shape, however, that society was gradually becoming Christian. This fact was to be of huge significance in relation to Dalriada's development.

Christianity appears to have reached Ireland by way of Roman, or Romanised, Britain. When this process started is uncertain. But it was sufficiently advanced by 431 for Pope Celestine, according to a Gaulish chronicler of the time, to have that year sent one Palladius as bishop 'to the Irish believing in Christ'. Palladius was followed in due course by the British-born, and much more renowned, St Patrick. And soon Irish Christianity was well enough established for it to have acquired its own particular characteristics. Of these, one of the most striking was the tendency in Ireland for church organisation to be based not so much on priests and bishops – who tended to dominate ecclesiastical structures elsewhere in early-medieval Europe – as on monks and abbots. Monasticism, it should be made clear, was not an Irish invention. Its originators were those Syrian and Egyptian Christians who, during the second and third centuries, began establishing communities of like-minded individuals in desert locations. But the practice – on word of it reaching Ireland by way, perhaps, of the trade routes which then linked that country with the Mediterranean – was one which, for some reason, seems to have appealed greatly to the Irish, or Gaelic, mind. By the sixth century, as a result, monastic settlements were being established both in Ireland itself and in Dalriada – where St Columba, in 563 or shortly after, founded the justly renowned monastery of Iona.[9]

Columba – or *Colum Cille* as he was, and is, known in his own language – was born in the opening years of the sixth century's third decade. His birthplace is believed traditionally to have been near Gartan in present-day County Donegal – where a modern heritage centre admits of no doubts as to the district's Columban associations. And though Adomnan – whose *Vita Columbae*, 'Life of Columba', is the principal source of such information as we nowadays possess about Colum Cille – does not confirm Gartan's claims, Adomnan does state specifically of the Iona monastery's founder: 'St Columba was born of a noble lineage.'[10]

Ancestry was, and would long continue to be, of critical importance among Gaelic-speakers. And Columba's ancestry was as prestigious as anyone could wish for. His great-grandfather was *Niall Noigiallach*, Niall of the Nine Hostages, a historically shadowy warlord who appears to have lived in the years around 400. At a time when overkings signalled their supremacy by taking hostage senior figures from among the different peoples who owed them tribute, Niall's household – hence the 'nine hostages' associated with his name – reputedly contained princes who had been removed from the five provinces of Ireland as well as others taken from the more distant realms of the Britons, the Picts, the Saxons and the Gauls. Niall's actual achievements were possibly less spectacular than stories of this sort suggest. But he nevertheless seems to have operated on a very wide front – probably conducting raids on Roman Britain and fighting sea battles, according to some accounts, in places as far apart as the English Channel and the Hebrides. The wealth resulting from their ancestor's freebootery may have been one factor in the subsequent rise to political supremacy of Niall's descendants, known collectively as the *Ui Neill*. By the start of the sixth century, at all events, the Ui Neill were effectively in charge of most of the northern half of Ireland. And Colum Cille, the future St Columba, as a high-born member of the *Cenel Conaill*, an Ui Neill kindred whose lands included modern Donegal, should in no way be considered, therefore, an unworldly and humble monk. Columba belonged to his society's ruling élite. Whether or not he caused King Bridei's doors to open miraculously before him, he would certainly have presented himself to Bridei, and to the more aristocratic of Bridei's retainers, as a man come among equals.

Nobody now knows why the young Colum Cille elected to become a churchman in preference to adopting the more roistering lifestyle which would have been readily available to someone of his background. Nor does anybody know for certain why it was that Columba, by this point a relatively senior cleric, chose to leave Ireland for Dalriada in 563. Regarding Colum Cille's departure, Adomnan wrote only: 'In the second year following the battle of Cul Drebene, when he was forty-one, Columba sailed away from Ireland to Britain, choosing to be a pilgrim for Christ.' This is less than informative. But on the basis of that single sentence and a further comment by Adomnan to the effect that Columba was expelled temporarily from the Church, whole theories have been erected to explain why Colum Cille acted as he did.[11]

At the centre of most such theories is the Battle of Cul Drebene – mentioned, in passing, by Adomnan and known to have taken place near present-day Sligo City in 561. Columba's closest kin among the Ui Neill were afterwards reported to have emerged victorious from this affray as a result of Columba having worked miracles on their behalf. That, it has been suggested, hints at Columba having become personally embroiled in the Cul Drebene fighting – which, if true, would have been in breach of the rules governing clerical conduct. Hence, it has been further suggested, Columba's expulsion from the Church and his enforced departure, by way of ecclesiastically imposed penance, for Alba.

Although such speculation has the merit of accounting for the way in which later Gaelic tradition persistently portrays Colum Cille as an exile from Ireland, it cannot be substantiated. Nor can accounts of how Colum Cille voyaged from Ulster to Scotland; pausing at islands such as Oronsay to check if Ireland could be seen from them; finding that it could; sailing on, therefore, until he came to Iona where, even from that island's highest point, Columba's native land – this land on which he had supposedly been instructed never to look again – was safely below the southern horizon.

Bede, commenting from a distance on matters about which he had heard only at second hand, was later to assert that Iona was gifted to Columba by the Picts. This is improbable. Mid-sixth-century Dalriada appears to have incorporated not just Mull – the much larger and more northerly island of which Iona is a south-westerly adjunct – but the neighbouring mainland localities of Morvern and Ardnamurchan.

In the 560s, therefore, Iona would have been well inside Dalriadan territory. This gives some plausibility to a comment made about Columba's contemporary, Conall mac Comgaill, king of the Cenel nGabrain, Dalriada's leading kindred, in the annals, or chronicle, afterwards compiled in one of Ireland's monasteries. 'He gave as offering the island of Iona to Colum Cille,' these annals state of Conall. And the possibility of some such transaction actually having occurred is made all the stronger, first, by Adomnan portraying Columba in Conall's company shortly after the former's departure from Ireland and, second, by the close association which subsequently developed between Columba and Conall's successor, Aedan mac Gabrain.[12]

Aedan, a great-grandson of Fergus Mor mac Eirc, had something of Niall Noigiallach about him. Irish annalists tell of Aedan having mounted, about 580, a military expedition to Orkney. He is known to have been at war, some twenty years later, with Northumbria. Other campaigns are hinted at. And in all such undertakings, it appears, Aedan had Colum Cille's blessing – with Adomnan mentioning, for instance, how the saint once told Iona's monks to 'pray fervently' for Aedan's success in battle.[13]

According to Adomnan, the mutually trusting relationship which evidently existed between Aedan and Columba had its origins in the latter having been instructed by an angel to ordain the former. If it took place as Adomnan described, the resulting ceremony – on Iona – was one of the first of its type in all of Europe. And when Aedan and Columba jointly attended an important convention or conference held some time afterwards at Druim Cett near Derry, it is likely that Columba, in the manner of many later medieval clerics, was acting as political and constitutional adviser to his king – the Druim Cett gathering, which also involved a number of Ulster's leading figures, having apparently dealt with the potentially delicate issue of relationships between Dalriada and Ireland.

The fact of his having put in an appearance at Druim Cett has the effect of negating the longstanding tradition that Columba, having once left Ireland, was not permitted to go back there. And his probable role on that occasion was such as to suggest that Colum Cille's encounter with King Bridei may also have had a worldly dimension. This is not to say that there was no religious purpose to Columba's travels in Pictland. In a Gaelic poem composed shortly after Colum Cille's death, the Iona monastery's founder is said to have preached to 'the tribes of the Tay' – tribes who, at that point, are likely to have been Pictish. Columba, then, may well have endeavoured to bring Christianity to those Picts – probably a large majority – who were still pagan. But it is by no means impossible, given his close links with Aedan and his obvious interest in Dalriada's politics, that Columba – who would not, in any case, have made our modern distinctions between secular and spiritual matters – appeared before Bridei in the capacity of Aedan's ambassador as well as in the guise of a Christian missionary. Adomnan's account of how his hero so spectacularly gained access to Bridei's presence can be interpreted, therefore, as an assertion of Dalriada's growing power as well as a demonstration of those outstanding personal qualities which, as far as Adomnan was concerned, Columba had been gifted by God.[14]

On summer mornings nowadays, the upper decks of the ferry which plies between Oban, on the Argyll mainland, and Craignure, on Mull, are invariably crammed with tourists. On disembarking, those tourists – regularly numbering several hundred in total – pile into waiting coaches which, in a long, convoy-like procession then set off along the mostly single-track road connecting Craignure with Fionnphort. Here the road ends beside the narrow stretch of water known as the Sound of Iona – this same sound across which, as Adomnan mentioned, travellers once shouted to attract the attention of the boatman serving Columba's monastery. Today a motor vessel has replaced the simpler craft of Adomnan's time. And there are hotels, restaurants and souvenir shops where, for centuries, there was nothing in the way of such facilities. But the essentials of the scene are as they have long been. Iona's outline has not altered over the years. Nor has the extraordinary way in which sunlight, reflected back from white shellsand on the ocean floor, can quickly transform the Sound of Iona's waters into a patchwork of translucent greens and turquoises. Iona now, as in the past, is beautiful. And the island's twenty-first-century visitors, although their numbers cause them to impact upon the place in a way that Columba's monks never did, see much that Colum Cille saw.

The buildings which constitute the modern Iona Abbey, admittedly, owe nothing to Iona's first monastic occupants. Those buildings are twentieth-century restorations of late-medieval originals. That is why it is a good idea, on getting to Iona, to walk in the direction of the little bay, some two miles south of the abbey, where Colum Cille is traditionally believed to have landed on the island which has ever since been associated with his name. Sitting on one of the knolls which rise behind that bay, seeing only the ocean and hearing only the sounds of gulls, it is easy to understand why, some centuries after Columba's death, a Gaelic poet should have envisaged the saint as longing, during an absence from Iona, to be in just this sort of situation:

> Delightful I think it to be in the bosom of an isle, on the peak of a rock, that I might often see there the calm of the sea.
>
> That I might see its heavy waves over the glittering ocean, as they chant a melody to their Father on their eternal course . . .
>
> That I might see its splendid flocks of birds over the full-watered ocean; that I might see its mighty whales, greatest of wonders.[15]

Walkers who, having reached Columba's reputed landing point, go on to make a circuit of the entire island of Iona, can opt to return to the abbey complex by way of Dun I, Iona's highest hill. Such walkers, on looking towards the abbey from Dun I's upper slopes, can readily pick out, in fields immediately below them, the remnants of the turf rampart which, with its accompanying ditch, denoted the boundary of the original monastic settlement. In the area thus enclosed there stood, in Colum Cille's day, the mostly wooden buildings comprising his monastery: a church, the huts that served as sleeping quarters, kitchens, a communal eating place, a guest-house, workshops, barns and storehouses. The timber that went into those buildings, according to Adomnan, came from places as far away as Ardnamurchan. There Iona's monks felled trees in the oakwoods and pinewoods still to be seen on the shores of Loch Shiel: floating the resulting logs down the River Shiel to the sea; towing the same logs for many miles to the west before rounding Ardnamurchan Point and turning south along Mull's Atlantic coast.

As well as labouring on his monastery's construction projects, an Iona monk was required to assist with the never-ending task of feeding the community to which he belonged. Archaeological investigations have demonstrated that beef, mutton, ham, horseflesh, venison, fish, sealmeat and whalemeat were all consumed on Iona. So were apples, nuts, milk, barley and other grains – such grains being grown, no doubt, on the notably fertile machair lands in which Iona abounds. But for all that Adomnan's book about Columba has a good deal to say – however obliquely – about farming, fishing and the like, all such activities, Adomnan made clear, were incidental to the Iona monastery's more central tasks. Foremost among these tasks, of course, was the worship of God – this worship taking the form of an almost ceaseless round of prayer, bible-readings, psalm-singing and the celebration of mass. But coming a close second to worship as a priority in the lives of Iona's 150 or so monks was the time-consuming job of copying and recopying the sacred texts on which Christianity rested its claims to spiritual supremacy over what had gone before.

It is impossible to be sure as to who or what was worshipped by the pre-Christian occupants of the Highlands and Islands. Archaeological evidence certainly points to religious convictions having been held by the area's inhabitants as long ago as the neolithic period. And it can reasonably be suggested, on the basis of research among modern hunter-gatherers, that belief both in an afterlife and in the supernatural reaches back, in a Highlands and Islands context, to the very start of human settlement. But what distinguished Christianity from all such previous belief – what distinguished it, for example, from faiths resting on the innumerable river spirits, sacred springs and hallowed groves which both the Gaels and the Picts appear to have honoured in pre-Christian times – was its huge reliance on the power of the written word.

The pagan priests, or druids, whom the Romans encountered everywhere among the Celts – and one of whose later representatives, Broichan by name, features in Adomnan's account of Columba's visit to King Bridei's court – were illiterate. This did not mean they were stupid but it did place them at something of a disadvantage in their dealings with Christian clerics whose religion – being dependent ultimately on books – was closely bound up with an ability to read and write. In a society which had never previously known such skills, enormous prestige naturally attached itself to those individuals who, like Columba, could both access the wisdom of past ages and make a permanent record of what was being said and done around them. His literacy, I suspect, was one of the attributes which made Columba so useful to Aedan mac Gabrain. And his awareness of the extent to which his authority arose from his literacy, I equally suspect, underpinned Columba's dedication – a dedication Adomnan stressed repeatedly – to the craft of penmanship.

A number of the more mundane episodes in Adomnan's account of his predecessor – such as one featuring a 'clumsy guest' who spills Columba's ink – are of interest precisely because they touch on the extent to which his work as a copyist was one of Colum Cille's constant preoccupations. And the wider significance of so many such trivial incidents having been included in Adomnan's *Vita Columbae* is to be found in the way they tend to underline the book's essential veracity. Adomnan, to be sure, took up his own pen primarily with a view to proving Columba's saintliness. Hence his book's preoccupation with what seemed to him to have been miracles: Columba's stilling of a storm; Columba's restoration of life to a dead boy; Columba's driving out of demons; Columba's triumphant passage through King Bridei's barred doors; Columba's effortless mastery over the Loch Ness 'water beast'. On being presented with such material, of course, the modern mind is instantly and understandably sceptical. But even if Adomnan's interpretation of events is rejected, one is left with much that should surely be allowed to stand. Adomnan, himself a significant figure, was a scholar of the sort not given to dealing in casual fiction. Nor would such fiction have been acceptable to his immediate audience. Although his *Vita Columbae* dates from a hundred years after its subject's death, Adomnan was writing in a place – Iona – where both Columba and his doings were well remembered. Earlier – now largely lost – writings about Columba were readily available in Iona's well-stocked library. And long after its founder's death the Iona monastery contained men – one of them being Adomnan himself – who had met people known personally to Columba. Adomnan, in other words, had both the incentive and the opportunity to get his facts right. It is not surprising, therefore, that his narrative's circumstantial detail has the ring of authenticity. To read of Columba 'sitting by the fire in the monastery', or 'sitting at the top of the hill that overlooks our monastery from a little distance', is to get as close as it is possible now to get to this wholly remarkable man.[16]

Adomnan's literary merits, which are considerable, can most clearly be discerned in his account of Columba's last weeks on Iona. One day in May 597, Adomnan wrote, Columba had himself taken in a cart – 'for he was an old man, worn out with age' – to visit 'the brethren at their work'. The monks in question, Adomnan added, were 'labouring on the west side of Iona'. And one can readily imagine them there on the machair which, at that time of year, would have been brightly speckled with wild flowers: breaking off from their various tasks to gather round their abbot; listening sadly as Columba talked to them of his forthcoming 'departure from the world'.[17]

On a Saturday in early June, Adomnan continued, Columba went with Diarmait, 'his faithful servant', to bless the contents of a barn. There Columba said, matter-of-factly, that his death was now imminent:

> The attendant, hearing these sad words, began to weep bitterly, and St Columba tried as far as he was able to console him.
>
> After this the saint left the barn and made his way back to the monastery. Where he rested halfway, a cross was later set up, fixed in a millstone . . . As the saint was sitting there for a few minutes' rest (for he was weary with age, as I have said), behold, a white horse came to him, the loyal work-horse which used to carry the milk pails . . . to the monastery. It approached the saint and – strange to tell – put its head against his bosom, inspired, I believe, by God . . . It knew that its master would soon be going away so that it would see him no more, and it began to mourn like a person, pouring out its tears in the saint's bosom and weeping aloud with foaming lips. The servant, seeing this, started to drive off the weeping mourner, but the saint stopped him, saying:
>
> 'Let him be! Let him that loves us pour out the tears of bitterest mourning here at my breast. Look how you, though you have a man's rational soul, could not know of my going if I had not myself just told you. But according to his will, the Creator has clearly revealed to this brute and reasonless animal that his master is going away.'
>
> So saying, he blessed the horse.[18]

Later that day, Columba 'sat in his hut writing out a copy of the psalms', stopping forever at the point, in Psalm 34, where the psalmist remarks: 'They that seek the Lord shall not want any good thing.'[19]

Afterwards, as a long summer's evening drew slowly to a close, Columba attended vespers in the monastery church, returning to his lodgings and lying down to sleep, as always, on his bed – 'where at night, instead of straw, he had bare rock and a stone for his pillow'. Then 'as the bell rang out for the midnight office', Columba 'rose in haste and went to the church, running in ahead of the others and knelt in prayer before the altar':

> In the same instant, his servant Diarmait, following behind, saw from a distance the whole church filled inside with angelic light around the saint. As he reached the door, the light quickly vanished, though some of the other brethren had seen it from further off.
>
> So Diarmait entered the church, crying in a tearful voice: 'Father, where are you?'

> The lamps of the brethren had not yet been brought, but feeling his way in the dark he found the saint lying before the altar. Raising him up a little and sitting down at his side, Diarmait cradled the holy head on his bosom. Meanwhile the monks . . . had gathered and they began to lament at the sight of their father dying. Some of those who were present have related how, before his soul had left him, the saint opened his eyes and looked about him with a wonderful joy and gladness in his face, for he could see the angels coming to meet him. Diarmait held up the saint's right hand to bless the choir of monks. The venerable father himself, insofar as he had the strength, moved his hand at the same time so that by that movement he should be seen to bless the brethren though, in the moment of his soul's passing, he could not speak. Then at once he gave up the ghost.[20]

It was two or three minutes into the morning of Sunday, 9 June 597. And Colum Cille, perhaps the most eminent individual ever to have lived in the Highlands and Islands, was dead.

Columba was by no means the only cleric to play a part in bringing Christianity to the Highlands and Islands. An Irish monk called Donnan – a man whose identity is still preserved in various Uist, Skye and Wester Ross placenames – established his own monastery on Eigg in the years around 600. Donnan was followed, in the later seventh century, by a further Irish missionary, Maelrubai, who based himself in Applecross. Numerous other individuals were to engage in similar endeavours: establishing churches and hermitages across the Highland mainland, throughout the Hebrides, in Orkney and in Shetland. But none of this activity, although it must have contributed enormously to the gradual Christianising of Pictland, resulted in the emergence of any real rival to Dalriada's Iona. There Columba was followed in office by abbots whom the Northumbrian historian, Bede, thought 'distinguished for . . . their love of God'. This, it should be underlined, was no routine compliment. Bede, for reasons mentioned subsequently, considered Iona to have gone seriously astray on important aspects of doctrine. But being conscious of what Northumbria's Anglian people owed to Columba's successors, he was careful to pay proper tribute both to these men and to their monastery.[21]

Today there is a widespread disposition to regard Iona as inaccessible and to think of its Columban monks as recluses who sought to isolate themselves from the world. In fact, Iona's monastic occupants mostly appear to have been outward-looking, rather than introspective, by inclination. And there was clearly nothing in their geographical position which got in the way of this tendency. That is because modern Iona's supposed peripherality – like the supposed peripherality of much of the rest of the present-day Highlands and Islands – is entirely a function of the way that society is nowadays organised. In a country which has long permitted a handful of mostly southern cities to exercise a controlling influence over its economy, its politics and its culture, it is extremely hard to envisage a quite different state of affairs. But just such a situation may well have existed during most of the millennia covered by this book. The neolithic inhabitants of the Highlands and Islands – people responsible for such indisputably assertive structures as the Calanais Stones and the Ring of Brodgar – are unlikely to have thought of themselves as living anywhere other than at the centre of things. The builders of Highlands and Islands brochs – irrespective of the words which Tacitus placed in the mouth of one of their contemporaries – are equally improbable candidates for the role of a marginal people. As for Columba and the abbots who came after him on Iona, their whole conduct and demeanour was such as to make clear they considered their monastery to occupy anything but some back-of-beyond location.

In an era when it was a lot easier to travel by sea than by land, Iona was actually situated very handily from the standpoint of anyone wishing to communicate with Ireland, with Dalriada or with the more westerly and northerly parts of Pictland. Its own rapidly increasing reputation as a place of piety and learning, moreover, bestowed on Iona something of the pulling power which was long afterwards to be exercised – not least in a Highlands and Islands context – by urban-based colleges and universities. It consequently seemed perfectly reasonable to Bede that the early-seventh-century King Oswald of Northumbria should, as a young man, have spent some years on Iona. There, Bede wrote, the future monarch was so impressed by what he saw and heard that, on his eventually taking charge of still-pagan Northumbria, he got in touch with Iona's monks – whose Gaelic language he had learned to speak – and 'requested them to send a bishop by whose teaching and ministry the English race over whom he ruled might learn the privileges of faith in our Lord and receive the sacraments'. Thus it came about that Aidan – 'a man of outstanding gentleness', in Bede's estimation – was despatched from Iona to Northumbria. Thus it came about, too, that the inhabitants of a large part of modern England, for a period at least, regarded Iona as their principal source of religious enlightenment. From Iona, Bede commented, there came to Northumbria 'many' Gaelic-speaking monks, 'preaching the word of faith with great devotion'. And on Lindisfarne, a North Sea island not far from Oswald's royal fortress at Bamburgh, Aidan himself founded, at this time, a monastery which was, in every sense, Iona's offshoot.[22]

Organisationally at any rate, Iona's influence on the present-day North of England was ultimately to lessen. Some years before Oswald welcomed Aidan to Northumbria, a papal emissary named Augustine had established a church at Canterbury in the Saxon, and heathen, kingdom of Kent. Augustine's variant of Christianity did not differ hugely from that associated with Columba – whose death, as it happened, coincided very closely with Augustine's arrival in England. But as a result of their being closely in touch with Rome, where the papacy was then acquiring its managing role in respect of ecclesiastical affairs, Augustine's successors were more attuned than Columba's to the various directives which the wider Church's ruling councils had circulated on matters such as how exactly to determine the date of Easter. Iona and Canterbury thus found themselves at odds on a topic to which – as is shown by the space Bede gave the Easter issue – the early-medieval mind attached enormous weight. And when, in 664, King Oswiu of Northumbria, Oswald's successor, convened a clerical assembly to decide whether his kingdom should adhere, as it were, to Canterbury or to Iona, the gathering – held at Whitby – came down in Canterbury's favour.

Iona itself was eventually to abandon its independent line on the Easter question. That can be interpreted as something of a setback to the island monastery. But this reversal, if reversal it was, had no permanent effect. Soon Iona's overall standing was higher, if anything, than it had ever been. According to Adomnan, who presided over the Iona monastery in the years around 700, this was exactly as Columba had foretold. Just prior to Columba's death, Adomnan wrote, the saint had prophesied that Iona would be well regarded, not just by his fellow Gaels, but by the peoples and rulers of 'foreign nations'. Before the end of the seventh century, this prediction – not least because of Adomnan's own efforts – had most definitely come true. The events of 664 notwithstanding, Iona's monks maintained close contact with Northumbria. In Pictland, meanwhile, Iona's authority, although subject to challenge on those fairly frequent occasions when Pictish kings were politically or militarily at odds with Dalriada, was still greater. The monastic settlements which Pictland had acquired in the course of its Christianisation appear mostly to have looked to Iona for spiritual guidance. And because the same was true of several Irish monasteries, there continued to be much regular coming and going between Ireland and Iona. Iona-trained churchmen, as a result, were among the Irish clerics who, during this period, came to exercise a great deal of influence in a number of continental Europe's post-Roman kingdoms.[23]

Iona's continental connections are responsible for the fact that the earliest surviving copy of Adomnan's *Vita Columbae* – dating from around the time of its author's death in 704 – is preserved today at Schaffhausen in Switzerland. This copy, made by the Iona monk Dorbbene whose name it bears, was one of many such books turned out in Iona's *scriptorium* – the Latin name given to buildings of the sort in which scribes like Dorbbene laboured. The basic raw material employed by those scribes was the cured calfskin known as vellum. On to this they painstakingly penned the words of the books from which there derived both Christianity and the whole corpus of learning and scholarship to which institutions like the Iona scriptorium were dedicated. Grammars, histories and other works of that kind – many of them deriving from Roman originals – were consequently duplicated over and over again. Had they not been, texts of the sort on which preceding pages have drawn so heavily – Tacitus's *Agricola*, Adomnans's *Life of Columba*, Bede's *History of the English People* – would not exist today. Even in our ever more secular age, then, there possibly continues to be some responsibility on us to accede to the request which Dorbbene entered on the last page of his carefully copied version of Adomnan's manuscript: 'Whoever may read these books about St Columba's miraculous powers, pray to God for me, Dorbbene, that after death I may have life eternal.'[24]

For all the importance which monks like Dorbbene attached to works like Adomnan's, it was on the gospels, the source of their Christian faith, that they inevitably placed most emphasis – and to the copying of which they devoted most attention. This is most evident in the so-called Book of Kells – generally considered to be an Iona product. In essence, the Book of Kells is merely the text of the four gospels: Matthew, Mark, Luke and John. But surrounding that text – and often, as it were, woven into its words – is the lavish and intricate decoration which ensures that the Book of Kells is nowadays regarded as one of the most outstanding creative achievements of early-medieval Europe. This monastic art – which, to be properly appreciated, needs to be seen, not read about – draws on many sources. Pictish and Northumbrian influences, as well as those which are Irish, Gaelic or Dalriadan, can be detected in it. That, in view of Iona's role and connections, is what one might expect. But what requires to be emphasised and re-emphasised about the Book of Kells, in a Highlands and Islands context, is the fact that there once existed here, in an area which even its own people have more recently tended to regard as far removed from the world's intellectual and artistic mainstreams, the capacity to create something of such enduring beauty.

The Book of Kells is written in Latin. That was the language employed by the Church throughout early-medieval Europe. And by mastering it, Iona's monks were able to access the literary heritage left by imperial Rome. This did not result, however, in those monks abandoning their native Gaelic. Adomnan, to be sure, thought Gaelic a 'poor . . . language . . . in comparison with the different tongues of foreign races'. But in Iona, as in other parts of the Gaelic-speaking world, monks who began by being literate in Latin went on to become literate in Gaelic also: applying to their own language a version of the Roman alphabet; setting down, in this new literary Gaelic, the *Tain* and other age-old epics of that sort; setting down, too, Gaelic poetry of their own devising. Thus Gaelic – routinely denounced as crude and barbaric by those who were one day to set about 'civilising' the Highlands and Islands – actually acquired both a written form and a vernacular literature in advance both of English and of most other modern European languages.[25]

This literature, it goes almost without saying, was the possession of a vanishingly small élite. The generality of eighth-century Gaelic-speakers – the generality of eighth-century Pictish-speakers, come to that – are unlikely to have so much as set eyes on the Book of Kells or on any other of the equally impressive volumes which possibly then existed. Either in response to the exhortations of monastic missionaries or on the instructions of their secular overlords, who expected to be obeyed in this respect as in so many others, practically all the people living in the eighth-century Highlands and Islands had certainly exchanged their former religions for Christianity. But their day-to-day existence, one suspects, had not altered greatly as a result. For every person who could read and write, there were hundreds upon hundreds who could not – those hundreds consisting mainly of the women, the men, the children who, week in, week out, year after year, were required to labour on the land. As had been true of their predecessors since farming first reached the Highlands and Islands in neolithic times, and as would be equally true of their successors for another thousand years or more, the lives of these men, women and children were shaped primarily by the demands made of them by the crops and by the animals on which they ultimately depended. Although – in the shape, for instance, of the story-telling tradition already referred to – these common folk had their own stake in the overall culture of which the Book of Kells was part, products of the latter type are unlikely to have impinged any more on the wider population of the eighth-century Highlands and Islands than the paintings produced in Renaissance Florence impinged on fifteenth-century Tuscan peasants.

That, of course, does not make the Book of Kells any less amazing. To examine the open pages of one of its four volumes – as displayed today in the library of Trinity College, Dublin – is to appreciate what was meant by the twelfth-century Welsh cleric to whom the Book of Kells, or some similar production, seemed 'the very shrine of art'. And another of this cleric's comments is as apt today as it was when first made. Fully to comprehend the 'fine craftsmanship' that long-ago Welshman discerned in the Book of Kells, it remains essential, as he instructed, to look as 'keenly' at its 'different designs' and at its 'tracery' as the book's custodians will permit. Then, 'you will make out intricacies so delicate and subtle, so exact and compact, so full of knots and links, with colours so fresh and vivid, that you might say all this was the work of an angel, and not of a man'.[26]

Equally deserving of close inspection are the stone slabs and crosses which constitute the other great artistic accomplishment of the early-medieval Highlands and Islands. Particularly in the more northerly and easterly parts of the area, such monuments – for all that the message they are intended to convey is a Christian one – are very evidently a development of pagan Pictland's symbol stones. Pictish sculptors may also have contributed to the fostering of stone-carving skills in Dalriada where there began to be produced, in the course of the eighth century, the high, wheeled crosses which have come to be so ineradicably associated with the Columban Church.

One of the most impressive of such crosses stands at Kildalton in the south-eastern corner of Islay. Twelve centuries of exposure to Hebridean wind and weather has inevitably had the effect of eroding the finer detail of its maker's work. But to run one's fingers over the Kildalton Cross's elaborately chiselled surface is to encounter, I think, a three-dimensional version of the Book of Kells. And to stand in front of any such memorial – the Kildalton Cross, its several Iona equivalents or the Nigg Cross in Easter Ross – is immediately to understand that the still-recently Christianised society which gave rise to such intrinsically authoritative creations could not have been other than immensely assured and self-confident.

Something of that self-confidence – verging, perhaps, on complacency – is encapsulated in the words of the early-medieval Gaelic poet who wrote:

> Paganism has been destroyed,
> though it was splendid and far-flung;
> the kingdom of God the Father
> has filled heaven and earth and sea.[27]

Although these lines are likely to have been first set down in Ireland, not Scotland, the 'paganism' to which they refer can legitimately be thought to encompass the beliefs of the pre-Christian Picts as well as those of the pre-Christian Gaels. And in view of what was accomplished by the Church in the Highlands and Islands in the two hundred years following Columba's journey to Bridei's hillfort, the Gaelic-speaking monk who produced this eighth-century poem can readily be excused his Christian triumphalism. Such triumphalism, however, was soon to be proved premature.

CHAPTER THREE

The broad loom of slaughter

794–1266

As determined by the method of calculation accepted so reluctantly by the Columban Church some 350 years before, Easter came late in 1014. Good Friday fell that year on 23 April. Despite their being especially exposed to chilling winds from the north and east, therefore, Caithness's wide, flat farmlands would have been tinged by springtime green when, on the morning of this holiest of Christian festivals, a Caithness man named Dorrud – or so it was afterwards remarked in the course of an Icelandic saga – 'saw twelve riders approach a woman's bower and disappear inside'. Cautiously stealing up to the dwelling in question, Dorrud, as foolhardy as he was curious, peered through one of its windows:

> Inside, he could see women with a loom set up before them. Men's heads were used in place of weights, and men's intestines for the weft and warp; a sword served as the beater, and the shuttle was an arrow.[1]

What had been granted to him, Dorrud realised, was a glimpse of the valkyries: harpy-like handmaidens of the Norse god Odin; blood-crazed females whose grisly task it was to choose who should die on any field of battle. And as they wove their ghastly fabric, it seemed to Dorrud, the valkyries chanted these verses:

> Blood rains
> From the cloudy web
> On the broad loom
> Of slaughter.
> The web of man,
> Grey as armour,
> Is now being woven;

The Valkyries
Will cross it
With a crimson weft.
The Valkyries go weaving
With drawn swords,
Hild and Hjorthrimul,
Sanngrid and Svipul.
Spears will shatter,
Shields will splinter,
Swords will gnaw
Like wolves through armour.[2]

Whether or not they had been orchestrated by the weird women whom Dorrud was reputed to have seen in Caithness, grim and gory events were certainly unfolding that Good Friday morning. At Clontarf, near the mouth of Ireland's River Liffey, on a piece of ground which has long since disappeared below Dublin's spreading streets, two armies were confronting each other. One was predominantly Irish, the other predominantly Norse. Among the leaders of this second army was Sigurd the Stout, Earl of Orkney and ruler of a realm which extended southwards and south-westwards across the Pentland Firth into both the Highland mainland and the Hebrides.

By his mother, it was said, Earl Sigurd had been given a banner which the compiler of one of Iceland's sagas subsequently described in detail. 'It was a finely made banner,' this sagaman observed, 'very cleverly embroidered with the figure of a raven, and when the banner fluttered in the breeze, the raven seemed to be flying ahead.'[3]

But much more than its appearance, the sagaman insisted, marked out Sigurd's raven banner. The earl's mother was 'a sorceress' and she had crafted her son's battle-flag with all the strange skills at her disposal. 'My belief is this,' his mother told Sigurd as she handed the banner to him, 'that it will bring victory to the man it's carried before, but death to the one who carries it.'[4]

So things turned out. In the course of a battle fought at Skitten in Caithness, Earl Sigurd lost one standard-bearer after another. But he emerged victorious all the same. And at Clontarf, Sigurd hoped to repeat his earlier triumph – causing to be unfurled there, beside the Liffey, the banner carrying his mother's magically endowed representation of the big, black, crag-haunting bird which, as Sigurd's men would have been well aware, was traditionally linked with Odin, master of the valkyries, god of slaughter, god of war.

'The armies clashed,' a further sagaman wrote of Clontarf, 'and there was bitter fighting.' One Irish soldier 'advanced with such vigour that he felled all those in the forefront. He burst through Earl Sigurd's ranks right up to the banner, and killed the standard-bearer.'[5]

A new standard-bearer was found. But soon both this man 'and all those who were near him' had died:

> Earl Sigurd ordered Thorstein Hallsson to carry the standard, and Thorstein was about to take it when Amundi the White said, 'Don't take the banner, Thorstein. All those who bear it get killed.'
>
> 'Hrafn the Red,' said the earl, 'you take the standard.'
>
> 'Carry your own devil yourself,' said Hrafn.
>
> The earl said, 'A beggar should carry his own bundle.' He ripped the flag from its staff and tucked it under his clothing.
>
> A little later Amundi the White was killed, and then the earl himself died with a spear through him.[6]

Back in Orkney, meanwhile, there waited a man called Harek who had been told by Sigurd that he would be the first of all the island earldom's people to learn the outcome of the earl's expedition to Ireland. On the same Good Friday that Dorrud saw the valkyries set up their gory loom in Caithness, the Good Friday on which the Battle of Clontarf was fought, Harek glimpsed Sigurd, as he thought, come riding towards his, Harek's, Orkney home. 'Harek mounted his horse and rode to meet the earl,' the relevant saga comments tersely. 'They were observed to meet and go riding behind a hill, but they were never seen again, and not a trace of Harek was ever found.'[7]

The story of Dorrud, the valkyries, Sigurd, Clontarf and the raven banner was one of many such tales to emerge from the society created by folk who first began to make their presence felt in the Highlands and Islands towards the end of the eighth century. These people, Scandinavian in origin, are known today as Vikings – a term which, in their own Norse language, was applied to individuals who made a career of piracy and plundering. The Vikings, then, can readily be portrayed as having been, almost by definition, robbers and cut-throats. That is certainly how they were regarded by those Picts and Gaels who were among the earliest victims of a people whose most distinguishing, and most terrifying, characteristic consisted of an unrivalled ability to descend, with next to nothing in the way of advance warning, on any spot within reach of their ships.

Exactly what propelled the Vikings outwards from Scandinavia remains a matter of contention. But there is no argument as to what enabled them suddenly to put in an appearance in places as far apart as Russia and Ireland, Greenland and North Africa. The key to Viking mobility consisted of the highly manoeuvrable and endlessly versatile craft which Scandinavian boatbuilders – after much experiment – appear finally to have perfected in the years just prior to 800.

By Norse poets, Viking ships were frequently compared to serpents. And there was much that was snake-like about them. Sleek, low, swift and sinuous, the archetypal Norse vessel – thanks to its shallow draught and to the suppleness inherent in a hull constructed from long, overlapping planks – could handle open sea and enclosed coastal waters with equal ease. Powered both by sail and by oar, such a ship could readily make a lengthy ocean voyage, reconnoitre a coastline and penetrate even the most confined estuary or inlet. Nor were the Vikings dependent on harbours and anchorages of the kind used by more conventional sailors. A Norse ship could readily be beached on any conveniently shelving strand of sand or gravel – on to which there then leaped the ship's crew who doubled invariably as heavily armed warriors.

Warriors of this sort made their first recorded visit to Scotland's coasts in 794 when they were reported by Irish chroniclers to have subjected island after island to 'devastation'. In 795 'Skye was pillaged' and Iona raided. In 798 'the Hebrides . . . were plundered by Scandinavians'. In 802 Iona's monastery was 'burned'. And in 806 no fewer than sixty-eight of the monastery's monks were 'slain' – at the spot, so Iona tradition insists, which has ever since been known as *Port nam Mairtear*, Martyr's Bay.[8]

Other parts of Europe suffered similarly. 'The number of ships increases,' lamented the mid-ninth-century Frankish chronicler, Erementarius of Noirmoutier:

> The endless flood of Vikings never ceases to grow bigger. Everywhere Christ's people are the victims of massacre, burning and plunder. The Vikings overrun all that lies before them, and none can withstand them.[9]

Most of the Norsemen who thus terrorised the Frankish realms in present-day Holland, Germany, Belgium and France were, in origin, Danes. Swedish Vikings, for their part, tended to concentrate on those more eastern lands to which access was gained, from the Baltic, by way of rivers like the Dvina and the Dneiper. But Vikings whose homelands were in Norway, for reasons which are obvious to anyone glancing at a map, tended to look to the west and south-west – where there lay, of course, the Highlands and Islands.

With the help of sun and stars, as well as by taking account of cloud formations, the movements of seabirds and even the varying colour of seawater, Norse navigators were perfectly capable, when occasion demanded, of making transoceanic voyages. They preferred, however, to keep in sight of land. Hence the attractiveness to Viking raiders of the route which took them from Norway to the Hebrides – and then on to Ireland, Spain and the Mediterranean – by way of Shetland and Orkney. Given an easterly or north-easterly wind of the sort common in springtime, when Viking expeditions usually commenced, it was possible to sail to Shetland from, say, Bergen in not much more than twenty-four hours. Depending on weather conditions, a skipper who had thus made the crossing of the Norway–Shetland gap might opt to round Muckle Flugga, the northernmost tip of the seventy-mile-long chain of islands making up the Shetland group, prior to turning south. But either by that route or by the more straightforward one along the Shetland Mainland's east coast, most Viking ships – when outward bound from western Norway – were likely to come eventually to Sumburgh Head, Shetland's most southerly point. From there, on days of reasonable visibility, Fair Isle can be seen. From Fair Isle, in turn, it is possible to pick out North Ronaldsay, Sanday and the other more northerly outliers of the numerous islands which make up Orkney. Beyond Orkney, from which it is separated by no more than seven or eight miles of open water, is the Highland mainland's northern coast. At that coast's western extremity is the exposed promontory of Cape Wrath. In English, its name seems singularly appropriate to a place surrounded by some of the world's angriest seas. But that name, in fact, derives from a Norse term meaning a turning-point – for Cape Wrath, on being rounded, gave Viking seamen access to southward-tending, and comparatively sheltered, sealanes. All around those sealanes were, and are, the Hebridean islands, Iona among them, which Vikings began regularly to raid in the course of the eighth century's last decade.

Physically and scenically, the Highlands and Islands – where, as has already been emphasised, a fragmented coastline encircles a mountainous interior – are very similar to Norway. Nor was the society which the Vikings encountered in the Highlands and Islands radically different from their own. Scandinavia's eighth-century inhabitants, just like their Celtic counterparts, were a tribal people. And one only needs to compare Norse sagas with their Gaelic equivalents – such as the *Tain Bo Cuailgne* – to glimpse the extent to which Vikings and Celts were virtually united in their views as to what was proper and meritorious. Sagas of the sort that contain the tale of Earl Sigurd's raven banner did not acquire a written form until Icelanders began to set them down on vellum in the twelfth century. But these sagas encapsulate at least something of the values of the earlier times they so dramatically describe. Embedded in many Icelandic sagas, moreover, are verses – of the kind telling, for instance, how the valkyries came to Caithness – which are known to be much older than the sagas themselves. Those verses were composed by Viking poets who were known as skalds and whose social position was identical to that of Gaelic bards. For all its undeniable power, much skaldic poetry – glorying as it does in violence, bloodshed and slaughter – tends to reinforce the longstanding notion that the Vikings were singularly destructive. But the *Tain*, it needs to be recalled in this connection, is no less given over to the glorification of war. And both Gaels and Picts – in the course of their numerous conflicts with each other and with their various neighbours – had proved every bit as capable as Norwegians of inflicting misery on their enemies. In truth, there was little that was novel about even the most eye-catchingly gruesome aspects of Viking behaviour. It was as ship-borne marauders, after all, that Picts and Gaels had originally been known to the inhabitants of much of Roman Britain. And it is highly doubtful, to say the least, if the Roman victims of pillaging Gaels or Picts were treated any less harshly than Picts or Gaels were treated, in their turn, by Norse raiders.

None of this, to be sure, excuses Viking conduct of the kind resulting in the martyrdom, in 825, of the Iona abbot, Blathmac, spiritual heir of Columba, whose relics, it appears, Blathmac defended – literally – to the death. Blathmac's murder was graphically described, some twenty years after its occurrence, in the course of a Latin elegy penned by Walafrid Strabo, then in charge of the monastery of Reichenau on Lake Constance and a man who, it can be assumed, had heard first-hand accounts of Blathmac's fate from one or more of the Gaelic-speaking monks then commonly to be found in continental Europe.

At some point, or so it can be deduced from Strabo, Iona's monks had arranged for the 'holy bones of St Columba', their monastery's revered founder, to be encased in a 'shrine' constructed of 'precious metals'. Knowing that such an object would be prized by Viking looters, who always valued gold and silver above all other booty,

Iona's monastic community – possibly as a standard precaution or possibly because they had some forewarning of this, the latest, Viking attack on their island – had taken care, prior to the commencement of the 825 raid, to remove Columba's shrine 'from its pediments' and to conceal it 'in the earth . . . under a thick layer of turf'. Abbot Blathmac, who would have been in charge of these proceedings, meanwhile continued to preside over Iona's religious routine. But no sooner had he celebrated mass than a gang of newly landed Norsemen 'came rushing through' the monastery's buildings – 'threatening cruel perils' and making clear to Blathmac, in particular, that he would be killed if he did not immediately reveal the whereabouts of such treasures as he had had a hand in hiding. Blathmac, Strabo wrote, stood his ground 'with unshaken purpose of mind'. Making clear he would never yield to any Viking, Iona's abbot said simply: 'Gracious God, to thy aid I commend me humbly.' Moments later, he was 'torn limb from limb'.[10]

In Colonsay, towards the end of the nineteenth century, there was discovered the grave of a Viking of the sort responsible for what was done to Blathmac. Beside this Viking's bones were the remnants of a sword, a knife, an axe, a spear and a shield. In addition to such warlike paraphernalia, however, the Colonsay grave contained a set of balances and a number of lead weights. So was this ninth-century Norseman – the date of whose death can be fixed, at least approximately, as a result of some coins having also been interred with him – a fighting man, as is suggested by his weapons, or a trader, as is suggested by the fact that he owned a set of scales? To pose this question is immediately to engage with much recent debate as to whether the Vikings were actually as barbaric as they have habitually been portrayed. Pointing out that monastic chroniclers who wrote negatively about Vikings were biased in consequence of their having been Viking victims, and adding that a growing body of archaeological evidence suggests that many Vikings were more interested in commercial exchange than in butchery, some modern historians have set out, as it were, retrospectively to enhance the Viking image. That Scandinavians were widely on the move in ninth-century Europe is not denied by such historians. But these Scandinavians, the same historians insist, were by no means the murderous thugs of legend. Instead they were itinerant merchants on the look-out for business – or emigrant farmers in search of new land.

When carried to extremes, the notion of the steadfastly peaceable Viking is rather hard to square with what happened to Blathmac and many others like him. That is why it might make most sense to think of Vikings as having been governed – like many other folk before and since – by all sorts of complex impulses. Is it not possible, maybe even probable, that an individual Norseman might have engaged, at different times and in different circumstances, in both barter and banditry? Is it not likely, too, that men who first came to the Highlands and Islands in order simply to raid and to pillage might ultimately have settled here as landholders of one kind or another? As far as the Hebrides at least are concerned, the archaeological record – exemplified by another ninth-century grave which was found to contain buckles and brooches of intermingled Norse and Celtic design – certainly suggests as much. Island placenames reinforce the point. Thus three-quarters of all the village names in modern Lewis – names like Habost, Laxay, Shawbost and Shulishader – are of Norse origin. Admittedly, the density of such names decreases as one moves southwards through the Hebrides and thus gets steadily further from Norway – Norse names being much more prevalent in Skye than in Islay, for instance. But there is no island in the Hebrides – known to the Vikings, incidentally, as *Sudreyjar*, the Southern Isles – which does not contain, even today, some trace of the impact made on it, eleven or twelve centuries ago, by immigrants from Scandinavia.

Among the more prominent of these immigrants was Ketil Flatnose who, according to the sagas, 'raided . . . extensively' in the Hebrides before making his home there. By the middle years of the ninth century, it seems, Ketil, although he owed a nominal allegiance to the kings of Norway, was effectively in charge of an extensive island realm and, as a result, sufficiently prestigious to contemplate the making of agreements and alliances with other Norse princelings whose position was analogous to his own.[11]

At the centre of one such agreement was Ketil's daughter, Aud the Deep-Minded, who, at her father's instigation, married Olaf the White, one of several Viking chieftains who had conquered territories in Ireland. On Olaf being killed in battle, Aud returned to the Hebrides with her son, Thorstein the Red, who was to become, in time, a noted Viking warrior in his own right. 'He raided far and wide throughout Scotland and was everywhere victorious,' an Icelandic saga notes of Thorstein whose conquests are said to have included a large part of the Highland mainland – where Aud, at some stage, joined him. But Thorstein, too, was ultimately to die in the course of one or other of the wars he helped unleash. On news of his loss reaching Aud's Highland home, a sagaman commented, 'she realised that she had no further prospects there'. Her father, her husband and now her son being dead, Aud's own position – given the often brutal and always male-dominated nature of the society to which she belonged – had evidently been rendered very vulnerable. She consequently decided to make yet another of the fresh starts which were one of her life's repeated features. 'Aud was in Caithness when she learned of Thorstein's death,' runs the relevant saga. 'She had a ship built secretly in a forest and, when it was ready, she sailed away to Orkney.'[12]

Aud's ultimate destination was Iceland. Its earliest inhabitants had been Gaelic-speaking monks who – venturing north from monasteries like Iona's and possibly deducing the existence of some such landmass from the migratory movements of geese – sailed there by way of Orkney, Shetland and Faroe. In that most remote of all the North Atlantic islands, it was observed of Iceland by one monastic scholar, the summer sun sank below the horizon for so short a time that, despite its having set, 'a man could do whatever he wished, as though the sun were still there, even remove lice from his shirt'. But for all its proximity to the Arctic, Iceland, as immediately appreciated by those Norsemen who landed on its southern shores in the 860s, was by no means inhospitable. Grass grew plentifully in the island's coastal valleys. There were even woods – afterwards felled and cleared – in more sheltered localities. In the ninth century's closing decades, therefore, thousands of Norse settlers were to make their way to Iceland. Among those settlers was Aud the Deep-Minded.[13]

Aud's voyage from Caithness to Iceland was far from hurried. On getting to Orkney, she stayed there for such time as it took to arrange for the marriage of her granddaughter, Groa, a daughter of Thorstein the Red, to one of Orkney's leading Norse families. A further granddaughter, Oluva, was similarly provided for in Faroe. And in Iceland itself – where Aud finally set up home in a previously unoccupied area in the north-western corner of the island – this most matriarchal of women took care to reserve her estate's most desirable holdings for the two dozen or so individuals she had brought with her from the Highlands and Islands.

The Book of Settlements, a medieval Icelander's account of his country's origins, has this to say about Aud's last days:

> Aud was a woman of great dignity. When she was growing weary with old age, she invited her kinsmen and relatives by marriage to a magnificent feast, and, when the feast had been celebrated for three days, she chose fine gifts for her friends and gave them sound advice. She declared that the feast would go on for another three days and that it would be her funeral feast. That very night she died.[14]

Aud's intelligence and perspicacity – the qualities which resulted in her being dubbed 'deep-minded' – were as renowned among her contemporaries as the fortitude she demonstrated in making herself one of the most successful of Iceland's pioneering colonists. She was, it is remarked in one of the several sagas dealing with the doings of her descendants, 'a paragon'. And since little or nothing is known today about most of the individuals, particularly the women, who inhabited the Highlands and Islands a thousand or so years ago, Aud, the outlines of whose biography can be recovered from Icelandic sources, more than merits the few lines devoted to her here.[15]

Born in Norway, her father's homeland, Aud the Deep-Minded also lived in, or visited, the Hebrides, Ireland, the Highland mainland, Orkney, Faroe and Iceland. The Viking world into which much of the Highlands and Islands had been drawn by the time of Aud's death, then, was an enormously extensive one. People from the Highlands and Islands consequently found themselves presented with the chance to make new homes in a variety of faraway places. As regards Iceland, in particular, that chance was clearly seized. Among the men and women who settled there in the years around 900 were many whose names were Celtic. Some of these folk were Irish. Others, however, had emigrated to Iceland from the Highlands and Islands. Nor was Iceland necessarily these people's final destination. From Iceland, families of Highlands and Islands extraction appear to have made their way to the Norse settlements which were established, during the tenth century, in Greenland. And when the Greenland Viking, Thorfinn Karlsefni, briefly attempted – around 1010 – to establish a colony even further to the west, in the North American locality he and his fellow-Greenlanders called Vinland, Karlsefni was accompanied by 'a Scottish couple' who, the chances are, were of Highlands and Islands origin.[16]

Vinland was almost certainly located on the Atlantic coast of the country now called Canada – a country which, as things turned out, was one day to attract huge numbers of emigrants from the Highlands and Islands. The Viking presence in North America, however, was destined to be extremely transient. Greenland, for its part, offered few opportunities for settlement. And even Iceland – one of the most successful Norse colonies and an island which remains Scandinavian in language and culture – was soon thought to contain all the settler families it could readily sustain. Although overseas emigration from the Highlands and Islands can be said to have started in Norse times, therefore, such emigration, by the standards of later periods, was not substantial. Of greater importance, in a Highlands and Islands context, was the extent to which the Viking impact on the Highlands and Islands resulted in the emergence, within the region itself, of self-governing principalities presided over by their own Norse rulers. Ketil Flatnose's Hebridean domain was one such principality. But of much more significance was the Viking realm which became known as the Earldom of Orkney.

Drive across Orkney's Mainland – much the largest, as its name suggests, of the seventy or more islands which make up the Orkney archipelago – and it is not hard to see why the Vikings so valued this place. By Norwegian standards, and by the standards, too, of almost all the other islands and island groups which Norway's Vikings incorporated into their sphere of influence, Orkney is remarkably fertile. In contrast to Shetland and most of the Hebrides, places given over largely to crofts or smallholdings, modern Orkney is a region of large farms – their substantial, stone-built farmhouses testifying to this landscape's age-old capacity to generate a lot more wealth than the rocky, boggy and generally unproductive terrain which is characteristic of much of the rest of the Highlands and Islands.

The names of Orkney's farms – Quanterness, Hobbister, Feolquoy, Vigga, Ocklester, Skaill, Mellsetter, Wasbuster, Hurkisgarth – are predominantly Norse. Indeed, so overwhelming was the Viking influence hereabouts that, despite the islands having been inhabited for thousands of years prior to the arrival of Norwegian immigrants, there exists in all of Orkney just a single placename – the name Orkney itself – which is indisputably of pre-Norse origin. That fact was once thought to point to Orkney's earlier inhabitants having been expelled or exterminated by Viking invaders. Today it is thought more likely that in Orkney, as in the Hebrides, Norse settlers – though they may have resorted to violence as a means of ensuring that they obtained the best available land – were perfectly prepared to live alongside other, much longer-established, populations. But for all that such populations almost certainly survived the Vikings' appearance among them, they probably did so in a distinctly subordinate position. Orkney's ruling class had previously been Pictish. Now it was Scandinavian – in language, in culture, in outlook. Soon that Scandinavian ethos had been embraced by the Orcadian population as a whole – with the Pictish language, in the process, becoming extinct.

Much the same was true of both Shetland and Caithness: the

former having constituted, from the Orcadian earldom's inception, a north-easterly extension of its territories; the latter being annexed by the earldom in the course of the ninth century.

Quite how the earldom itself emerged remains obscure. *Orkneyinga Saga*, an Icelandic account of its history, tells how Orkney was given by Harald Finehair, a ninth-century king of Norway, to one of his noblemen, Rognvald, Earl of More. Rognvald, *Orkneyinga Saga* goes on, then gifted his new possession to his brother, Sigurd the Powerful, whom King Harald, in due course, made Earl of Orkney. That seems clear enough. But despite the saga's author having had on his side a longstanding tradition to the effect that there were kinship ties between later Earls of Orkney and the family of More, whose Norwegian lands lay in the vicinity of Trondheim, there is something suspiciously straightforward about this *Orkneyinga Saga* version of the earldom's beginnings. The truth is probably more complex. Irrespective of what went before, however, Sigurd the Powerful definitely governed Orkney in the middle decades of the ninth century when, in alliance with Thorstein the Red, son of Aud the Deep-Minded, he appears to have waged a series of campaigns with the objective of bringing much of the Highland mainland under Norse control. 'Earl Sigurd became a great ruler,' *Orkneyinga Saga* remarks. 'He joined forces with Thorstein the Red . . . and together they conquered the whole of Caithness and a large part of Argyll, Moray and Ross.'[17]

Given Thorstein's connections – through his grandfather, Ketil Flatnose, and his father, Olaf the White – with the Hebrides and Ireland, it is possible to envisage, on the basis of that *Orkneyinga Saga* sentence, how Thorstein and Sigurd might jointly have waged war on such Gaels and Picts as tried to resist their advance. Thorstein, one imagines, would have fought his way north-eastwards across the Highlands from Argyll, by way of the Great Glen, to those 'Moray and Ross' lowlands which adjoin the Beauly and Cromarty Firths. Sigurd, for his part, would have thrust southwards across Caithness and Sutherland prior to crossing, or rounding, the Dornoch Firth and linking up with Thorstein in the vicinity of, say, Tain.

That, of course, is supposition. But whether such overlordship was accomplished by Sigurd and Thorstein or by others, the Vikings certainly succeeded, at some point, in establishing their jurisdiction over virtually the entire Highland mainland to the north of a line extending roughly from Dingwall to Ullapool. The placename record demonstrates as much. Both Ullapool and Dingwall – the latter denoting, like Tingwall in Shetland or Thingvellir in Iceland, a place of assembly – were named originally by Norse-speakers. Between the Cromarty and Dornoch Firths, admittedly, Norse placenames are none too plentiful. North of the latter inlet, however, they are notably thicker on the ground – especially in Caithness where, in the more low-lying and fertile parts of the county at any rate, the Vikings seem to have settled almost as densely as they did in nearby Orkney.

Caithness – where a Norseman called Dorrud was said to have seen the valkyries on the day of the Battle of Clontarf – is almost as treeless today as any of the islands across the Pentland Firth. There are plenty of woods in Sutherland and Easter Ross, however. Could it have been in one of these localities rather than in Caithness – given the difficulties which Icelandic sagamen had with Scottish geography – that Aud the Deep-Minded built the ship in which she sailed to Iceland? And could it have been his interest in obtaining supplies of the timber needed by his shipbuilders which lay behind the Highland mainland campaigns of Sigurd the Powerful?

The sagas cast no light on these possibilities. They confine themselves to noting the deaths both of Sigurd and Thorstein the Red. And they dwell, in particular, on the peculiar way in which Sigurd, first Earl of Orkney, met his end.

Among the Scots, or Gaels, with whom Sigurd warred, it seems, was one Maelbrigte. A 'meeting', it further seems, was arranged 'at a certain place' between Sigurd and Maelbrigte. At this meeting, the two principals were 'to settle their differences' and each, it had been agreed, was to be accompanied by no more than forty men. By way of guarding against the possibility of double-dealing on the part of Maelbrigte and his followers, however, Sigurd 'had eighty men mounted on forty horses'. On the earl's ensuing encounter with Maelbrigte quickly and inevitably degenerating into 'a fierce fight', his two-to-one superiority in numbers naturally enabled Sigurd to score an easy victory. 'It wasn't long,' *Orkneyinga Saga* comments, 'before Maelbrigte and his men were dead.' The saga continues:

> Sigurd had their heads strapped to the victors' saddles to make a show of his triumph, and with that they began riding back home, flushed with their success. On the way, as Sigurd went to spur his horse, he struck his calf against a tooth sticking out of Maelbrigte's mouth and it gave him a scratch. The wound began to swell and ache, and it was this that led to the death of Sigurd the Powerful. He lies buried in a mound on the bank of the River Oykell.[18]

Such thousand-year-old tales ought not to be taken literally. It is in their nature to have grown a good deal in the telling. But for all that the historian does well to approach this and other *Orkneyinga Saga* episodes with a degree of scepticism, the story of Maelbrigte's posthumous revenge on Earl Sigurd is one that is corroborated – to some extent at any rate – by the existence of the Sutherland farm of Cyderhall. This farm is located at the northern end of the bridge which carries the modern Inverness-Caithness road across the Dornoch Firth. The firth, as it happens, is the seaward extension of the River Oykell on whose banks Sigurd the Powerful was said to have been interred. And the farm which is presently called Cyderhall is known to have had, in the thirteenth century, the name Syvardhoch – which translates as the howe, or burial mound, of Sigurd.

Of most of the various earls who ruled Orkney in the century or so following the death of Sigurd the Powerful, not a great deal is known beyond their names: Guthorm, Turf-Einar, Hallad, Arnkel, Erlend, Thorfinn Skull-Splitter, Arnfinn, Havard, Hlodvir, Ljot and Skuli. Then, towards the end of the tenth century, there emerged Sigurd the Stout with whom this chapter began. Sigurd, according to *Orkneyinga Saga*, was a 'great chieftain' who 'ruled over several dominions . . . and used to go on viking expeditions every summer as well, plundering in the Hebrides, Scotland and Ireland'. From this and several other scraps of testimony to the same effect, it can be deduced that Sigurd's territorial ambitions were nothing if not far-reaching; that his jurisdiction, as noted previously, extended from his Orkney powerbase across much of the Highlands and Islands including, very possibly, parts of Argyll and the Hebrides; that he aspired, in due course, to extend his influence into Ireland; that he became embroiled, as a result, in the events which culminated in his being killed, in 1014, at Clontarf.[19]

Despite its having ended his life, Sigurd's Irish foray is indicative of the extent to which the Orkney earldom had become, by his time, a power of real reach and significance. Nor was this a transient phenomenon. Thorfinn the Mighty, Sigurd's son and successor, is reputed to have campaigned 'deep into Scotland' and to have ruled 'the whole of the Hebrides' as well as 'a considerable part of Ireland'. Some subsequent weakening of the earldom's position is implied by the *Orkneyinga Saga*'s Icelandic author noting that Thorfinn 'was the most powerful of all the Earls of Orkney'. But his realm, for all that, continued to be important for decades, indeed centuries, after Earl Thorfinn's death in 1065.

Among the enduring attractions of *Orkneyinga Saga* are its detailed word-portraits of some of Norse Orkney's leading personalities. Here, for instance, is the saga's description of Earl Thorfinn:

> He was unusually tall and strong, an ugly-looking man with a black head of hair, sharp features, a big nose and bushy eyebrows, a forceful man, greedy for fame and fortune. He did well in battle, for he was both a good tactician and full of courage.[20]

And here is the saga on one of its most rumbustious characters, the twelfth-century magnate and freebooter, Svein Asleifarson of Gairsay:

> This is how Svein used to live. Winter he would spend at home on Gairsay, where he entertained some eighty men at his own expense. His drinking hall was so big there was nothing in Orkney to compare with it. In the spring he had more than enough to occupy him, with a great deal of seed to sow, which he saw to carefully himself. Then, when that job was done, he would go off plundering in the Hebrides and in Ireland on what he called his 'spring-trip', then back home just after mid-summer, where he stayed until the cornfields had been reaped and the grain was safely in. After that he would go off raiding again, and never came back until the first month of winter was ended. This he used to call his 'autumn-trip'.[21]

On the basis of such accounts, it is easy to imagine men like Thorfinn and Svein to have been little more than warlords and gangsters. But there was much more to the Earldom of Orkney than its role as a springboard for forays of the sort which Svein Asleifarson's Norse predecessors had been mounting in places like the Hebrides for the better part of three centuries. The society described in *Orkneyinga Saga* was, by medieval standards, remarkably prosperous, cosmopolitan and sophisticated. Several of the sea routes which were the key to Viking domination of the North Atlantic intersected in Orkney's vicinity – with the result that Orcadians were in regular contact not just with mainland Scandinavia and its oceanic outliers, but with England, with Ireland, with France and with several lands around the Mediterranean. When Thorfinn the Mighty toured Europe, visited Rome and met the Pope in or about 1050, therefore, he most certainly did not travel in the guise of frontiersman or barbarian. The earl was, and knew himself to be, a man of substance. And in the residence which he had constructed for himself at the former Pictish centre of Birsay on Orkney's Atlantic coast, Thorfinn, it can safely be surmised, lived in the carelessly lavish style then thought appropriate to a great ruler.

Among the courtiers whom Thorfinn the Mighty gathered around him at Birsay was Arnor Thordarsson, the Icelandic skald or bard whose verses can still be read, some nine hundred years after their composition, in *Orkneyinga Saga*. 'The bright sun will turn black,' runs Arnor's magnificent eulogy for his patron, 'the earth sink into the dark sea . . . before a chieftain finer than Thorfinn shall be born in the Orkney Isles.'[22]

Just as their Gaelic-speaking counterparts dealt ceaselessly in traditions stemming ultimately from Ireland's pagan past, so skalds like Arnor steeped themselves in the mythology and outlook of pagan Norway. But this, even in the era of Earl Thorfinn, was consciously to be archaic. Eleventh-century Orcadians, like their contemporaries elsewhere in the Nordic world, were Christians. Many Vikings, admittedly, may well have embraced Christianity in much the same tentative spirit as Aud the Deep-Minded's kinsman, Helgi the Lean – of whom it was recorded that he 'believed in Christ and yet made vows to Thor when it came to voyages and difficult times'. The Norse gods, after all, had held sway in Scandinavia from a time beyond reckoning. And these gods – Thor, Odin and the rest – were not ejected easily from the Viking mind. This makes it all the more noteworthy that by far the most spectacular of all the Earldom of Orkney's surviving monuments is a church.[23]

Of the several visits I have made to the church in question, the Cathedral of St Magnus in Kirkwall, the most memorable took place amid the swirling rain and sleet of a December evening. At nine o'clock or thereabouts, it had been dark – in a town which shares its latitude with St Petersburg, with Anchorage and with the northern part of Hudson Bay – for five or six hours. Kirkwall's streets and pavements, long since abandoned by the last of the day's shoppers, gleamed emptily in the wet. A westerly gale eddied among homes which, consisting of one or two storeys at most, seemed almost to be hunkering down in the face of the storm. Then, on turning a corner, I was confronted by the great bulk of St Magnus's Cathedral, completely dwarfing every other building in its vicinity. The church's stained-glass windows were brightly lit from inside. Rising above the noise of the wind there came the sound of singing. Christmas carols,

I surmised, were being rehearsed for the coming Sunday's service – one more link in an unbroken sequence of weekly worship which stretches virtually all the way back to the day in 1137 when, at the behest of Earl Rognvald Kali Kolsson, work began on this most impressive of churches. Slipping in by way of a side door which I found ajar, I stood, in my dripping waterproofs, listening to what was being sung. A woman approached, and I began to apologise for having entered uninvited. 'No, no,' she said in the unmistakable accents of Orkney. 'You're very welcome. Everyone is very welcome here.'

Magnus, the earl and saint whom Kirkwall's great church commemorates, is portrayed in *Orkneyinga Saga* as 'a man of strict virtue, successful in war, wise, eloquent, generous and magnanimous'; a man who 'believed divine justice to be more important than social distinctions'; a man who 'always gave the greatest comforts to the poor'. Such assessments would not have gone unchallenged in Magnus's lifetime. They would certainly have been disputed by Hakon – Magnus's cousin and the man with whom Magnus wrangled and fought in the course of one of the protracted succession disputes which were the Orkney earldom's most constant source of weakness. But had Magnus not possessed some underlying nobility of character, then *Orkneyinga Saga*'s highly coloured account of his death would have lacked all credibility. Equally lacking would have been any reason to expect Magnus's demise to be followed, as the saga claims it was, by a whole series of miracles.[24]

At Easter in 1117, it appears, Hakon enticed Magnus to the small Orkney island of Egilsay. There Hakon, having ensured that Magnus's men were hugely outnumbered, 'ordered his cook, Lilof, to kill Magnus'. When Lilof responded to this command by starting 'to weep out loud', Magnus immediately tried to comfort him:

> 'This is nothing to weep over,' said Magnus. 'A deed like this can only bring fame to the man who carries it out. Show yourself a man of spirit and you can have my clothes according to the old laws and customs. Don't be afraid. You're doing this against your will and the man who gives you the order is a greater sinner than you are.'
>
> At this, Earl Magnus took off his tunic and gave it to Lilof, then asked for leave to pray. This was granted, and he prostrated himself on the ground, committing his soul to God and offering himself as a sacrifice. He prayed not only for himself and his friends but for his enemies and murderers,

> forgiving them with all his heart for their crimes against him. He confessed his own sins before God, praying that his soul might be washed clean by the spilling of his own blood, then placed it in God's hands. He asked that he might be greeted by God's angels and carried by them into the peace of paradise.[25]

Moments later, Magnus was dead, killed by a blow to the head. 'The place where this happened,' *Orkneyinga Saga* reports, 'was rocky and overgrown with moss, but soon God revealed how worthy Earl Magnus was in his eyes, for the spot . . . turned into a green field.'[26]

With Magnus's posthumous reputation growing by leaps and bounds, it made good sense for Magnus's nephew, Rognvald Kali Kolsson, to promise – during a further struggle for control of the earldom – that, should he succeed in taking power in Orkney, he would establish a church dedicated to his uncle. On Rognvald becoming earl, he made good this pledge. The result is the cathedral of St Magnus. And it should maybe be mentioned by way of a footnote to what *Orkneyinga Saga* has to say about Earl Magnus's assassination that when, in 1919, there was discovered inside one of the cathedral's internal pillars the skeleton of a man thought to have been Magnus himself, the skeleton's skull was found to bear the marks of just the sort of mortal wound which *Orkneyinga Saga* describes the earl suffering in Egilsay at the hands of a tearful Lilof.

In Ireland the Vikings founded trading towns which eventually developed into cities like Cork, Waterford, Wexford, Limerick and Dublin. In the Highlands and Islands, where Norse immigrants seem mostly to have preferred agriculture to commerce, no substantial urban centres emerged in the Viking period. But the fact that a number of twenty-first-century Kirkwall's streets have obviously Nordic names ought not to be regarded as just another manifestation of the way in which modern Orcadians like to emphasise and underline their Viking roots. Thorfinn the Mighty may have regarded Birsay as his earldom's foremost place. By Earl Rognvald's time, however, Kirkwall – already a merchant settlement – had emerged as Orkney's capital. It has held that title ever since. And this little town's crowning glory remains the architectural masterpiece which Earl Rognvald caused to be erected here in honour of the saint who was his uncle. Other than where they are concealed by seventeenth-century tombstones or by the tapestry gifted some years ago to the people of Orkney by residents of Bergen and its hinterland, the red and cream sandstone walls and columns which constitute the interior of St Magnus's Cathedral are much as their medieval builders left them. Not least because their grace impresses every bit as much as their scale, these walls and columns serve to make the point that the Vikings, for all the negative connotations which still cling to their name, brought much that was positive to the Highlands and Islands. And there is one more message which Rognvald's church conveys to its twenty-first-century visitors. Our world may believe Orkney to be a remote and marginal locality of little contemporary consequence. Our world, in making this assessment, may be right. But Rognvald's church reminds us that things were not always so. It reminds us that the Earldom of Orkney exercised enormous influence, commanded considerable wealth and was capable of great accomplishments.

Well to the south of Orkney, meanwhile, a new kingdom was emerging. Eventually to be known as Scotland, this kingdom was to devote a good deal of its collective energies to bringing the Highlands and Islands within its boundaries and under its control. That process took a long time to complete. In much of what follows, therefore, it constitutes something of an underlying theme. The story thus to be unfolded, of course, is one which lots of other writers have told at some length. But this book views Scotland's expansion from a standpoint which differs, in one key respect, from that adopted in most accounts of the country's history. As their published output amply testifies, Scotland's historians incline generally to the view that the emergence and growth of the Scottish state – the political entity which gave shape and definition, of course, to Scottish history's subject matter – was an unrelievedly positive development. From the perspective of the Highlands and Islands, however, that judgement is open to challenge. It is certainly challenged here. Scotland's territorial expansion, it is argued in the course of this and subsequent chapters, impacted on the Highlands and Islands in a manner which was almost wholly adverse. The area's people, for instance, were gradually deprived – often forcibly – of their autonomy. That autonomy had been theirs since the Highlands and Islands were first settled in the millennia following the ice age. It had endured in the face of Roman invasion. It had survived, if in a necessarily adapted and modified form, the arrival of the Vikings. And its loss – first to Scotland and then to the wider United Kingdom of which Scotland eventually became part – was to have consequences so debilitating for the Highlands and Islands that the region is only beginning again today, at the start of the twenty-first century, to realise something of the potential which, whether in Dalriadan Iona or Norse Kirkwall, made the Highlands and Islands of eight, nine, ten or more centuries ago an area of outstanding creativity.

It is more than a little ironic, then, that the Scottish state was, in some respects, a Highlands and Islands creation, its founding dynasty having been, in essence, the Cenel nGabrain who – in the person particularly of a king known nowadays as Kenneth MacAlpin – migrated eastwards from Dalriada and took over what had previously been the southern, and latterly the most important, part of Pictland. This migration took place some three or four decades into the ninth century. What prompted it is far from certain – though it could well have been precipitated, to some extent, by the activities of Ketil Flatnose and those other Norsemen who were then assuming a dominant position in the Hebrides and, as a result, encroaching into what had been the Cenel nGabrain heartland. But if the causes of Kenneth MacAlpin's departure from Argyll are obscure, its consequences are clear enough. There now took shape, in much the same strategically significant locality that Rome's Inchtuthil garrison had been intended to dominate eight centuries before, the nucleus of a new realm. In Gaelic, the language of its creators, this realm was called *Alba*. In Latin, the language employed by its church-educated clerks and chroniclers, Alba became *Scotia* – the country of the *Scoti* or Gaels. And in English, Scotia, in due course, became Scotland.

To travel on the often tortuous roads linking modern Argyll with the district which Kenneth MacAlpin so triumphantly appropriated is immediately to suspect that neither Kenneth nor his successors would have had much reason to mourn their abandonment of their former homeland. Those roads may provide today's tourists with access to some of the finest mountain scenery in Europe, but mountain scenery was of little value to an early-medieval monarchy. Of infinitely greater interest, as far as such a monarchy was concerned, were vistas of the sort that open up when – having reached Strathtay by way of Tyndrum, Killin and Aberfeldy – you turn south towards Dunkeld and Perth. The countryside hereabouts is hugely more productive than any part of Argyll. And this countryside – even when farmed by folk whose agricultural techniques could deliver no more than a small fraction of present-day yields – was capable of supplying its ninth-century masters with wealth of a sort that never came their way in Dalriada.

Not surprisingly, then, the MacAlpin dynasty quickly set about staking an enduring claim both on Strathtay and on the lands around it. To their new territories they may have brought from Argyll the slab of rock, long afterwards called the Stone of Destiny, which was installed, during this period, at Scone, just to the north of Perth. There the stone – which, irrespective of its provenance, was a semi-mystical totem of huge significance – played a major role in the rituals surrounding the inauguration of Scotia's kings. Since they were predominantly pagan in nature, it is maybe appropriate that these rituals were conducted on an artificial mound – still to be seen in the grounds of the modern Scone Palace – which was itself of prehistoric origin. But the MacAlpin monarchs, though they thus took care to nurture ancestral customs deriving ultimately from pre-Christian Ireland, were equally concerned to safeguard the close association which the Cenel nGabrain had long had with the Columban Church – and especially with Colum Cille's own monastery of Iona.

In the 830s and 840s, in response to continued raids of the sort which had led to Abbot Blathmac's martyrdom, the Iona monastery's remaining treasures – among them a number of relics and other items reputedly connected with Columba himself – were conveyed from Iona to places where, it was hoped, they would be less susceptible to Viking depredations. Some of these valuables, including the gospel books which thus acquired their link with that particular location, were shipped to the monastery of Kells in Ireland. Others – at Kenneth MacAlpin's personal instigation, it appears – were conveyed to a monastery at Dunkeld. Of that monastery, there is nothing now to be seen. Some of the materials from which it was constructed, however, are believed to have been incorporated into the later Dunkeld Cathedral which, though a good deal less remarkable than its Kirkwall counterpart, has the merit of occupying one of the most attractive ecclesiastical sites in all of Scotland. Its lushly wooded precincts on the banks of the Tay, about fifteen miles upstream from Scone and within two or three hours' march of Inchtuthil, may lack an oceanic ambience of the kind that makes Iona so unforgettable. But any Iona monks who came here – and some would have done so – are unlikely to have been any more regretful than Dalriada's kings about their having swapped Argyll's stormy and vulnerable coasts for the comparative tranquillity of their new home.

There were times, admittedly, when Norse armies threatened even Dunkeld. But Scotia, having weathered such crises, both survived and expanded.The former Pictish territories in eastern localities like Angus and Fife came under Scottish control at an early stage. And during the two centuries following Scotia's establishment, its frontiers were pushed steadily southwards. The kingdom of Strathclyde, having first become a Scottish dependency, eventually became an integral part of the Scottish realm. So did the still more valuable area between the Forth and the Tweed – an area which had earlier been part of the kingdom of Northumbria. By the eleventh century, therefore, Scotland's southern boundary lay more or less where it has lain ever since.

The state which had thus been formed was, by the standards of its time, a notably successful one. Neither then nor later were Wales and Ireland – both of which remained under the jurisdiction of numerous local rulers – to produce a national monarchy of the type created by Kenneth MacAlpin and his successors. And even England – where the Saxon kingdom of Wessex undertook much the same unifying, or aggrandising, task as Kenneth MacAlpin's Alba – was to prove, in some respects, a decidedly shakier entity than its northern neighbour. Early-medieval England, it needs stressing in this context, was conquered twice – first by the Danes, then by the Normans. Early-medieval Scotland avoided such a fate.

Alba's expansion had the inevitable effect of shifting the Scottish kingdom's centre of gravity still further to the south and east – its monarchs eventually quitting Strathtay for the former Northumbrian stronghold of Edinburgh. But the kingdom's Dalriadan – and ultimately Irish – roots remained long in evidence. Until the end of the eleventh century, for example, most of Scotland's kings were buried on Iona. And for the first few hundred years of its existence, Scotland was overwhelmingly Gaelic in speech. In what had previously been Strathclyde, for instance, Welsh gave way totally to Gaelic. In the greater part of what had once been Pictland, Pictish did the same. Hence the very large extent to which the present-day placenames of areas like Angus and Fife are Gaelic in origin. Hence, too, the fact that Scotland's earliest surviving fragments of written Gaelic – dating from the twelfth century – are to be found in the margins of a Latin gospel book which belonged to a monastery at Deer in what was then the solidly Gaelic-speaking district of Aberdeenshire.

It can be difficult to pin down exactly what determines the abandonment of one language and the adoption of another. In Shetland, Orkney and the north-eastern corner of Caithness – just about the only parts of modern Scotland, incidentally, where Gaelic has never been spoken by any substantial number of people – the replacement of Pictish by Norse was doubtless related, as previously noted, to the fact that, from the ninth century onwards, Norse-speakers constituted this area's ruling order. The much more widespread shift from Pictish to Gaelic must similarly have been connected with the way in which Gaelic-speakers, also from the ninth century onwards, took charge in places where Picts had previously dominated. There are circumstances, however, in which the language of a society's governing orders is not adopted by the same society's lower strata. Thus Norman French, despite its being the speech of England's ruling class in the era following the Norman Conquest of 1066, did not displace English in England as a whole. Indeed it was English, in the later middle ages, which finally got the better of Norman French. A virtually identical process, as it happened, was to occur in the south-eastern part of Scotland.

Although it was certainly spoken in the Lothians, not least by early Scottish kings and by their courtiers, Gaelic seems never to have been anything like so dominant there as it was to the north of the Forth. Unlike Orkney and Shetland, the Lothians have their share of Gaelic placenames – Balerno, for example. But around Edinburgh, the formerly Northumbrian settlement which gradually took on the role of Scotland's capital, the Anglian language – itself stemming from a dialect brought across the North Sea by Northumbria's Germanic originators – continued to be spoken by the population at large. In time this language, in the form nowadays called Broad Scots or Lallans, was actually to take over from Gaelic – in a development paralleling the triumph of Lallans' close linguistic relative, English, over Norman French – as the speech of the people who mattered at the centre of the Scottish kingdom. The influence and prestige thus gained by the Lallans of the Lothians were factors in the subsequent spread of that language into the rest of Lowland Scotland. The consequent demise of Gaelic to the south and east of the Highlands and Islands was, in turn, indicative of the Scottish kingdom's wider tendency, starting in the eleventh and twelfth centuries, to turn its back on its Highlands and Islands beginnings.

Rather like modern business corporations, medieval monarchies typically sought to swallow up their rivals – in the manner, for instance, that Alba acquired Strathclyde – while also trying to avoid their own subordination to others. And just as the modern corporation tends both to borrow management methods and to recruit senior managers from its competitors, so medieval monarchies, not least the monarchy of Scotland, both adopted institutions which had been devised elsewhere and imported personnel with the skills required to ensure that such transplanted institutions worked effectively. In the Scottish case, the institutions in question were predominantly those associated with the social order historians have since labelled feudal. To the increasingly feudalised Scotland which thus began to emerge in the twelfth century, there were accordingly enticed or attracted substantial numbers of the medieval equivalents of those present-day executives and directors who – in return for appropriately enhanced prospects – migrate so readily from one company boardroom to the next. Such individuals mostly consisted, in twelfth-century circumstances, of Norman or Normanised aristocrats whose fathers or grandfathers had moved from France to England as a result of events in 1066 and who – in the manner of those other Normans who turned up, at this time, in places as far afield as Palestine, Sicily and Ireland – hoped to carve out new niches for themselves in Scotland.

The Normans, as their name suggests, had begun as Vikings. That is how there came to be a family connection between Orkney's earls and the dukes of Normandy – of whom by far the most renowned was the eleventh-century Duke William who, following his invasion and subjugation of England, acquired the title of William the Conqueror. William's undoubted aggressiveness may conceivably have owed something to his Viking ancestry. But a couple of centuries spent on the western margins of France, one of Europe's most heavily feudalised countries, had resulted, well before 1066, in Normans putting their Norse past behind them and taking on behavioural characteristics of the sort held to be archetypally feudal. The standard modern portrayal of medieval Normans features mounted, armoured knights who lived in castles and paid homage to a king to whom they, in return for the extensive estates which their king granted them, owed military service in time of war. That particular image, as such images go, is broadly accurate. When Scotland's kings set out to strengthen their realm by feudalising it, knights, castles and the concept of homage, or fealty, were among the novelties – mostly Norman in origin – which resulted.

Among medieval Scotland's feudal immigrants was a family whose earliest known representatives held senior positions in the household of the bishops of Dol, a locality on the borders of Normandy and Brittany. In the years around 1100, a member of this family, one Alan by name, attached himself to Henry, youngest son of Duke William of Normandy, conqueror of England. In his capacity as Henry's feudal subordinate, Alan received estates in Shropshire. But these, it seems, were insufficient to provide for Alan's third son, Walter, who, around 1136, found his way to Scotland where he entered the service of

David I – one of the most feudally inclined of all Scotland's medieval monarchs. On Walter, who became one of his most steadfast supporters, David bestowed substantial landholdings in and around Renfrew, Paisley and Pollok on the southern bank of the River Clyde. On Walter, in due course, David also bestowed the office of royal purseholder or steward. From this office, subsequently made hereditary, Walter's descendants – many of them kings and queens of Scotland – derived their surname, Stewart. In one capacity or another, as things turned out, holders of this surname, over many generations, were to play a hugely significant part in the process of integrating the Highlands and Islands into the Scottish kingdom.

That could not have been foreseen in the twelfth century. But what was clearly perceived even then by David I and by other Scottish monarchs of the period was the manner in which feudalism could be of enormous help to kings aiming – as Scotland's twelfth-century kings certainly were – to expand their authority. Pre-feudal realms were governed in accordance with traditional values which, as mentioned in the previous chapter, meant kingship was dispersed among a whole variety of potentially competing kin-groups. Not only did this result in a highly localised, as opposed to centralised, society, but it also meant that subordinate rulers could, and did, aspire to displace their superiors. Just such displacement occurred in Dalriada. It also occurred, as will be seen shortly, in eleventh-century Scotland. To a king like David I, therefore, one of feudalism's most alluring qualities lay in the extent to which it appeared – assuming that it could be imposed widely and forcefully enough – to eliminate such threats to himself and to his dynasty. All Scotland's territories, feudalism's advocates insisted, were, in effect, the personal property of a single, hereditary monarch. The occupiers of these territories, it followed, held their lands by virtue of a contractual relationship – spelled out in the charters which were one of feudalism's defining features – with that monarch. And because the social and political hierarchy thus established had no room for rival power centres, the feudal king, conceptually at any rate, was enormously less challengeable than his pre-feudal predecessors. He was, quite literally, monarch of all he surveyed.

In the nature of things, feudal theory and practice never coincided completely. But feudalism, for all that, provided a centralising and expansionist monarchy with a critically important means of promoting a kingdom's development. If a region which had customarily been governed by its own local notables could be parcelled out among incoming feudal magnates who owed their position to a king whose authority over that region had previously been nominal or non-existent, then the king in question had enhanced his position in a readily measurable fashion. An area that had previously been outside the monarch's jurisdiction was now firmly within it. Should any of that area's inhabitants be disposed to challenge the monarch's rule, they would find themselves confronting his newly installed feudal nobility in that nobility's role as heavily armed cavalry operating out of strongly fortified keeps. And by way of underlining his control of such newly feudalised localities, a king might also take the opportunity to make additional changes of a type which – while not strictly feudal – had the effect of underlining his overall ascendancy. A unified legal system – operated by royal officials of the sort known in Scotland as sheriffs – might take the place of customary, and often highly diverse, law codes. Ecclesiastical structures might be overhauled in such a way as to turn the Church into an instrument of central government. Merchant settlements – of the kind which Scots, significantly enough, were to call royal burghs – might be established in order to give an economic dimension to monarchical policies of an increasingly ambitious and interventionist type.

Right across Europe, from Spain to Silesia, medieval kings employed such methods as a means to the overriding end of bolstering their power and augmenting their dominions. It is not surprising, then, that Scottish monarchs were to deploy feudal techniques in the course of their various attempts to gain more leverage over the Highlands and Islands. Nor is it surprising that the first part of the Highlands and Islands to be subjected to these techniques was the locality called Moray. Its rulers, after all, came close – in the course of the eleventh century – to supplanting Kenneth MacAlpin's heirs as kings of Scotland.

Moray in the middle ages was much larger than the relatively restricted county or district of more recent times. Extending from the North Sea to the Atlantic, its heartland comprised all the coastal lowlands to the south of the Moray and Beauly Firths – while its hinterland included Strathspey, Badenoch, Lochaber and the highly fragmented mountain country stretching westwards from the Great Glen into Knoydart and Lochalsh. Roughly conterminous, very possibly, with the Pictish province administered in Columba's day by King Bridei, this entire region became, in the course of the ninth and tenth centuries, a Gaelic-speaking area governed by men who claimed descent from the Cenel Loairn, one of the kindreds originally constituting Dalriada. Although nothing is known for certain as to how this particular transition came about, the Cenel Loairn, whose Dalriadan territories were located around Loch Linnhe, appear to have moved up the Great Glen into Moray in much the same way, and at much the same time, as the Cenel nGabrain migrated eastwards into Strathtay. The end result was the emergence of Moray as a regional power of some considerable importance. Several of the 'Scottish kings' who feature in *Orkneyinga Saga* – including Maelbrigte with whom Sigurd the Powerful tangled so fatefully – appear to have been rulers of Moray rather than rulers of Scotia. And it is suggestive of Moray's strength that its governing dynasty managed to preserve their kingdom's independence in the face of the obvious threat posed to that independence by successive Earls of Orkney.

As to the relationship between Moray and the Scottish state put together by Kenneth MacAlpin and his heirs, it was probably analogous to that between the Cenel Loairn and the Cenel nGabrain in Dalriada. Moray's ruling family – whose principal base, like that of Bridei before them, was probably in or around present-day Inverness – may have acknowledged Scotland's monarchs to be, in some sense, their overkings. But like their Cenel Loairn forebears, Moray's leading men, sometimes known as *mormaers*, were also kings in their own right. And just as the Cenel Loairn sometimes managed – if only occasionally and briefly – to replace the Cenel nGabrain as the supreme authority in Dalriada, so Moray's kings, given appropriate circumstances, could aspire to become monarchs of Scotland as a whole. This is exactly what happened in 1040 when the most famed of Moray's rulers, a man known to history as Macbeth, first defeated Scotland's King Duncan in battle and then assumed control of Duncan's kingdom.

Macbeth governed Scotland for more than ten years. In 1054, however, he was ousted by Duncan's son, Malcolm, who had meanwhile been living in exile in England and who, with English backing, had mounted a successful cross-border invasion of Macbeth's realm. At this point, significantly enough, Macbeth simply withdrew to Moray which remained, equally significantly, beyond Malcolm's jurisdiction. Another three years passed before Malcolm judged it safe to move north. And such was Moray people's determination to resist Malcolm's encroachments that, following Macbeth's death in the course of the fierce fighting which now ensued, they promptly proclaimed the late king's stepson, Lulach, as their ruler. Not until Lulach had himself been ambushed and killed in the early part of

1058 was Malcolm's position finally rendered more or less secure.

As *Calum Ceann Mor*, or Malcolm Canmore, the king who thus replaced Macbeth was to reign in Scotland until 1093. And his descendants were to occupy the Scottish throne for most of the next two hundred years. From the perspective both of this Canmore dynasty and of the Stewarts, their eventual successors, Macbeth, of course, was simply a usurper. That is how he was portrayed by the Scottish monarchy's propagandists. And that is how he is depicted, needless to say, in the early-seventeenth-century play which has resulted in Macbeth's name having acquired such universal familiarity. William Shakespeare – writing from London and wishing to curry favour with the Stewart monarch who, in 1603, had become England's king as well as Scotland's – stuck firmly with what had long been the Scottish crown's standard line on the events of the 1040s and 1050s. Shakespeare's Macbeth, as a result, is a blood-drenched villain of whom Scotland was well rid.

The reality, not least from a Highlands and Islands standpoint, was altogether more ambiguous. As far as Malcolm Canmore was concerned, his victories over Macbeth and Lulach may have resulted in Moray, like Strathclyde or Lothian before it, becoming just another piece of Scottish territory. But its consequent loss of its earlier autonomy was bitterly resented within Moray itself.

From the eleventh century until the eighteenth, practically all the advances made by Scotland's central government in the Highlands and Islands were met with violent resistance – resistance which, while it appeared perfectly legitimate to those who engaged in it, was inevitably regarded, in the south, as insurrection and insurgency of a most disloyal and treacherous kind. Events in Moray, during the period following the deaths of Macbeth and Lulach, conformed exactly to this pattern. Malcolm Canmore had to lead an army into a still restless Moray in 1078. Malcolm's son, Alexander I, had to do the same in 1116. And in 1130 one of Lulach's grandsons, Angus, gained widespread backing in Moray for his attempt to overthrow Alexander's younger brother, David I, in much the same way as Macbeth had toppled David's grandfather some ninety years before. Angus's uprising failed. But he was able to menace the Lowlands with an army which reportedly sustained 4,000 casualties before being overwhelmed. Twelfth-century Moray, these facts suggest, was anything but reconciled to Canmore rule.

It was in order to deal with this situation that David I, in his capacity as one of feudalism's most enthusiastic advocates, set out – in the aftermath of Angus's rebellion – to make Moray loyal by making it feudal. Having presumably expropriated Gaelic-speaking landholders of the sort who rallied to Angus in 1130, David established a number of foreign-born magnates in the area. Of these, the most significant was a man called Freskin who was granted substantial estates in the vicinity of Elgin – where King David, at this point, created a royal burgh. Probably of Flemish origin, Freskin was the founder of an aristocratic family whose members were known initially by their Latinised territorial designation, *de Moravia*, and afterwards by the name of Murray. But neither this family nor others of the same type were to find it easy to profit from their new possessions. Moray's glens and mountains continued to shelter Gaelic-speaking kindreds, most notably the MacHeths and the MacWilliams, who remained committed to the much older social order which feudalism was intended to destroy. Over and over again, these kindreds and their followers took up arms against Scotland's kings. Over and over again, they were crushed. But it was more than a decade into the thirteenth century before his agents were able to present a Scottish monarch with the severed head of the last of his MacHeth opponents. And not until 1230, a full century after David I undertook Moray's pacification, was MacWilliam rebelliousness finally snuffed out. That year, according to one of Scotland's medieval chroniclers, the one surviving representative of the principal MacWilliam family was seized by knights loyal to Alexander II, king of Scotland and a great-grandson of Malcolm Canmore. The MacWilliam heir in question was a little girl 'who had not long left her mother's womb'. Soon her captors had rode with her into Forfar. There, in a gesture which points to feudal nobles having been rather less chivalrous than their romanticisers like to believe, this infant symbol of Moray's persistent rejection of Scotland's monarchy had 'her head . . . struck against the column of the [market] cross and her brains dashed out'.[27]

Having thus disposed of the former Kingdom of Moray, Scotland's central government turned its attention to the mainland territories of the Earldom of Orkney. Partly in response to the threat thus posed to its interests, the earldom, particularly in the person of Harald Madaddson who became Orkney's ruler in the later part of the twelfth century, had increasingly identified itself with the cause of the MacWilliams and the MacHeths – Harald Madaddson's second wife, for example, being of MacHeth extraction. But Orcadian alignments of this sort served mainly to make Scottish kings all the more determined to safeguard their earlier gains by extending their rule into present-day Sutherland and Caithness. Nor was Earl Harald's position helped by the fact that Norway's monarchy – for reasons virtually identical to those shaping Scottish policy in the Highlands and Islands – was also making efforts to exert its authority both in the Earldom of Orkney and in more outlying parts of the Norwegian mainland. During the 1190s, as a result, Harald became embroiled in what was, in effect, a war on two fronts. This war went very badly for Orkney's ruler. By way of punishment for his having participated in a Norwegian rebellion organised by men who were seeking to thwart the centralising ambitions of Norway's King Sverre, Harald found himself deprived of Shetland – now detached, on Sverre's orders, from the Orkney earldom and governed, for most of the next two centuries as things turned out, by Norwegian officials appointed by Sverre and his successors. South of the Pentland Firth, meanwhile, Earl Harald was having no more luck than had come his way in Norway.

An Orcadian invasion of Moray in 1196, far from assisting Earl Harald's MacWilliam and MacHeth allies, precipitated a counter-invasion of the earldom's mainland possessions by an army under the personal command of the Scottish king, William the Lion, a man every bit as committed as his father, David I, to securing greater royal control of the Highlands and Islands. Scotland's monarchs had long asserted that their realm included the entire Highland mainland and that Orkney's earls were, in consequence, the Scottish crown's feudal subordinates – in respect, at least, of the earldom's landholdings in Sutherland and Caithness. Now William, the first Scottish king to venture so far north, gave real meaning to these claims. When, in 1197, his army reached Ousdale, a glen which lies just inside modern Caithness's boundary with Sutherland, William's camp was reported to have 'extended from one end of the valley to the other'. Soon Thurso, then the site of Harald's foremost mainland stronghold, had been captured by the Scots. Although such blows by no means destroyed the Orkney earldom, they unmistakably signalled that, relative to an increasingly assertive kingdom of Scotland, the earldom was very definitely on the wane.[28]

William the Lion's 1197 campaign ended Orcadian control of Sutherland. And despite the Earls of Orkney managing to retain a presence in Caithness, this presence was a good deal less secure than it had been in former times – with the earls' hold on their Caithness possessions becoming conditional on their paying homage, in their role as Caithness landholders, to Scotland's kings.

Those same kings' steadily tightening grip on both Sutherland and Caithness was also evident in the ecclesiastical sphere. The wider Scottish Church, it should be mentioned in this connection, had itself been radically reorganised in the course of the various reforms – feudalism's introduction pre-eminent among them – which Scotland's medieval monarchy so vigorously promoted. The monastery-based Church of Columban times had consequently given way to one where authority resided, as had long been the case in England and in continental Europe, with priests and bishops rather than with monks and abbots. The Scottish crown inevitably took a close interest in appointments to this Church's upper echelons – most such appointments going, during the twelfth and thirteenth centuries, to men belonging to the recently installed feudal élite whose primary function, in the Highlands and Islands anyway, was to assist the growth of royal power. Hence the significance attached, both by the crown and by its Highlands and Islands opponents, to the issue of who exactly should have jurisdiction over ecclesiastical matters in Sutherland and Caithness.

When Orkney's earls were unreservedly in charge of the northern Highland mainland, Orkney's bishops – men whose background was naturally Norse rather than Scottish – were regarded as the Church's leading figures in the region. By 1200, however, the Scottish monarchy was imposing its own bishops on the north. This was inevitably resented both by the Earls of Orkney and by a population whose language and culture were still predominantly those of the Vikings. In 1202, as a result, the Scrabster residence of one of the Scottish king's Caithness and Sutherland bishops was stormed, and the unfortunate bishop, on being taken captive, was ritually mutilated – his eyes being put out and his tongue being cut from his mouth. Twenty years later, the 1202 victim's successor, Bishop Adam, suffered an even grimmer fate at the hands of a party of Caithness men who burst into his home at Halkirk. 'Like wolves against the shepherd, degenerate sons against their father, and satellites of the devil against Christ the Lord,' according to one Scottish account, Bishop Adam's assailants 'stripped him of his proper vestments, stoned him, wounded him . . . with a double-sided axe and roasted him to death in his own kitchen'.[29]

Modern Halkirk, a stone-built village straddling the River Thurso, contains no visible remains of Bishop Adam's house. But anyone who travels south from Halkirk on the modern Thurso-Inverness road – a road which, incidentally, traverses Ousdale where William the Lion once camped – can still visit, in the Sutherland town of Dornoch, the cathedral to which the murdered Bishop Adam's remains were moved in 1239. Adam's disinterment and reburial were ordered by his successor as bishop of Caithness and Sutherland, Gilbert de Moravia, previously archdeacon of Moray and a man whose family had been intimately identified, for more than a hundred years, with the cause of subjecting the Highlands and Islands to the rule of Scotland's kings. The death of Bishop Adam represented something of a setback to that cause. And so, it might be argued, did Gilbert's decision to establish his diocesan headquarters in Dornoch rather than in a more northerly centre like Halkirk. But Bishop Gilbert knew exactly what he was doing. Dornoch's cathedral, Scotland's smallest, might today be rather grander if Gilbert had been better placed to access the ecclesiastical revenues generated by Caithness's rich farmlands. By establishing his cathedral in Dornoch, however, Gilbert achieved the more immediately important objective of placing himself beyond the reach of his predecessor's killers – thirteenth-century Dornoch being surrounded by territories dominated by the bishop's close relatives. Prominent among those relatives was Gilbert's cousin, William de Moravia, who – at about the time that Bishop Adam's corpse was being laid finally to rest in Dornoch Cathedral – had been created Earl of Sutherland. William owed his earldom, just as Gilbert owed his bishopric, to King William the Lion's son and successor, Alexander II. That, no doubt, is why earl and bishop alike were firmly in agreement with the forward policy which Alexander showed himself determined to pursue – not just in Caithness and Sutherland but in the Highlands and Islands as a whole.

As far as the wider Highlands and Islands were concerned, Alexander II's ambitions were most evident on the western seaboard. Under Norse domination since the ninth-century heyday of Ketil Flatnose, much of this area had formally been annexed to Norway in 1098 – when one of that country's kings, Magnus, mounted a major naval expedition to the Hebrides. Intended to demonstrate exactly who was ultimately in command of the islands, Magnus's expedition certainly achieved its purpose – according at least to the account contained in bloodcurdling lines composed by the Norwegian monarch's palace poet or skald, Bjorn Cripplehand. In Lewis, Bjorn claimed, 'fire . . . played high in the heaven', as 'flame spouted from the houses'. In Uist, 'the king dyed his sword red in blood'. In Skye, 'he sated the eagles' hunger' with human flesh. In Tiree, 'the glad wolf battened his teeth . . . in many a mortal wound'. In Mull, 'the people . . . ran to exhaustion' and the king 'caused maids to weep'. In Islay, too, Magnus 'plundered . . . and burned' – while 'the sons of men south in Kintyre bowed beneath swords' edges'.[30]

Having thus given practical expression to his territorial ambitions in the Hebrides, Magnus, so Norwegian sources insist, negotiated a treaty with the king of Scotland – this treaty's key clause being to the effect that 'Magnus was to own all the islands . . . to the west of Scotland . . . between which and the mainland a ship could pass'. In an attempt to add the Kintyre peninsula to his dominions by showing that it was an 'island' in the sense this term was employed in his agreement with the Scottish monarch of the day, Magnus, or so it was said, had one of his vessels dragged across the half-mile-wide neck of land which separates Kintyre from the rest of Argyll. In the event, this particular feat – which one sagaman attributed to a well-founded Norse conviction that Kintyre was 'more valuable than the best of the Hebridean islands' – failed in its aim. Kintyre, unlike the Hebrides, did not become part of Norway. But this, as far as the Scottish monarchy was concerned, was no great gain. Irrespective of where the boundary between Scotland and Norway was judged to lie in 1098 and in the years that followed, virtually the whole of the West Highland mainland, together with the islands claimed by Magnus, remained the preserve of locally based rulers who – as had been the case since Ketil Flatnose's time – were more interested in preserving their own independence than in accepting either Norwegian or Scottish governance.[31]

Of these rulers, easily the most significant was Somerled who was probably born within a year or two of King Magnus's 1098 expedition and who was certainly to nullify a good deal of that expedition's impact by asserting his own sovereignty, in effect, over much of the Hebrides. There is thus an important truth embedded in a Gaelic tradition – first set down in writing in the seventeenth century – which traces Somerled's rise to power from his reported encounter with 'a large force' of Norwegians 'in the mountains and woods of Ardgour and of Morvern'. The tradition in question tells how Somerled first defeated those Norwegians and then 'drove them northwards across the River Sheil'. That might not be quite what occurred. But Somerled's ascent to prominence in the West Highlands and Islands was very definitely achieved at the expense both of the Norwegian crown and the kings of Man – rulers of Norse extraction who had previously held sway over many of the territories which ultimately came under Somerled's control.[32]

Somerled's name was Norse and some, perhaps many, of his ancestors were Norwegians. But Somerled's genealogy – preserved in Gaelic tradition and accepted as broadly authentic by modern scholars – places most emphasis on his descent from Gofraid, son of Fergus, an Ulster chieftain who was himself descended, or so it was claimed, from one of the leading families of Gaelic Ireland. Gofraid, according to entries in Irish annals dealing with the ninth century, came to Dalriada in the 830s at the invitation of Kenneth MacAlpin, king of Alba. By Ireland's annalists, Gofraid was called *toiseach Innse Gall* – a phrase denoting lordship over the Hebrides which Gaelic-speakers had dubbed *Innse Gall*, islands of the foreigners or strangers, in the wake of their occupation by Vikings. Somerled was to aspire to, indeed achieve, a similar status. And for all that he and his successors continued to be influenced by the Norse element in their complex background, Somerled was, and clearly thought himself to be, primarily a Gael – his rule, not coincidentally, being accompanied by a marked resurgence of Gaelic culture in localities from which that culture had retreated in the aftermath of Viking settlement.

But despite his Gaelic affinities and despite his ancestor's links with Kenneth MacAlpin, the kingdom of Scotland's principal founder, Somerled was by no means engaged in promoting Scottish, as opposed to Norwegian, interests in the area which became his principal theatre of operations. That area included islands like Islay, Jura, Mull and Tiree – as well as the West Highland mainland between Kintyre and Ardnamurchan. This region is roughly equivalent to modern Argyll. In making himself its political master, which he did in the years around 1150, Somerled, in a very real sense, had recreated Dalriada. And for all that his island territories were nominally subject to Norway, just as his mainland dominions were nominally subject to Scotland, Somerled was very much his own man. A Latin document of his day entitles him *regulus*. Irish sources call him *ri*. Both terms, especially the latter, imply that Somerled – just like his earlier counterparts in Moray – was regarded as a king in his own right. His kingship, to be sure, may have been of a somewhat more subordinate variety than that, say, of David I, Somerled's close contemporary. But this kingship was sufficient to elevate Somerled – both in his own opinion and in the opinion of his followers – to a status well beyond that enjoyed by any merely feudal magnate of the sort David so favoured.

One of Somerled's sisters married Malcolm MacHeth, an eminent representative of the grouping which so strongly resisted the Scottish monarchy's claims to Moray. Malcolm's daughter became, in turn, the second wife of Harald Madaddson, Earl of Orkney, another of the Scottish crown's principal antagonists in the Highlands and Islands. At a time when most such marriages were a means of cementing dynastic alignments, these connections point to the existence, at a minimum, of some loose identity of interest as between Argyll, Moray and the Orkney earldom. Had that identity of interest been translated into an enduring and effective alliance, the Scottish monarchy's advance into the Highlands and Islands might have been decisively stalled. But the Highlands and Islands – then and later – were nothing if not disunited. The several members of what might have been transformed into an effective anti-monarchical coalition, therefore, only very occasionally succeeded in co-ordinating their strategies. At different times and in separate places, Highlands and Islands rulers thus tended to confront Scotland's medieval kings very largely by themselves. So it was with Somerled.

From the perspective of Somerled's Argyll-centred kingdom, a serious threat was posed by those previously mentioned estates, in the vicinity of the Clyde estuary, which were granted by David I to Walter the Steward, progenitor of so many of Scotland's future monarchs. In much the same way as their Moravia counterparts were doing – or were to do – in Moray and Sutherland, the Stewarts clearly hoped to expand these landholdings both in their own interests and in the interests of their royal backers. Any such expansion was likely to be at the expense of Somerled's territories in Argyll. And it may have been in the hope of thwarting such designs that Somerled, in 1164, sailed up the Clyde at the head of some 160 warships manned by several thousand armed men.

Although Somerled was probably aiming merely to strengthen his own eastern borders, his thrust up the Clyde may just possibly have had as its ultimate objective the throne of Scotland – on which Somerled conceivably had Macbeth-like designs. His actions were certainly interpreted, by the Scottish kingdom's chroniclers, as those of a man who was 'wickedly rebelling . . . against . . . the king of the Scots, his natural lord'. By the same chroniclers, Somerled's Gaelic-speaking troops – in a phrase that was to be deployed against the people of the Highlands and Islands for centuries to come – were portrayed as 'barbarous hordes'. And the eventual defeat of those troops – a defeat which culminated in the killing of Somerled himself – was attributed, by the Scottish monarchy's backers, to God having wreaked 'divine vengeance' on Argyll, its population and its ruler.[33]

Somerled's realm, though divided between his heirs, survived his death. Nor was this realm, despite Scottish propaganda to that effect, some sort of isolated and benighted backwater on Scotland's margins. Somerled's Argyll produced no single surviving structure on a par with the cathedral which Earl Rognvald was then establishing in Kirkwall; but the impressive monastic buildings which tourists today discover on Iona – buildings which these same tourists sometimes mistakenly associate with the Columban era – were commenced, around 1200, on the orders of Somerled's son, Ranald. Saddell Abbey and Ardchattan Priory, the one in Kintyre and the other on the north shore of Loch Etive, date from the same general period. So do some of the most impressive of all the numerous fortifications to be found in the Highlands and Islands – such as Castle Sween in Knapdale, Duart Castle on Mull and Dunstaffnage Castle to the north of Oban. Like the many smaller buildings of similar vintage whose remnants are still to be observed across the West Highlands and Islands, most notably in the shape of tumbledown parish churches and chapels, Argyll's medieval castles, abbeys and priories suggest that Somerled and his successors were capable of mobilising and deploying substantial resources. Equally illustrative of Somerledian Argyll's overall character is the fact that its architecture was of a most up-to-date variety. When he gave instructions for a new monastery to be built on Iona, Ranald was no doubt conscious of paying a retrospective tribute to St Columba. But there was no question of Ranald's monks adhering to what little then remained of the Columban church. Iona's thirteenth-century monastery belonged to the Europe-wide Benedictine order. Its cosmopolitan connections were deliberately reflected in the outward-looking style of its construction.

None of this, of course, made Argyll any less desirable to the Scottish monarchy. Hence the extent to which Alexander II, who became Scotland's king in 1214, pursued much the same sort of aggressive strategy on the western seaboard as he did in localities like Sutherland and Caithness – where, for example, he intervened forcibly in the wake of the 1222 murder of Bishop Adam at Halkirk. Nor were Alexander's ambitions confined to mainland Argyll. He wanted also to undo the agreement made between the Scottish and Norwegian kingdoms in 1098. Alexander, as a pro-Norwegian source puts it, was 'very covetous of dominion in the Hebrides' and 'constantly sent men to Norway' with a view to negotiating this island group's transfer to Scotland.[34]

On the Norwegians refusing to accede to his requests, Alexander decided on war. Taking personal command of the fleet he mobilised with a view to invading the Hebrides, the Scottish king, in the early summer of 1249, set sail from the Clyde, rounded the Mull of Kintyre and made his way northwards into the Firth of Lorne. There, while his ships were anchored off Kerrera, a small island to the west of Oban, Alexander took ill and died – an event which the Norwegians and their Hebridean allies promptly hailed in much the same fashion as the Scottish monarchy's supporters had earlier hailed the death of Somerled.

It was left to the dead king's son and successor, Alexander III, to complete what his father had begun by making the Hebrides formally Scottish. This process is one which modern Scotland's historians – who dignify it with titles like 'the winning of the west' – habitually describe in ways which imply that Scotland's appropriation of the islands approximated to a modern war of liberation. But contemporary Hebrideans, like the inhabitants of the rest of the Highlands and Islands, had no very good reason to associate the Scottish monarchy with freedom and progress. Rather the reverse. It is of some passing significance, in this regard, that the most Hebridean – but also the most Gaelic – of saints, Columba, was reported to have featured in Alexander II's troubled dreams as he lay dying near Kerrera in July 1249. A 'frowning' figure who 'was very bald in front', Colum Cille, having ascertained that Alexander 'intended to go plundering in the Hebrides', apparently instructed the king to 'turn back'.[35]

That story comes from the Norwegian side, not the Scottish one. But the fact that Columba could thus be posthumously deployed against Alexander II is indicative of the extent to which Hebrideans found it perfectly possible, in the thirteenth century, to combine a strong awareness of their Gaelic heritage with an equally strong desire to remain outside the jurisdiction of monarchs who had once been representative of that heritage – but who were increasingly regarded, quite correctly, as being representative of it no longer. In this respect, Alexander II's replacement by Alexander III signalled no improvement from the perspective of a Hebridean population which, despite that population's continuing links with Norway, was becoming steadily more Gaelic both in speech and in culture. The new king's inauguration at Scone in 1249 had been marked, as it happened, by the recitation in Gaelic of his genealogy – a genealogy which firmly rooted the Scottish monarchy in exactly the same Dalriadan and Irish world to which Columba had belonged. But Alexander's outlook was shaped much less by Gaelic tradition than it was by the centralising and feudalising stance adopted by forebears who were a lot closer to him in time than the kings of Dalriada. Hebrideans had every reason, then, to be suspicious of the Scottish monarchy's motives. And such suspicions could only have been intensified by the behaviour of

Alexander III's lieutenants. When the soldiers of the Scottish king stormed through Skye in 1262, or so it was alleged at the time, they 'burned farms and churches and slew very many men and women'. Alexander's troops had also 'taken small bairns and spitted them on their spear-points' – prior to holding their spears aloft and shaking them in such a way that the skewered corpses of Skye infants 'fell down . . . dead . . . on their hands'.[36]

On reports of these atrocities being drawn to the attention of Norway's King Hakon, Norwegian chroniclers asserted, the king was greatly 'touched'. Maybe so. But Hakon – whose predecessor, Magnus, had treated Hebrideans every bit as appallingly as the Scottish monarch's representatives were reported to have done – also had a self-interested agenda to advance in places like Skye. This agenda, a mirror image of the one pursued by Alexander III, amounted to a more ambitious version of the policy which had earlier been applied to Shetland. That policy had resulted in Shetlanders having been subject, from the 1190s onwards, to direct rule from Norway. Hakon, on becoming Norway's king, managed to impose similar arrangements on other Norse outposts, most importantly Iceland, which had been virtually independent since Vikings first occupied them. When Hakon sought to counter Alexander by embarking on his own military expedition to the Hebrides in 1263, therefore, it was not with the aim of safeguarding the considerable autonomy enjoyed by Somerled's successors. Rather it was with a view to transforming the Hebrides into a Norwegian province of the wholly subordinate sort which Iceland had become a year or two before.[37]

Hakon began by holding 'a general assembly in Bergen' where he proclaimed, according to a saga-writer, that 'he intended to go west beyond the sea' in order 'to avenge the warfare that the Scots had made in his dominions'. That was in the spring or early summer of 1263. In July, Hakon loaded a sizeable army into an equally sizeable fleet and set sail in a style which inspired skaldic verses of the sort that had always surrounded such forays:

> The host of the king,
> As it skimmed over the main,
> Was like unto lightning
> That springs from the sea.[38]

Having spent two nights *en route* from Norway, Hakon reached Shetland where his fleet anchored for a time in Bressay Sound off Lerwick. From Shetland, following the Viking route of long before,

Hakon pushed on to Orkney. Pausing there, the Norwegian king turned his attention to Caithness which consequently found itself, for some weeks, at the centre of what was rapidly turning into a major trial of strength between Hakon and Alexander III.

Many, perhaps most, Caithness people were still Norse-speaking in 1263. Many, perhaps most, Caithness people might still have identified, at that point, with the Earldom of Orkney – possibly even with Norway – rather more than they identified with Scotland. During the preceding sixty or seventy years, however, Caithness's inhabitants had more than once been confronted with what it meant to antagonise Scotland's monarchy. They were probably disinclined to run the risk of doing so again. But Alexander, just to be on the safe side, despatched a military force northwards and forcibly removed a number of Caithness's leading men to Inverness. There the Scottish king's Caithness hostages were kept in confinement as a means of ensuring that their relatives and neighbours did nothing to aid Hakon. Nothing is what Caithness people duly did.

Nor were developments elsewhere in the Highlands and Islands significantly more favourable from the Norwegian king's point of view. In the course of the century which separated Somerled's death from Hakon's 1263 campaign, the Hebrides and much of the adjacent mainland had effectively been parcelled out among a number of semi-autonomous kindreds. The most powerful of these kindreds or clans – as it now begins to make sense to call such groupings – were headed by men descended from Somerled. These men had made an art of preserving their considerable independence by means which typically involved them in declining to be wholly aligned with either of their nominal royal masters – the kings of Norway and Scotland. This balancing act, however, was impossible to sustain in the face of pressures of the sort generated by the events of 1263. Although some West Highlands and Islands clans stuck with Hakon and the Norwegians, others began to throw in their lot with Alexander – for reasons, it can be assumed, which had less to do with pro-Scottish sentiment than with a shrewd appreciation of the extent to which Alexander's claims on the Hebrides were becoming irresistible.

Despite this crumbling of his local support, and despite the fact that autumn storms were more likely with every day that passed, Hakon, some time during August, opted for an offensive strategy. With the king still personally directing its operations, the Norwegian fleet left Orkney, rounded Cape Wrath and headed for the Mull of Kintyre by way of Skye, Kerrera and Gigha. Soon Hakon's ships were in those Firth of Clyde waters where Somerled had earlier come to grief and where Hakon, as matters turned out, was to do little better.

The Norwegians began, admittedly, by scoring a spectacular success. Reviving tactics which the Vikings had once employed, a detachment of Hakon's men sailed up Loch Long to Tarbet where, as a Norse account puts it, 'they took their boats and drew them . . . over the land to the great lake which is called Loch Lomond'. The Norse narrative continues:

> There are . . . very many islands in that lake, [islands which are] well-inhabited. The Norwegians wasted these islands with fire. They burned, too, the whole district around the lake and wrought there the greatest mischief.[39]

Much of the area affected by these actions was in the possession, by the mid-thirteenth century, of the same Stewart family whose expansion Somerled had tried in vain to check. Given this family's longstanding intimacy with Scotland's kings, to raid Stewart lands and to burn Stewart homes was to attack the Scottish monarchy itself. But it was by no means to bring Alexander to his knees. Only a decisive Norwegian victory could do that. And no such victory was forthcoming.

What finally ensued, at the start of October, was the Battle of Largs. Less a single encounter, more a series of skirmishes, Largs – though not the Scottish triumph it was afterwards made out to be – ended in Hakon's ships, which had been damaged rather more by gales than by the Scots, withdrawing from the Clyde and returning to Orkney. There Hakon – whom one Norse account describes, accurately enough, as having endured 'much care' and enjoyed 'little peace' since leaving Bergen – became seriously ill. He was conveyed to the Kirkwall palace of the bishops of Orkney. This palace's impressive ruins can be found just across the street from St Magnus's Cathedral. And on a wild winter's night of the sort that must have occurred in the course of the November and December weeks which Hakon spent in Kirkwall in 1263, it is easy, while standing in the lee of the palace's remaining walls, to imagine the king lying here in a candle-lit room and listening to the sound of one of his attendants reading aloud at his insistence. 'He let Latin books be read to him at first,' it was reported of Hakon's last days. But on his condition worsening, and his grasp of Latin slipping, the king asked to hear the Norse sagas dealing with the deeds of his ancestors. So it came about that Hakon died, in mid-December, with the history of the Viking era ringing in his ears.[40]

That, perhaps, was appropriate. Although Orkney and Shetland were to elude the Scottish monarchy's grasp for another two hundred years, both the failure of his 1263 expedition and Hakon's own subsequent death marked the end of a Highlands and Islands epoch which had begun with the first Norse raids of more than four and a half centuries before. In 1266, Hakon's son, Magnus, bowing before the inevitable, made peace with Alexander III and, in terms embodied in that year's Treaty of Perth, granted to Alexander both the Hebrides themselves and 'all right which he [Magnus] and his progenitors had of old therein'.[41]

CHAPTER FOUR

Children of Conn

1267–1493

On driving out of Inverness on the Aberdeen road and following that road eastwards through Nairn and Forres to Elgin, it quickly becomes apparent why – despite the many options offered by what was then a large province – the more influential of twelfth-century Moray's newly arrived feudal families were particularly anxious to set up home here. This locality's land is first-rate. So is its climate. Sheltered from the Atlantic's rain-bearing winds by mountain ranges to the west and to the south-west, Moray's coastal plain – on which Forres and Elgin are situated – is much drier, and noticeably milder, than adjacent areas. Hence the extent to which the lower-lying part of Moray was transformed, just as Scotland's monarchs had hoped, by its feudalisation. Substantial numbers of people – from the Scottish Lowlands and from further afield – appear to have settled in the vicinity of Forres and Elgin following the arrival thereabouts of King David I's protégé, Freskin. And despite some 850 years having passed since this immigration occurred, its effects remain obvious to anyone whose ear is sufficiently well attuned to detect the linguistic boundary encountered in the neighbourhood of Auldearn, a village on the Forres side of Nairn.

To the west of that boundary, people mostly employ today – as they do in Inverness itself – a variant of English which, for all its highly distinctive accent, uses grammar and vocabulary of a sort that would be regarded as fairly standard in more southerly parts of the United Kingdom. East of Auldearn, however, people's speech patterns – especially the speech patterns of long-established residents – become those of the zone, stretching on into Aberdeenshire, where the predominant *spik*, or dialect, is the variant of Broad Scots or Lallans nowadays called Doric. Differing noticeably from English in both sound and structure, that dialect was introduced to Moray – which had previously been Gaelic-speaking – by Lowland folk who came north, around 1150, in Freskin's wake. Eight or nine centuries later, its Lallans speech continues to distinguish the Forres and Elgin area from those other Highlands and Islands localities – including Auldearn and all points west – where Gaelic persisted until it gave way, in more recent times, to English instead of to Broad Scots.

As well as being Scots-speaking when neighbouring regions – southwards in the direction of Strathspey and Badenoch as well as westwards in the direction of Inverness – were still Gaelic-speaking, the Moray coastal plain, in the later medieval period, was notably wealthier than places which did not possess its high-yielding soils and comparatively good weather. The results are plain to see if, on entering Elgin, you take the ringroad which skirts the modern town centre and, turning off this ringroad to the north, visit what remains of Elgin Cathedral. Built at about the same time as its more modest Dornoch counterpart, this was once the grandest ecclesiastical structure to be found between the Scottish Central Belt and Kirkwall. Something of that grandeur is evident still. For even in the ruined condition into which it fell during the seventeenth and eighteenth centuries, Elgin Cathedral continues to impress – the houses constructed in the cathedral precinct in Victorian times being wholly overshadowed by the remnants of its soaring towers. Those same towers must have seemed all the more spectacular when, as would have been the case in the fourteenth century, Elgin consisted largely of low-walled, timber-built and thatch-roofed homes. It is perfectly understandable, then, that Moray people were outraged and infuriated by the actions of the 'wild, wicked, Highland men' – as they were called by one contemporary – who, in June 1390, set fire both to Elgin Cathedral and to the dwellings occupied by the cathedral's clerics.[1]

No less than eighteen 'noble and beautiful mansions of canons and chaplains' were reported to have been destroyed in the ensuing conflagration. But causing more 'bitter pain' than the loss of those fine residences was the fate of a church described, at the time, as an 'ornament of the kingdom'. Elgin Cathedral's walls were left standing, but the building's interior furnishings, together with 'all the books, charters and other goods of the countryside preserved there', were totally lost.[2]

The 'Highland men' responsible for these atrocities swept into Elgin from the hill country constituting the town's hinterland. This hinterland can readily be accessed from modern Elgin by way of a road which, on reaching Rothes, broadly follows the course of the River Spey to Grantown, Aviemore and Kingussie. Those Strathspey and Badenoch villages are mostly located within the borders of what were once – long before such villages existed in their present form – the principal landholdings belonging to the eminent, if singularly disruptive, individual who, as fourteenth-century observers made clear, personally supervised Elgin Cathedral's burning. By Scots-speakers, whether in Elgin or elsewhere, this individual – in a back-handed acknowledgement of his notoriety – was known as the Wolf of Badenoch. To his own mostly Gaelic-speaking followers, however, the Wolf was *Alasdair Mor mac an Righ*, meaning Big Alexander, the king's son. That last phrase, at least, stuck strictly with the facts. For Alexander Stewart, Wolf of Badenoch, was indeed a younger son of Scotland's first Stewart monarch, Robert II.

As such, Alexander's role in the Highlands and Islands might be expected to have conformed a lot more closely than it did to that of the feudal nobles – the Wolf's own ancestors among them – whose function it had been, when such nobles were first brought to Scotland by kings like David I, to add to the authority of the country's central government. But this is to assume that men of Norman ancestry and feudal background were bound to respond to the social and cultural environment they encountered in the Highlands and Islands by seeking to modify that environment in a manner which made it more akin to the society from which they sprang. Sometimes, as on Freskin's Moray estates, this clearly happened. But sometimes it did not. There were incoming magnates who, on finding themselves in a Gaelic-speaking and traditionally orientated milieu of the kind which existed in fourteenth-century Strathspey and Badenoch, reacted to that milieu, not by trying to change it but by endeavouring to make themselves a part of it. This was exactly what happened in the case of Alexander Stewart.

There are conflicting theories as to why feudal aristocrats, as the middle ages advanced, became increasingly prone to go native, as it were, when residing in Gaelic-speaking areas. But go native they indubitably did – in Ireland, incidentally, as well as in localities like Badenoch and Strathspey. Their consequent loss of leverage over men they had regarded as their agents was a development of some concern to governments in both London and Edinburgh – the one trying desperately to consolidate the Irish conquests made by thirteenth-century English kings and the other trying equally hard to sustain the Scottish monarchy's gains in the Highlands and Islands. As stressed in the preceding chapter, Scotland's rulers, from the reign of David I onwards, had attempted to gain greater influence in the Highlands and Islands by installing externally recruited noblemen in the region.

But such an approach made little sense if the noblemen in question chose simply to merge into the Gaelic-speaking society they had been expected, by the authorities in Edinburgh, to subject to external control.

Hence the Scottish monarchy's adoption of a new approach to the Highlands and Islands – an approach exemplified by the manner in which Scotland's kings and their Edinburgh-based administrations took to making alliances with already established Highlands and Islands families who, usually in return for some ensuing enhancement of their own prospects, could be persuaded to identify themselves, to some extent at any rate, with the Scottish crown. The beginnings of such practices are detectable as early as the start of the thirteenth century when Alexander II, in the course of his efforts to exterminate the MacHeths, turned for help to one of the latter grouping's local rivals, *Fearchair mac an t-Sagairt* or Farquhar MacTaggart, whom Alexander afterwards rewarded with the newly created Earldom of Ross – a district, extending from the Black Isle to Applecross, which had earlier been claimed both by Moray's Cenel Loairn rulers and by the Norse Earls of Orkney. The tactics from which Farquhar thus benefited were to feature in governmental dealings with the Highlands and Islands until the eighteenth century. They were certainly to loom large in the thinking of Alexander II's successor, Alexander III, when, during the 1260s, he set out to extend his realm westwards.

Many of the gains the Scottish monarchy made in the West Highlands and in the Hebrides during the later thirteenth century stemmed ultimately from Alexander III's success in winning to his side (prior to the Battle of Largs) Ewen of Argyll, Somerled's great-grandson. Ewen's clan, the MacDougalls, was one of three – the others, also headed by descendants of Somerled, being the MacDonalds and the MacRuaris – which were, by that stage, in control of Somerled's former realm. Such clans, as noted in the previous chapter, had long managed to avoid wholehearted identification either with the kings of Norway, to whom they owed a nominal allegiance in respect of their island territories, or with the kings of Scotland, to whom they owed an equally nominal allegiance in respect of their mainland possessions. But having made an accurate guess as to who was likely to emerge victorious from the developing confrontation between Alexander III and King Hakon, Ewen of Argyll broke with past practice and threw in his lot with Alexander. This helped to bring about the Scottish kingdom's expansion, as confirmed by the Treaty of Perth, into the Hebrides. But it also helped

Ewen, who thus stole a march on his MacDonald and MacRuari counterparts, to emerge from the Scottish-Norwegian war of 1263 as one of the Scottish monarchy's right-hand men.

That was a position which Ewen's successors were to retain for the remainder of Alexander III's long reign. During this period, as a result, the MacDougalls – while continuing to profess their loyalty to the Scottish crown – consolidated their grip on the North Argyll mainland, Jura, Lismore, Mull, Coll and Tiree. Also during this period, a MacDougall chief, Alexander, Ewen of Argyll's son, wed a daughter of John Comyn, a feudal baron who possessed extensive landholdings in Strathspey, Badenoch and Lochaber. The Comyns, who were of Norman extraction, had obtained those landholdings in the early thirteenth century when the family played a leading role in suppressing the last of the uprisings initiated by the Scottish crown's opponents in what had previously been the Kingdom of Moray. Alexander MacDougall's marriage to John Comyn's daughter was thus of huge significance. It showed that the MacDougalls, for all their deep roots in one of the most Gaelic parts of the Highlands and Islands, had acquired a status on a par with that enjoyed by those much more recently established members of the Highlands and Islands nobility, such as the Comyns, who had been sent north with a view to making the Highlands and Islands an integral part of Scotland. Like Farquhar MacTaggart before them, therefore, Ewen and Alexander MacDougall gained greatly by co-operating with the Scottish monarchy – rather than by resisting royal expansionism in the way the MacHeths, the MacWilliams or, for that matter, Somerled had done.

The MacDougalls seemed set to acquire still more influence when, in the 1290s, their Comyn connection opened up the prospect of this Argyll and Hebridean clan being in close and cordial contact with a new king of Scotland. That king was John Balliol, who obtained his throne as a result of a wholly unforeseen sequence of events which began in March 1286 when Alexander III, journeying from Edinburgh to Fife on a dark and stormy night, fell from his horse and broke his neck.

One of Alexander's two sons had died in 1281, the other in 1284. His daughter, Margaret, who had married King Erik of Norway as a result of post-1263 efforts to improve relations between Scotland and Erik's kingdom, was also dead. Alexander's only direct heir, therefore, was the daughter of Margaret and Erik – a little girl who became known, in due course, as the Maid of Norway.

Having been accepted as Alexander's heir by the leading men of his realm, this small child was despatched to Scotland by her father in the early autumn of 1290. She never reached Scottish territory. At Kirkwall, where her accompanying party made a landfall, the Maid took ill and died – very possibly in the same Bishop's Palace where Hakon had expired a quarter of a century before.

On Scotland thus being left without a recognised ruler, several individuals staked a claim to the country's kingship. With a view to obtaining an independent verdict on the issue, the Scottish nobility decided – somewhat rashly – to invite England's king, Edward I, to select Scotland's next monarch. Because they were generally considered to be the main contenders, Edward was obliged to choose, in effect, between two men. One was John Balliol, Lord of Galloway. The other was Robert Bruce, Earl of Carrick. Edward selected Balliol. And since Balliol was closely related to John Comyn whose daughter was their chief's wife, the MacDougalls, as already noted, had every reason to anticipate further enhancements of their already considerable power.

But Edward, who had earlier conquered Wales and who was actively pursuing territorial gains in Ireland, had his own self-interested reasons for welcoming the chance which had come his way to intervene in Scotland. The English monarch, it emerged, was determined to make himself master of the entire British Isles – an ambition which, if it were to be realised, required both Balliol and his subjects to recognise Edward as their feudal superior. This the Scots refused to do. There followed a series of English invasions and Scottish uprisings which culminated, in February 1306, in another Robert Bruce, grandson of Balliol's original rival, proclaiming himself Scotland's rightful king and pledging himself to restore the country's independence which Balliol, by this point, was widely thought to have surrendered to Edward.

On 25 March, Bruce was crowned at Scone. In June, however, the force which passed for Bruce's army – but which, for obvious reasons, had been cobbled together at some speed – was routed by the English at Methven, a little to the west of Perth. Soon Bruce had been reduced to the status of a fugitive. Reversing the route taken by Kenneth MacAlpin when he left Dalriada for Strathtay nearly five hundred years before, Scotland's aspiring king now fled for his life into the mountains of Argyll. In September, Bruce was reported to be in Kintyre. Then, with winter coming on, he went totally to ground – most probably in the Hebrides.

That Robert Bruce should thus have sought refuge in the Highlands and Islands appears to run counter to the previous chapter's thesis that the Scottish monarchy's role in the region had been such as to give the population of the Highlands and Islands no reason to rally to any king of Scotland – even one as charismatic as Bruce was quickly to prove himself to be. But it would hardly have improved Highlands and Islands prospects, it needs emphasising in this context, had the region come under the control of Edward I – a ruler who had shown himself, both in Wales and in Ireland, to be every bit as hostile as any Scottish king to localised power structures of the type which had for so long been characteristic of the Highlands and Islands. Nor did Bruce, for his part, regard the Highlands and Islands with the mistrust and hostility so many of his royal predecessors had displayed in their dealings with the region.

In origin, the Bruces – like their Comyn rivals – were Normans who had come to Scotland in the early twelfth century at the invitation of David I. But his remote ancestry was a much less important factor in the life and character of Robert Bruce than the future king's own upbringing. This took place in his grandfather's earldom of Carrick – a hilly, south-western segment of Ayrshire and a district which, partly because of its proximity to Ulster, had long been predominantly Gaelic in speech. Even today, the names of Carrick's farms and villages have a strongly Gaelic ring to them. And though Gaelic there, as in the rest of west central Scotland, eventually gave way to Broad Scots of the kind that Robert Burns (born in the same locality as Bruce) was to employ in his poetry, no such transition had taken place in Robert Bruce's day. Bruce, whom Highland tradition regards as Scotland's last Gaelic-speaking king, was certainly raised among Gaelic-speakers. Some of his earliest political dealings, moreover, were with Gaelic-speaking Highlanders from Kintyre – which can readily be seen from the Carrick coastline. The fact that he was thus perfectly at home both with their language and with their overall perspective on the world must have contributed to the relative ease with which Bruce – during the winter of 1306–7 when, on any objective assessment, his prospects seemed utterly hopeless – obtained the backing of some key personalities in the Highlands and Islands.

While it would be an exaggeration to depict Robert Bruce's subsequent triumphs as amounting to a replay of Macbeth's emergence from Moray to seize the throne of Scotland, the Highlands and Islands – which Bruce clearly felt it politic to secure prior to embarking on more southerly campaigns – were certainly critical to his eventual success. It was fitting, therefore, that the brigade which Bruce commanded personally in June 1314 at Bannockburn – where this, the most renowned of Scotland's kings, won his most acclaimed victory over his English enemies – was one which included many men from the Highlands and Islands. It was equally fitting that Bruce took care to ensure the presence at Bannockburn of the very ancient reliquary known as the *Breccbennach Choluim Chille*. Still to be seen in the National Museum of Scotland, this is a tiny and intricately decorated box which, though empty today, was considered, in the fourteenth century, to contain a relic of St Columba. The Breccbennach, then, was a most emotive talisman. By associating himself with it, Bruce was seeking to link his own kingship with that of the Gaels who had founded Dalriada and gone on to establish Alba. Nor did this appeal to Gaelic sentiment miss its mark – as is amply evident from the almost supernatural attributes which were afterwards attached to Bruce's name in Gaelic-speaking parts of the Highlands and Islands. Formally and constitutionally, Alexander III and his forebears might have incorporated the greater part of the Highlands and Islands into the kingdom of Scotland. But it was Robert Bruce who – for a time at least – made many people living in the Highlands and Islands feel themselves part, emotionally as well as legally, of the country which had thus been brought into existence.

Like most such contests, however, Scotland's wars of independence were civil conflicts as well as struggles for national self-determination. There were those in Scotland, in 1306 and afterwards, to whom Robert Bruce seemed anything but a liberator. Balliol, when Bruce launched his attempt on the throne, might have long since been reduced to the status of Edward I's puppet. But he had been crowned Scotland's king. And, though in exile in England, he was still alive. To Balliol's adherents, the Comyns and the MacDougalls prominent among them, Robert Bruce, therefore, was a usurper. He was a usurper, in addition, whose bid for power had begun with the murder, in Dumfries, of his leading opponent. This opponent was John Comyn, possessor of extensive lands in the Highlands and Islands, close ally of John Balliol and equally close ally of the MacDougalls. Unsurprisingly, both the dead John Comyn's family and their MacDougall kin were henceforth to be Bruce's unrelenting enemies. If his cause was to prevail, Bruce thus knew very well, he would have to shatter the power both of the Comyns and the MacDougalls. That was why, having come out of hiding in the early part of 1307 and having campaigned briefly in Carrick and Galloway, Bruce next marched north: capturing the Comyn stronghold of Inverlochy Castle in Lochaber; heading up the Great Glen; taking Castle Urquhart by Loch Ness; occupying Inverness; winning either the support or the neutrality of Ross, Sutherland and Caithness; heading into Moray by way of Forres and Elgin; ruthlessly terminating Comyn influence everywhere in the Highlands and Islands prior to thrusting deep into Argyll, during the summer of 1308, with a view to next destroying Clan MacDougall.

Given the way his name came to be inextricably linked with iniquity and depravity of one kind or another, it is singularly appropriate that Alexander Stewart, the Wolf of Badenoch, should have occupied a castle in as bleak a location as the Highlands and Islands have to offer. That castle's ruins stand on a small island in the two-mile-long stretch of water called Lochindorb – situated, at an altitude of nearly a thousand feet, on the northern fringes of Strathspey. In the middle ages, to be fair, Lochindorb may well have been surrounded by pinewoods. Today, however, those woods – other than where they survive in the shape of one or two windblasted trees – have long gone. The former forest's place has been taken by moorland. Especially in winter, when snow streaks this moorland's coating of dark heather and when Lochindorb's peat-stained water looks as black as it is possible for water to be, the resulting landscape might have been designed as a backdrop for some of Alexander Stewart's more notorious escapades.

Built when the Comyns were dominant hereabouts, Lochindorb Castle passed – following Robert Bruce's destruction of Comyn authority – into the hands of Thomas Randolph, one of Bruce's leading supporters and a man on whom Bruce bestowed several of John Comyn's Highlands and Islands possessions as well as the title of Earl of Moray. By the 1340s, however, Randolph's line had run out. Into the vacuum there eventually stepped, towards the end of the 1360s, Robert Stewart, a direct descendant of Walter the Steward to whom David I, more than two hundred years earlier, had given such generous landholdings in the vicinity of Paisley and Renfrew.

Surviving the attacks mounted against it both by Somerled and by followers of King Hakon, that Stewart powerbase had been steadily expanded by successive generations of this most acquisitive of families. Westwards, the Stewarts had moved into the Cumbraes, Bute and Cowal. Northwards and north-eastwards, they had made themselves the possessors of territories around Loch Lomond and in Atholl. This latter locality, on the Highland fringes of what had once been Alba's Strathtay heartland, contains the principal route – now followed by road and railway alike – from the south, across

Drumochter Pass, into Badenoch and Strathspey. These districts, then, were doubtless regarded by Robert Stewart – who, as a result of his father having married Robert Bruce's daughter, was to become king of Scotland in 1371 – as a logical extension to his domains. In 1355, by marrying the widow of the third and last Randolph, Earl of Moray, Robert equipped himself with the beginnings of a claim to lands beyond Drumochter. That claim, for various tactical reasons, was subsequently pursued in the name of Robert's younger son, Alexander. And even when the much greater prize of Scotland's kingship had come the Stewart family's way, Badenoch and Strathspey were not forgotten. With his father safely installed on the throne as Robert II, the way became clear, during the early 1370s, for Scotland's parliament – a relatively new institution that seldom got in the way of royal policy – to recognise Alexander Stewart as Lord of Badenoch and master, in addition, of the castle of Lochindorb.

Prior to this point, as it happened, other heirs of the Randolphs had managed to get their hands on some of the more desirable portions of the Moray earldom – including the locality with which this chapter began. But Alexander was soon to overshadow all such potential competitors. As other Stewarts had done before him, he added landholding to landholding until, within just a few years, his estates spanned both the Monadhliath and Cairngorm mountains from the Great Glen in the west to Strathavon in the east. A marriage to the widow left by an heirless Earl of Ross – a marriage modelled, perhaps, on his father's similar union with a Moray earl's widow – put Alexander in charge of territories stretching all the way to the Atlantic coast. On his father granting him various royal offices, as well as the custody of a number of royal fortresses, Alexander's position – already strong – seemed to have become virtually unassailable.

But it was one thing to control, as the Wolf of Badenoch controlled by the 1380s, strongholds like Urquhart Castle, Dingwall Castle and Inverness Castle. It was quite another thing to ensure that such control was genuinely grounded in the society over which it was exercised. Alexander Stewart had definitely become a very substantial figure in the Highlands and Islands – where he wielded power so great that its possessor looks, at first glance, to have been in the same league as Thorfinn the Mighty, Macbeth and Somerled. Those three, however, were products of their social and cultural settings in a way the Wolf of Badenoch was not. He had been imposed – or had imposed himself – on the Highlands and Islands. This fact accounted both for growing local resistance to the Wolf's authority and for his own reliance on armed force of a most unruly and indisciplined kind.

Hence the extent to which Alexander Stewart, despite his father having made him the leading enforcer of royal justice in all of Scotland to the north of the Forth, became inescapably pursued by allegations that he was a major cause of the disorder with which, during his lifetime, Lowland Scots were beginning to associate the Highlands and Islands.

The troops who burned Elgin Cathedral in 1390, on the orders of the man they knew as Alasdair Mor mac an Righ, were of the sort called *ceatharn* in their native Gaelic. Such ceatharn were professional soldiers whose services were available to magnates with the necessary cash. Their two main areas of operation, in the later fourteenth century, were Ireland – where Hebridean *kerne*, or ceatharn, featured in war after war – and the Highland mainland localities dominated by Alexander Stewart. Had he truly been what he seems to have aspired to be, a clan chief on the lines of the MacDougall notables with whom the Wolf's Comyn predecessors had been allied, Alasdair Mor would have been able to rely on a fighting force of the kind which Highlands and Islands clans, then and later, could so efficiently generate from within their own ranks. As it was, the Wolf of Badenoch, being very much an incomer in a Highlands and Islands context, had no clan from which to derive an armed following. If he was to have military backing, and he needed such backing to maximise his power, then the Wolf simply had to pay for it. Hence Alexander Stewart's hiring of those ceatharn whom he ultimately deployed in much the same way as twentieth-century Chicago gangsters deployed their gangs.

The Wolf's ceatharn were unleashed on the Moray coastal plain in 1390 as a result of their employer's mounting detestation of Alexander Bur, Bishop of Moray, one of the few individuals whom the Wolf failed completely to intimidate. From his diocesan headquarters in Elgin Cathedral, Bur presided over church estates which Alexander Stewart inevitably coveted and some of which he seems simply to have seized. But Bur, instead of acquiescing in his losses as most of the Wolf's victims appear to have done, protested noisily about them. This, from the Wolf's point of view, was bad enough. What was worse was the fact that the bishop also had the temerity to take the side of Alexander's wife, Euphemia, the formerly widowed Countess of Ross, in the course of the latter's repeated altercations with her husband – altercations arising from the Wolf's tendency to spend more time with a mistress than with the wife whom he had probably wed primarily as a means of getting Ross into his possession. Between Bishop Bur and the Wolf of Badenoch, then, there was very bad blood – something of the tone of their quarrels being preserved in a book written by the sixteenth-century church historian, Hector Boece.

Alexander Stewart, according to Boece, was a man 'whose wickedness had earned him universal hatred'. Stewart 'divided as he pleased . . . lands stolen from the church and gave them to be cultivated by certain wicked men who had no regard for God'. Those 'wicked men', it is safe to guess, were of the same provenance as the 'wild' Highlanders responsible for the destruction of Elgin Cathedral. They were, in other words, the Wolf's ceatharn whom Boece went on to accuse of killing Moray people 'in the most high-handed way'.[3]

While there may be doubt as to whether Alexander Stewart's ceatharn actually behaved more violently than fighting men had been behaving for centuries, their 1390 descent on Moray – where they attacked Forres as well as Elgin – was distinguished by one highly significant circumstance. Had such an attack been launched in earlier times, its victims, as well as its perpetrators, would have been Gaelic-speakers. As a result of linguistic developments which had occurred during the preceding two or three hundred years, however, much of Moray, as noted at this chapter's outset, had become Scots-speaking. So had the Angus lowlands which, within a year or two of Elgin's burning, suffered similarly at the hands of a further ceatharn band headed, it appears, by the Wolf of Badenoch's illegitimate sons, Duncan and Robert Stewart. The term ceatharn, as a result, now entered Broad Scots as 'cateran' – a wholly pejorative noun afterwards applied to armed robbers, bandits and law-breakers of all kinds. The manner in which this occurred was indicative of a much wider shift in Lowland opinion – a shift which ended in Lowlanders regarding almost every inhabitant of the Highlands and Islands in a highly unfavourable light.

Some importance attaches in this context to a passage written, towards the close of the fourteenth century, by a Lowland chronicler, John Fordun. Two languages were spoken widely in the Scotland of his day, Fordun observed, those languages being Gaelic and Broad Scots – which Fordun, in a conscious or unconscious tribute to the Scots tongue's German origins, called 'Teutonic'. The 'customs and habits' of Scotland's people, Fordun continued, varied with this 'difference of language'. Thus Scots-speakers were 'home-loving, civilised, trustworthy, tolerant and polite, decently attired, affable and pacific'. Gaelic-speakers, on the other hand, were 'a wild and untamed race, primitive and proud, given to plunder and the easy life'. Although Fordun did not go as far as those later Lowlanders who described Gaelic-speakers simply as 'savages', the import of his comments was clear enough. Linguistic distinctions between Gaelic-speakers and Scots-speakers, John Fordun believed, were accompanied by other differences. Those differences arose from the fact, as Fordun saw it, that Gaelic-speakers, were a lot less advanced – culturally, socially, intellectually – than their Scots-speaking neighbours.[4]

Such judgements, of course, were hardly novel. Somerled's Gaelic-speaking troops had been called barbarians by their enemies. So had those still earlier Gaels who had raided Roman Britain. But in remarking that Scots-speakers occupied Scotland's plains while Gaelic-speakers lived either among the country's mountains or on its 'outlying islands', Fordun identified a new aspect of the distinction he was trying to make. The Highland Line – to employ the name traditionally applied to the border between Fordun's 'plains' and the hillier terrain on those plains' northern and western fringes – had existed since humans arrived in Scotland. But this boundary's significance, prior to the fourteenth century, had been purely geographical. Now, because of the way Gaelic had retreated from the Lowlands, it was becoming a linguistic frontier as well. Extending north-eastwards from the Clyde estuary by way of the lower end of Loch Lomond to the Braes of Angus, then turning northwards through Deeside and Donside to reach the Moray Firth in the neighbourhood of Auldearn, that linguistic frontier was to remain in being until, during the nineteenth and twentieth centuries, Gaelic withdrew still further. South and east of the Highland Line, as thus defined, people – by the fourteenth century's end – generally spoke Scots. North and west of that same divide, most folk spoke Gaelic.* The way in which society was organised in the Scots-speaking zone, moreover, was also diverging – again by the fourteenth century's end – from the way it was organised in Gaelic-speaking areas. For all his evident prejudices, therefore, John Fordun was right to recognise that the Highland Line had come, by his time, to divide populations separated by more than language. Whatever might have been the case in former periods, the Lowlands, for example, no longer contained anything quite like the clans – another Gaelic term incorporated into Broad Scots at this point – which were, if anything, looming larger and larger in the life of much of the Highlands and Islands.

Was Alexander Stewart, the Wolf of Badenoch, seeking to equip himself with his own instantly created clan when he hired so many

* Other than in the Northern Isles and parts of Caithness where, as explained later in this chapter, Norse was beginning to give way to Broad Scots.

ceatharn, or caterans, of the kind who devastated Elgin? If he was, and if he had succeeded, then the Wolf might have managed to establish something by way of an enduring political entity in the part of the Highlands and Islands which he dominated throughout the 1370s and 1380s. As matters turned out, however, the Wolf's attack on Elgin was followed by his being forced increasingly on to the defensive. Having lost royal backing, because his father died within months of the Elgin episode, he was deprived both of his royal offices and many of his lands. The once feared Alexander Stewart, as a result, lived out the closing phases of his life in an obscurity which eventually became so all-embracing as to have ensured that nobody today knows exactly when or where he died.

At some point in the fifteenth century's opening decade, or so it has long been claimed, Alasdair Mor mac an Righ was buried in Dunkeld Cathedral. There visitors are directed nowadays to a tomb surmounted by a carved stone effigy of a man in armour. Below this effigy, the same visitors are told, there lies the Wolf of Badenoch. Actually, as with so much else concerning Alexander Stewart's ultimate fate, some doubt surrounds the precise place of his interment. But what can be said with certainty is that the Wolf of Badenoch's accomplishments, such as they were, had been wholly overshadowed, well before his demise, by the latest power to have arisen in the Highlands and Islands. This power was the MacDonald Lordship of the Isles.

Like Alexander Stewart's castle of Lochindorb, the principal residence of the Lords of the Isles, at Finlagan on Islay, was surrounded by water. This was all the two dwellings had in common, however. As is evident even from its ruins, Lochindorb Castle was primarily a military stronghold. The Islay home of the Lords of the Isles, in contrast, was wholly unfortified. That is a fact of some significance. Unlike the Wolf of Badenoch, it suggests, the Lords of the Isles had little or nothing to fear from the population they lived among. And it is tempting to see something of this reflected in the place they chose as their base. Loch Finlagan, the body of water containing the island where successive Lords of the Isles maintained both a household and an administrative headquarters, is situated towards the head of a wide, low-lying and – by Hebridean standards – extremely fertile valley. The hills around this valley are green, grassy and well grazed. So are the fields in Loch Finlagan's more immediate vicinity. And despite its former buildings having long since been reduced to a clutter of nettle-covered stones surmounted by a couple of crumbling gable-ends, the small island once occupied by the Lords of the Isles engenders none of the atmosphere of desolation which seems to have attached itself to Lochindorb's bleak setting. Finlagan was, and remains, a most pleasant locality.

This locality's historical importance derives from a family whose rise to prominence can be traced to Robert Bruce's decision, following his defeat at Methven in June 1306, to withdraw into the Highlands and Islands. Bruce's route, in all probability, took him westwards by way of Comrie, Glen Ogle, Glen Dochart and Strathfillan. There, in the neighbourhood of Tyndrum, Bruce's already depleted band of followers encountered a force commanded by the MacDougall chief, John of Argyll, a close ally, as already noted, both of the Comyns and of John Balliol. Fighting followed. That fighting deprived Robert Bruce of what little remained of his army, and he consequently fled from Strathfillan with virtually nothing in the way of resources or prospects. Whatever motivated the folk who now came to the fugitive king's aid, therefore, it was not the hope of rapid preferment. With his relatives, friends and associates being hunted down and hanged on the orders of Edward I, Robert Bruce, in the summer and autumn of 1306, was in no position to offer patronage to anyone. But there were men and women who rallied to him nevertheless. Among the most significant of these was *Aonghais Og*, Young Angus, the leading man among the MacDonalds whose territories, at this point, consisted mostly of Islay and Kintyre.

Like the MacDougall chief, John of Argyll, Angus Og was a direct descendant of Somerled. But between the MacDougalls and the MacDonalds there had for some time been rivalry. This is not to say that Angus Og MacDonald backed Robert Bruce solely because Bruce had become, as it were, his MacDougall enemies' enemy. But considerations of that sort undoubtedly played some part in Angus Og's decision to come to Bruce's aid in 1306. And the alignment thus put in place was certainly to be to the long-term advantage of Angus Og's family. It resulted, on Bruce commencing his successful comeback during 1307 and 1308, in the MacDonalds playing a leading part in the destruction of Clan MacDougall's former hegemony in Argyll. It ensured that the MacDonalds had a substantial role in the army which won the Battle of Bannockburn. And it meant, when the time came for Bruce to reward his supporters, that Angus Og's clan gained substantially increased landholdings – both in Argyll, where the MacDonalds profited from the collapse of the MacDougalls, and in

Lochaber, where they picked up possessions previously in the hands of the Comyns.

Angus Og's alliance with Bruce, therefore, benefited the MacDonalds in much the same way as Ewen of Argyll's earlier alliance with Alexander III had benefited the MacDougalls. The MacDonalds, however, were to capitalise more effectively on their position than their former rivals had done. Thus Angus Og's son, John, by marrying the heiress to the last chieftain of the MacRuaris, a clan whose lands lay to the north of those belonging to the MacDonalds, added enormously to the territories he had inherited from his father. By the 1330s, then, John MacDonald, as well as controlling much of the mainland between Kintyre and Knoydart, had made himself the supreme authority in virtually the whole of the Hebrides. To that extent, John's Latin designation, *Dominus Insularum*, Lord of the Isles, can be interpreted as no more than a statement of fact. As John MacDonald would have been well aware, however, his Latin title was eloquent with all sorts of historical resonances. Implicit in that title was its holder's affirmation that his status was to be understood as akin to that enjoyed by his great-great-great-grandfather, Somerled. The latter, of course, had been no mere *dominus*. He had been, to his own Gaelic-speaking adherents at any rate, *Ri Innse Gall*, an island king. A similar claim to kingship, or to something very like it, is apparent in the way successive MacDonalds conducted themselves at Finlagan.

The regal aspirations of the Lords of the Isles are especially evident in the ceremonies surrounding their inauguration. According to Hugh MacDonald, a seventeenth-century *seannachaidh* or tradition-bearer, those ceremonies took place at Finlagan and featured 'a square stone' in which there was incised the shape of 'a man's foot'. Just such a stone, as mentioned previously, had been a central element – prior to its having been taken from Scone to Westminster by Edward I – in the enthronement rites of Scotland's kings. And an incised footprint of the Finlagan type, as also mentioned previously, is still to be seen on the summit of Dunadd – where, as an earlier chapter stated, Dalriada's overkings may have been crowned. It seems likely, therefore, that the Finlagan rituals described by Hugh MacDonald were, in essence, many hundreds of years old. It seems equally likely that their sheer antiquity served to make the point that the Lordship of the Isles was the inheritor, not simply of Somerled's realm, but of a culture and a civilisation which long antedated Somerled – the culture and civilisation in question being those both of Dalriada and of the country from which Dalriada's Gaelic-speaking founders had come.[5]

Not coincidentally, the Gaelic genealogy of the Lords of the Isles reached back beyond Somerled into this distant past. Intended to add to the Lordship's prestige by providing its ruling family with an appropriate pedigree, that genealogy, as noted in the preceding chapter, included historical figures like Somerled's ninth-century ancestor, Gofraid. But it was rooted ultimately in the time of semi-mythical Irish hero-kings, such as Conn of the Hundred Battles, who, if they existed at all, must have lived in the period – a thousand years before the Lordship of the Isles took shape – when migration from Ulster to Dalriada was just getting under way. The lordship, then, was thought by its governing élite to be the concrete expression, in late-medieval circumstances, of ideas and ideals deriving ultimately from the sort of society which had produced both the *Tain Bo Cuailgne* and innumerable other tales – lots of them in circulation among the lordship's population – stemming from the epoch in which the *Tain* was set.

Lords of the Isles, on being inaugurated at Finlagan, were consequently given to understand that their position was underpinned by their remote antecedents as well as by the power they exercised. That was why, at the moment when a Lord of the Isles first stepped on to the lordship's equivalent of Scotland's Stone of Destiny, a Gaelic bard 'rehearsed a catalogue of his [the latest lord's] ancestors'. Scotland's monarchs, on taking over their kingdom, were apparently content to sit on the slab of rock kept for that purpose at Scone. A Lord of the Isles, however, entered into his inheritance while standing – his erect posture, Hugh MacDonald commented, 'denoting that he should walk in the footsteps . . . of his predecessors'. Wearing 'a white habit' in order to demonstrate 'his innocence and integrity of heart', each new Lord of the Isles was handed, in turn, 'a white rod' and 'his forefathers' sword': the one 'intimating that he had power to rule . . . with discretion and sincerity'; the other signifying his duty 'to protect and defend' the Lordship's people 'from the incursions of their enemies'.[6]

It is indicative of the fundamentally pagan origin of these formalities that Christianity intruded only towards their close. True, prayers were eventually said and mass celebrated. But such religious observances, one senses from Hugh MacDonald's account, were of rather less moment than the partying which followed – mass being the prelude to feasting and to the bestowal of gifts by the 'new created Lord' on the 'poets . . . and musicians' who had come to Finlagan to assist with what amounted to a coronation.[7]

Today the only sounds to be heard in the part of Islay where those celebrations occurred are the calls of gulls and the noise of water lapping on Loch Finlagan's shore. On great occasions such as Hugh MacDonald described, however, this long-deserted spot would have been as noisy as it was congested. Harpists would have played the instruments whose string-pins have been found by modern archaeologists among the foundations of what was once Finlagan's great hall. Gaelic songs would have been sung. Gaelic verses would have been recited. For just as skalds like Arnor Thordarsson clustered around Thorfinn the Mighty in the Birsay palace that was Finlagan's eleventh-century Orkney counterpart, so the leading Gaelic bards of the fourteenth and fifteenth centuries looked to successive Lords of the Isles for the support and sustenance such bards believed to be their due.

The most prominent of the lordship's bards were men belonging to a single family, the MacMhuirichs. Ever since this extraordinary dynasty's founder arrived in Scotland from Ireland in the early thirteenth century, generation after generation of MacMhuirichs had been poets. During the fourteenth and fifteenth centuries, in return for lands which they were granted in Kintyre, successive MacMhuirichs served as bards to successive Lords of the Isles. In that capacity, the MacMhuirichs – as well as composing poems in praise of their patrons – made it their business to be repositories of the Gaelic-speaking world's history, myth and lore. Enormous esteem attached itself to the MacMhuirich name as a result – so much so that Hugh MacDonald, when telling of a banquet given by a particular Lord of the Isles, took care to make clear that the principal MacMhuirich of the day, a guest at the banquet, was reckoned to be among the most eminent of all the lordship's inhabitants.

In so honouring its poets, the Lordship of the Isles – as it also did by engaging in those Finlagan rituals which have already been described – demonstrated the extent to which the lordship was shaped by the Gaelic world's past. Thus a bard's functions and status in the fifteenth-century Lordship of the Isles were identical to the functions and status of a bard as laid down, hundreds of years earlier, by the compilers of early-medieval Ireland's law tracts. And what was true of its bards was equally true of the lordship's other professions. Its physicians, its law-officers, its music-makers and sculptors were the readily recognisable representatives of learned orders whose responsibilities – and overall standing – had been carefully delineated, centuries previously, by men who belonged to the same Gaelic-speaking society as Dalriada's early kings and Iona's early abbots.

Those abbots' Benedictine successors – their monastery established by Somerled's son, Ranald, from whom the MacDonald Lords of the

Isles traced their descent – were as much involved in the politics of the lordship as Columba had been involved in the politics of Dalriada. When under Benedictine jurisdiction, however, Iona's monastery possessed little of the reputation, whether for learning or sanctity, that its Columban forerunner had enjoyed – the island abbey's increasingly dubious character being highlighted by the fact that one of its fifteenth-century abbots, having first broken those monastic vows dealing with chastity, succeeded in having his son follow him into high office in the Church.

This, admittedly, was exactly what the Lordship of the Isles tended to encourage in more secular walks of life. The remarkable case of the MacMhuirichs has already been mentioned. And all sorts of skills other than versifying tended similarly to remain the prerogative of particular families – the MacMhuirichs having their medical counterparts in the Beatons and their legal equivalents in the Morrisons. The former practised here and there throughout the West Highlands and Islands. The latter were especially associated with Lewis. And there were other family groupings, no doubt, who monopolised musicianship or who specialised in the production of the intricately carved tombstones which are still to be seen in several of the places once subject to the Lords of the Isles.

Those tombstones, as placed over the graves of the lordship's leading men, typically show these men in military garb of the sort mentioned in a sixteenth-century account of how a Hebridean of that era equipped himself for battle. Such a Hebridean's 'defensive armour', it appears, consisted of 'an iron headpiece' and 'a coat of mail formed of small iron rings' – this chainmail jacket 'frequently reaching to the heels'. The favoured offensive weapon, it seems, was the bow – its arrows 'barbed with iron' in such a fashion as to ensure that no arrow, on entering an enemy's flesh, could be withdrawn 'without widely enlarging the orifice of the wound'. The bow, however, is a relatively long-range weapon. To assist with close-quarter combat, therefore, island fighting men also carried 'swords or . . . axes'.[8]

Such axes – the lineal descendants of weapons wielded by Vikings – constitute a reminder that the Lordship of the Isles, although wholly Gaelic in speech, had been brought into existence by men whose ancestry and background was partly Norse. That background is evident in the domestic architecture of the lordship – architecture which, as demonstrated by archaeological investigations at Finlagan and elsewhere, owed a good deal to Viking building styles. But the lordship's Norse inheritance was most obvious in the ships on which Lords of the Isles, as rulers of an essentially maritime realm, necessarily relied. The builders of such ships – including, one gathers, a family resident at Colbost near Dunvegan in Skye – were yet another of those Lordship castes whose skills were handed on, through the years and through the centuries, from father to son. Those skills, however, were ultimately of Norwegian provenance. That is clear from the appearance of the lordship's galleys – craft strongly reminiscent, in everything from the method of their construction to the way they were sailed, of those other ships which had long before brought the Vikings to the Hebrides.

It comes as no surprise, then, to learn that many of the Gaelic terms relating to boats are of Norse origin. Nor is it coincidental that a medieval Gaelic bard, searching for words that could be applied to galleys mustering for an attack upon some well garrisoned strongpoint, employed images and vocabulary of a sort that might easily have been used by a Viking skald. 'Tall men are arraying the fleet which swiftly holds its course on the sea's bare surface,' this bard wrote. Each crewman held 'a trim warspear'; each man's shield was 'polished and comely'; each man's fist clenched the 'gold and ivory' hilt of his much decorated sword. When shiploads of such men bore down on communities unfortunate enough to be targeted by a Lord of the Isles, the impact on such communities must have been practically indistinguishable from that which would have resulted had they attracted the attentions, in a previous period, of Ketil Flatnose or Thorstein the Red.[9]

The military forces commanded by Lords of the Isles were more than once deployed against Scottish kings and their governments – relations between the lordship and the monarchy having tended to deteriorate steadily in the decades following the passing from the scene of Angus Og and Robert Bruce. Given the way in which Lords of the Isles conducted themselves as if their territories amounted to an independent state, this deterioration was probably inevitable. Its effects were somewhat masked in the middle years of the fourteenth century when, after the death of his MacRuari wife, John MacDonald, Angus Og's son, married Margaret Stewart, Bruce's great-granddaughter. John thus became the Wolf of Badenoch's brother-in-law. More significantly, he also became the son-in-law of the future King Robert II who, partly as a result of this connection, was on relatively good terms with the lordship throughout most of his reign – which lasted from 1371 to 1390. Thereafter, however, the lordship and

Scotland's government tended to regard each other with a mutual hostility which, in 1411, boiled over into actual fighting.

The immediate cause of this outbreak of hostilities was the lordship's expansion – masterminded by John's son, Donald – into the area which the Wolf of Badenoch had tried, and failed, to make his personal fief. Particularly at stake was the future of the Earldom of Ross on which Donald, Lord of the Isles, had a claim arising from his marriage to the daughter of an earlier earl. This claim was strongly contested by the Duke of Albany, a Lowland nobleman then serving as Scotland's regent – the country's king, James I, having had the misfortune to be taken prisoner by the English with whom, throughout this period, Scots were semi-permanently at odds. Albany's motives with regard to Ross were not entirely disinterested – he wanted to bring the earldom under his own control. That, however, did not make any less momentous Donald MacDonald's decision to pursue his territorial objectives by means which involved his making war on the recognised representative of Scotland's absent monarch.

Having marched out of the lordship's West Highland heartland at the head of an army said to have numbered six thousand men, Donald first seized Inverness Castle, the Scottish government's foremost Highland outpost. Next he headed eastwards and southwards, by way of Forres and Elgin, into Aberdeenshire – reaching Harlaw, just north of Inverurie, on the evening of 23 July 1411. At Harlaw, early the following morning, the Lord of the Isles was surprised by a government force commanded by the Earl of Mar. The fighting which ensued, on a tract of moorland since reclaimed for agriculture, was so intense as to ensure that Harlaw long rivalled Bannockburn in its grip on the Scottish people's collective imagination.

To Lachlan Mor MacMhuirich, *ollamh* or bard to Donald, Lord of the Isles, Harlaw was an opportunity for the MacDonalds – descendants, so Lachlan believed, of the endlessly celebrated Conn of the Hundred Battles – to prove themselves worthy of their ancestors:

> O children of Conn, remember
> hardihood in time of battle:
> be watchful, be daring,
> be dexterous, winning renown;
> be vigorous, pre-eminent;
> be strong, nursing your wrath;
> be stout, be brave,
> be valiant, triumphant . . .

O children of Conn of the Hundred Battles,
now is the time for you to win recognition:
O raging whelps,
O sturdy bears,
O most sprightly lions,
O battle-loving warriors,
O brave, heroic firebrands,
the children of Conn of the Hundred Battles.[10]

Whether or not they were stirred to great deeds by such sentiments, the men of the Lordship certainly fought spiritedly at Harlaw. This was acknowledged by an Aberdeenshire balladeer whose perspective on the conflict was that of a soldier in the Earl of Mar's army:

They fell fu' close on ilka side,
Sic fun ye never saw;
For Heilan' swords gaed clash for clash,
At the Battle o' Harlaw.
The Heilan' men wi' their lang swords,
They laid us on fu' sair;
And they drave back our merrymen
Three acres breadth or mair.[11]

Although it did not last as long as this Aberdeenshire song suggests, Harlaw was bitterly contested, with heavy casualties being suffered on both sides:

At Monday at morning,
The battle it began;
On Saturday at gloamin',
Ye'd scarce tell wha had wan.
And sic a weary burying,
The like ye never saw,
As there was the Sunday after that,
On the muirs down by Harlaw.[12]

While it is hard to be sure who exactly got the better of the Harlaw fighting, Donald, in the days following that fighting, withdrew northwards. Mar duly claimed victory. And as is stated on the plaque attached to the commemorative monument which Aberdeen Town Council erected at Harlaw on the occasion of the battle's five-hundredth anniversary, the events of July 1411 came to be regarded –

both in Aberdeen and in the rest of Lowland Scotland – as having amounted to a 'great deliverance' from the threat posed to Lowland life, Lowland values and Lowland culture by the lordship's Gaelic-speaking troops.

In a number of key respects, the Battle of Harlaw was actually less of a Highland–Lowland clash than is often supposed. The Earl of Mar, for example, was himself a Gaelic-speaker. He was, moreover, both a cousin of Donald, Lord of the Isles, and a son of Alexander Stewart, Wolf of Badenoch – a pedigree which, to put it mildly, made him an unlikely champion of John Fordun's 'home-loving, civilised, trustworthy, tolerant and polite' Lowlanders. But Mar, despite having begun his career as one of his father's caterans, had since come to the conclusion that he had more to gain from serving Scotland's rulers than from defying them. Donald, on the other hand, seems to have been more and more set on taking the opposite course. So what was the Lord of the Isles hoping to achieve when he embarked on the campaign which culminated in his invasion of Aberdeenshire?

Donald's stated objectives were nothing if not modest. He simply wanted, he said, to secure a number of Banffshire and Aberdeenshire estates which, in his view, were detached portions of the Earldom of Ross. Those estates, however, scarcely warranted operations on the scale undertaken by the lordship in the summer of 1411. Hence the longstanding suspicion that Donald wanted to topple the Duke of Albany's régime as a prelude to placing himself on the throne which the captive King James I had, for the moment, been obliged to leave empty.

Nor was this, in principle, an unattainable ambition. Donald, as James's cousin and as the son of Robert II's daughter, had close family links with Scotland's royal line. As Lord of the Isles, he had also been accustomed and encouraged from birth to think of himself – in ways which this chapter has already touched on – as something of a king in his own right. While Donald is unlikely to have been aware that in striking southwards from Moray, he was – quite literally – following in the footsteps of Macbeth, both he and others of the lordship's leading men might readily have considered Lords of the Isles to have had an absolute right to do what Macbeth once did. Just as one of its subordinate kings could aspire to the overkingship of Dalriada, and just as the similarly subordinate ruler of eleventh-century Moray could aspire to the kingship of Alba, so the Lord of the Isles, Somerled's successor as *Ri Innse Gall*, could well have been thought – by his own people at any rate – to be entitled to supplant a Scottish monarch who, as luck would have it, was in no position to preserve his kingship.

There is a sense, moreover, in which the spirit of the times favoured Donald's bid – if that is what it was – for supreme power in Scotland. Throughout the British Isles, the years around 1400 witnessed something of a resurgence on the part of Celtic groupings and cultures which had seemed, for two hundred years or more, to be in irreversible decline. In Wales, where English rule had been imposed by Edward I, the revolt of Owain Glyn Dwr – at its height in the run-up to the Harlaw episode – re-established, for some years at least, Welsh autonomy of a kind which nobody had expected to see again. In Ireland, where the English monarchy had earlier looked to be about to repeat Edward's Welsh successes, a series of native lordships – all of them organised along much the same lines as their Hebridean and West Highland counterparts – had so aggressively reasserted themselves as to have confined English influence, together with the English language, to the area immediately around Dublin. Had Harlaw turned out differently, something similar could conceivably have occurred in Scotland. In the manner of their Gaelic-speaking counterparts in Ireland, the Gaelic-speaking people of the Highlands and Islands might have begun to reverse the processes which had made Broad Scots, not Gaelic, the language of localities such as the one where the Battle of Harlaw took place.

Aberdeenshire Scots-speakers were definitely aware of this possibility. That is why Harlaw's outcome, as their ballads make clear, mattered so much to such folk. As far as the Lordship of the Isles itself was concerned, however, Harlaw seemed less significant. It might have curtailed such plans as Donald MacDonald had of making himself Scotland's king. It certainly resulted in his formally submitting to the Duke of Albany, at Lochgilphead, during 1412. But neither the Battle of Harlaw nor anything else which happened during the first half of the fifteenth century impinged on the lordship's internal workings. Despite their being nominally answerable to ministers and kings in Edinburgh, both Donald and his son, Alexander, who became Lord of the Isles in 1423, continued to preside – just as their predecessors had done – over what was, in effect, their own government. That government, known as the Council of the Isles, was dominated by the heads of the lordship's leading families. It met, for the most part, in Islay. 'There was a table of stone where this council sat in the Isle of Finlagan,' Hugh MacDonald commented. At that table, one surmises, there were taken the decisions which led, among other things, to the issuing of the lordship's surviving charters – charters which show, incidentally, that each successive Lord of the Isles, for all his careful cultivation of a Gaelic and Celtic persona, was quite capable, when it suited him, of adapting feudal techniques to his own purposes.[13]

The most pressing such purposes, of course, were those deriving from the lordship's need to ensure its continuation as, at the minimum, a semi-autonomous realm. This was less a matter of charters and feudal legalities, more a matter – as a German statesman famously remarked in a much later context – of blood and iron. It is of no small significance, therefore, that the Lordship of the Isles, under Alexander MacDonald's leadership, emerged triumphantly from the conflict precipitated, in the mid-1420s, by James I's much-delayed release from custody in England.

James, who accorded a high priority to bringing the lordship to heel, began by enticing a number of Highlands and Islands magnates – including Alexander MacDonald – to Inverness where the magnates in question were promptly seized and imprisoned. Alexander was taken to Perth where some attempt was made, it appears, to persuade him to assume the role of courtier. This prospect, it seems, Alexander rejected. Instead he turned his energies to escaping from the king's custody. That was quickly accomplished and soon Alexander, by way of getting his revenge on James, had burned the royal burgh of Inverness and laid siege to its castle.

James responded by personally leading a government army into the lordship and forcing Alexander's surrender. Hauled before Scotland's king in the unconvincing guise of penitent and supplicant, Alexander MacDonald was again incarcerated. His relatives and supporters, however, were still battling enthusiastically on his behalf. And soon they had won a famous victory – Alexander's uncle, a man known as Alasdair Carrach, routing a royal force at Inverlochy, close to modern Fort William, in September 1431. That particular success was made all the sweeter, from the lordship's standpoint, by the fact that Alasdair Carrach's opponent at Inverlochy was none other than the Earl of Mar, architect of the lordship's earlier reverse at Harlaw. This time, MacDonald tradition reports gleefully, Mar met with what such tradition portrays as a deserved comeuppance – the earl having been ignominiously obliged, in Inverlochy's aftermath, to take to his heels and to flee for his life into the Lochaber hills.

Now it was King James's turn, in effect, to sue for terms. Alexander was restored to the lordship and, having also been confirmed formally as Earl of Ross, he was, by the mid-1430s, in undisputed control of the bulk of the Highlands and Islands. Skye, the one Hebridean island which had previously been outside the lordship's jurisdiction, was gained along with the Ross earldom. On the west coast of the mainland, Alexander's territories extended, virtually unbroken, from the Mull of Kintyre to Achiltibuie. Those territories also stretched eastwards, through Lochaber, to the fringes of Badenoch – while, further north, in his capacity as Earl of Ross, Alexander was master of the highly productive farmlands around the Beauly and Cromarty Firths. It was in this latter area, in fact, that both Alexander MacDonald and his son and successor, John, were to spend a good deal of their time – members of the lordship's council, judging by the charters they issued, meeting in Dingwall, from the 1440s onwards, as often as they met in Finlagan. And if its Ross involvements can be seen retrospectively as one cause of the lordship's ultimate demise, in that they drew Alexander and John away from the real sources of MacDonald power, this was certainly not suspected in the middle decades of the fifteenth century. Then the Lordship of the Isles looked to have undone much of what the Scottish monarchy had been trying for centuries to accomplish in the Highlands and Islands – by restoring to the region a good deal of its age-old independence.

Because of its ruling family's tendency to behave as if the Lordship of the Isles was a sovereign power, that family's members clearly thought themselves entitled to deal, from time to time, with governments other than Scotland's. Among the more controversial outcomes of such dealings was a secret treaty – finalised at one of the lordship's castles, Ardtornish in Morvern, during 1462 – between John MacDonald, Lord of the Isles, and Edward IV, King of England. This agreement had at its core the notion that, should Edward find himself at war with Scotland, John MacDonald would come to his assistance and would, by way of reward, be recognised by Edward as the ruler of those parts of Scotland to the north of the Forth–Clyde line. Although disaffected Lowland nobles were also involved in the 1462 negotiations, the Lord of the Isles was undoubtedly the key player. In that capacity, he was clearly prepared to envisage the partitioning of Scotland between England, the Scottish kingdom's longstanding enemy, and his own lordship – which would have assumed control, had the 1462 treaty ever taken effect, of the lands which, six centuries before, had constituted the core of Kenneth MacAlpin's Alba.

Would the state thus envisaged have been one which could have preserved its autonomy and permitted the Highlands and Islands to develop in their own way and at their own pace? Or would its emergence have simply been a prelude to English rule extending across all the territories between the Tweed and the Pentland Firth? There can be no definitive answer to such questions – which, for better or worse, are wholly hypothetical. Nor is it possible to be certain as to John MacDonald's motives. Perhaps he genuinely aspired to an untrammeled kingship of the kind his Ardtornish agreement was ostensibly intended to bring him. Perhaps he simply wanted to access the English gold the 1462 treaty appears to have channelled in his direction. Perhaps – and this may be the most plausible explanation of John's conduct – he was merely endeavouring to find some means of countering the Scottish monarchy's continued enmity towards his lordship. Edward IV, on this reading of what happened in 1462, was being invited by John MacDonald to fulfil the function which Norway's kings had fulfilled in Somerled's time. He was being introduced into Highlands and Islands affairs in the hope that the resulting Scotland–England tensions would provide the Lordship of the Isles with rather more room for manoeuvre.

John MacDonald's father, Alexander, had tried to pull off much the same trick in the course of his quarrels, during the 1420s, with James I. In contrast to John, however, Alexander looked to Scandinavia, not England, for prospective allies. He looked, in particular, to King Erik of Denmark. The latter's country, in 1380, had assumed control of Norway. The Danish monarchy, as a result, acquired its Norwegian predecessor's overseas possessions. Those possessions no longer included the Hebrides which Norway had ceded to Scotland in 1266. The terms of that year's Treaty of Perth, however, had obliged the Scottish crown, in return for undisturbed occupancy of the Hebrides, to make stipulated annual payments to Norway's rulers – meaning, after 1380, Denmark's kings. Because no such payments had been made for a long time, it followed – or so Alexander MacDonald appears to have suggested to King Erik – that the Danish crown, as the Norwegian monarchy's inheritor, was entitled to assert some sort of claim to the Hebrides.

Of course, there was never more than the slightest chance that King Erik might actually seize islands like Skye or Lewis in lieu of the sums owed to him by James I. And in raising the possibility of Danish intervention in the Hebrides, Alexander MacDonald – who may have made noises to the effect that he would positively welcome such intervention – was probably trying mainly to bolster his own position at James's expense. The Scottish king, however, was sufficiently alarmed to take the precaution, in 1426, of negotiating a deal with Erik whereby the Danish monarch, in return for a promise that future payments would be unfailingly forthcoming, cancelled more than a century's worth of arrears.

Alexander MacDonald's Danish liaisons might have had the unintended consequence of reminding James that the Lordship of the Isles was not the only part of the Highlands and Islands where the Scottish monarchy – if it was to be completely in charge of the region – still had work to do. The lordship's territories, for all the difficulties James confronted when attempting to exercise royal jurisdiction over them, were at least within the internationally recognised boundaries of his kingdom. That was not true of Orkney and Shetland. Those island groups had been left in Norway's possession in 1266. Along with Faroe, Iceland and Greenland, they had been gained from Norway by Denmark in 1380. By this point, however, it was beginning to be felt in Edinburgh that both Orkney and Shetland ought ultimately to be acquired by Scotland's Stewart monarchy. This feeling was to harden into a profound conviction in the course of the fifteenth century.

Especially in the case of Orkney, Stewart ambitions were assisted by developments similar to those which had already enabled Scottish kings to consolidate their grip on Caithness. There a series of immigrant landholders, most of them of Lowland stock, managed – with royal encouragement – to establish themselves during the thirteenth and fourteenth centuries. Those landholders naturally tended to congregate most thickly in the more productive, and more low-lying, north-eastern part of the area. It is a measure both of their numbers and of their influence that – at a time when Gaelic was tending to take over from Norse in the hillier terrain further west – this corner of Caithness became the one segment of the Highland mainland, other than the district to the east of Auldearn, where Broad Scots had managed to obtain a significant toehold by the fifteenth century's end. By then, too, significantly enough, Broad Scots was well on the way to displacing Norse as the preferred means of communication among Orcadians.

Orkney's agricultural potential made its component islands as attractive to fourteenth-century Scots as they had earlier been to Vikings. And Scots, being fully in charge of nearby Caithness, could now move to Orkney much more easily than comparatively distant Danes and Norwegians. Such movement could, in principle, have been resisted by the Norwegian and Danish monarchies. Neither, however, was inclined to adopt such a course. And so extensive was Scottish migration across the Pentland Firth during this period that, long before Denmark was persuaded to relinquish its sovereignty over Orkney, the island group's earls, holders of the title once held by Sigurd the Powerful and Thorfinn the Mighty, were themselves Scots rather than Scandinavians – the most famed of those Scots earls being members of a family by the name of Sinclair.

The Sinclairs – who had originally accompanied the Bruces, the Stewarts and other feudal notables from France or England to Scotland in the twelfth century – became Earls of Orkney in 1379. In their Orcadian capacity, of course, they owed allegiance to successive kings of Denmark. But they also held Scottish estates in places like Aberdeenshire, Fife and the Lothians. They were actively involved, very often, in Scotland's politics. And it suited them gradually to surround themselves, both at their Kirkwall base and in the rest of Orkney, with more and more of their fellow nationals. Soon virtually all Orcadian administrators, and virtually all Orcadian churchmen of any seniority, were Scots – it being a measure of this group's growing influence that, after 1443, Norse ceased to be used in documents generated from within the earldom.

Matters were very different, it should be noted, in Shetland. Because it was more difficult than Orkney for Scots to reach, and because it had been ruled since the 1190s by directly appointed representatives of Norwegian and Danish kings, Shetland, throughout the fourteenth and fifteenth centuries, remained overwhelmingly Norse in language, culture and outlook. The intermarriage which occurred at this time between Shetlanders and the inhabitants of Faroe – with which Shetland may have shared administrators – is one piece of evidence to the effect that Shetlanders continued to identify primarily with the wider Scandinavian world to which they had belonged for several hundred years. Equally suggestive of such identification are fifteenth-century Shetland's trading links with Bergen – trading links which ensured it was fairly common, at this time, for individuals to own property in both Shetland and Norway.

There was some Scottish infiltration into mid-fifteenth-century Shetland, admittedly. But it was not on anything like the scale required to produce changes of the kind which had so transformed Orkney. Despite that island group's Norse antecedents, and despite its still being technically subject to Danish rule, Orkney, by the 1450s and 1460s, approximated much more to the Scottish Lowlands, not least in speech, than any other part of the Highlands and Islands – excepting only the Moray coastal plain and the north-eastern corner of Caithness. Many Orcadians were now of Lowland extraction. The public life of Orkney was entirely in this recently arrived population's hands. And from the standpoint of contemporary Edinburgh, as a result, Orkney, for all its distance from Scotland's capital, was much less alien a place than, for instance, the areas comprising the Lordship of the Isles – areas where neither Lowlanders nor their culture had impacted in any comparable way.

Partly because of their own Lowland connections, moreover, Orkney's earls, in contrast to Lords of the Isles, were generally on good terms with the Scottish monarchy – William Sinclair, who was Earl of Orkney in the middle decades of the fifteenth century, taking much more to do with Scotland's Stewart kings than he ever took to do with the Danish sovereign, Christian IV. By the 1460s, in fact, relations between Christian and Earl William had deteriorated so markedly that Christian, in a desperate attempt to re-exert his authority over Orcadians, gave up completely on the earl and appointed Orkney's bishop, William Tulloch, the Danish crown's principal representative in Kirkwall. Tulloch, however, was promptly imprisoned by Earl William's son. And Christian, clearly concluding that Orkney was anyway slipping out of his control, decided to make the best of a hopeless situation by entering into diplomatic discussions which ended in the island group's acquisition by Scotland.

At the centre of those discussions – conducted in Denmark and involving, on Scotland's side, ambassadors appointed by the Scottish parliament – was a suggested marriage between Scotland's young king, James III, and Christian IV's daughter, Margaret. This marriage, it was agreed, should take place – if only for the reason that it would enable Christian to claim some sort of gain, in the shape of a royal son-in-law, from negotiations otherwise characterised by his making concession after concession. Margaret, it was next agreed, should bring with her to Scotland a dowry of 60,000 Rhenish florins.* This was a sum which, as its Scottish proposers knew very well, could not possibly be raised by Christian – who, like most monarchs of that era, was exceedingly short of ready cash. Hence the further agreement that Christian would be required merely to make a down payment of 10,000 florins – with James III to have possession of Orkney until such time as the balance of his bride's dowry was forthcoming.

This deal was finalised in September 1468. By the following spring, however, Christian had managed to scrape together only one-fifth of the promised 10,000 florins. A further remarkable bargain was consequently struck by Scotland's negotiators – who, in addition to having obtained 2,000 florins and a wife for their king, had also persuaded the Danes to surrender their right to payments of the sort guaranteed by the two-hundred-year-old Treaty of Perth. In lieu of the missing 8,000 florins, it was now conceded by the Danish side, James

* Equivalent to many millions of pounds at modern values.

III, already in charge of Orkney, would also be granted Shetland.

The 1468 and 1469 arrangements regarding Orkney and Shetland may have been thought by Danish ministers to be reversible – in that the two sets of islands, in principle, could have been regained by Denmark if, or when, its king's financial situation improved. The Scottish government, however, was strongly of the view, from the outset, that the Northern Isles had unalterably become part of Scotland – as, in the event, matters turned out. And it was with a view to asserting the country's absolute sovereignty over its new possessions that Scottish ministers now moved decisively against the man who had been their leading Orcadian ally. Earl William's offhand attitude towards his royal masters had been positively encouraged by the Edinburgh authorities when these masters had been in Denmark. But now that Orkney was firmly in Scotland's grip, it rapidly became apparent, William Sinclair's usefulness to Edinburgh was at an end. The earl was provided with a castle in the Lowlands – where, as mentioned previously, his family already had substantial interests. But he was stripped of his Orkney estates which now became the property of the Scottish monarchy. And that same monarchy, it was made clear to Shetlanders and Orcadians, would henceforth be the ultimate arbiter of their fate. In future, the Scottish parliament ruled in 1472, only sons of Scotland's kings would be entitled to style themselves Earls of Orkney or Lords of Shetland.

Those events brought to a close a process which had commenced when Malcolm Canmore, having forcibly removed Macbeth from Scotland's throne, sent an army into Macbeth's own kingdom of Moray. Bit by bit, piece by piece, decade by decade, all of the Highlands and Islands had been brought inside the frontiers of the Scottish state. With Orcadians and Shetlanders firmly under its jurisdiction, it remained only for that state to deal finally with the one remaining threat to what its rulers had accomplished over the preceding four centuries. This threat was posed by the Lordship of the Isles – the last surviving bastion of anything approximating to political autonomy in a region where such autonomy had once been virtually universal. Neutralising the lordship, still presided over by John MacDonald, was thus something of a priority for James III. And in 1475, when the existence of the lordship's 1462 treaty with Edward IV became known in Edinburgh, James, much boosted by his annexation of the Northern Isles and his deposing of Earl William, was presented with the perfect opportunity to move against the one person in the Highlands and Islands who continued to be capable of causing the Scottish monarchy real trouble.

On 16 October 1475, a royal messenger rode up to the gates of John MacDonald's castle at Dingwall – a castle which has long since been demolished but which then served as the administrative centre of John's Earldom of Ross – to inform the Lord of the Isles that he was required to appear before parliament in Edinburgh, on 1 December, to answer charges arising from what were viewed as his treasonable dealings with the King of England. On John declining to go south, he was tried, and found guilty, in his absence. Various nobles were next invited to invade John's territories and assured that, if they judged it expedient, they could go so far as to kill John himself. The latter, reckoning his position hopeless, eventually submitted to James III in the course of 1476. Although permitted to retain the title of Lord of the Isles, together with the bulk of the lordship's original lands, John was stripped of the Earldom of Ross. As King James intended, this enormously eroded the lordship's power. It also precipitated a debilitating breach between John and his son, Angus – the latter being of the opinion that his father should have done battle with the Stewart monarchy rather than cravenly relinquish Ross.

John, from this point forward, became an increasingly marginal figure who was content, or forced, to allow the lordship to fall gradually under the control of his more assertive son and heir. Although the details of what followed are both scanty and confusing, it seems that a substantial proportion of the lordship's leading figures endorsed Angus's view that the time had come for renewed war with Scotland's monarchy. Angus was certainly able, in the early 1480s, to put an army in the field, to mount an attack on Inverness Castle's royal garrison and to defeat at least one of the troop detachments which James III deployed against him. The king's resources, however, were now considerably greater than those available to the lordship. And for all Angus's evident skills as a military commander and tactician, it is improbable that, even had he lived, he would have been able to restore his family to its previous position. As it was, Angus having being assassinated in 1490 and his place having being taken by his cousin, Alexander MacDonald of Lochalsh, the overall Highlands and Islands situation, as viewed from within what remained of the lordship, deteriorated still further. When Alexander mounted a series of raids into the former Earldom of Ross, Scotland's latest Stewart king, James IV, responded by deciding to extinguish the Lordship of the Isles in much the same way as his father, James III, had earlier extinguished the Earldom of Orkney. In 1493, the already weakened lordship was declared by the Scottish parliament to have ceased, in effect, to exist. It was not to be recreated.

CHAPTER FIVE

No joy without Clan Donald

1494–1659

From Craig Phadraig, where Columba may have met King Bridei, the sheer size of modern Inverness is immediately apparent. The town, one of Britain's most rapidly growing urban areas at the twentieth century's close, practically fills the northern end of the Great Glen. But for all that Inverness seems so extensive when inspected from the elevated viewpoint provided by Craig Phadraig, its expansion has not yet been so great as to deprive visitors of a sense that, even when looking round the town centre, they are within easy reach of countryside of the sort that makes the Highlands and Islands so appealing. From the Ness Bridge, as focal a point as Inverness possesses, the view downstream and to the north-west is dominated by the bulky shape of Ben Wyvis – its upper slopes snow-covered for several months each year. As for the waters of the River Ness itself, so unpolluted are they that, from the Ness Bridge, it is possible to watch an angler hook and land a fresh-run salmon in a setting which one might think unspoiled, even natural, if – by some trick of the light – the buildings on the river's bank were momentarily to vanish from view.

Easily the most prominent of those buildings are a couple of office blocks which, by virtue of their jointly overlooking the Ness Bridge's eastern end, guard the approaches to Inverness's High Street. On encountering this pair of concrete monstrosities while visiting the Highlands in the mid-1990s, Bill Bryson, a best-selling travel writer, expressed himself astonished 'that an entire town could be ruined by two inanimate structures'. Built in the 1960s, that most architecturally disastrous of decades, the structures in question seemed to Bryson to be 'madly inappropriate to the surrounding scene'.* It is hard, on strolling uphill from the Ness Bridge to the High Street, to disagree with that verdict – a verdict which Bill Bryson might have

* This particular pile, it should be admitted, houses the headquarters of Highlands and Islands Enterprise.

delivered with even greater force had he known what was demolished to make way for the larger of the two edifices to which he took such exception. On this edifice's riverside site there previously stood a house dating from the sixteenth century – a house which, prior to its being bulldozed, was one of modern Inverness's few links with its distant past.[1]

By more recent standards, the town inhabited by that house's original occupants was very small. Inverness, for several hundred years, consisted of just four thoroughfares: present-day High Street, Bridge Street, Castle Street and Church Street. Those streets are now given over generally to shops – most of them branches of the nationwide chains which came to dominate British retailing in the later part of the twentieth century. But if few of Inverness's modern stores have been present in the town for more than three or four decades, the activity in which they and their customers are engaged is of much more ancient origin. From their remotest beginnings, towns were places where buyers and sellers met to engage in commerce. Inverness was no exception.

When exactly Inverness became a trading centre is unclear. If indeed Craig Phadraig was – during the reign of Bridei or later – a Pictish hillfort, then the chances are that, as was certainly true of Craig Phadraig's Dalriadan equivalents, merchants from the southern half of the British Isles, even from continental Europe, would have been among the hillfort's regular visitors. Might such merchants or their successors have established some sort of semi-permanent settlement near the spot – since occupied by the Ness Bridge – where the River Ness was traditionally forded and where the Great Glen, giving access to the west, intersects with other routes leading south, east and north? Such a settlement, if it existed, could conceivably have become the nucleus of the town, or burgh, which eventually emerged here. All we know for sure about Inverness's origins, however, is that the place was first formally designated a burgh by Scotland's twelfth-century monarchs who were then incorporating into their realm this and other parts of the former Kingdom of Moray.

Two further burghs, Elgin and Forres, were also founded in twelfth-century Moray. Both became locally significant centres. And not least because of its possessing so spectacular a cathedral,* Elgin, in particular, acquired some wider importance. Medieval Inverness was of much less account ecclesiastically. But Inverness – a place which may well have had associations with Macbeth and other members of

* Although again ruinous, this cathedral was rebuilt and reroofed in the period following the Wolf of Badenoch's attack on it.

Moray's previously ruling dynasty – nevertheless became the Scottish monarchy's principal outpost in the Highlands and Islands. The town's present-day role as the region's administrative capital – symbolised by its housing the headquarters of central government agencies like Highlands and Islands Enterprise and the Crofters Commission – is thus a longstanding one. From the twelfth century onwards, Scotland's Edinburgh-based rulers regarded Inverness as a key factor in their plans for the entire territory of which it was part. That was why the newly established burgh was immediately equipped with one of the most potent emblems of centralised and centralising authority: a royal castle.

Despite its mock battlements, the Victorian building which currently occupies this castle's site, on steeply rising ground a couple of hundred yards upstream from the Ness Bridge, is of no military consequence. But matters were very different in the past. The timber palisade that went up here in the twelfth century, and still more the stone-built fortifications which afterwards took the initial palisade's place, were intended to provide Scottish kings with a Highlands and Islands base of a sort that the region's – habitually mistrusted – inhabitants could not easily threaten.

As for the town which gradually took shape to the north of the castle hill and to the east of the River Ness, there was about it, too, a good deal that was indicative of its having been the product of policies intended to bolster royal influence in an area where such influence, in the opinion of Scotland's kings at any rate, badly needed bolstering. Thus the merchants who constituted early Inverness's dominant social group – and who were expected to assist with, and promote, the Scottish kingdom's northwards expansion – were mostly drawn, like the feudal noblemen then installing themselves in the Moray countryside, from the Lowlands, from England and from mainland Europe.

The essentially colonial nature of medieval Inverness's mercantile population is evident in that population's surnames. As late as the fifteenth and sixteenth centuries, Inverness traders were typically called Marshall, Burr, Cuthbert, Vass, Birnie, Barbour, Scott, White, Fleming and Winchester – names which owed nothing to the Highlands and Islands. In Inverness, it followed, the dominant language – among the town's leading families at all events – was Scots or English, not Gaelic. As an early-eighteenth-century observer of the Inverness scene was perceptively to comment, the burgh community's sense of its separateness from its surroundings was partly rooted in this fact:

> The natives [of Inverness] do not call themselves Highlanders . . . because they speak English . . . Yet although they speak English, there are scarce any who do not understand the [Gaelic] tongue; and it is necessary they should do so [in order] to carry on their dealings with the neighbouring country people; for within less than a mile of the town, there are few who speak any English at all.[2]

Nor was it only because of its townsfolk's choice of language that Inverness, in relation to the burgh's rural hinterland, was a place apart. Medieval towns, whether in Scotland or elsewhere in Europe, were legally and fiscally privileged in all sorts of ways. Those privileges were owed ultimately to kings who, if only as a means of generating higher returns from taxation, were everywhere endeavouring to promote trade. Because all such trade was dependent ultimately on traders, and because traders needed a mix of assurances and incentives in order to persuade them to embark on new ventures, medieval monarchies found themselves engaged, in effect, in state-sponsored development of their countries' economies. Just as twentieth-century governments were to establish enterprise zones, proffer grant aid to inward investors and otherwise attempt to foster economic growth, so twelfth-century rulers founded burghs like Inverness with a view to creating circumstances of a kind meant both to attract merchants to particular localities and to guarantee those merchants a reasonable return on such commercial activity as they were able to conduct there. To be a burgess – the term applied to a member of a burgh's governing élite – was thus to be exempted from various royal tolls and impositions while simultaneously having the right to take part, with other burgesses, in the administration and public life of the burgh in which one resided. To be a burgess, moreover, was automatically to gain access to what amounted to a regally enforced monopoly – each burgh's burgesses being entitled in law to have sole rights to buy and sell over a very wide area.

In Inverness's case, this area amounted to the greater part of the Highlands and Islands. And the burgh council – composed of the town's leading burgesses – was not at all hesitant about insisting on Inverness's privileges. When the name of a certain 'Gillespyk MacGregor' appears in the burgh's sixteenth-century records, for example, it is as a consequence of this freelance trader having had the temerity to despatch to Perth, from Strathglass and Glen Urquhart, a consignment of goods consisting of, among other things, twenty dozen lamb skins, twelve dozen kid skins, six dozen calf skins and five stones of wool. Having been seized by the Inverness authorities and promptly confined to the town jail, MacGregor was ordered to make arrangements either to have his goods returned north – for sale, as the law required, in Inverness – or to make over to the burgh council a cash sum equivalent to his consignment's market value.[3]

The unfortunate Gilleasbuig MacGregor – whose name shows that, in contrast to most Inverness burgesses, he was of Highland origin – may have traded illegally with the folk of Strathglass and Glen Urquhart. But the commodities in which he dealt were very much the Highlands and Islands staples of his time. Rather like the frontier towns which Highlanders would later help to found in eighteenth-century North America, Inverness, during the middle ages and afterwards, channelled hides, pelts and other items of that kind in the direction of Europe's more advanced economies – such economies, in the twelfth, thirteenth and fourteenth centuries, being confined to continental locations, most notably Flanders. Medieval Inverness's exports to such locations consisted of furs, salmon, herring, timber and the like. Imports, for their part, were mostly made up of goods which the Highlands and Islands could not readily produce – salt, wines and spices, for example.

Since Inverness did not possess anything approximating to its modern harbour until the later seventeenth century, visiting ships simply anchored in the river mouth or off the Longman – an area immediately to the east of the Ness's estuary. It was in this same general vicinity, presumably, that there were built those other ships which are known to have been constructed in the burgh – from timber, it is safe to guess, felled in places like Glen Moriston and floated seawards by way of Loch Ness and the River Ness. So well-built was one such ship – ordered, in 1247, by a continental nobleman, Count Hugh of St Pol – that it caught the attention of a contemporary English writer, Matthew Paris. It says a good deal for the skill of the medieval town's shipwrights that this Inverness-built vessel, which must have been one of many, was sufficiently seaworthy, as Paris noted, to convey crusader troops from the Pas de Calais to the Holy Land.

Its shipwrights were only one among the several sets of craftsmen to be found in Inverness in the centuries following the burgh's creation. Ironworkers, candlemakers, hatters, tanners, weavers, butchers, bakers, brewers and shoemakers all plied their trades here. Those tradesmen's business premises, the remote predecessors of today's shops, occupied the lower storeys of the houses that lined each side of the burgh's streets. Above and behind such frontages were the homes where there lived the families of tradesmen, merchants and other burgh residents. By the sixteenth century, one or two of those homes – such as the one demolished to make way for the office block which so offended Bill Bryson – were built of stone and roofed with slates or tiles. Prior to that point, however, Inverness houses, by subsequent standards, were very flimsily constructed. A few stones might go into their underpinnings. But their walls consisted primarily of wattle – made by weaving hazel or willow wands through slender timber uprights and plastering the resulting framework with clay.

Roofs consisted universally of thatch and, in such circumstances, fire, on taking hold, tended to spread rapidly from home to home, street to street. Hence the ease with which Donald, Lord of the Isles, was reported to have burned 'most of the town' when he and his army came this way in the weeks preceding the Battle of Harlaw. Also burned by the lordship's forces was an earlier version of the modern Ness Bridge. That bridge, one Invernessian commented, had been 'the famousest and finest of oak in Britain'.[4]

Inverness's pre-Harlaw conflagration was started deliberately. Others came about by accident. And it was in an attempt to minimise such disasters that the burgh authorities – in Inverness as elsewhere in the middle ages – made it an offence to carry an uncovered candle, or any other naked light, through the town's streets. Although patrolled each night by watchmen drawn from among the ranks of the burgesses' servants, those streets, in consequence, were dark and scary places: lit only by moon and stars; given over, in large measure, to the rats which scurried furtively from one midden or open sewer to the next.

In the total absence of mains drainage, Inverness, for the greater part of its existence, must have stunk. The fosse or ditch which, for defensive purposes, was dug around the burgh's perimeter in the twelfth century seems gradually to have been transformed into a gigantic and uncovered septic tank known – appropriately enough – as 'the Foul Pool'. The backyards and gardens at the rear of each row of houses appear to have filled up, in many instances, with garbage of one kind or another. And since Inverness's tanners – of whom there were a substantial number – were anyway in the habit of curing hides in enormous vats of urine, it must have been impossible, in so tiny a town, to get away from lingering odours of the most pungent kind.[5]

Nor would the interiors of most Inverness houses have offered much in the way of sanctuary from the discomforts of the burgh's streets. Few homes, prior to the sixteenth century, had glazed windows – such windows as existed being merely shutter-covered apertures in houses' exterior walls. Other fitments were equally rudimentary. Light possibly came from lamps fuelled by seal oil. But it was more probably confined, for the most part, to such natural light as found its way inside during daytime – and to the glow given off by kitchen fires at night. Floors were covered with sand, rushes or straw. And while wealthier merchants might own bedsteads, chests, tables, chairs, pewter plates and silver spoons, there were few such possessions to be found in homes occupied by the poorer people. Such folk's beds consisted mainly of heather, straw or bracken; their furnishings were limited to two or three roughly made benches; their utensils might consist of a cooking pot, some wooden plates, a handful of wooden or clay cups and two or three knives.

Partly because homes were small and public buildings – other than the town's church – virtually non-existent, much of Inverness's commercial and social life, prior to modern times, was conducted in the open air. 'There they stand in the middle of the dirty street,' an eighteenth-century visitor remarked of the way the burgh's merchants customarily did business with one another, 'and are frequently interrupted in their negotiation by horses and carts which often separate them from one another in the midst of their bargains or other affairs.' And what was true of Inverness's business class was even truer, of course, of the burgh's less well-to-do inhabitants. 'Poor women, maidservants and children' were to be observed about the streets even 'in the coldest weather, in the dirt or in snow, either walking or standing to talk with one another, without stockings or shoes'. Down by the river, meanwhile, it was customary to come upon 'women with their coats tucked up, stamping, in tubs, upon linen by . . . way of washing; and not only in summer, but in the hardest frosty weather when their legs and feet are almost literally as red as blood with the cold'.[6]

Edinburgh, in the 1380s, was said to contain four hundred houses. Inverness, whether then or two hundred years later, would have been still more diminutive. But the burgh, for all that, was, as it has since remained, by far the largest town in the Highlands and Islands. Throughout the middle ages and into the sixteenth century, in fact, Inverness was virtually the region's only urban centre of any consequence – its few early rivals, such as Dingwall, Tain, Dornoch and Kirkwall, then being little more than hamlets.

To leave sixteenth-century Inverness by any route other than the one leading to Forres and Elgin, therefore, would have been to find oneself in an unrelievedly rural landscape. Today such landscapes are thought benign and attractive. But to read one of the earliest published accounts of the Highlands and Islands is immediately to grasp the extent to which the region's appearance, in the past, seemed anything but reassuring:

> The Highlands are but little known even to the inhabitants of the low country of Scotland, for they have ever dreaded the difficulties and dangers of travelling among the mountains; and when some ordinary occasion has obliged any one of them to such a progress, he has, generally speaking, made his testament before setting out, as though he were entering upon a long and dangerous sea voyage, wherein it was very doubtful if he should ever return.[7]

The dangers supposedly inherent in Highlands and Islands travel were no doubt believed to derive, in large part, from the region's human residents. But there were other hazards, too. The lynx became extinct in the neolithic period; bears had been wiped out by Macbeth's time. During the sixteenth century, however, wolves remained sufficiently common, even in the vicinity of Inverness, for one of the town's burgesses to have blamed their maraudings for his loss, in December 1569, of a 'blak oxe of five yeiris auld'.[8]

The night-time howling of the area's wolves – a sound that had long ceased to be heard in the rest of Britain – was one of the factors which resulted in people from England or the Lowlands treating the sixteenth-century Highlands and Islands as wild and off-putting. But the region's mountain scenery – for all that it was afterwards to be so highly esteemed – was also disliked by the first outsiders to venture north. 'An eye accustomed to flowery pastures and waving harvests is astonished and repelled by this wide extent of hopeless sterility,' one early visitor commented. To such visitors, Highland peaks seemed 'frightful', 'monstrous', 'dreary' and 'most horrible'.[9]

As noted previously, Highlands and Islands hillsides were once clothed in trees. Those trees had been under human assault ever since the region's hunter-gatherers started turning them into spears and harpoon shafts. But because Lowland Scotland had been almost totally deforested, the sixteenth-century Highlands and Islands – outside Shetland, Orkney and the more exposed parts of the Hebrides at any rate – were thought comparatively well-wooded by travellers from the south. Unlike their twenty-first-century successors, moreover, the forests encountered by such travellers consisted entirely of native tree species – larch, sitka spruce and the other exotic conifers which dominate many modern plantations having not yet put in an appearance. The absence of such conifers, were we able to experience the sixteenth-century Highlands and Islands at first hand, we should find a little odd.

We should find much else odd as well. The Highlands and Islands of four or five hundred years ago, for example, were almost as roadless as the area had been when its brochs were built or when Roman legionaries set about constructing their Inchtuthil fortress. 'The ways are so rough and rocky', it was observed of the age-old bridle paths leading westwards from Inverness, 'that no wheel ever turned upon them since the formation of [the] globe.' In the absence of carts and wagons, let alone trains, cars, trucks and aircraft, much of the sixteenth-century Highlands and Islands – outside Inverness – would thus have been extremely quiet. The loudest noises most of the area's inhabitants ever heard were the sounds generated by wind, by running water, by their family's domestic animals, by the human voice, by musical instruments or by hammer-wielding craftsmen working metal into new shapes.[10]

For all their relative silence, however, the sixteenth-century Highlands and Islands consisted overwhelmingly of peopled landscapes. Inverness apart, substantial towns, as already remarked, were nowhere to be found. But the lack of any worthwhile urbanisation was more than counterbalanced by people having spread themselves across practically every piece of land capable of sustaining them. This meant that glens and islands which have since been emptied of their occupants were thickly settled. The northern half of Scotland, as a result, contained a far higher proportion of the country's total population in the sixteenth century than it did four hundred years later. Everywhere there were clusters of homes – each cluster constituting one of the *clachans* or townships which were so central, in the sixteenth century and for some time afterwards, to Highlands and Islands society.

In 1577, having put in to Orkney in the course of a voyage from England to the Arctic, the explorer Martin Frobisher penned this account of an Orcadian township's homes:

> Their houses are verie simply builded with pebble stone without any chimneys, the fire being in the middest thereof. The good man, wife, children, and others of the familie, eate

> and sleepe on one side of the house and their cattell on the other.[11]

For all their rudimentary character, houses of the type Martin Frobisher described had one huge advantage. The materials needed for their construction were readily to hand and could be easily assembled. In Orkney, as had been the case since Skara Brae was first settled, the exterior walls of most homes appear to have consisted largely of stone. Elsewhere in the Highlands and Islands countryside, houses – while they might have had somewhat more solid foundations – were frequently made from nothing more substantial than turf or wattle. As in Inverness, roofs were thatched. And since the building of such dwellings required no very great expertise, a township's whole population – men, women and children – could be mobilised to assist with a house's construction. As would subsequently occur on the North American frontier, where a newly arrived pioneer family's neighbours took pride in ensuring that such a family's log cabin went up in a single day, the people of a Highlands and Islands township regularly got together in numbers sufficient to ensure that entire homes were put up between the sun's rising and setting.

Although every bit as sparsely equipped as most of their Inverness equivalents, the homes thus provided, as remarked in the course of a sixteenth-century account of the Highlands and Islands, were by no means comfortless:

> In their houses . . . they lie upon the ground, strewing fern, or heath, on the floor with the roots downward and the leaves turned up. In this manner they form a bed so pleasant that it may vie in softness with the finest down.[12]

This was a society which lacked modern communications media every bit as much as it lacked modern furnishings. There were few books, and certainly no newspapers, magazines, radios or television sets, in the sixteenth-century Highlands and Islands. As they had done for millennia, therefore, the area's inhabitants made their own entertainment. On the mainland and in the Hebrides, there were endlessly rehearsed those Gaelic tales – concerning Cu Chulainn and his like – which had already been told for a thousand years or more. In Orkney and still more in Shetland, where the common speech remained the Norse dialect known as *Norn*, the dominant folklore was Scandinavian rather than Celtic in both origin and content. But it would have been none the less esteemed for that.

Irrespective of the language they spoke, each township's inhabitants, as well as drawing on more widely circulating traditions, had their own supply of highly localised stories. Such stories – featuring families and places with which their hearers were personally familiar – served both to encapsulate a township's sense of identity and to cement the longstanding linkages between a particular community and that community's physical surroundings. Nor were such purposes served only by the spoken word. Song and music – in which the Highlands and Islands have, for centuries, been very rich – similarly celebrated the manifold connections between each piece of territory and the people who occupied it, managed it, worked it.

And work, it goes almost without saying, was each township's constant preoccupation. Some of that work was of a specialist kind – the prerogative of the local smith, miller or shoemaker, for example. Some of it was deemed the preserve of women – cooking, mending, child-rearing, for instance. But virtually every one of its residents – male or female, young or old – was involved in the effort required to provide a township with its food.

As contemporary accounts of it make clear, there was little that was elaborate about the sixteenth-century Highlands and Islands diet:

> They make a kind of bread, not unpleasant to the taste, of oats and barley, the only grain cultivated in these regions, and, from long practice, they have attained considerable skill in moulding the cakes. Of this they eat a little in the morning, and then contentedly go out a-hunting, or engage in some other occupation, frequently remaining without any other food till the evening.[13]

Of course, folk living in the Highlands and Islands did not subsist exclusively on the oatcakes thus described. Their 'grettest delyte' was reported to be beef – which they ate regularly. Milk and cheese were common. Fish were to be got from the sea and from rivers. Coastal and island communities, as they had probably done since the beginning of human settlement in such places, sometimes slaughtered seals or even whales. And in the sixteenth century, just as in the more distant past, there were lots of berries and nuts to be gathered, plenty of birds and game to be taken by hunters.[14]

Although plain, the traditional Highlands and Islands diet was by no means bad. Oatmeal, its staple component, is rich in vitamins and, especially when combined with fish and dairy products, is perfectly capable of sustaining health. Such nutritional difficulties as confronted the inhabitants of the sixteenth-century Highlands and Islands, therefore, did not stem directly from their choice of foodstuffs. Those difficulties came, rather, from the fact that a cereals-based diet of the Highlands and Islands sort was inherently vulnerable in a region where the weather was seldom reliable and where arable land has always been at a premium. All Highlands and Islands communities, therefore, were obliged to give a great deal of time and attention to the management of such potentially cultivable land as was available to them.

⁂

During the seventeenth and eighteenth centuries, Highlands and Islands townships – their layout probably much the same as it had been for some time – were variously reported to consist of 'halfe a scoare cottages', 'a few huts for dwellings' and 'about eight or ten houses together'. In the immediate vicinity of those closely grouped dwellings, each of them built within yards of its neighbours, were a number of 'barns' or 'stables'. All around the clachan which thus resulted were the fields on which that clachan's occupants depended for their survival.[15]

Those fields looked nothing like the neatly fenced, and usually flat, enclosures in which crops are raised today. They consisted instead of a mass of separate plots. Each plot was heaped up in such a way as to turn it into an elongated, low-crested ridge. And since the terrain surrounding a township might contain scores – even hundreds – of such ridges, their cumulative impact on the Highlands and Islands landscape was clearly immense. Whole localities must have had something of the appearance of an ocean petrified at a point when it was affected by a steeply rolling swell.

Cultivation ridges of the sort thus described – the overwhelming majority of them given over, year in, year out, to cereals – were known, in Scots, as rigs. The type of land management to which they gave rise was called, in turn, runrig.

In the sixteenth century, runrig was to be found throughout Scotland. Here and there in the Highlands and Islands, it was to endure into the twentieth century. In most places, however, runrig has long faded both from view and from memory – its remaining traces being generally confined to ground markings which have been so smoothed out and worn away in most Highlands and Islands settings that they are nowadays revealed only by the melting of wind-blown snow or by the long shadows cast by a setting sun.

As such ground markings demonstrate, rigs came in all shapes and sizes. They might be twenty or thirty feet across. Their length might be as much as ten times greater than their breadth. They were higher in the middle than at the edges because the soil which they contained was worked in such a way as to turn it constantly towards their centres. And between any two rigs was a stony or marshy hollow which, in an era prior to the invention of subsoil drainage, served to channel away surplus rainwater.

Each of the several families occupying the average township had the use of a whole series of rigs. But a family's rigs were seldom adjacent to one another – being typically scattered across a wide area and interspersed, therefore, with other people's landholdings. Because of our modern tendency to think of a farm as a single piece of land, runrig strikes us as untidy. That untidiness had a purpose, however. It made for a high degree of equitability in the sharing-out of a township's resources – runrig making it impossible for any one family to be better provided for, in an agricultural sense, than their neighbours. This was ensured by allocating to all township landholders equal numbers of rigs in each of several categories – ranging from the highest-yielding to the lowest-yielding.

In a further attempt to give township residents a fair share of what was to be had in the way of land, a township's rigs might also be redistributed on a fairly regular basis. But irrespective of who exactly was responsible for particular rigs at a particular moment, their use was always in accordance with a standard pattern. If a rig was one of those constituting a township's 'infield', the name given to the more productive area in the immediate vicinity of the township's homes, then that rig was cropped continually. It was also manured intensively: with dung from its cultivator's cattle, with discarded thatch and other organic debris from its cultivator's home, with turf stripped from nearby hillsides and, where circumstances permitted, with seaweed. If, in contrast, a rig lay in the less fertile and more marginal part of a township's total landholding, the part known as 'outfield', then such a rig was permitted, on occasion, to lie fallow. Outfield rigs, moreover, received much less in the way of manure – having to rely, for the most part, on dung provided by the livestock which were folded, or penned, in the temporary enclosures erected on such rigs during their fallow periods.

Rigs might be cultivated with the help of ploughs drawn by horses or oxen. They might be cultivated manually. Either way, they were mostly sown, right across the Highlands and Islands, with oats or bere – the latter being a pre-modern variety of barley. Returns on such crops were generally low – much lower than those produced by the scientifically bred cereals of modern times. Hence the importance of ensuring that maturing crops were given every possible protection – something which necessitated the exclusion from a township's arable land, during the growing season, of all its livestock. This was achieved each spring by driving cattle and other animals beyond each township's head dyke – the wall marking the boundary between a township's rigs and its hill pastures.

Everywhere in the Highlands and Islands, in places which have long been deserted as well as in places which are still inhabited, one comes across the remnants of those head dykes. Nowadays, they are long, meandering, grass-grown mounds of around three feet in height. When newly built, however, the standard head dyke – consisting of layer after layer of freshly cut turf – was some six feet high. It was also unbroken by gates or other features of that kind. When the time came to move livestock on to the grazings lying beyond the head dyke, a part of the dyke was simply taken down. The township's animals, typically comprising sheep, goats and horses as well as cattle, were then driven through the resulting gap – which had afterwards to be speedily repaired.

Each township's hill pastures constituted, as those of crofting communities in the twenty-first-century Highlands and Islands still do, a common grazing. As its name indicates, all families residing in the community are entitled to pasture their stock on such a grazing. In order to avoid their over-exploitation, therefore, common grazings have always had to be carefully controlled. In a modern crofting township, management of the common grazing is the responsibility of a grazings committee and its clerk. In runrig townships of the sixteenth and seventeenth centuries, control rested with barony courts and their constables – the latter having the job of enforcing the regulations which emanated from the former. Unlike present-day grazings committees, which are elected by crofters having shares in the grazings, barony courts answered primarily to the countryside's leading men – its gentry and its aristocracy. Because all concerned had a vested interest in effective land management, however, barony court proceedings were often broadly consensual in nature. It is unlikely, for example, that anyone took exception to a Glenorchy Barony Court ruling of 1631 to the effect that every township's stock had to be 'outwith the head dyke from the 1st of May and, from the 8th day of June, [had] to pass to shielings'.[16]

Shielings were those higher altitude grazings to which the folk of most Highlands and Islands townships took their cattle and other animals in summer. Since a township's shielings might be several miles distant from the glen, the lochside or the coastal spot where the township was itself located, shielings were equipped with huts in which the community – especially women and children – lived for much of each June, July and August. Such seasonal migrations, quite apart from their keeping a township's livestock well away from its growing crops, enabled the Highlands and Islands population to make use of mountain pastures that would otherwise have been inaccessible to its livestock. There was thus a great deal to be said – from a resource-management perspective – for the shieling system. And the practice of moving annually into shieling huts was consequently to endure in some localities – particularly Lewis – into the twentieth century. As a result of land-use changes examined in subsequent chapters, however, shielings were generally abandoned long before that. The majority of shieling sites are nowadays indicated, therefore, by little other than those green and grassy patches which anyone hillwalking in the Highlands and Islands comes across in the remotest locations – locations made permanently more fertile than their heather-clad surroundings by the droppings deposited in such spots by the animals once pastured here.

Shielings did not exist everywhere in the Highlands and Islands – they were more or less unknown in Shetland, for instance. And there were other variations, between one district and another, in the way land was managed – with so-called bailie courts taking the place of barony courts in Orkney, for example. Irrespective of how exactly they organised their agricultural activities, however, inhabitants of the sixteenth-century Highlands and Islands, to an extent now almost unimaginable, were responsible for supplying their own wants, meeting their own needs. A community's homes, as already noted, were constructed by the community's members from locally sourced stone, timber, turf and thatch. Those homes were heated with locally extracted peat or locally cut firewood. Townships grew and ground their own meal, reared and killed their own cattle and sheep, turned out their own dairy products, caught their own fish, spun their own wool, made their own tools. Inverness's modest import-export trade apart, there was thus no sixteenth-century equivalent of the complex commercial interchanges – often featuring commodities as basic as clothing and foodstuffs – which bind the modern Highlands and Islands to the rest of Britain, the rest of Europe, the rest of the world.

The self-sufficiency, not just of the Highlands and Islands in their entirety but of even the smallest Highlands and Islands localities, helped frustrate the intentions of the Scottish politicians who, in the sixteenth century as in earlier times, expended so much energy on attempts to impose externally conceived agendas on the region. Because Highlands and Islands communities mostly stood on their own feet economically, it was much easier for key individuals in those communities to be at odds with Scotland's government than would have been the case had such individuals, or the wider population of which they were part, been more reliant on trading links with the Scottish monarchy's southern heartland.

The political autonomy which much of the Highlands and Islands had earlier enjoyed was not recreated during the sixteenth century. But the constitutional arrangements which ended that autonomy continued to be resented. Since they were intended to subordinate Highlands and Islands interests to Scotland's national interest as defined by the country's Edinburgh-based administrators, the arrangements in question were regularly challenged by folk who wanted the Highlands and Islands, whether in whole or in part, to be ruled again from within the area's own borders. Among the most effective such challenges – for a period at least – were those emanating from the two island groups which, in 1468 and 1469, the Scottish kingdom had so triumphantly brought within its jurisdiction.

To one of Scotland's sixteenth-century monarchs, James V, Orkney and Shetland seemed so many 'scattered isles in the polar ocean'. They were far away, in other words, from the Lowland areas where rulers like James V habitually located themselves. By taking advantage of this fact, a succession of island strong men managed to wreck the Scottish monarchy's plans for its most northerly possessions.[17]

On acquiring Orkney and Shetland from Denmark, Scotland's kings had begun by exiling William Sinclair, Earl of Orkney, whose island estates, having been appropriated by the Scottish monarchy, were administered on the monarchy's behalf by Orkney's bishops. The Sinclair family's consequent eclipse did not last long, however. By the 1490s, a new generation of Sinclairs, most notably Earl William's grandson, Lord Henry Sinclair, had succeeded in manoeuvring themselves into key positions in Orkney. Much the same was true of Shetland where Lord Henry's uncle, Sir David Sinclair of Sumburgh, managed to make himself that island group's *foud* or administrator. As the sixteenth century opened, therefore, the Northern Isles were dominated by a powerful family grouping who, while theoretically subject to Scotland's kings, were in practice almost as free as their

Norse predecessors had been to manage Orkney and Shetland affairs in accordance with locally determined priorities.

The Sinclairs, as noted earlier, had originally moved north from the Scottish Lowlands. But they had long been perfectly at ease in an island *milieu* that still owed a good deal to Scandinavia. This is evident from the complex career of Shetland's late-fifteenth-century foud, David Sinclair. Nominally answerable to Edinburgh, he held an office which carried a Norse title and which – for all that Shetland had ostensibly become a part of Scotland – regularly obliged its holder to intervene in disputes arising from a legal system that was almost entirely Norwegian in character. Among the more distinctive features of this system was udal law – a set of principles encapsulating a peculiarly Scandinavian approach to landholding. As the island group's foud, David Sinclair, had he wished to integrate Shetland more fully into the Scottish kingdom, might have sought to undermine this key aspect of Shetland's Norse heritage. Revealingly, he did not do so. Udal law remained in being. Shetland land transactions continued to be registered, as had been the practice for centuries, in Norwegian courts. And Shetland's foud, as if by way of underlining the extent of his own affinities with Scandinavia, dabbled ceaselessly in the politics of Danish-ruled Norway – eventually managing to have himself made governor, by Denmark's king, of Bergen Castle.

David Sinclair's Orkney-based nephew, Lord Henry, although less involved with Norway and Denmark than his uncle, was little more inclined to subordinate his interests to those of Scotland's kings. And had the Sinclair family been able to capitalise more effectively on the power which its various members wielded, a sixteenth-century version of the Norse earldom of several hundred years before might have taken shape in the Northern Isles. Rather like their Norse predecessors, however, the Sinclairs – who loomed almost as large in Caithness, incidentally, as they did in Shetland and Orkney – suffered from an ineradicable tendency to fall out among themselves. The result, on a particular quarrel getting completely out of hand, was open warfare which culminated in one Sinclair faction mounting an armed invasion of Orkney with the aim of ousting the other Sinclairs then in charge there. The invasion in question took place in 1529. It culminated, among hills south of Stenness, in the Battle of Summerdale – an encounter followed, so Orkney tradition insists, by horrific violence on the part of the victorious Sinclair faction. This faction – of which the leading light was the now dead Lord Henry's nephew, Sir James Sinclair of Brecks – was itself to fall victim to further feuding. Thus there was opened the way for a new attempt by Scotland's central government to make its weight felt more effectively in the Northern Isles. The outcome, in the middle years of the sixteenth century, was the imposition on Orkney and Shetland of Robert Stewart – who rapidly took control of both island groups and who, being a son of King James V, was expected by the authorities in Edinburgh to be more responsive to their wishes than the Sinclairs had been.

This expectation proved unfounded. Soon it was clear that the latest master of the Northern Isles – utilising methods reminiscent of those associated with that earlier Stewart freebooter, the Wolf of Badenoch – meant to exercise his newfound power as he, and he alone, saw fit. That was equally true of Robert Stewart's son and heir, Patrick. In the course of their successive reigns as Earls of Orkney and Lords of Shetland, titles recreated and bestowed on them at their insistence, Robert and Patrick were to be accused of crimes and misdemeanours ranging from the arbitrary imprisonment of their critics to the levying of unlawful taxes. As is evident from the still spectacular ruins of the palace built for them at Birsay, once the centre of Thorfinn the Mighty's Viking empire, Earl Robert and Earl Patrick certainly lived in a style suggestive of their having had incomes far larger than any likely to have been yielded by honest endeavour. But for all that Robert and Patrick Stewart attracted a bad press, both in their own day and afterwards, it does not do – from a Highlands and Islands perspective anyway – to portray them as mere hoodlums.

That, admittedly, is exactly how some Shetlanders and Orcadians portrayed the Stewart earls in representations made about their conduct to government ministers in Edinburgh. But most such representations, it is worth stressing, emanated from a relatively small segment of Orkney and Shetland society. This segment consisted, for the most part, of individuals who, during the decades on either side of 1560, migrated from the Scottish Lowlands to the Northern Isles in the hope of acquiring estates there. Those incomers were professional men – lawyers and the like – who, with a view to enhancing both their financial position and their social status, were looking to become landed proprietors, or lairds, of the sort then beginning to be common in more southerly parts of Scotland. To individuals of this type, Orkney and Shetland, so recently added to the Scottish realm, seemed almost in the nature of colonies which they, as colonisers, were entitled to recast in the image of the Lowlands they had just left. To be a newly arrived laird in the sixteenth-century Northern Isles, in other words, was to promote Scots law at the expense of Scandinavian law; it was to favour the Scots language at the expense of the Norse, or Norn, still spoken by many longer-established islanders; it was, in short, to identify strongly with those Scotticising processes which, even in advance of 1468, had been under way in Orkney and which, since 1469, had begun to affect Shetland also.

The slow but steadily accelerating demise of Norn, originally introduced to the Northern Isles by the Vikings, constitutes one obvious indicator of how profoundly Orkney and Shetland were being altered by the time the sixteenth century gave way to the seventeenth. As Scots-speakers consolidated the grip they had earlier obtained on the public life of Orkney, as other Scots-speakers acquired a similar hold on public office in Shetland, and as further Scots-speakers took over more and more land, so Scots became the language in which all sorts of vital transactions had to be conducted. Norn, for its part, was inevitably deprived both of utility and prestige. In much the same way as it had itself replaced Pictish, the speech of the Vikings thus began to vanish from the Northern Isles.

When exactly Norn became extinct is a matter of dispute. Well into the eighteenth century, it seems to have been spoken on one or two more isolated islands. And as late as the nineteenth century, especially in some parts of Shetland, it was still possible to hear the occasional Norn phrase, even a line or two of Norn verse. But Norn's ultimate fate, it is clear, was sealed during the sixteenth and seventeenth centuries – when, for better or worse, the common speech, first of Orkney and then of Shetland, began to be the dialect of Scots that most Orcadians and Shetlanders employ today.

Embedded in that dialect, to be sure, are lots of Norn terms. And there were to be other Norse survivals. Traces of the Viking naming system – which continues to be employed in Iceland and which prefers patronymics to surnames – were to be found in nineteenth-century Shetland, for example. Thus the father of Magnus Davidson, who died on Yell in 1862, was not, as might be expected, a man who went also by the surname of Davidson. He was someone whose first name was David – someone who had chosen to name his son in accordance with exactly those Norse practices which, in modern Iceland, produce names like Magnus Magnusson.

Even more persistent has been udal law – which continues to govern some aspects of landholding in twenty-first-century Orkney and Shetland. But such Norse law as survives in today's Northern Isles is the merest remnant of the highly detailed legal codes once enshrined in manuscript volumes like the Shetland lawbook – Shetlanders' main source, until the sixteenth century's end, of guidance on how to punish crime, handle property transfers and generally ensure social order. Not coincidentally, other formerly Norse realms, like Faroe, possessed equivalent texts. Such texts – some of them still in existence – were to be long consulted in those areas, Faroe being one, which remained Scandinavian in culture. Shetland's lawbook, however, did not survive the upheavals which affected the Northern Isles in the opening years of the seventeenth century.

That was when Patrick Stewart's enemies succeeded in having Black Pate, as the earl was called, deposed, imprisoned and, in the end, executed by the Scottish government of the day – a government which, acting in conjunction with the island lairds who had been Black Pate's sternest critics, promptly proceeded to introduce the institutional changes required to make Orkney and Shetland the sort of places those same lairds wanted them to be. Of the reforms which ensued, one of the most significant occurred in 1611 when the Scottish Privy Council, then the principal executive arm of the country's government, declared that Scandinavian law, other than in cases relating to locally unique landholding practices, must immediately give way, throughout the Northern Isles, to Scots law – to 'the proper laws of the kingdom', as the privy council put it. By the lairds who had pressed for just such a declaration, this edict was warmly welcomed. But it was an edict made possible only by Patrick Stewart's downfall. In this fact there can be discerned ambiguities of a type which make the overall role both of Earl Patrick and his father – especially in relation to this book's central theme – a good deal less clear-cut than that role has frequently been made to appear.[18]

Stand today amid the ruins of the Stewart earls' palace at Birsay and it is at once apparent that such a building, on such a site, could only have housed men for whom self-aggrandisement was something of a religion. Surrounded invariably by an armed retinue, preceded everywhere by trumpeters, Earl Robert and Earl Patrick were by no means devoted to the wellbeing of the Orkney and Shetland commonalty. But unlike the lairds who helped engineer their downfall, the Stewart earls were committed to the maintenance of much of what the Northern Isles had inherited, by way of legal systems and the like, from their Norse past. This was not because Earl Robert and Earl Patrick had become, by adoption, Orkney and Shetland patriots. The earls' relatively high regard for traditional practices was entirely a consequence of the fact that such practices lent themselves to highly personal, indeed autocratic, rule of the type in which Robert and Patrick Stewart specialised. But the termination of that rule was not followed, as far as the mass of Orcadians and Shetlanders were concerned, by some generalised liberation. It was followed instead by island régimes which were very much the creation of the lairds who had been the Stewart earls' principal antagonists. Those lairds, in contrast to the Stewarts, posed no threat to the Scottish state. As a later chapter will make clear, however, they deployed their locally enhanced power in ways which, especially in Shetland, were far more oppressive than the conduct of either Earl Robert or Earl Patrick had been.

Perhaps suspecting that the Stewart earls – for all their faults – were to be preferred to the lairds then taking their place, the farming folk of the Northern Isles rallied in substantial numbers to Earl Patrick's son, Robert, when, in 1614, the latter mounted a rebellion intended to restore his family to the prominence it had lost. That rebellion failed. But if its collapse constituted something of a success from the standpoint of the Edinburgh politicians who devoted so much time during the sixteenth and seventeenth centuries to obliterating such vestiges as remained of the Highlands and Islands autonomy of previous periods, developments elsewhere in the Highlands and Islands were, from the same politicians' perspective, less encouraging.

Just as the deposition of Earl Patrick resulted in rebellion, so did the earlier expropriation, by the Scottish monarchy, of the MacDonald Lordship of the Isles. The troubles precipitated by the lordship's forfeiture, however, were hugely more hazardous to Scotland's rulers than those troubles' Orkney and Shetland equivalents. In the course of the half century following the lordship's 1493 demise, there were no fewer than six armed attempts to restore it. And the strength of the MacDonald lordship's hold over the imaginations of its former subjects is indicated by the fact that the best organised of those half-dozen rebellions was the last one – which occurred in 1545.

At the head of this 1545 rising was a charismatic individual whom one Gaelic account describes as 'Donald Dubh, son of Angus, son of John of Islay, son of Alexander of Islay, son of Donald of Islay, son of Angus Og'. The last of those names, of course, belonged to the man who, not least as a result of his military backing for Robert Bruce, had long before laid the foundations for the rise to eminence of the Islay-based kindred known to Gaelic bards as Clan Donald – the kindred headed by Alexander MacDonald, John MacDonald and other Lords of the Isles. Donald Dubh, the rebel leader of 1545, was – as his Gaelic *sloinneadh*, or lineage, demonstrates – those men's direct descendant.

By virtue of that fact, as far as his followers were concerned, Donald Dubh was *Ri Innse Gall*, Lord of the Isles. As such he was duly proclaimed.[19]

The planners of the 1545 rebellion had picked their moment well. England's monarch, Henry VIII, was then seriously at odds with Scotland. And with the active encouragement of English envoys, Donald Dubh entered into what was, in effect, an alliance with Henry – an alliance directed against the Scottish king, James V. 'It is to be remembered,' Donald's representatives informed Henry, 'that we have always been enemies to the realm of Scotland.' Was Donald aspiring, as more than one of his ancestors may have aspired, to seize Scotland's throne? Or was he merely trying to avenge himself on the latest of those Stewart monarchs who, as his agents told Henry VIII, had 'hangit . . . presoned and destroyed many of our kyn, friendis and forbears'? Nobody now knows for certain. Either way, Donald posed a major threat to the Scottish monarchy's entire position in the Highlands and Islands.[20]

Having summoned a new Council of the Isles and having recruited practically all the leading families of the former lordship, Donald Dubh was able to put himself at the head of a fighting force consisting of no fewer than 180 galleys and some 8,000 men. In the course of subsequent manoeuvrings, however, the rising's initial impetus was lost. And when, towards the end of 1545, Donald Dubh took ill and died, all serious hopes of restoring the Lordship of the Isles – Donald having left no heir – died with him. A Gaelic bard, possibly a MacMhuirich, articulated the consequent, and widespread, sense of loss:

> Alas for those who have lost that company; alas for those who have parted from that society; for no race is as Clan Donald, a noble race, strong of courage.
>
> There was no counting of their bounty; there was no reckoning of their gifts; their nobles knew . . . no end of generosity . . .
>
> For sorrow and for sadness, I have forsaken wisdom and learning; on their account, I have forsaken all things: it is no joy without Clan Donald.[21]

All vanished powers and principalities tend to take on, in the wake of their disappearance, something of a rosy glow. Lamenting the passing of the Duchy of Brittany, destroyed by French kings at much the same time as the Stewart monarchy was launching its final assaults on the

MacDonald lordship, a Breton writer remembered the fifteenth-century duchy as 'a veritable earthly paradise . . . a country at peace, rich and opulent in every kind of wealth'. The Lordship of the Isles was to be recalled in virtually identical terms. That is evident from the Gaelic poem already quoted. It is equally apparent in the writings of a sixteenth-century Scottish churchman whose career took him to many parts of the Highlands and Islands. 'In thair time,' this churchman wrote retrospectively of the lordship's MacDonald rulers, 'thair was great peace and welth in the Iles throw the ministration of justice'. That was to exaggerate. But such exaggeration seems pardonable in view of the many ills afflicting the sixteenth-century Highlands and Islands – ills which arose, in many instances, from circumstances created by what the Scottish monarchy had done in 1493.[22]

Although the Scottish state possessed sufficient resources to overthrow the Lordship of the Isles, the same state's organisational capabilities were so limited as to make it impossible for Scotland's kings to provide the West Highlands and Islands with administrative structures of the kind the lordship had earlier sustained. Something very close to anarchy thus ensued in much of the area which the lordship had previously dominated. Clan Donald fragmented into its component groupings – with MacDonalds of Sleat, of Glengarry, of Clanranald, of Glencoe, of Ardnamurchan, of Islay and of various other places emerging, in effect, as clans in their own right. Others of the lordship's previously subordinate kindreds endeavoured to stake out equivalent claims to clanship – as MacLeods of Lewis, MacLeods of Dunvegan, MacNeils of Barra and MacLeans of Duart. The inevitable outcome – made all the more certain by the way in which this emphasis on local territoriality quickly became universal in the Gaelic-speaking Highlands and Islands – was a constant jockeying for land and position. That jockeying, in turn, spiralled readily into open conflict.

Not for nothing does the sixteenth century feature in Gaelic tradition as *linn nan creach*, the time of raids or forays. In Skye, one group of MacDonalds fought repeatedly with MacLeods to determine who should hold sway over the island's Trotternish peninsula. In Islay, a second set of MacDonalds battled with MacLeans to decide who should control the district called the Rinns. Other such wars were fought elsewhere – with comparatively organised hostilities of the MacDonald–MacLeod type frequently giving way not to peace but to a still more unsettling and disruptive tendency towards generalised banditry and violence.

Internecine and intercommunal warfare is always singularly brutal and unforgiving. So it was in those extensive areas of the sixteenth-century Highlands and Islands which were affected by burnings, massacres and the further miseries to which clan rivalries gave rise. But to the Gaelic bards of that era, immersed as they were in tales of Cu Chulainn and other legendary or semi-legendary warriors of the distant past, it seemed almost as if Gaeldom's heroic age had been reborn. Employing techniques used by their predecessors of a thousand years before, sixteenth-century bards peopled their poems with men who were invariably brave, youthful and handsome; men whose swords were unfailingly burnished, well-balanced and bejewelled; men whose spears and arrows always struck true; men whose overriding ambition and duty it was to fight well and die better. During the sixteenth and seventeenth centuries, admittedly, the longstanding bardic monopoly of Gaelic literature was starting to be challenged by new, less traditional, poets. And in verses composed by this latter group there are to be discerned sensitivities of a type that older-fashioned bards would have been inclined to scorn. Such sensitivities are certainly present in lines dating from the early seventeenth century and supposedly crooned by a woman who, in the aftermath of a clan battle fought in 1601 at Carinish, North Uist, nursed a badly wounded MacDonald fighting man, *Domhall mac Iain `ic Sheumais*:

> Your noble body's blood
> lay on the surface of the ground.
>
> Your fragrant body's blood
> seeped through the linen.
>
> I sucked it up
> till my breath grew husky.[23]

But even that song exhibits a degree of contrivance. The suffering of which the singer tells was clearly real enough. That suffering, however, is formalised, ritualised, almost sanctified, in ways designed to usher both Domhall mac Iain `ic Sheumais and his nurse into the age-old Gaelic pantheon already inhabited by Niall of the Nine Hostages, Conn of the Hundred Battles and all those other champions to whom Highlands and Islands bards had long made repeated reference. There was thus a strong tendency, on the part of the region's Gaelic poets at any rate, to conceptualise one society (the one to which Domhall mac Iain, for instance, actually belonged) in a manner deriving ultimately from another society (one which had arguably ceased to exist several centuries before Domhall mac Iain was born). But by thus blurring the distinctions between their own epoch and its remote precursors, Gaelic poets of the years around 1600 were – consciously or unconsciously – drawing attention to something which, if one wishes to comprehend what was then going on in the Highlands and Islands, it does not do to ignore. The world which such poets inhabited – this world of clans, battles, forays and the rest – was one which actually did bear some resemblance to the much earlier world depicted in the *Tain Bo Cuailgne*.

Here, by way of reinforcing that point, is an eighteenth-century account of how island aristocrats of the previous century – the MacLeods of Dunvegan or the MacLeans of Duart, perhaps – marked their homecomings from war:

> When the Hebridean chiefs and captains returned . . . after a successful expedition, they summoned their friends and clients to a grand entertainment. Bards . . . flocked in from every quarter, pipers and harpists had an undisputed right to appear . . . These entertainments were wild and cheerful . . . The bards sang, and the young women danced. The old warrior related the gallant actions of his youth, and struck the young men with ambition and fire. The whole tribe filled the chieftain's hall. Trunks of trees covered with moss were laid, in the order of a table, from one end of the hall to the other. Whole deer and beeves [oxen] were roasted and laid before [the crowd] . . . After the feast was over, they had . . . entertainments . . . Then the females retired, and the old and young warriors sat down in order from the chieftain, according to their proximity in blood to him. The harp was then touched, the song was raised and the *sliga-crechin*, or the drinking shell, went round.[24]

Other than in its featuring of bagpipes – then displacing the more traditional harp in the affections of the region's Gaelic-speakers – that scene could as readily have occurred in the Highlands and Islands of the tenth, fifth or even first centuries as in the Highlands and Islands of just three or four hundred years ago. Svein Asleifarson of Gairsay, I suspect, would more than once have organised just such festivities on his getting back to Norse Orkney at the end of one of his buccaneering voyages. Dalriada's kings, it can reasonably be postulated on the basis of what is known of the period in which they lived, would regularly have staged similar celebrations. So, it can safely be guessed, would Caledonian head men of the sort who once lived in Highlands and Islands brochs and accompanied Calgacus to Mons Graupius.

Having been deprived by Scotland's monarchs of the overarching political structures provided by the Lords of the Isles, by the Earls of Orkney, by Somerled and by other indigenous rulers of that sort, the sixteenth-century Highlands and Islands – the Scottish state's impact on the region having been far more disruptive than constructive – tended to revert to older, indeed largely tribal, forms of social organisation. This happened, to some extent, in Orkney and Shetland where first various members of the Sinclair family, then Robert and Patrick Stewart, established, in ways already noted, their own local supremacies. But it was in the Gaelic-speaking Highlands and Islands that such reversion was most complete. Even when subsumed into larger entities such as the Lordship of the Isles, of course, this area's population had been governed by men steeped in traditions stemming ultimately from tribal civilisations of the Dalriadan or Irish variety. Perhaps because they so strongly featured highly localised power of a kind that was also common in the sixteenth-century Highlands and Islands, those same traditions seem somehow to have acquired renewed vitality in the wake of the lordship's destruction. Hence the remarkable extent to which a sixteenth-century clan and its chief, in both character and conduct, were recreations of the *tuath* and *ri* of a millennium before.

Because a tribal society's most powerful bonds are those of blood relationship, and because an individual's status within that society is consequently defined very largely in terms of his or her ancestry, the chiefs of sixteenth-century Highlands and Islands clans, just like the men who had dominated Dalriada and Ireland in Colum Cille's time, set enormous store by their ancestry. All clan chiefs claimed prestigious forebears. And by far the most esteemed such forebears, it scarcely needs commenting, were the long-dead Irish warrior kings whose great deeds had for so long been recounted around innumerable Highlands and Islands firesides.

The men who headed the various branches of Clan Donald could claim Irish descent with some degree of plausibility – by virtue, first, of their undoubted connections with Somerled and by virtue, second, of Somerled's own genealogy having reached deep into Ireland's past. But many other such claims were more tendentious. Some chieftainly families – the MacLeods of Dunvegan and the MacLeods of Lewis are examples – were more Viking than Celtic. Others – the Frasers of Lovat and the Stewarts of Appin, for instance – were descended from men whose origins are to be found among migratory Norman noblemen of the sort who had helped feudalise the medieval Scottish kingdom. Distinctions of this variety ought not to be over-emphasised, however. Irrespective of whose blood was to be found in their veins, sixteenth-century clan chiefs were invariably immersed – as clan chiefs then had to be – in the culture of the communities they presided over. And this culture, as immediately preceding paragraphs have stressed, was the one first brought to the Highlands and Islands by Fergus Mor mac Eirc and those other people who, during the fifth and sixth centuries, swapped Ulster for Argyll.

In Gaelic, *clann*, or clan, means 'children'. That points to there having been a strongly paternal aspect to a chief's relationship with his clansfolk. The bonds between chief and clan, however, were of greater complexity than a simple father–child analogy might suggest. Clansfolk certainly benefited – particularly in the context of the unsettled conditions prevailing in the sixteenth-century Highlands and Islands – from their chiefs' ability to protect them from attack. But Highlands and Islands chieftains were every bit as dependent on their clans as those clans were on their chieftains – a chief's power resting very largely, for example, on his clansmen's willingness to fight, and sometimes die, for him. It is to this mutuality of interest – as between leader and led – that many of the key attributes of clanship can be traced.

If they were to retain the respect and affections of those around them, chiefs had to behave as custom – much of it very old – dictated. They had, as one seventeenth-century Gaelic poet put it, to be 'generous' and 'free-handed'; they had to ensure that their castles resounded to 'the sound of harps' and 'the roar of pipes'; they had to be supportive of 'bards and makers of song'; they were expected, in short, to live in much the same way as Niall of the Nine Hostages or Conn of the Hundred Battles were thought to have lived. And with that expectation, during the sixteenth century anyway, most clan chiefs complied.[25]

Despite their having presided over a wholly rural society, men like Niall, Conn and their counterparts had not deigned to work the land. That task was one which such Celtic aristocrats assigned to those of lesser rank. This continued to be the case throughout the Gaelic-speaking parts of the sixteenth-century Highlands and Islands. In much the same way as Dalriada's farmers were obliged to render tribute to their kings, the generality of clansfolk were thus expected to make regular deliveries of foodstuffs – by way, as it were, of rent – to their chiefs. A considerable proportion of the grain that was grown on township rigs, together with a further proportion of the dairy produce yielded by herds pastured on township common grazings, thus found its way to the stone-built strongholds – some still occupied today, most now in ruins – maintained by clan chieftains.

Charged with ensuring the prompt rendering of all such tribute were the individuals who, in Broad Scots and English, were called tacksmen. They constituted an influential grouping known in Gaelic as *daoine uaisle* – gentry, in effect. Standing just one step behind chiefs in clanship's overall pecking order, tacksmen were frequently chiefs' blood relatives – their nephews or cousins, perhaps. And with a view to reinforcing such kinship linkages, a chief's sons were frequently brought up in the households of his tacksmen – fosterage of this type, incidentally, being yet another of the practices carried forwards into the sixteenth-century Highlands and Islands from the *tuatha* of ancient Ireland.

When a clan mobilised for war, its tacksmen became its officers – taking their orders from the clan's chief and giving orders, in turn, to those lower-ranking clansmen who, during periods of peace, lived in clachans and townships of the sort described in this chapter's opening pages. A tacksman's duties, however, were by no means confined to military matters. Tacksmen, for example, commonly supervised the various agricultural arrangements discussed earlier: dividing arable land between one township and the next; making sure that each township's rigs were fairly distributed among its occupants; generally attending, in short, to all the day-to-day administrative tasks so vital to a clan's existence.

The district for which a sixteenth-century tacksman was responsible generally consisted of a tract of territory which he leased from his chief. However, this is not to say that tacksmen were tenant farmers. Farmers involve themselves directly in agricultural production. Tacksmen, in contrast, were every bit as disinclined as their chiefs to engage in manual labour – their role with regard to agriculture being, as already indicated, more supervisory than hands-on. But there is much that is significant, all the same, about the fact that the *daoine uaisle* owed their English designation to their possession, in the sixteenth century and still more in the seventeenth, of written leases – which, in Scots, were called *tacks*. The gradual proliferation of such documents can be seen as an early indication of the way that clanship, for all the intrinsically tribal nature of its origins, was capable of evolving in directions which would ultimately result in chiefs being transformed into landlords.

This same transformation would lead to tacksmen's tenures being commercialised in a manner which eventually resulted in a tacksman's hold on the land becoming dependent on the prompt payment of a money rent. But for the duration of the sixteenth century, it must be stressed, strictly commercial considerations of that kind barely intruded on relations between tacksmen and their chiefs. The latter certainly made land available to the former. Little cash changed hands as a result of such transactions, however. Nor did money feature greatly in the dealings which tacksmen had with the subordinate tenants among whom they, in their turn, parcelled out rigs and grazings. Such tenants handed some part of their farming output to the appropriate tacksman. This tacksman, by way of facilitating renders or tribute of the sort already described, conveyed some part of his total take to a chief. And if those arrangements caused resentment at the township level, as they probably did, such resentment may have been tempered by a realisation that the system in which tenants, tacksmen and chiefs were jointly involved was one that conveyed some degree of benefit to all who participated in it. The chief gained an assured supply of the foodstuffs needed to sustain his household and to supply the lavish hospitality his clansfolk thought their due. The tacksman, who also tended to live in some style, was assured – as long as he carried out the managerial or military tasks assigned him – of his occupying a comparatively comfortable place in the overall scheme of things. The tenant's reward – apart from his attendance at such clan feasts and festivities as his labour had made possible – consisted of chief and tacksman extending to him a degree of security, both physical and tenurial, which was generally sufficient both to protect him from marauding enemies and to enable his family, through generation after generation, to maintain a tight grip on the land.

During the sixteenth century and subsequently, the importance of this link between tenant and land was reflected in the concept of *duthchas* – an almost untranslatable Gaelic term which encapsulated a pervasive belief that clansfolk were entitled to a permanent stake in the territories pertaining to their clan. Although its precise implications are difficult to pin down, this entitlement was thought to extend to all grades of landholder: to the occupier of a few scattered rigs, at one extreme; to tacksmen, at the other. Between the notion of *duthchas* and the leases beginning to be issued to *daoine uaisle*, admittedly, there was a fundamental incompatibility: the one implied a right to occupy land in perpetuity; the other, as a result of leases running for specified periods, introduced a degree of time-limitation into such occupation. Neither in the sixteenth century nor in the opening decades of the seventeenth, however, was there any appreciation of the desperate insecurity which was one day to arise from time-limitation of this sort. The clan chief in his eventual guise of evicting landlord still lay in the future. For the moment, as in this early-seventeenth-century evocation of life in the Dunvegan stronghold of a MacLeod chieftain, clan chiefs, to their clansfolk anyway, seemed essentially benevolent:

With Roderick Mor,
MacLeod of banners,

In his great house
I have been joyful,

Dancing merry
on a wide floor:

The fiddle-playing
to put me to sleep;

The pipe-playing
to wake me in the morning.[26]

Both clanship and the Gaelic culture which underpinned it were regarded with growing dislike by members of sixteenth-century Scotland's governing class. That class wanted to reshape Scottish society in such a way as to enable the country to participate effectively in an international order dominated by Spain, France and England. Those were powers whose muscle was considered to be a consequence, in part, of their internal unity. That unity was not merely territorial. Increasingly, it involved centrally directed efforts to ensure, as far as possible, that all the people living within a state's borders spoke the same language, shared the same beliefs and generally identified with the same nationally accepted institutions. Cohesion of this type, needless to say, was nowhere achieved totally. But it seemed, to Scotland's sixteenth-century monarchs and their ministers, to be particularly lacking in the Scottish state – a state which, or so the country's rulers were understandably disposed to conclude, was bound to remain prone to disharmony, unrest and even fragmentation until the clansfolk of the Highlands and Islands were persuaded, or forced, to organise their communities in accordance with the social and other values prevailing in the Scottish kingdom's Lowland core.

In the wake of the religious revolution, or reformation, which occurred in Scotland during the 1560s, those values tended to be aggressively Protestant in tone. But that did little or nothing to make them more acceptable to the typical clan chief and his adherents. The Scottish reformation – a localised manifestation of doctrinal upheavals which undermined or destroyed the medieval Catholic Church across much of Europe – was, in essence, a phenomenon of the Central Belt. Its impact certainly extended into the Highlands and Islands where the former ecclesiastical order – its origins traceable to Columba's time – disintegrated almost completely in the course of the sixteenth century's third quarter. Among the more evident symbols of that disintegration was the appropriation by secular property-owners of the extensive estates which various abbeys and bishoprics had earlier accumulated. This secularisation of church lands had important consequences. In Orkney, for instance, it enabled incoming Lowlanders – with results already touched on – to acquire the estates which made them lairds. But such developments were not usually accompanied in the Highlands and Islands, as they were in more southerly parts of Scotland, by a generalised and enthusiastic adoption of the new faith. Although Catholicism quickly ceased to exist in any very structured form on either side of the Highland Line, Scotland's Protestant Church attracted little more backing in the Highlands and Islands than the Scottish government – a government which had itself, of course, become insistently Protestant in the reformation's aftermath. Here and there, most notably in Argyll, Protestantism did achieve a genuine popularity – that popularity being due largely, in this instance, to the work of a Gaelic-speaking churchman called John Carswell. For the most part, however, the people of the Highlands and Islands, and especially of the more clan-dominated parts of the region, became Protestant in name only. Many decades after the reformation, for example, Lewis folk, for all that they had ostensibly given up Catholicism, were observed 'to kneel' and say 'their paternoster' when they came in view of any of the island's churches. Other localities were reputed to have reverted to still older forms of belief. From Wester Ross, for example, there emanated allegations of communities marking the feast day of Maelrubai, the seventh-century missionary who had first brought Christianity to the district, by engaging in the essentially pagan rite of sacrificing bulls in Maelrubai's honour.[27]

All such reports served to fuel antagonisms and animosities of the sort which, towards the sixteenth century's end, were expressed repeatedly by James VI, Scotland's latest Stewart monarch, and by

James's advisers. Official documents of the period are consequently replete with bloodcurdling denunciations of practically the entire population of the Highlands and Islands. Being 'void of the knawledge and feir of God', the area's inhabitants, it was claimed, were 'wild savageis': constantly 'batheing thameselfis in the blude of utheris'; taking a perverse delight in 'all kynd of barbarous and bestlie cruelteis'.[28]

Throughout the middle ages there had persisted in Scotland some small awareness of the kingdom having originated in Gaelic-speaking Dalriada. Thus William Elphinstone, the scholarly churchman who became Bishop of Aberdeen in 1483, had been anxious to discover 'the antiquities of the Scottish people, especially in the Hebrides, where are preserved the sepulchres of our ancient kings and the ancient monuments of our race'. By James VI's time, however, the Highlands and Islands, far from being regarded as the cradle of Scotland's nationhood, were viewed by most Lowlanders – including the king himself – as irredeemably foreign. Gaelic – increasingly called *Erse*, or Irish, by Scots-speakers – had come to be considered a wholly alien tongue. More than ever before, it was also thought a backward one. It comes as no surprise, therefore, to find the Scottish parliament insisting that Gaelic should be 'abolisheit and removeit' from Scotland on the grounds that it was 'one of the chief and principall causis of the continewance of barbaritie and incivilitie amongis the inhabitantis of the Ilis and Heylandis'.[29]

As already noted, Lowland colonisation of Orkney and Shetland had gone some way, by James VI's reign, to effecting irrevocable changes both in the ethnic composition and linguistic identity of those island groups. From the king's standpoint, the Hebrides – which James thought the most uncivilised part of a generally uncivilised region – cried out for similar treatment. Hence the commencement, during the 1590s, of attempts to settle Lowlanders in Lewis – an island which, prior to those Lowlanders' arrival, was formally declared to have been forfeited by the MacLeod chieftains who had been its masters for generations.

If necessary, King James wrote, Lewis's colonisers were to proceed 'not by agreement with [Lewis people] but by extirpation of thame'. In the event, however, the five or six hundred Lowlanders who arrived in the vicinity of Stornoway towards the end of 1598, were themselves obliged to fight for their lives. Unlike Orcadians and Shetlanders, who mounted no effective resistance to settlers from the Lowlands, Lewis people subjected their aspiring colonisers to a succession of ferocious attacks. These had the effect of so undermining the incoming community's morale as to make the entire colonising venture unsustainable. Just a few years into the seventeenth century, therefore, it was abandoned.[30]

The failure of their Lewis colony was accompanied by a change of tack on the part of James VI and his government. In 1608 they despatched to the Hebrides a naval force whose commander, having first invited a number of island chiefs to join him aboard his ship, informed those chiefs that they were to be conveyed south as his captives. In 1609, after being held through the winter in Lowland castles, the imprisoned chiefs were released on condition that they gathered on Iona, where they were obliged to put their names to a document containing a series of clauses, or 'statutes', of a kind intended to undermine clanship by rather more subtle tactics than those involved in sending Lowlanders to Lewis. Clan chiefs, it was laid down by the Statutes of Iona and by a series of similar measures which followed, were to be legally responsible for the conduct of their clansfolk; they were to appear regularly in Edinburgh to answer for that conduct; they were to build Protestant churches; they were to dispense with the services of Gaelic bards; they were to have their eldest sons educated in the Lowlands; they were to assent, in short, to their being assimilated into a society from which they had hitherto kept determinedly aloof.

More than fifteen centuries previously, Cornelius Tacitus had written of how Agricola, when Roman governor of Britain, subverted Celtic culture in what afterwards became England. 'He educated the sons of the chiefs in the liberal arts,' Tacitus commented. 'The result was that instead of loathing the Latin language they became eager to speak it effectively.' The Statutes of Iona were meant to have a broadly similar effect. And it is something of a tribute to the deeply rooted nature of the society which the statutes were designed to destroy that the men who framed the Iona edicts of 1609 found it necessary to single out Gaelic bards for particular attention. Those bards' predecessors of one and a half millennia before had been described by the Romans as the most steadfast defenders of the Celtic value-systems which Agricola and his like were anxious to root out. The Gaelic versifiers who featured prominently in the retinue of seventeenth-century clan chieftains were committed to much the same value-systems and were to be duly horrified when their chiefs began gradually to adopt the southern habits and tastes which the Scottish authorities – their policies originating in thinking identical to Agricola's – were so eager to promote.[31]

That is to anticipate, however; for the Statutes of Iona, although retrospectively significant in that they denoted the adoption by Scotland's rulers of a strategy that was eventually to erode both clanship and its associated ethos, were quickly overtaken by events in the shape of the various commotions which occurred in the Highlands and Islands during the 1640s.

Those commotions had their origins in James VI, on the death of Queen Elizabeth I in 1603, becoming England's king as well as Scotland's. James, who inherited the English throne as a result of earlier marriages between his Stewart predecessors and Elizabeth's Tudor forebears, promptly moved from Edinburgh to London. This meant that the monarchy's superintendence of affairs in Scotland, which retained its own national parliament and government, became necessarily remote. That did not pose undue problems for James who was very much a Scot by upbringing. But it was certainly one of the factors making for the many difficulties in which James's son and successor, Charles I, became embroiled in the course of the 1630s. Because he believed firmly that public policy should be shaped primarily by himself, Charles managed to alienate key sections of opinion in each of his two kingdoms. In England, the king found himself confronting an increasingly antagonised parliament whose members and backers were eventually to take up arms against him. In Scotland, meanwhile, royal power was challenged by the political and religious grouping known as the Covenanters – a set of nobles, lairds and others who pledged, or covenanted, themselves to resist Charles's attempts to tamper with the ecclesiastical structure which had evolved in the aftermath of the Scottish reformation. This structure had become partly presbyterian in form. It had vested a good deal of influence, therefore, in kirk sessions and general assemblies in which the laity, as well as the clergy, participated. When Charles – with a view to aligning this Scottish variant of Protestantism with England's equally Protestant but differently organised Church – set out to reduce all such lay influence, the outcome was the Covenanter-led revolution which placed Scotland's government, as well as the country's Church, under the control of presbyterians of a most extreme and uncompromising variety.

With London dominated by a parliament with which he was soon to be at war, and with Edinburgh in the hands of his Covenanter opponents, Charles sought support wherever it was to be got. Hence the emergence of a somewhat unlikely alliance between the Stewart monarchy and a number of the Highlands and Islands clans which the same monarchy had so recently been endeavouring to destroy. Perhaps, as has sometimes been suggested, there was a natural affinity between a king committed to his own absolute rule and clan chieftains who were equally in thrall to the notion of personal dominion. But of possibly greater relevance in this context was the fact that the Campbells – a clan whose Argyll heartlands, as already indicated, were more presbyterian in sympathy than most other parts of the Highlands and Islands – aligned themselves with the Covenanters. This immediately made pro-monarchy men of clan chiefs who reckoned themselves the Campbells' enemies. And of the latter, as it happened, there were a lot.

During the sixteenth century, Scotland's central government, as a consequence of the persistent weakness of its own position in the region, had acquired the habit of making allies of clans whose chiefs were prepared to co-operate with Edinburgh as long as such co-operation enabled the chiefs in question to expand and to consolidate their territories at the expense of those other – more numerous – clans who preferred to keep the government at arm's length. On the easterly fringes of the mainland Highlands, the Gordons of Huntly served as Edinburgh's principal proxies. In the north-west, the MacKenzies – who were permitted to seize Lewis from the MacLeods following the abandonment of James VI's colonising schemes – fulfilled the same role. But it was in the south-western corner of the Highlands and Islands that such arrangements were especially evident and especially enduring. There the clear and repeated beneficiary of government favours was Clan Campbell whose chiefs, before 1493, had been overshadowed by the MacDonald Lords of the Isles but who were ultimately to eclipse every one of the lordship's successor clans – including all the various branches of Clan Donald itself.

Lords of the Isles had tried – and failed – to preserve their pre-eminence by confronting the Scottish state and by emphasising their separateness from it. Earls of Argyll, as Campbell chiefs were soon titled, pursued an entirely opposite – and much more successful – strategy. With just one or two exceptions, Campbell earl after Campbell earl lined up behind whoever was in charge of Scotland's government at any given moment: the Stewarts and their ministers during the sixteenth and early seventeenth centuries; the Covenanters and their supporters for a time thereafter. While maintaining – when in the Highlands and Islands anyway – their Gaelic identity, the chiefs of Clan Campbell, by repeatedly making themselves useful to the Scottish authorities, were able so skilfully to combine governmental interests with their own as to render the two indistinguishable. When deployed by Edinburgh administrations against this or that other clan, for example, the Campbells usually managed to expand their own landholdings under the guise of putting down rebellion. And since the Earls of Argyll – by virtue of their growing involvement in southern politics – could as readily mobilise lawyers and bureaucrats as they could mobilise swordsmen, Campbell gains tended to be far less transient than those made by clans still relying on more traditional methods of securing their positions. 'The sharp strokes of short pens protect Argyll,' a MacDonald bard complained. Addressing the Campbells, the same bard continued: 'By falsehoods you deprived us of Islay green and lovely, and Kintyre with its verdant plains.'[32]

Any Earl of Argyll, of course, would have emphatically rejected this charge of duplicity. But irrespective of the precise means by which their annexation had been accomplished, the Campbells had certainly seized, in the course of the seventeenth century's opening decades, several of the localities – Islay and Kintyre among them – which had once been the basis of MacDonald power. In the process of thus adding to their domains, however, the Earls of Argyll made a bitter enemy of a man who was eventually to prove himself the most formidable of the Campbells' numerous adversaries. This man, better known in the seventeenth-century Highlands and Islands by his Gaelic designation of *Alasdair MacColla*, was Alexander MacDonald. His family's former possessions in Argyll having passed into Campbell hands, MacColla had moved to Ireland where he became caught up in that country's variant of the conflict which, during the 1640s, was to convulse the entire British Isles. As was also true of the fighting then going on in Scotland and England, the Irish war was ostensibly intended to clarify the future role, if any, of Charles I who, as England's monarch, also ruled Ireland. That country, by the end of the sixteenth century, had effectively been transformed into an English colony. But more than the king's constitutional claims were at stake among the inhabitants of England's Irish possessions. Ireland's population included, by the 1640s, a community composed of people who were the exact equivalents of the settlers James VI had sent to Lewis. This community's component families – most of them presbyterians from the Scottish Lowlands – had, for some decades past, been moving into Ulster. There they displaced other families who were both Gaelic-speaking and – the reformation having made no impact to the west of the Irish Sea – Catholic. This latter group, needless to say, had been cordially despised by James VI – who was as dismissive of Ireland's Gaels as he was of Gaels residing in the Highlands and Islands. But for much the same reason as he was obliged to seek military assistance from the Highlands and Islands clansmen his father had so badly treated, the beleaguered King Charles was forced to look for help to the native, and Catholic, Irish – whose main objective, once hostilities commenced, inevitably turned out to be the eradication of as many as possible of Ulster's recently arrived Scots presbyterians. Those presbyterians, in their turn, immediately appealed for and received assistance both from Scotland's Covenanter régime and from that régime's Campbell allies. It was by way of responding to this Scottish intervention in Ireland that some of King Charles's backers there conceived the notion of mounting a counter-strike against Scotland. This took the form of the expeditionary force – consisting partly of Irishmen and partly of émigré Highlanders like himself – which Alasdair MacColla, having successfully negotiated the well-travelled seas between Ireland and Argyll, brought ashore in Morvern during the summer of 1644.

Soon MacColla had met up in Atholl with James Graham, Marquis of Montrose and the man whom Charles had placed in overall command of his backers in Scotland. At the head of a steadily growing body of men, drawn largely from those clans whose chiefs felt themselves most threatened by the growth of Campbell power, Montrose and MacColla now marched south. At Tippermuir near Perth, on an unusually hot September Sunday, they met and rapidly overwhelmed a numerically superior force of Covenanters. That force's loss turned out to be the first of several shattering defeats which Scotland's Covenanter government suffered at the hands of what, despite its Irish core, was essentially a Highlands and Islands army. It was to Alasdair MacColla that there was owed much of the credit for this army's remarkable success.

During the middle ages, the Highlands and Islands fighting man had usually been a semi-professional soldier who – being burdened with chain mail and normally wielding a heavy, two-handed sword – was anything but quick on his feet. Troops of this sort had been deployed against similarly arrayed opponents both by the Lordship of the Isles and by the many Irish principalities which, prior to their conquest by the English, were given to employing Highlands and Islands mercenaries. By the end of the sixteenth century, however, the development of firearms – to which a slow-moving warrior of the former type was extremely vulnerable – had made it essential for Highlands and Islands clans to devise a new way of waging war. The tactics which were accordingly developed might not have been Alasdair MacColla's personal invention, but it was certainly he who refined them, perfected them and – both at Tippermuir and elsewhere – put them triumphantly to the test.

The tactics in question depended on a clan's ability to mobilise substantial numbers of men who, though they received little in the way of formal training, were more than capable – when handled in the way MacColla handled such troops – of routing opponents who, from a purely theoretical perspective, should have been unbeatable.

Instead of the much weightier weapons favoured by their predecessors, seventeenth-century clansmen relied primarily on the single-handed and basket-hilted sword which became known, in time, as the claymore. With its 'cleaving, sharp, blue edge of steel', as a Gaelic bard put it, such a sword was capable of inflicting terrible damage on an enemy. And for all that such an enemy – because he normally belonged to a formation equipped with muskets – should in principle have been able to stop a detachment of sword-bearing clansmen in their tracks, this seldom happened in practice. Instead, clan armies, their individual members holding aloft their claymores and screaming Gaelic battlecries, typically advanced at such an extraordinarily rapid rate that their adversaries, having fired a single volley, were – because the muzzle-loading guns of the period took so long to reload – seldom able to discharge another. It was for this reason that one survivor of a 'Highland charge', as such an onslaught came to be called, urged his fellow soldiers to hold their fire until the last possible moment:

> If . . . fire is given at a distance, you probably will be broke, for you never get time to load a second cartridge, and if you give way you may give your [infantry] for dead, for they [the Highlanders] being without a firelock or any load, no man, with his arms, accoutrements, etc., can escape them, and they give no quarter.[33]

So great was the terror engendered by a Highland charge, however, that its victims seldom followed this advice. More often, they loosed off their muskets prematurely, panicked, turned and ran – only to be hacked into pieces by such clansmen as overhauled them. That was what happened at Tippermuir. It was to happen again and again in the months which followed.

By the time the winter of 1644–45 came on, MacColla and Montrose, having made themselves the masters of much of the rest of the Highlands and Islands, felt sufficiently confident to march into Campbell territory. 'Throughout all Argyle,' it was reported in a despatch which may have been penned by Alasdair MacColla himself, 'we left neither house nor hold unburned'. And when the understandably demoralised Campells, at the start of 1645, finally organised themselves sufficiently to mount a pursuit of Argyll's now withdrawing invaders, both the Campbells' clan levies and the Lowland Covenanters who accompanied them were utterly and disastrously outmanoeuvred. Having first made a forced march through snowbound and supposedly impassable mountains to the south-east of the Great Glen, MacColla and Montrose descended on their pursuers at Inverlochy – where the forces of the Lordship of the Isles had routed the Earl of Mar more than two hundred years before. As at Tippermuir, battle was joined on a Sunday. And as at Tippermuir, victory was engineered, or so a MacDonald bard asserted, by 'Alasdair of the sharp, cleaving blades', this 'spirited, princely youth who would rouse thousands'.[34]

That same bard ghoulishly exulted in the fact that Inverlochy earth had been 'manured, not by the dung of sheep or goats, but by the blood of Campbells'. He gloried, too, in 'the wailing of the women of Argyll' – women whose husbands had been reduced to so many 'unclothed bodies', 'their sinews severed', 'their heads battered with sword blows', 'the film of death on their lifeless eyes'. Apart from gratifying MacDonalds who wished simply to kill Campbells, however, bloody affrays of the Inverlochy sort achieved rather less, from a Highlands and Islands perspective, than their victors were inclined to suppose. Viciousness, admittedly, was a fairly generalised feature of seventeenth-century warfare. And Covenanter troops – their banners at Tippermuir chillingly inscribed with the words 'Jesus and no quarter' – could be as bloodthirsty as any clansman. But the atrocities which MacColla's Gaelic-speaking followers undoubtedly perpetrated, both on the battlefield and in the course of such forays as they managed to make into Lowland centres like Aberdeen, nevertheless served to intensify Lowlanders' already considerable detestation of practically everyone and everything associated with the Highlands and Islands. Irrespective of who might have had right on their side in the Scotland of the mid-1640s, therefore, the overall effect of what then occurred was to make it more, not less, likely that the population of the Highlands and Islands would ultimately be deprived of such freedom as they still retained to live their lives in accordance with their own beliefs, their own traditions. This was because Montrose, MacColla and their clan-dominated army managed to terrify and to antagonise Lowlanders while failing, in the end, to conquer them. It followed that any southern government which afterwards chose, and had the ability, to impose its will firmly and absolutely on the Highlands and Islands was almost bound, however oppressively it behaved, to have Lowland Scotland's enthusiastic backing.[35]

Montrose and Alasdair MacColla separated during the summer of 1645. Shortly afterwards, the forces remaining at the former's disposal were broken by the Covenanters. Montrose now fled abroad – while Alasdair, after an abortive attempt to regain Clan Donald's lost lands in Argyll, returned to Ireland where, towards the end of 1647, he was killed in battle. Montrose, still endeavouring to win Scotland for the Stewarts, succeeded in returning to the Highlands and Islands, by way of Orkney, in 1650. But there was to be no repeat of the dazzling campaign he and MacColla had mounted five years earlier. About a thousand men were persuaded to leave their Orkney townships and accompany Montrose to Caithness – prior to striking south towards Inverness. But at Carbisdale, near the head of the Dornoch Firth, the Orcadians crumpled in the face of a Covenanter cavalry charge. And Montrose, on being taken prisoner, left the Highlands and Islands for Edinburgh 'upon a little shelty horse,' as was remarked at the time, 'his feet fastened under the horse's belly.'[36]

Executed by his captors, Montrose shared the fate, perhaps appropriately enough, of Charles I – who was beheaded at the instigation of England's parliament. Between that parliament and Scotland's Covenanter administration, however, there were growing tensions. These culminated, during 1651, in an invasion of Scotland by an army headed by England's military strongman, and eventual dictator, Oliver Cromwell. Having first occupied the Lowlands, Cromwell's troops swept north into the Highlands and Islands – an area whose inhabitants, the invaders reported, were 'cruel', 'covetous', 'treacherous', 'wild', 'base' and 'beggarly'. But for all their evident dislike of the folk they encountered there, the Cromwellian conquerors of the Highlands and Islands showed every sign of wishing to make their presence permanent – establishing well-garrisoned strongpoints in Argyll, Lochaber, Lewis, Orkney, Shetland and Inverness. The Inverness fortification's position, a mile or so north of the modern town's centre, is indicated by the present-day Cromwell Road. This street, close to Inverness's harbour, gives access to a sprawling complex of oil storage tanks. Nothing remains in its vicinity of the bastions and gun emplacements which began to go up here in 1652. But what was done in places like this by Oliver Cromwell's troops was of long-term significance all the same. Those troops proved that a well-resourced army could impose its will completely on the Highlands and Islands. That would not be forgotten.[37]

CHAPTER SIX

Moments when nothing seemed impossible

1660–1791

In summer, night comes suddenly to North Carolina's Cape Fear River country. At an hour when – back in the Highlands and Islands – the day would have a way to go, the sun, hardly less broilingly hot than at its height, dips behind a middle-distance stand of longleaf pines. A ground mist forms over maize and tobacco fields. Crickets strike up the strangely soothing racket with which, as I have learned in the course of my occasional visits to the American South, they always greet dusk's onset. But mosquitoes, too, have put in an appearance. So Jane McNeill and I, seated on the porch of a timber-built farmhouse first occupied by Jane's Gaelic-speaking great-great-great-grandparents, decide to leave the gathering darkness to its insects. We step indoors, talking all the while of what it was that caused families like Jane's to come to North Carolina and the several other transatlantic locations where, during the eighteenth and nineteenth centuries, there were established communities which, even today, exhibit something of their Highlands and Islands origins.

It has been my good fortune to spend time in several such communities: in Nova Scotia's Cape Breton Island and in Ontario's Glengarry County as well as in the area of the Cape Fear River.* I have met, as a result, a lot of Americans and Canadians whose ancestry is similar to Jane McNeill's. I have heard story after story of how those folk came to be where they now are. And in home after home, I have been shown treasured mementoes – Gaelic bibles are among the commonest such objects – of a past which folk like Jane, despite there being an ocean's breadth between us, share with residents of the modern Highlands and Islands. Hence Jane McNeill's appearance in this narrative at a point when many thousands of men, women and

* Those and other localities feature in the same author's book, *A Dance Called America: The Scottish Highlands, the United States and Canada*.

children from the Highlands and Islands were about to be scattered all around the world.

This dispersal was caused by the impact on those people's homeland of extraneous, and increasingly disruptive, influences. But of the cataclysmic effect those influences were shortly to have, it has to be acknowledged, there was little indication in the later seventeenth century. Particularly from the perspective of Gaelic-speaking districts, then accounting for a large majority of the total Highlands and Islands population, the period was, if anything, characterised by clans and clan chieftains shaking off the controls imposed on them in Oliver Cromwell's time.

For reasons having more to do with political manoeuvrings in the south than with developments in the Highlands and Islands, Cromwell's death in 1658 was followed, in 1660, by the restoration – to both the Scottish and English thrones – of the Stewart monarchy in the person of Charles II. The new king was understandably anxious to undo as much as possible of what Cromwell had done. As a result, the latter's militarily enforced Anglo-Scottish union was speedily dissolved and the governance of Scotland became again the responsibility of the country's Edinburgh-based parliament – a parliament which, by withdrawing Cromwell's Highlands and Islands garrisons in order to save money, helped accidentally to reinvigorate clanship of the type the Cromwellian army had devoted so much effort to curtailing.

Prominent among the clans thus permitted to regain some freedom of action were several whose leading men – by backing Montrose and Alasdair MacColla – had extended a badly needed helping hand to the Stewart cause during the 1640s. And when, in 1661, the restored Charles II sanctioned the execution of the Earl of Argyll who – in his overlapping guises of Scottish statesman and Campbell chief – had supported the Stewart monarchy's Covenanter opponents, it must have seemed to the dead earl's numerous enemies in the Highlands and Islands that royal policies of the kind pursued in the region ever since James IV's destruction of the Lordship of the Isles were at last being put decisively into reverse. With the Campbells – formerly Edinburgh's principal proxies in the Highlands and Islands – having so spectacularly fallen from favour, the time was propitious, or so it may plausibly have been calculated in more than one chieftain's castle, for something of a comeback on the part of those other clans on to whose territories the Campbells had encroached. Since such clans tended – in their own estimation at any rate – to be more truly committed than the Campbells had recently been to Gaelic song,

Gaelic poetry and the like, everything pointed, or so it could reasonably have been concluded in the heady period following Charles II's restoration, to there being created in the Gaelic-speaking Highlands and Islands another golden age of the type supposed to have existed prior to the lordship's disintegration.

Clan Campbell, however, had not achieved its previous predominance without acquiring, in the process, a quite outstanding capacity for adaption and self-renewal. Within remarkably few years of his father's beheading, a new Earl of Argyll successfully engineered his family's rehabilitation and, indeed, made himself the restoration régime's most indispensable agent in the Highlands and Islands. As the 1660s gave way to the 1670s, therefore, a Campbell earl – with the freely bestowed blessing of Charles II's Scottish ministers – was once more in a position to ensure that Edinburgh's edicts were given effect in the Highlands and Islands in ways that also benefited his clan. Foremost among the victims of this most skilfully conducted strategy – a mix of political influence, legal machination and brute force – were the MacLeans whose clan lands in Mull, Morvern and Tiree were taken over by the Earl of Argyll in what amounted, in the years around 1680, to an all-out war of conquest.

Campbell fortunes, admittedly, took a marked turn for the worse when, following the death of Charles II in 1685, the Earl of Argyll – in an apparent abandonment of his clan's custom of keeping always on the right side of Scotland's rulers – launched a vain attempt to bring about, by force of arms, the downfall of James VII, King Charles's successor. But for all that the failure of the earl's rising meant he had to flee the country, it was to his long-term benefit to have thus thrown in his lot with James's political opponents. The latter saw in the latest Stewart monarch, Charles's younger brother, an autocratic and pro-Catholic ruler who, from the perspective of his many critics, was bidding to undo both the previous century's reformation and the constitutional settlement – a settlement guaranteeing a degree of wider, if still mostly aristocratic, participation in government – which Charles II had accepted prior to acceding to the Scottish and English thrones in 1660. James's actual intentions remain unclear. But his policies were certainly more than sufficiently repressive to foster a growing antagonism towards him. During the winter of 1688–89, in consequence, the king was deposed, forced into exile and, in both England and Scotland, replaced by William of Orange – a Dutchman whose foremost attraction, as far as his Scottish and English backers were concerned, lay in his combining a staunch Protestantism with a willingness to give parliaments, whether in

London or Edinburgh, some worthwhile jurisdiction over affairs of state. Confidently expecting to play a prominent part in those affairs, it hardly needs mentioning, was the Earl of Argyll whose anti-Stewart credentials had been impeccable since 1685 and who, by 1689, had resumed control of his clan's extensive territories.

Although William of Orange managed rapidly to win widespread support, there continued to be opinion to the effect that James Stewart remained the legitimate monarch of both Scotland and England. People who professed this belief were known as Jacobites – a term deriving from the exiled James's Latin designation, *Jacobus*. With the Campbells firmly linked to William of Orange, Jacobitism inevitably attracted countervailing support from those Highlands and Islands clans whose chiefs, having rejoiced in the Campbells' post-1685 fall, were correspondingly alarmed by the Earl of Argyll's subsequent return to his ancestral possessions. It was to such clans that John Graham of Claverhouse, Viscount Dundee, appealed for aid when launching, in the spring of 1689, a military campaign on behalf of the Stewart cause. This campaign began slowly. But it was greatly boosted, on 27 July, when Dundee – a distant kinsman of that other Graham, the Marquis of Montrose, whose exploits had so electrified the Highlands and Islands a generation earlier – encountered and defeated a Williamite force at Killiecrankie to the north of Pitlochry.

Although heavily outnumbered, Dundee's army, consisting mainly of men from the western periphery of the Highlands and Islands, came hurtling down Killiecrankie's hillsides in as devastating an example as has ever been experienced of the sort of charge Alasdair MacColla had pioneered at Tippermuir and Inverlochy. Minutes later, the grassy slopes on which this Killiecrankie charge terminated – slopes visible today from the main Perth–Inverness road – were strewn with Williamite dead. The surviving remnant of Dundee's opponents had meanwhile fled the scene. And had it not been for one piece of bad luck, Dundee's fatal wounding, the Jacobite triumph would have been complete. As it was, the loss of their commander proved the prelude to the Jacobite clans demonstrating, not for the last time, that it was a good deal easier for such clans to win occasional, if spectacular, victories than it was for them to sustain the drawn-out campaigning needed to defeat a relatively well-resourced government of the kind William of Orange had established, by the summer of 1689, in Scotland's capital. Among that government's most determined backers, predictably, were those plentiful Lowland presbyterians who thought themselves the spiritual heirs of the preceding era's Covenanters. And it was, to say the least, unfortunate for the Jacobites that Alexander Cannon, the professional soldier who took Viscount Dundee's place in Killiecrankie's aftermath, should have encountered, at Dunkeld, a Williamite detachment drawn from the most extreme of just such presbyterians. The fighting which ensued in the vicinity of Dunkeld Cathedral – where Colum Cille's relics had once been preserved – was peculiarly bitter. And despite this fighting's immediate outcome being inconclusive, it was followed by a gradual fading away of Highlands and Islands resistance to King William's rule.

Neither the Highlands and Islands nor Scotland more generally had heard the last of Jacobitism, however. Pro-Stewart feeling survived both the setback sustained at Dunkeld and the rout of what remained of Dundee's forces at the Haughs of Cromdale in Strathspey on 1 May 1690. Nor was support for the Stewarts entirely eradicated by the numerous other reverses which Jacobites were soon to suffer. The crushing of Irish Jacobitism at the Battle of the Boyne in July 1690 was the most dramatic such reverse. But possibly more threatening, from a Highlands and Islands point of view, was the Scottish government's decision to re-establish, in a number of Highlands and Islands locations, a permanent military presence of the sort removed from the region at the close of the Cromwellian period. If, subsequent to this latter development, there were any remaining doubts among Highlands and Islands Jacobites as to the seriousness of Williamite intentions, those doubts were dispelled by the massacre, on 13 February 1692, of the MacDonalds of Glencoe.

The Glencoe massacre tends to be interpreted nowadays as a manifestation of the inter-clan feuding long common in the Highlands and Islands. This interpretation gains some slight credence from the involvement in the Glencoe killings – as victims and perpetrators respectively – of members of two famously antagonistic clans, the MacDonalds and the Campbells. But the fact that there were Campbells in Glencoe in February 1692 was a consequence of their having been recruited by the Williamite military. Far from acting on their own volition, then, those Campbells were the instruments of Scotland's government. And what that government was attempting to arrange, at the point it ordered its troops into action in Glencoe, was nothing less, as contemporaries recognised, than the wiping out of a whole community.

When the elderly Alasdair MacDonald, Glencoe's chieftain, narrowly failed to meet the deadline – 1 January 1692 – by which Scotland's Williamite ministers expected the heads of pro-Jacobite clans like the Glencoe MacDonalds to have sworn loyalty to the country's new king, those same ministers treated the Glencoe chief's lapse as the perfect opportunity to teach the wider population of the Highlands and Islands an unforgettable lesson. 'It would be a proper vindication of the public justice,' one Scottish politician commented of Glencoe's inhabitants, 'to extirpate that sept of thieves.' But despite the MacDonalds of Glencoe, as this politician implied, being no angels, their offences – such as their involvement in cattle raiding – would not have been thought to justify their slaughter had it not been for the extent to which, as is demonstrated by ministerial correspondence dating from 1692, the inhabitants of the Highlands and Islands had come to be viewed, by lots of Lowlanders, as an inferior species. Had he been dealing with a Lowland locality which had fallen foul of the government of Scotland, Robert Campbell of Glenlyon, commander of the military detachment sent to Glencoe within weeks of Alasdair MacDonald's tardy registering of his loyalty oath, might have been tacitly encouraged – in an age invariably careless of such civil rights as it acknowledged – to rough up that locality's residents. In such circumstances, however, genocide would not have been contemplated. Only the Highland identity of his prospective victims, in other words, made it possible for Campbell to be instructed that 'the good and safety of the country' required him 'to put . . . to the sword all [Glencoe MacDonalds] under seventy'.[1]

The Massacre of Glencoe, as matters turned out, was botched – with the result that a substantial proportion of the glen's occupants survived to fight, sometimes literally, another day. But the official thinking underpinning Robert Campbell's orders was such as to give some credence to the notion, discernible here and there in the compositions of Jacobitism's many Gaelic poets, that the Jacobite clans of the Highlands and Islands were fighting, in the seventeenth century and later, for the preservation of their way of life – even their very existence – as well as for a Stewart restoration. This is not to claim that the divide between Jacobite and non-Jacobite neatly followed the Highland Line – with Gaelic-speaking clansfolk on the one side and Scots-speaking Lowlanders on the other. There were Lowlanders who were Jacobites; there were also clans – the Campbells and several others – whose opposition to Jacobitism was one of the reasons why the Stewarts never did regain power. And while aspects of Highlands and Islands Jacobitism – such as its links with clanship – were peculiar to the region, it was also the case that Highlands and Islands Jacobites had much in common with Jacobites elsewhere. Just like their Lowland counterparts, for example, the Stewarts' Highlands and Islands backers tended to be people whose religious beliefs were such as to make them less than wholehearted supporters of the presbyterian supremacy which took shape in Scotland following William of Orange's emergence as the country's king. Presbyterianism's opponents, who had enjoyed royal favour during the reigns of the mildly agnostic Charles II and the fiercely anti-presbyterian James VII, consisted mainly of episcopalians (Protestants favouring a Church run by bishops rather than by presbyteries) and Catholics. Both groups were well represented in the Highlands and Islands where presbyterianism had made relatively few inroads and where, in the course of the seventeenth century's opening decades, missionaries from Ireland – following, as it were, in Columba's footsteps – had been able to revive Catholicism in places like Barra, South Uist, Arisaig and Morar.

Since Jacobite chiefs who were not Catholic tended to be episcopalian and since such chiefs' dislike of the staunchly Hanoverian Campbells stemmed – to some degree at least – from the Campbells' longstanding identification with presbyterianism, a good deal of pro-Stewart sentiment in the Highlands and Islands can arguably be traced to Jacobitism's religious dimension. Elsewhere in Scotland, however, individuals became Jacobites for more diverse reasons – among them Jacobitism's propensity, after 1707, to serve as a convenient vehicle for Scottish nationalism.

Scotland's parliamentarians, when they agreed to the country's 1707 merger with England, acted out of a perfectly reasonable conviction that Scotland's interests would be well served by an arrangement which opened English markets – including England's colonies in North America – to Scottish merchants and to Scottish goods. But opinion in Scotland at large was less favourably disposed to union with England than was opinion in Scotland's parliament. And the pro-union case was not made any more convincing by the fact that it took a long time for the bulk of the Scottish population to derive any economic benefits from the United Kingdom into which their rulers had propelled them. For several decades after 1707, therefore, it was easy to obtain endorsement in Scotland for the proposition that the country's previous independence should be restored. Shrewder Jacobites, capitalising on this conviction, maintained that just such an outcome would result from a reinstatement of the Stewarts. And when, in 1714, the single Anglo-Scottish throne created by the 1707 union was made over by the United Kingdom's London-based parliament to yet another continental, George I, who had previously ruled only the small state of Hanover, Scotland's Jacobites – stridently resentful of their being governed in the name of this 'wee bit German lairdie' – were presented with an opportunity to transform the Stewart cause into something approximating to an all-Scotland crusade.

That opportunity was not well taken. The Jacobite rebellion of 1715, though more strongly backed than Dundee's rising in 1689, failed, like its predecessor, to break decisively out of the Highlands and Islands. An ensuing revolt, in 1719, was still more of a Highlands and Islands affair. By the 1730s and 1740s, therefore, even the most Jacobite of Highland chieftains, men like Cameron of Lochiel and the leaders of Clan Donald's various segments, had taken to insisting they would not again make war on the United Kingdom and its Hanoverian kings in the absence of a cast-iron guarantee to the effect that they could depend, from the start of any such enterprise, on the direct military involvement of France – whose government the exiled Stewarts had, for some time, been cultivating.

Conveniently for the Jacobites, steadily worsening relations between France and the United Kingdom led, in March 1744, to the two countries going to war. The ensuing hostilities appeared, at first, to have created circumstances conducive to a French expedition of the kind demanded by Lochiel and his fellow chiefs. Indeed Prince Charles Edward Stewart, grandson of James VII and the young man on whom Jacobite aspirations mostly depended by this stage, journeyed eagerly to the Channel coast from the Stewart family's Italian headquarters in the firm belief that the French monarch, Louis XV, would at once invade the United Kingdom in order to oust George II – who had succeeded George I in 1727. As 1744 advanced and no French invasion was forthcoming, however, it became apparent that Prince Charles Edward's optimism as to France's intentions had been unfounded. He conceived, therefore, an altogether desperate plan. Because the French were reluctant to move until a new Jacobite rebellion had broken out, and because the putative rebels were equally unwilling to commit themselves until French troops had landed in the United Kingdom, Prince Charles Edward decided to sail – virtually unaccompanied – for the Highlands and Islands where he intended, by sheer force of personality, to persuade the area's Jacobite chiefs to commence a rising which, in turn, would have the effect, or so Charles Edward calculated, of inducing Louis XV at last to sanction an assault on Britain – the name by which the United Kingdom was beginning to be known. Hence Charles Edward Stewart's arrival, with just seven followers, in Loch nan Uamh, Moidart, on 25 July 1745.

Perhaps because it ended so catastrophically for the region, there has long been a widespread disposition in the Highlands and Islands to assume that the Jacobite rebellion of 1745 could not have turned out other than it did. But such determinism can be overdone. It is no bad thing, therefore, that an effective antidote to it is available in the writings of one of the 1745 rising's earliest historians, John Home. Those writings include a brilliant summary of the opportunities so remarkably opened up by the adventure which commenced that summer's day in Moidart:

> The conclusion of this enterprise was such as most people both at home and abroad expected, but the progress of the rebels was what nobody expected; for they defeated more than once the king's troops; they overran one of the united kingdoms and marched so far into the other that the capital trembled at their approach; and during the tide of fortune, which had its ebbs and flows, there were moments when nothing seemed impossible; and, to say truth, it was not easy to forecast, or to imagine, anything more unlikely than what had already happened.[2]

That the Jacobites did better than anyone anticipated in 1745 was due, in large part, to Charles Edward Stewart, then just twenty-four years old. It is with some justice, therefore, that the prince features as a messiah-like figure in many of the Gaelic poems and songs he inspired. On his becoming king, it was claimed by a whole series of versifiers, warm winds would figuratively take the place of cold; frost and snow would be banished; 'every hill' would be 'laid in smooth rigs'; wheat would grow on the highest mountainsides; and Scotland's Gaels – despite their having become confined, as one Jacobite poet lamented, to the 'narrow corner' constituted by the Highlands and Islands – would reclaim the much grander inheritance that had been theirs when Gaelic-speaking monarchs ruled in Alba. The promised land thus envisaged was to remain beyond the reach, as events demonstrated, of Prince Charles Edward's Highlands and Islands followers. But what they and he jointly accomplished, as John Home pointed out, was astonishingly impressive all the same. On 19 August 1745, Charles Edward, having unfurled the Stewart standard at Glenfinnan, some ten miles east of Loch nan Uamh, formally commenced his uprising. On 17 September, less than a month later, he marched in triumph into Edinburgh.[3]

Nothing testifies more eloquently to the youthful Prince Charles Edward's remarkable personal qualities than the fact that he was able,

Iona and its restored medieval abbey

Standing stones at Calanais

Cattle have been a part of the Highlands and Islands scene for thousands of years

Oil rigs at anchor in the Cromarty Firth

A livestock sale in Benbecula
© Highlands and Islands Enterprise

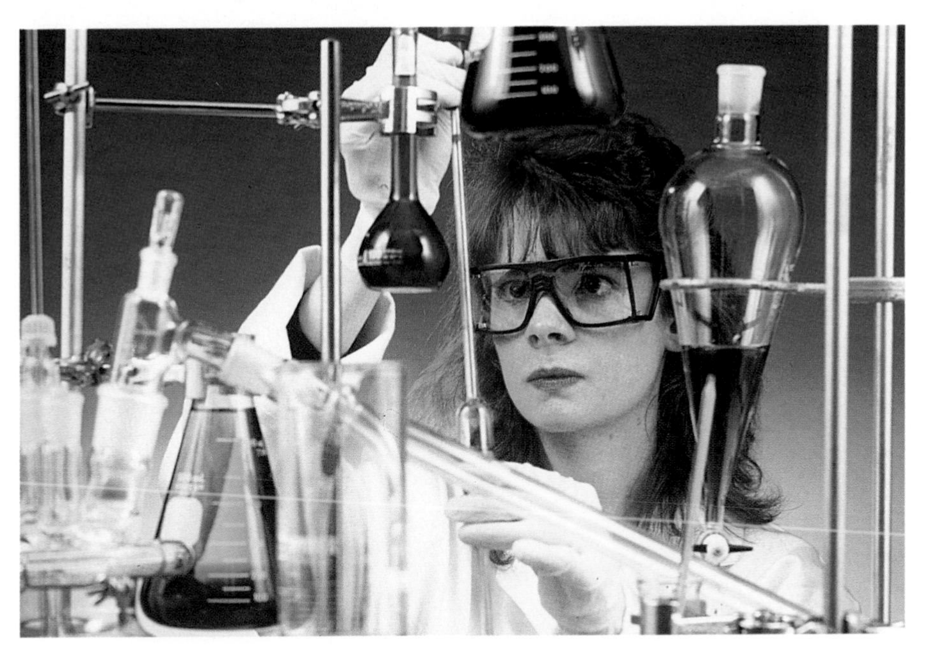

A pharmaceuticals laboratory in Lewis
© Highlands and Islands Enterprise

Utilising boat-building skills that stem from the Viking era

Jewellery manufacture: a modern industry with roots deep in the past

Fishing has gone on in the Highlands and Islands
since people first settled here

The clarsach, or harp, has been played in the
Highlands and Islands for at least two millennia

Artillery piece at Fort George: symbol of the United Kingdom's eighteenth-century pacification of the Highlands and Islands

ABOVE AND BELOW: Gaelic, spoken in the Highlands and Islands since the time of Columba, is today being promoted actively among the region's children
© Highlands and Islands Enterprise

Sutherland crofter Allan MacRae celebrates his community's purchase of the North Assynt Estate
© John Paul

Inverness High Street – at the centre of a centuries-old town

Farmland in the Black Isle

Up-Helly-Aa: Shetlanders celebrate their Norse heritage

despite his having come to Moidart with none of the French aid the Jacobite chiefs had said would have to be available before they joined in any revolt, to get much older and more worldly-wise men such as Donald Cameron of Lochiel to risk everything – their clans, their lands, their lives – in pursuit of a goal which many of them, in their more cautious moments, considered unattainable. True, there were those among the ostensibly leading Jacobites of the Highlands and Islands – including clan chiefs like MacLeod of Dunvegan and MacDonald of Sleat – who remained stubbornly at home throughout the hectic period Gaelic-speakers ever afterwards called *Bliadhna na Thearlaich*, Charlie's year. But from the Camerons, from the Clanranald MacDonalds, the MacDonalds of Glencoe, the Stewarts of Appin, the MacPhersons and others, sufficient support was forthcoming to enable Charles Edward Stewart to equip himself with the clan-based army which, from Glenfinnan, he first marched eastwards into the Great Glen, then ordered south by way of Badenoch. On 27 and 28 August, in the vicinity of the Corrieyairack Pass, Charles Edward easily outmanoeuvred the Hanoverian commander in Scotland, General Sir John Cope, who chose to occupy – pointlessly as it proved – Inverness rather than to give battle. Days later, having set a cracking pace through Atholl and Dunkeld, the prince recruited the Perthshire aristocrat, Lord George Murray, an outstandingly able field commander. And on the morning of 21 September, with Murray's help, Charles Edward Stewart engineered, at Prestonpans near Edinburgh, the annihilation of those forces which Cope had meanwhile brought south from Inverness by sea – the Jacobites, in a matter of minutes, killing three hundred of the Hanoverian general's troops, wounding another five hundred and taking some fifteen hundred prisoners for the loss of just seventy of their own men.

In the late summer and early autumn of 1745, then, Prince Charles Edward did what only two others – Macbeth and Robert Bruce – had managed previously to do. Starting from a Highlands and Islands base, he successfully took over Scotland.

As he himself recognised, however, Charles Edward's achievements depended almost entirely on the extraordinary momentum he had maintained since reaching Loch nan Uamh. He never deployed more than five or six thousand men at any one time. He possessed no worthwhile cavalry or artillery. His financial assets were vanishingly slender. And arrayed against him was all the very considerable power at the disposal of a country, the United Kingdom, which – both militarily and economically – was one of the eighteenth-century world's most formidable states.

Charles Edward Stewart's rebellion is best understood – in terminology devised by twentieth-century Marxists and anarchists – as a revolution of the will. Its key figure, the prince, paid less attention to objective realities, in other words, than to his own fervent, and utterly sincere, conviction that he could decisively alter those realities by acting in ways which, considered logically, were little short of crazy. Charles Edward had arguably behaved irrationally by coming to Moidart with no French backing. He had manifested further irrationality by contending, in the face of any amount of evidence to the contrary, that a handful of clansmen could conquer Scotland. And he continued to disregard the facts by asserting over and over again in Edinburgh, during the autumn of 1745, that his tiny army should immediately march on London. The clan chiefs who dominated Charles Edward's war council – and who tended, a little paradoxically, to become steadily more fearful as success followed success – were unconvinced by such thinking. The prince, however, was repeatedly proved right. This made it difficult for more prudent spirits to get any leverage over him. And it was not until 4 December – having, in the interim, struck deep, at Charles Edward's insistence, into England – that the prince's council, Charles Edward only dissenting, opted for caution and calculation in place of recklessness. The Jacobites resolved, that December day, to turn back. They had just entered Derby. In London, 120 miles away, one of the city's more eminent residents was writing of 'a panic scarce to be credited'. 'There never was so melancholy a town,' another Londoner noted gloomily. 'I . . . fear the rebels beyond my reason.'[4]

Most modern historians are of the opinion that the Jacobite clansmen who occupied Derby in December 1745, though they had demonstrably shaken Britain's Hanoverian régime to its foundations, could not ultimately have caused that régime's collapse. Such historians may be right. But what those same Jacobite clansmen had already accomplished, as John Home emphasised long ago, was no less inconceivable, when they set out from Glenfinnan, than the possibility of their forcing their way into London. Few seizures of power – as is evident from lots of twentieth-century instances – have seemed likely until they have actually occurred. And for all that Prince Charles Edward Stewart's army, as it marched south by way of Carlisle and Manchester into the English Midlands, had attracted little support, neither had it encountered any meaningful opposition. The men who then ran Britain were heartily disliked, even detested. Only a small minority of the country's citizens, as a result, were prepared to rally in support of its government. And on the day of their Derby deliberations, though neither Charles Edward nor his council knew this at the time, no substantial military force stood between that government and the Jacobite army. Of course, there were excellent reasons – most of them arising from the obvious, though actually exaggerated, risk of their troops being surrounded and trapped far from home – as to why the members of Charles Edward's council reached their fateful decision. But had his few thousand Highlanders and Islesmen been ordered on 4 December 1745 to push on, as the prince wanted, it is by no means inconceivable that the cracks already discernible in the structure of the Hanoverian state would rapidly have widened sufficiently to bring the entire edifice tumbling down. As it was, the Jacobites, by withdrawing, provided their opponents with the desperately needed breathing space King George II and his ministers had feared might be denied them. A French descent on England's south coast, a real likelihood had Jacobite nerves held, ceased again to be a serious prospect. So did any chance of pro-Stewart unrest inside England itself. And though Lord George Murray's generalship was such as to ensure that Charles Edward's army was brought back to Scotland with scarcely a single casualty, retreat was rapidly to become almost as addictive as advance had formerly been.

A Jacobite victory at Falkirk in January was not followed up. Instead the bulk of Charles Edward Stewart's forces – their morale crumbling perceptibly – were pulled back to Inverness. From the south, meanwhile, there gradually advanced, by way of Aberdeen and Moray, newly assembled Hanoverian formations under the personal command of King George's younger son, the Duke of Cumberland. Charles Edward – his earlier *élan* having given way to depression which led, in turn, to his seeking solace in alcohol – refused to confront Cumberland until the latter, by this stage fully seized of the strategic initiative, had brought his infantry, his dragoons and his heavy guns to ground of the Jacobite prince's choosing. That ground – high, flat, windswept and marshy – lies some four or five miles to the east of Inverness. The place is called Culloden Moor. It was as ill-suited as any spot could have been to the battle tactics – most notably the downhill charge – on which clan armies had relied since the era of Montrose and Alasdair MacColla. As such, Culloden, where his remaining troops assembled on the morning of 16 April 1746, should never have been occupied, let alone defended, by Charles Edward Stewart. The prince was told as much by Lord George Murray. But with Lord George, Charles Edward had long since fallen out. He consequently pressed on regardless with his plans: plans which exposed the prince's amazingly loyal following, for ages as it doubtless seemed, to a withering artillery bombardment; plans which could have come to fruition only if, despite their being massively outnumbered by soldiers who were better armed than themselves, Charles Edward's clansmen had somehow managed to press home a frontal assault of the kind that carries all before it.

No such assault was organised by the Jacobites at Culloden. Such suicidally heroic attacks as were mounted on Cumberland's lines resulted, predictably, in little other than the deaths of the attackers. The wider battle ended, equally unsurprisingly, in Charles Edward's total defeat. The prince was left to commence his ignominious, though still romanticised, 'flight in the heather' – a flight which ended with his return, in October 1746, to the continent. The prince's surviving troops, for their part, were abandoned to whatever fate the Duke of Cumberland might have in store both for themselves and for the wider Highlands and Islands society – this society built on clans and on clanship – to which they and their families belonged.

Among the Hanoverian army's officer corps were individuals who, being interested in classical history, were aware of the parallels between the Duke of Cumberland's 1746 campaign and the one conducted in 83AD by Gnaeus Julius Agricola. Cumberland's route to Culloden, as commented earlier, was much the same as Agricola's route to Mons Graupius. Cumberland, like Agricola, was the military representative of an imperial power seeking to counter a challenge posed to its authority by the inhabitants of the Highlands and Islands. And though the clans Cumberland confronted were by no means identical – either in their overall composition or in the way they made war – to the Caledonian tribes Agricola's legions had encountered, both Culloden and Mons Graupius were battles in which technologically sophisticated and highly disciplined armies easily outperformed less well equipped and more informally organised adversaries. There is, however, one key difference between what occurred in 83AD and what took place in 1746. This difference lies in the sharply contrasting outcomes of Agricola's and Cumberland's victories.

The Caledonians lost the Battle of Mons Graupius. But they by no means lost the war of which Mons Graupius was part. The Romans did not remain long in the Highlands and Islands; they did not even maintain a lengthy presence on the region's borders; they certainly made no attempt to alter, in any fundamental fashion, the nature of Caledonian society. The eighteenth-century United Kingdom, on the other hand, was intent on making its Highlands and Islands conquests permanent. That was why, as became starkly apparent in the months following Culloden, the United Kingdom's newly installed representatives in the Highlands and Islands were not prepared to confine themselves to eliminating Highlands and Islands Jacobitism. What the Duke of Cumberland and his successors intended was nothing less than the complete destruction of the region's clan-based social structures which, because of their age-old potential for making war, had made it comparatively simple for Prince Charles Edward Stewart, on his reaching Moidart, to raise the fighting force the prince had marched so spectacularly – and, from a Hanoverian standpoint, so terrifyingly – to Derby.

The concept of eradicating clanship was not at all a new one, of course. Successive governments of Scotland, as previous chapters stressed, had more than once set out to secure exactly that objective. But those governments had always lacked the capacity – because of the relatively underendowed character of the country over which they presided – to acquire anything approximating to absolute mastery of the Highlands and Islands. Hence the survival in the region, until 1746, of modes of life which had little in common with those then – and for hundreds of years previously – regarded as the norm in areas immediately to the south. Hence, too, the significance, in a Highlands and Islands context, of the fact that the Duke of Cumberland took his orders from London rather than from Edinburgh. Since England was considerably larger, more populous and a great deal wealthier than Scotland, an administration which could mobilise English as well as Scottish resources with a view to implementing its Highlands and Islands policies was more likely to get its way in the region than an administration limited to Scotland alone. Oliver Cromwell had briefly proved as much during the 1650s. And the United Kingdom government to which the Duke of Cumberland reported was better endowed – in territory, revenues and manpower – than Cromwell's régime had ever been.

Britain was the eighteenth-century world's major trading nation. Partly as a result of the investment capital its buoyant commerce had made available to its entrepreneurs, the country, at much the same time as its rulers were dealing with the consequences of Charles Edward Stewart's uprising, had become the first on earth to start industrialising. The economic clout which eighteenth-century Britain thus acquired was naturally reflected in its military standing. British fleets and British armies – partly funded from the profits accruing to the businesses whose interests those same fleets and armies often served – were regularly deployed to defend and to enlarge a colonial empire which extended, by the 1740s, from North America to India. Although none of this – not its colonies, not its sailors, not its soldiers, not its commerce – made eighteenth-century Britain invulnerable, as Charles Edward Stewart had so signally showed, the country's enormous financial and other assets certainly provided its politicians with the means they required to underwrite their planned new departure in the Highlands and Islands.

Just how far-reaching this departure was intended to be had been made clear by the Duke of Cumberland on his arrival in Scotland in January 1746. He had come north, Cumberland announced, to 'burn and destroy'. Soon he and his men, the duke continued, would be in the Highlands and Islands. There they would promptly 'crush' the 'thieves', 'plunderers' and 'robbers' who, in Cumberland's opinion, inhabited much of the region. He was relishing his chance, he said, to 'extirpate' a 'race' whose conduct had so jeopardised the existence of his father's kingdom. He was particularly looking forward, Cumberland concluded, to terminating Highlands and Islands 'clannism'.[5]

Cumberland's language is reminiscent of that employed by the organisers of the Glencoe massacre. It is reminiscent also of comments made routinely, over a lengthy period, by those Lowland Scots – most notably, perhaps, King James VI – who, by engaging in this sort of racist stereotyping, were looking to win acceptance for what would otherwise have been unacceptable. If, by virtue simply of their living there, the people of the Highlands and Islands, particularly the Gaelic-speakers among them, were inferior to people living in the Lowlands, then Lowlanders, or so it seemed to the proponents of such beliefs, were perfectly entitled to dominate their northern neighbours. Might it not be the case, indeed, that Lowlanders had a moral duty thus to impose their will on the Highlands and Islands? For how otherwise were the inhabitants of that benighted region to be brought within the ambit of the United Kingdom and taught to see the error of their ways?

So Lowland Scots had thought for long enough. So the English, as a result of what occurred in 1745, began to think as well. The human inhabitants of the Highlands and Islands, it was declared on all sides during Charles Edward Stewart's rebellion, were on a par with 'animals', 'vermin', 'wild beasts', 'wolves' and 'monsters'. The typical clan consisted largely of 'barbarians', 'banditti', 'fiends', 'arrant scum'. So wholly unforgiving was the political climate created by this outpouring of vilification that it comes as little surprise to learn that Cumberland, on getting to the Highlands and Islands, was urged by one southern aristocrat to 'starve the whole country indiscriminately' or, failing this, to 'put all to fire and sword'. Nor is it surprising that the duke – his own, already quoted, view of his Highlands and Islands mission chiming perfectly with the wider mood – took care, during the spring and summer of 1746, to leave nobody in the Highlands and Islands in any doubt as to the totality of the United Kingdom's post-Culloden ascendancy over the region. In June, one of Cumberland's officers was pleased to report that several hundred homes had been 'burned already' in the Highlands and Islands district for which he was responsible. It was disappointing, this same officer conceded, that there were 'still so many more houses to burn'. But further batches of Highlands and Islands homes, to such men's gratification, would go up in flames before the year was done.[6]

Contrary to the expectations engendered by Hanoverian propaganda, the Jacobite army, when taking Lowland towns like Edinburgh and when invading England, had conducted itself in a highly disciplined fashion. 'The rebels behaved tolerably well in their march southwards,' one London newspaper felt constrained to admit.[7]

As is amply demonstrated by the extent of their house-burning activities, the troops who constituted Britain's army of occupation in the Highlands and Islands felt under no reciprocal obligation to show a comparable restraint. Women were raped. Men were summarily shot and hanged. Crops were destroyed. Cattle and other livestock were rounded up, seized, driven off.

The United Kingdom's parliament, meanwhile, passed laws intended both to punish Highlands and Islands people for misdeeds they had allegedly committed in the past and to ensure that no further such misdeeds could be committed in the future. The lands of those clans which had taken part in Prince Charles Edward's rebellion were declared forfeit and expropriated by the British state. Chieftains – Jacobite and non-Jacobite alike – were legislatively deprived of their traditional powers over their followers. The keeping of weapons – not least the claymores which clansmen had been wielding to such effect since the seventeenth century – was prohibited. Presbyterianism, being pro-Hanoverian and anti-Stewart, was assiduously promoted at the expense of other faiths. And with a view to striking a further, intentionally demoralising, blow at clansfolk's sense of their distinctiveness, Britain's government – by means of a measure which one politician hoped would have the effect of 'undressing those savages' – made it a crime for the men of the Highlands and Islands to wear the checked, or tartan, plaids which had long distinguished them from breeches-wearing Lowlanders.[8]

Subsequent to the earlier Jacobite risings of 1715 and 1719, the British authorities had begun to build roads and – following Cromwellian and Williamite precedent – to establish permanently garrisoned strongpoints, such as Fort Augustus and Fort William, in various parts of the Highlands and Islands. Now further activity of this type was undertaken. Among the results were the barracks and batteries which together constitute the most formidable military complex to have been constructed in or near the Highlands and Islands since the Romans began work at Inchtuthil. This complex, still a British army base and still bearing the name of the Hanoverian king the Jacobites tried vainly to overthrow in 1745, is Fort George. Commanding the seaward approaches to Inverness and covering more than forty acres, Fort George stands, some seven or eight miles from Culloden, on a low, exposed peninsula jutting northwards into the Moray Firth. And should you want to understand what happened to the Highlands and Islands in the later 1740s, you could do no better than to make that peninsula your starting point.

I first heard of Fort George from my father who, when conscripted at the start of twentieth-century Britain's war with Adolf Hitler's Germany, became, as a nineteen-year-old recruit, one of the innumerable soldiers who have been marched interminably backwards and forwards across the fort's cold and blowy parade ground. Although my own connections with Fort George have been – thankfully – a lot more transient than my father's, I can understand, when I go there and stroll below the fort's stone walls, why he and many others came so to hate this place. Fort George is, and was meant to be, intimidating. It reeks, as it was planned to do, of the harsh and utterly unyielding hegemony which, in the middle years of the eighteenth century, the United Kingdom imposed on the Highlands and Islands.

**

There were some bold spirits in the Highlands and Islands who, even after Culloden, continued to resist Hanoverian rule. Prominent among them was a minor chieftain, Archibald MacDonnell of Barrisdale, whose clan lands were located in Knoydart and who, despite his having been formally attainted or outlawed, managed always to elude the military patrols sent in pursuit of him. This, as a government representative reported wearily in 1753, was because MacDonnell's people remained stubbornly loyal to him:

> They have the insolence, ever since the year 1746, to pay their rents to the attainted Barrisdale who, since that time, absolutely rules them, and ranges up and down that country and the neighbourhood with a band of men dressed, as well as himself, in the Highland habit.[9]

To defy the law by wearing a plaid – which is what was meant by 'the Highland habit' – was to do little more than thumb one's nose, gratifyingly but not very menacingly, in the direction of Britain's Hanoverian establishment. Actually to take up arms against an official of the British state was to pose a threat of a much more serious kind. That was why, when one of the men employed to administer confiscated Jacobite lands was killed at Lettermore, near Ballachullish, in May 1752, the Hanoverian authorities were anxious to respond in a manner calculated to discourage any further such episodes. That meant finding someone to hang. The person against whom charges were quickly framed – frame being a most appropriate term in the circumstances – was James Stewart, tacksman of Acharn in Duror.

Perhaps because I played regularly in the ruins of his Duror home while growing up in that vicinity, once one of the mainland possessions of the Lordship of the Isles and afterwards occupied by the Stewarts of Appin, I have always harboured a good deal of affection for *Seumas a'Ghlinne*, James of the Glen, as this eighteenth-century tacksman was known locally. Seumas a'Ghlinne had his own reasons – stemming from the dead estate administrator having turned him off the lands in Glen Duror to which he owed his Gaelic designation – for wishing harm on the man murdered at Lettermore. But Stewart's principal offence, if he committed one at all, was to have come publicly and courageously to the aid of a group of tenants whom the assassinated official, during the weeks prior to his being shot by a concealed marksman, had been planning to evict. A number of those threatened tenants lived in the Duror township of Achindarroch – less than half a mile from Acharn. They were, in consequence, James Stewart's neighbours. But that, as far as Hanoverian officialdom was concerned, mattered not at all. The fate of the Achindarroch tenants was the British government's business, it was thought in high places, not James Stewart's. By taking up the case of the Achindarroch people, and by going so far in his espousal of that case as to have travelled to Edinburgh with a view to mounting a court action on the Achindarroch folk's behalf, Seumas a'Ghlinne had thus made himself a marked man. That was why, on his being accused of having some hand – as an accessory, it was claimed, of a gunman who could not be found – in the Lettermore killing, the Acharn tacksman had no chance of receiving much in the way of justice. He was hanged on a knoll overlooking the tidal narrows giving entry to Loch Leven. The inscription to be seen on the memorial now standing on that same knoll – a memorial I visit, on occasion, prior to heading north across the nearby Ballachullish Bridge – unambiguously and, I believe, correctly, declares James Stewart to have been 'executed . . . for a crime of which he was not guilty'.

James Stewart – whose half-brother commanded, at Culloden, some three hundred men from Duror and adjacent districts – was a member of his traditionally Jacobite clan's ruling élite. And in his readiness to come to the assistance of his Achindarroch neighbours, whose status was much lowlier than Seumas a'Ghlinne's own, there is to be glimpsed one of the more attractive features of clanship: its capacity to engender solidarities of a sort which transcended social division. James Stewart gained nothing – indeed he lost all he had to lose – as a result of his identifying so visibly with Achindarroch's tenants. But he identified with them all the same. The ethics and ethos of clanship, as men like Stewart understood those things, demanded nothing less.

By 1752, however, beliefs of the type held by James Stewart were beginning to look decidedly anachronistic in a Highlands and Islands context. Much more representative of what clanship's upper echelons henceforth thought appropriate behaviour was the conduct of a man who assisted with James Stewart's prosecution. This man was Simon Fraser. At the insistence of the same Hanoverian authorities whom he served so diligently at James Stewart's trial, Simon's father, Lord Lovat, had been beheaded on charges of treason arising from his involvement, as chief of Clan Fraser, in Charles Edward Stewart's rebellion. Indeed Simon, also active on the Jacobite side in the run-up to Culloden, had himself been imprisoned for some years – with other Jacobites – in Edinburgh Castle. But far from plotting revenge on the Hanoverian politicians who – metaphorically at least – were both his gaolers and his father's executioners, Simon Fraser determinedly and methodically set out to curry favour with them. While still a prisoner, he deployed his considerable influence with his Fraser clansmen to ensure that franchise-holders among those clansmen used their votes in an Inverness-shire parliamentary election in such a manner as to secure the return of the British government's favoured candidate – a candidate whose victory was gained, incidentally, over one of Simon's own kinsmen.

His pro-Hanoverian credentials having thus been established,

Simon Fraser gained release from custody, took a law degree and, on graduating, tried to find further ways – as he so signally did when helping send James Stewart to the gallows – of enhancing his reputation as a Highlander on whom the United Kingdom's government could rely. Nor was it simply as a lawyer that Fraser served the state which, in addition to executing his father, had deprived the youthful Simon himself, as his Jacobite father's allegedly Jacobite heir, of estates which he would otherwise have inherited. When, in 1756, Britain – then trying to expel other European powers from North America – found itself embroiled in a new war with France, Simon Fraser personally recruited, in the Highlands and Islands, a regiment whose soldiers, known as Fraser's Highlanders, were to have a major role in the campaign which led to Britain taking Quebec and the rest of Canada from the French. The North American performance of Fraser's Highlanders, which Simon personally commanded, attracted plaudits from contemporaries. But what most pleased Simon Fraser about his regiment's exploits, it can safely be guessed, was the contribution those exploits made to persuading parliament that Simon had done enough to merit a 'particular act of grace'. That act took the form of legislation which, in 1774, restored to Simon Fraser, this former state prisoner, the lands which had earlier been taken from his father.[10]

There was nothing unprecedented, it should be acknowledged, in a man of Simon Fraser's background taking the side of a southern government which sought, as eighteenth-century Britain's governments were certainly seeking, to subjugate the Highlands and Islands. Scotland's kings, in the course of their protracted attempts to make the Highlands and Islands securely Scottish, had obtained invaluable assistance, after all, from many of the region's leading men – whether Farquhar MacTaggart in the thirteenth century or successive Campbell chiefs in the period after 1493. But MacTaggart (one may surmise) and the Campbells (very definitely) made their alliances with Scotland's monarchs in order to bolster the prospects of the kin-groups they headed. This is not to claim that Campbell earls of Argyll (whose motives are easier to discern than those of their thirteenth-century precursors) were unselfishly devoted to the wellbeing of their clan. It is simply to make the point that it was impossible, until well into the eighteenth century, for any Highlands and Islands magnate – in the Gaelic-speaking part of the region at any rate – to operate other than as a clan chief. And to be a clan chief, as emphasised previously, was automatically to be constrained both by that position's responsibilities and by the expectations which chieftainship automatically engendered among a chief's clansfolk. Hence the novelty, from a Highlands and Islands perspective, of the career path chosen – and so profitably pursued – by Simon Fraser. Here was a man who, though not above appealing to clan loyalties when looking to get Fraser families to put their young men into British uniforms, felt himself free from pressures of the sort the clan-based society of the Highlands and Islands had previously exerted on people of his rank. James Stewart of Acharn might have behaved in 1752 in ways that custom decreed. Simon Fraser set such custom brutally aside. Charmlessly but shrewdly, he conducted himself as self-interest demanded – rather than with a view to advancing, as precedent would have dictated, the wider cause of the kinship-linked collective over which his forebears had presided as Fraser chiefs.

Men like Simon Fraser – and there were to be many such in the Highlands and Islands of the later eighteenth century – constitute something of a testimony to humanity's adaptive capabilities. The young Simon Fraser, who marched to Culloden at the head of a detachment of armed clansmen, conformed – superficially at least – to behavioural codes of the sort Gaelic bards had been celebrating since the time of Fergus Mor mac Eirc. The older Simon Fraser, a United Kingdom parliamentarian as well as a major-general in the British army, succeeded in having himself accepted as an equal by Britain's southern rulers – to whom bardic poems, along with all the other trappings of clanship, seemed so many barbaric inanities. Viewed simply as an exercise in transcending cultural boundaries, then, Simon Fraser's achievement has to be reckoned remarkable. It was, in a sense, as if the Sioux and Cheyenne chiefs, Sitting Bull and Crazy Horse, had gone on from their nineteenth-century wars with General George A. Custer's Seventh Cavalry to become, in the fullness of time, United States congressmen. But between Sitting Bull and Crazy Horse on the one side, and those men's Highlands and Islands counterparts on the other, there were, of course, a number of distinctions. Not the least significant of these is to be found in the fact that, even before clanship was legislatively swept away, the ruling orders of the clans were beginning to turn their backs – in a way Crazy Horse and Sitting Bull never did – on the society of which they had long been an integral, indeed an absolutely central, component.

The divide between chief and clan which began to emerge as a result of this development, and which would ultimately separate clearing landlord from evicted crofter, can be attributed – partly at least – to the long-run effects of actions taken by Scottish governments, particularly the government answering to King James VI, in the opening decades of the seventeenth century. The Statutes of Iona might not have immediately transformed clan chieftains into Lowland lairds, but both the statutes and other measures of that sort, as noted earlier, did oblige chieftains to spend more and more time in Edinburgh. In that money-orientated and Scots-speaking city, needless to say, there was little prestige to be gained from activities such as the patronising of bards, pipers or harpists which, back in the Gaelic-speaking Highlands and Islands, were thought to define aristocratic success and accomplishment. If he was to cut a dash in Edinburgh society – and nobody was keener on cutting just such a dash than the typically status-obsessed clan chief – a chieftain needed to behave, therefore, in ways that would scarcely have occurred to him had he remained permanently in the Highlands and Islands. He needed to spend more lavishly, live more fashionably, dress more elaborately than when at home. And this sort of lifestyle, once adopted, proved impossible to give up.

As indicated previously, Gaelic bards, in their role as repositories and propagators of traditional values, were appalled by the extent to which chieftains began to behave, and even look, like the Edinburgh courtiers and Lowland gentry with whom such chieftains mingled increasingly. 'I would prefer you in a coat and plaid,' one seventeenth-century chief was informed by a contemporary poet, 'than in a cloak which fastens.' And for all that such admonitions constitute an unprecedented theme in a Gaeldom which had formerly made idols of its chieftains, they struck a note which, having once been sounded, was to be heard repeatedly. 'He comes out of the shop with the latest fashion from France,' one especially disillusioned bard claimed of his chief, 'and the fine clothes worn on his person yesterday, with no little satisfaction, are tossed into a corner.'[11]

Nor was it the case that Jacobite chiefs were any less susceptible to the undoubted attractions of the southern mode of life than were chiefs who inclined towards a pro-government stance. The latter, exemplified by those Campbell chieftains who had been dabbling in Lowland affairs since the sixteenth century, could not help but be drawn more and more deeply into the non-Gaelic world to the south and east of the Highland Line. But rebellions of the kind in which many of the Campbells' Highlands and Islands rivals engaged during the seventeenth and eighteenth centuries also tended to entangle their leading participants in Lowland, even English, politics. Earlier Highlands and Islands rebellions, to be sure, had not had this effect. But that was because such rebellions were undertaken solely with a view to achieving Highlands and Islands objectives. Later risings, in contrast, were themselves partly a product of the various external involvements which, by the middle years of the seventeenth century, were beginning to shape the pattern of events right across the Highlands and Islands. Hence the distinctions which can be drawn between successive Highlands and Islands rebellions – distinctions which emerge clearly if one compares Donald Dubh's rising of 1545 with the Marquis of Montrose's rising of a century later and with Charles Edward Stewart's rising of a hundred years after that.

Donald Dubh was very much a product of the Highlands and Islands. Although he made a tactical alliance with an English king, Henry VIII, he did so mainly with a view to advancing the wholly Highlands and Islands cause – the restoration of the Lordship of the Isles – for which he fought. Both his background and his aims, therefore, differentiated Donald Dubh from the Marquis of Montrose. Unlike Donald, the latter was a Lowlander. And while this could not be said of Montrose's close colleague, Alasdair MacColla, whose commitment to reviving Clan Donald power was firmly in the Donald Dubh tradition, it was Montrose, not MacColla, who took the lead in determining the goals of their joint uprising – an uprising which, despite its Highlands and Islands base, was undertaken to serve the interests of a monarch, Charles I, to whom the Highlands and Islands, other than as a source of military manpower, were of little ultimate account. And what was true of Charles I was truer still of Charles Edward Stewart. For all the extravagant hopes vested in him by Gaelic bards, the Jacobite prince treated the Highlands as a means to an end. Because most of them – whatever their other qualities – were highly intelligent men, this was evident from the outset to such clan chiefs as followed Charles Edward south. The participation of those chiefs in what turned out to be the last Jacobite rebellion can plausibly be regarded, therefore, as evidence not of the chieftainly class's isolation from the Lowlands and from England but as a pointer, in fact, to this class's growing eagerness to perform on a wider, more southerly, stage.

It is of some significance in this context that Donald Cameron of Lochiel – the clan chief whose support for Charles Edward Stewart went a long way to enabling the prince to launch his 1745 campaign with at least some prospect of success – was about as far removed as anyone could be from the warrior chieftain of legend. When engaged in hand-to-hand combat with one of the Cromwellian officers charged with the task of establishing a fort at Inverlochy in the 1650s, Donald's grandfather, Ewen Cameron, was reputed to have disposed of his adversary – and the story has all the panache of some ancient

Gaelic saga – by biting through the unfortunate officer's throat. But between that mid-seventeenth-century Cameron chieftain and his mid-eighteenth-century successor, this Donald Cameron who so crucially joined Charles Edward Stewart at Glenfinnan in the summer of 1745, there was only the most tenuous of connections beyond the fact of the latter's descent from the former. Donald Cameron's English, revealingly enough, was more fluent than his Gaelic. Instead of inhabiting a castle, he lived, in much the same way as Lowland or English country gentlemen of the time, in a well-appointed mansion house. And in order to finance this comfortable existence, Donald Cameron – who was, in 1745, well into middle age – actively involved himself in a variety of business ventures. He attempted, for example, to exploit the considerable commercial potential of the woodlands in the neighbourhood of his Lochaber home. He also engaged in trade with the West Indies.

Because people – being invariably complex – can seldom be placed in categories which do not sometimes overlap, it would be wrong to insist that Donald Cameron, in 1745 and 1746, was fighting for reasons that had absolutely nothing to do with the motivations of those other Highlands and Islands Jacobites who had gone to war in defence of what the several poets among them considered an endangered Gaelic civilisation. Even the briefest study of Donald Cameron's outlook and mindset, however, suggests that – had the Jacobites somehow triumphed in 1745 and had Culloden, in consequence, never occurred – the old order in the Highlands and Islands would have collapsed anyway. The destruction of clanship, then, cannot and should not be blamed entirely on the Duke of Cumberland. What Cumberland did to the Gaelic-speaking population of the Highlands and Islands was assuredly nasty, brutal and vindictive. But Hanoverian nastiness, brutality and vindictiveness, though they helped to accelerate clanship's disintegration, did not, of themselves, bring it about. The real reasons for the root-and-branch transformation of so much of the Highlands and Islands in the eighteenth century, to return to a point made a page or two previously, are to be found in those processes – processes well under way by the seventeenth century's end – which had the effect of integrating clan chieftains into first the Scottish, then the British, ruling class.

This is not to suggest that chieftainship of the traditional sort was destroyed because chieftains put away their tartan plaids and took to wearing the coats and breeches which Gaelic bards regarded with such evident contempt. But it is to suggest that the acquisition, by chief after chief, of expensive garments – along with elaborately constructed homes, imported furniture, fine wines and all the other trappings of southern gentility – could not be undertaken without altering, in a very fundamental fashion, those chiefs' relationships with their clans.

Clan chieftains never had lived modestly. As noted earlier, however, their customary feastings and festivities could readily be sustained by a system of food renders which was of immemorial antiquity and which, as a result, had long been incorporated into clanship's overall structure. What could not be thus incorporated – what, in fact, proved desperately disruptive – were the consequences of the novel forms of consumption in which clan chiefs began to indulge during the seventeenth century. Foremost among those consequences was an ever more urgent need – a need which, for reasons already touched on, cut across the Jacobite and non-Jacobite divide – for hard cash. Hence the extent to which the surviving seventeenth-century accounts of various chieftainly families tend to tell – though in a less entertaining manner – much the same story as the one told by the period's bards. Expenditure was universally on the up and up. Debts were everywhere increasing. Creditors were pressing. The unavoidable outcome was a growing tendency, on chieftains' part, to explore the possibility of their deriving a higher money income from their clan lands.

Many such lands had been leased, since the sixteenth century or perhaps for even longer, to tacksmen. To that extent, therefore, the commercialised landholding arrangements which eventually took clanship's place had been incubated, as mentioned in the previous chapter, inside clanship's essentially tribal framework. But the money rent which the typical tacksman traditionally made over to his chief in return for his tack was, as also mentioned earlier, extremely low. And this was a situation which even the hardest-pressed of hard-pressed chieftains hesitated to alter. Among tacksmen's many functions, it has to be remembered, was their role in readying clans for war. So vitally important was this role that most chieftains – even when faced by escalating debts – were not inclined to run the risk, prior to the last Jacobite rebellion, of antagonising tacksmen by sharply upping their rents. Just one substantial chief chose, in advance of the 1740s, to implement such a rent hike. That chief – a man who afterwards had cause to regret his decision – was Archibald Campbell, twelfth Earl and third Duke of Argyll, who, from his home in Inveraray, presided over the thousands of square miles of territory his predecessors had so aggressively amassed.

Their dukedom, it should be mentioned, was one of many rewards to have come the Campbells' way as a result of their having collaborated so closely with the Lowland gentry who had taken the lead both in removing the last of Scotland's Stewart kings from his throne and in ensuring that no Stewart sat on that throne again. But the more the Campbells worked with Lowlanders, lived among Lowlanders and adopted Lowland modes of thought, the more they became dissatisfied with customary ways of managing their Argyll landholdings. That dissatisfaction first manifested itself, during the seventeenth century, in initiatives such as the large-scale importation into Kintyre of Lowland farming families – some of whose descendants, incidentally, are still to be found there. The Campbell organisers of this colonising venture were motivated, to begin with, by a need to obtain replacements for the MacDonald tacksmen who had previously occupied Kintyre and who had been evicted as a result of MacDonald opposition to the Campbells' acquisition of the peninsula. But because Kintyre's Lowland settlers were readier than tenants of Highlands and Islands extraction would have been to accept what were – from a Highlands and Islands standpoint – comparatively onerous conditions of tenure, the Kintyre experiment also served to illustrate the extent to which Campbell finances might be boosted if, as had actually been done in Kintyre by the seventeenth century's close, a rent-driven management system could be imposed on the rest of the Campbell empire.

It was with exactly this aim in view that Archibald Campbell set out, in the 1730s, to revolutionise the way his clan lands were allocated to their occupants. Like other chiefs, earls of Argyll had formerly looked to their landholdings principally as a means of shoring up and cementing kin-based loyalties of the sort carried over into clanship from the tribal antiquity which, even in the eighteenth century, continued to shape most clansfolk's approach to such matters. Ever since written leases and other such contrivances had been imported into the Highlands and Islands in medieval times, of course, clanship had been moving away from its tribal origins. But both this fact and its wider implications had been disguised by the extent to which a particular clan's tacksmen – because of their generally being recruited from that clan's leading families – were usually the people who, had a less adulterated form of tribalism persisted, would have occupied an identical position to the one they did, in fact, occupy in such a clan's power structure. That was why tacksmen tended to regard their role as one sanctified, as indeed it truly was sanctified, by age-old tradition – tradition which, from his tacksmen's perspective, Archibald Campbell was set on recklessly disrupting for entirely selfish reasons.

Tacks, it was decreed by the third Duke of Argyll in 1737, were no longer to be let to men whose claims to preference rested primarily on their family connections with himself. Tacks, instead, were to be let competitively to the highest bidders.

This was to break boldly, decisively and, as it proved, irrevocably with the past. By insisting on commercially letting his tacks, Archibald Campbell was both abandoning the role of chief and taking on the role of landlord. But in so doing, as he and his aides were quickly to discover, the duke – while indubitably adding to his revenues – was jeopardising the armed support on which his family had previously relied in times of trouble. Because many Campbell tacksmen of the older type were dispossessed – or, if not actually dispossessed, left hopelessly insecure – in 1737 and subsequently, it was impossible after that date for Archibald Campbell to mobilise his clan in the way his ancestors had mobilised it. Such Campbell tacksmen as survived the duke's reforms were not inclined, understandably enough, to rally to the defence of a man who, they considered, was riding roughshod over their time-honoured rights and privileges. That was why Charles Edward Stewart's Highlands and Islands backers – Inveraray's chiefs having lost much of their war-making capacity – encountered unexpectedly little resistance from the nominally Hanoverian Clan Campbell.

Other chieftains were well aware of the extent to which Archibald Campbell's reforms had made his clan a much less effective fighting force. Despite a number of those chieftains – Donald Cameron of Lochiel among them, one suspects – being every bit as anxious as the Duke of Argyll to expand their incomes, there was thus no immediate rush to follow Archibald Campbell's example. That rush came only in the wake of Culloden – when, as a result of Britain's military occupation of the Highlands and Islands, and as a result, too, of the British government's highly effective assault on clanship, there ceased to be any prospect of chiefs being again dependent, as they had so often been dependent in the past, on clansmen's willingness to take up arms on their chieftains' behalf.

In ways that have seldom been emphasised sufficiently, therefore, Culloden and its aftermath liberated clan chiefs from many of the constraints under which they had previously operated. Freed from the need to retain the loyalties and affections both of their tacksmen and of other clansfolk, Highlands and Islands chieftains were able, after 1746, to complete the transformation on which they had begun to embark some decades previously. They became, in effect, full members of the southern establishment which their ancestors, in lots of instances, had battled against. And with a view to enhancing their position within that establishment, clan chieftains more and more took on identities and personas of the sort their bards so disliked: marrying Lowland or English wives; sending their children to Lowland or English schools; giving up their patronage of poets; ceasing, as Cameron of Lochiel had even before 1746, to speak Gaelic; abandoning also the Broad Scots which, in many cases, had been their forebears' second language; adopting, in place of forms of speech now widely considered uncouth, the aristocratically accented English which, in the course of the eighteenth century, became the *lingua franca* of the recently formed United Kingdom's Anglo-Scottish ruling class.

In 1746, and for some time afterwards, the suggestion was occasionally made in London that the clan chieftains of the Highlands and Islands – Jacobite and non-Jacobite alike – should be subjected to much the same treatment as had already been meted out to their Irish counterparts. In Ireland, during the seventeenth century, the leading men of a Gaelic-speaking people – a people from whom the Gaelic-speaking population of the Highlands and Islands had, of course, originally stemmed – were mostly exiled, executed or otherwise dispossessed by their island's English conquerors. The Irish territories thus acquired by the English state were handed over, in short order, to immigrant English landlords who, owing their position entirely to England's government, were most unlikely to foment rebellion of the sort in which their Gaelic-speaking predecessors had habitually engaged. But for all that there were evident attractions – from a United Kingdom standpoint – in dealing similarly with the post-Culloden Highlands and Islands, this proved unnecessary. United Kingdom politicians certainly wanted to have the Highlands and Islands dominated, as Ireland had for some time been dominated, by men who were English-speaking landlords rather than Gaelic-speaking chieftains; men who would manage former clan lands in much the same commercially orientated fashion as the aristocracies of England and Lowland Scotland already managed their estates; men who, in this and all sorts of other ways, would contribute to the process of ensuring that the Highlands and Islands became an integral part of the Hanoverian-ruled country Charles Edward Stewart had come so close, in 1745, to conquering. But those objectives, it gradually became apparent, could be achieved by means which were very different from those employed in Ireland. If, as soon proved to be the case, Highlands and Islands chieftains were themselves willing, indeed eager, to become Highlands and Islands landlords of the type the United Kingdom wished to create, then the British state – famously flexible in its approach to conquered territories – was more than happy to encourage and to make it easy for chief after chief to move in that direction.

That was why, having already restored his clan lands to Simon Fraser, the United Kingdom government decided, in 1784, to be equally generous to the heirs of other Jacobite chiefs whose lands had also been expropriated. The beneficiaries of this measure, as government ministers were well aware, had not the slightest interest in reinstating clanship or promoting Jacobitism. They simply wanted to have the chance to turn the estates in question into money-generating assets. And British politicians were more than willing to make that possible.

From today's vantage-point, the evolution of the region's clan chiefs into landlords can be seen as constituting the single most defining episode in the entire post-medieval history of the Highlands and Islands. Among the consequences of that episode are some with which inhabitants of the Highlands and Islands are living still. Also living with the results of landlordism's emergence are the innumerable folk descended, like Jane McNeill in North Carolina, from Highlands and Islands emigrants whose departure was closely bound up with actions taken by, or on behalf of, Highlands and Islands landlords. Those actions were frequently harsh. And while most of the more brutal things done to the population of the Highlands and Islands by landlords were done more than a century ago, many of us who live there continue to be aware of the cruelties with which Highlands and Islands landlordism thus became inextricably associated. We have heard – and even at the twentieth century's close it was possible to talk to people who, when children, met with eye-witnesses of the horrors in question – how community after community was destroyed to make way for new, more lucrative, types of agriculture. We have seen the ruins of homes which were forcibly emptied in the course of that terrible time; we have walked in uninhabited glens that were once densely populated; we have had our emotions stirred by songs and poems arising from our people's dispossession and dispersal. There are few of us, as a result, without some opinion of the landlords who did so much to shape the Highlands and Islands we know today. Almost all such opinions, it must be said, are adverse.

It is important, therefore, to make clear that Highlands and Islands landlords were every bit as human as their victims. It is equally important to make the point that Highlands and Islands landlords were themselves the product – prior to their beginning to be replaced, in the nineteenth century, by landowners whose origins lay elsewhere – of the society they did so much to demolish. This made for an often overlooked degree of complexity in the way that Highlands and Islands landlords responded, during the later eighteenth century and afterwards, both to the opportunities and to the difficulties confronting them.

Something of this complexity is observable in the thought processes surrounding the adoption of a landlord's lifestyle by individuals in whom there was still to be discerned a little of a clan chief's attitudes. Not every emergent landlord was in this category, admittedly. There were chieftains or the sons of chieftains – Simon Fraser being the outstanding exemplar – who appear to have experienced absolutely no compunction about abandoning clanship's moral codes. But there were other – possibly fairly numerous – members of chieftainly families to whom the business of being a landlord was forever rendered more problematic than might otherwise have been the case by the persistence of beliefs and feelings deriving from a past that had ostensibly been set aside.

Much the most fascinating insight into such people's thinking is provided by the posthumously published *Memoirs* of Elizabeth Grant whose family's ancestral lands were located at Rothiemurchus in Strathspey and whose father, John Peter Grant, found himself, in the years around 1800, trying to play – with mixed success – the then well-understood role of an upwardly aspiring country gentleman of the type featured prominently in the novels of his daughter's contemporary, Jane Austen. At one level, the young Elizabeth Grant's existence was that of every other youthful representative of the class her father was endeavouring to join. Thus she spent a great deal of time doing fashionable things in fashionable places – Edinburgh, London, Ramsgate and the like. But what distinguished Elizabeth Grant from the Austen heroines whom she otherwise resembled was the fact that her family, not many generations back, had been clan chieftains – fairly minor chieftains maybe, but chieftains nevertheless. That clearly made it hard both for Elizabeth and for others of the Grants to treat Rothiemurchus – where people of their name had lived for several centuries – in the way they might have treated this Strathspey estate had their connections with it been of a more transient, more straightforward, nature.

She never did manage, Elizabeth Grant observed, to interest one of her aunts in 'the improvements' her father – attempting, in his own small way, to emulate Archibald Campbell's trailblazing transformation of a set of clan lands – had implemented at Rothiemurchus:

> She said it was all very proper, very necessary, very inevitable, but not agreeable. She liked the Highlands as she had known them . . . when nobody spoke English, when all young men wore the kilt, when printed calicoes had never been seen, when there was no wheaten bread to be got . . . when there was no tidy kitchen range, no kitchen even . . . It was all very correct, the increase of comfort and the gradual enlightenment etc., but it was not the Highlands.[12]

Nor was Elizabeth Grant, despite her English mother and her southern education, personally unaffected by sentiment of this sort. To Elizabeth, Rothiemurchus – where 'every face . . . met revealed a friend's' – was her 'beloved Duchus'. And in her use of that term there is much that is revealing. To the most recent editor of Elizabeth Grant's writings, *duchus* is 'a Gaelic word having much the same signification as domain'. But a domain is merely a possession, a property. And *duthchas*, as hinted earlier, had long meant something very different. It denoted the entire, multi-faceted relationship between a clan's territories and the folk residing on those territories. Formally, of course, this relationship had been ended by the various legislative enactments of the post-Culloden period and by families like the Grants having adopted land management techniques of a sort which defined them as landlords rather than clan chiefs. But their former role, as far as Rothiemurchus's proprietors were concerned, did not instantly give way to their new one. For all that John Peter Grant organised the felling of his estate's extensive woodlands in order to raise the cash needed to sustain the status to which his family – now moving in circles dominated by the south's landed gentry – aspired, Grant clearly could not rid himself completely of the conviction that Rothiemurchus, in addition to its being an asset to be developed and exploited commercially, was also a place which imposed on him and on his family all the strictly non-commercial duties and obligations bound up with what Elizabeth Grant called 'duchus'.[13]

At Rothiemurchus, in Elizabeth Grant's time, there was constructed a home which subsequently became ruinous and which the present-day Grant family, who live in that same home, have partly restored. In comparison with the dwellings which the generality of Strathspey folk occupied in Elizabeth Grant's day, this home, when first built, was both large and imposing. In comparison with the houses erected to accommodate those more substantial Highlands and Islands landlords whose territories far exceeded the relatively limited acreages available to Rothiemurchus's lairds, however, this Grant home was notably modest – just how modest being apparent when it is contrasted, for example, with the quarters which Archibald Campbell, that most pivotal of eighteenth-century figures, provided for himself at Inveraray.

But if Inveraray Castle – a towered and turreted residence on a truly gigantic scale – is an enduring memorial to landlords whose regard for themselves could scarcely have been greater, it ought not to be assumed that such landlords expected the Highlands and Islands' future to be given over entirely to their glorification. While Archibald Campbell and his immediate successors certainly anticipated further increases in the revenues flowing into their Inveraray coffers, later-eighteenth-century dukes of Argyll – together with many of those other Highlands and Islands landlords who then looked to the Campbells for signals as to what policy stances they ought to be adopting – would have been most aggrieved, and with some justification, had they thought posterity would accuse them of being motivated by nothing other than personal gain.

The second half of the eighteenth century, both in the Scottish Lowlands and in much of England, was one characterised by breakneck economic growth stemming, as already indicated, from the world's first industrial revolution. The dukes of Argyll, together with Highlands and Islands landlords more generally, very much wanted their part of Britain to share in that growth and, in consequence, did everything they could to foster the region's overall development. To be a Highlands and Islands landlord in the later eighteenth century was thus to be committed to what was then called – by Elizabeth Grant among others – 'improvement'. And to be committed to improvement, as far as Highlands and Islands landlords were concerned, was very definitely to favour progress of every sort. Although the progress in question certainly involved changes of a kind intended to profit the landlords who were improvement's most enthusiastic advocates, the wider population of the Highlands and Islands, such landlords argued, also gained from what they, the region's landed proprietors, were about. This was because the total improvement package provided, in theory at least, for enhanced spending on infrastructure projects – roads, bridges and the like – from which all Highlands and Islands residents, improvers said, derived some advantage. In improvement, therefore, men like the dukes of Argyll discovered – and eagerly embraced – a set of ideas which arguably served to absolve them from some at least of such guilt feelings as they might have experienced on their having given up being chiefs. Protection and security of the kind his ancestors had once extended to their clansfolk might no longer be on offer from Inveraray Castle's ducal occupant. But by the dukes of Argyll and by numerous lesser landlords, the people of the Highlands and Islands would – to their own advantage – be shepherded into a new, more prosperous, social order.

So Highlands and Islands landlords claimed, at all events. And in so claiming they were at one with the United Kingdom government which, having instigated so much repression in the course of the British army's post-Culloden occupation of the region, was very much in the market for alternative – and somewhat more positive – ways of convincing the people of the Highlands and Islands that the British state's growing involvement in their affairs need not invariably work to their disadvantage.

Collaboration between the United Kingdom government and Highlands and Islands landlords was fostered by the emergence of semi-official bodies in which leading Highlands and Islands estate owners were often involved. Those bodies anticipated, in some respects, the public sector development agencies of more recent times. And their objectives were by no means ignoble in conception. Eighteenth-century improvers envisaged, for instance, the further expansion of the Highlands and Islands road network on which the military had been labouring for some time. They envisaged also the provision of strategically located canals, the establishment of harbours, the construction of towns and villages, the launch of new industries and the teaching of new skills.

Thus summarised, the Highlands and Islands development programme which took shape during the eighteenth century's second half may seem excessively, even crazily, ambitious. But this was a period when – to apply John Home's words in an economic, as opposed to a military, context – almost nothing seemed impossible; a period when Britain's ruling élite considered themselves equal to any challenge; a period when Highlands and Islands landlords, as recently recognised members of that élite, were understandably determined to make their own distinctive contribution to the unending success story, as it then appeared, that was the United Kingdom.

Much, in fact, was achieved. Just a mile or two from Inveraray Castle is the little town with which the castle shares its name. An attractive place of wide streets and spacious prospects, Inveraray was laid out by eighteenth-century dukes of Argyll. And there are lots of other Highlands and Islands population centres which could boast – if they so chose – a very similar pedigree. Sometimes those centres, as in Inveraray's case, were the work of individual landowners. Sometimes they were created by partnerships in which both landlords and government had a hand. But almost always they were imaginatively conceived and well designed. That much emerges from a stroll around a representative sample: Grantown-on-Spey to the south of Inverness; Bowmore or Port Charlotte on Islay; Tobermory on Mull; Ullapool in Wester Ross; Bonar Bridge and Lochinver in Sutherland; Thurso in Caithness. Some such towns and villages were founded, in the later eighteenth century, on what were then entirely vacant sites. Others were grafted on to earlier settlements. But all of them owe a great deal of their present-day shape – and a pleasing shape it usually is – to the eighteenth-century lairds who had such a key role in their planning.

The origins of a good deal of the modern communications system of the Highlands and Islands can also be traced to this era of state-aided, but usually landlord-driven, improvement. Roads were built to places which had previously been roadless; rivers were bridged; the opening of the Crinan Canal enabled seagoing vessels to get from the Firth of Clyde to the Hebrides without having to round the Mull of Kintyre; the construction of the Caledonian Canal made it possible for ships to sail through the Great Glen from Fort William to Inverness. And as a result of the enhanced business opportunities which its merchants and traders derived from the Highlands and Islands having thus been made more accessible, Inverness itself began to be extensively reconstructed. Described in 1769 as 'large', 'well built' and 'very populous', the town, by the eighteenth century's end, had ceased to be the congested medieval community described earlier and had begun to acquire its modern appearance.[14]

Of the industries then being established in more southern parts of Britain, admittedly, there were few traces in the eighteenth-century Highlands and Islands. Attempts were made to provide the region with a manufacturing sector. But for locational and other reasons those attempts largely foundered. And in this failure there can be discerned the root causes of some of the structural weaknesses from which the Highlands and Islands economy has arguably suffered ever since. In the later eighteenth century, however, those weaknesses were less apparent than they seem in retrospect. Then the Highlands and Islands economy, just like the economy of the rest of the United Kingdom, looked set to expand indefinitely. Lead began to be mined in Strontian; slate began to be quarried in Ballachullish and Easdale; huge tonnages of timber, as Elizabeth Grant's *Memoirs* make clear, began to be floated down the Spey and other rivers; whisky, which had been distilled here and there in the Highlands and Islands for several hundred years, began to be produced in larger and larger quantities.

Although generally considered by its eager consumers in the south to be superior to the spirits produced in city distilleries, whisky of the Highlands and Islands sort was usually turned out in defiance of laws which had been enacted with a view to safeguarding the interests of urban producers. Those laws made it illegal to operate farm-based stills of the type on which the Highlands and Islands industry mostly depended. But for all that lots of such stills were confiscated and smashed by the customs officers who became locked in an unceasing – and occasionally violent – struggle with Highlands and Islands whisky-makers, the latter, throughout the eighteenth century anyway, were very much in the ascendant. This was possibly no bad thing. Being primarily dependent on barley – traditionally the region's staple crop – and being a high-value commodity which could be produced on a small scale with easily acquired equipment, whisky-making, as conducted in much of the eighteenth-century Highlands and Islands, was a highly efficient means of extracting a worthwhile financial return from the region's relatively limited agricultural resources.

Much the same was true of the still more rapidly expanding trade in cattle. This trade's beginnings can be traced to the sixteenth century when sizeable numbers of young cattle were first driven south from the Highlands and Islands each autumn – with a view to their being fattened and slaughtered in the Lowlands. But it was during the eighteenth century that demand for Highlands and Islands cattle really started to expand – the Anglo-Scottish union of 1707 having opened up the English market at a point when a speedily industrialising, and speedily urbanising, England required huge quantities of beef as well as hides and other products of that kind.

The drovers who organised the cattle trade, and who came mostly from the Highlands and Islands, seemed, to the southerners with whom they dealt, decidedly unprepossessing: 'great, stalwart, hirsute men'; 'shaggy and uncultured and wild'; 'dressed usually in home-spun tweeds which smelt of heather and peat smoke'. But for all their rough and ready appearance, drovers were men to be reckoned with. Like the nineteenth-century American cowboys – themselves, very often, of Highlands and Islands extraction – whose job it was to get millions of cattle annually out of localities like Texas and Montana, eighteenth-century drovers typically combined immense physical stamina with entrepreneurial abilities of an extremely high order. Travelling to the Hebrides, Orkney, Caithness, Sutherland, Wester Ross or Argyll in the late summer, drovers bought batch after batch of cattle from their producers; shipping those cattle, where necessary, across wider sea passages like the Minch and the Pentland Firth; swimming herds across narrower straits and inlets like Kylerhea and Loch Leven; driving thousands of animals through the glens and passes which eventually gave access to the great trysts, or fairs, held every September and October in Lowland centres like Crieff and Falkirk; spending, in some instances, a good deal of their profits there on the drink, prostitutes and other attractions with which, at that time of year, both Crieff and Falkirk were, it seems, awash.[15]

The various pressures exerted by the droving business on its Highlands and Islands suppliers had the effect of commercialising a farming structure which had previously been geared largely towards subsistence. Although cows had been kept in the region since neolithic times, their customary role had been to supply Highlands and Islands families with milk, butter, cheese and, on occasion, meat. By the eighteenth century's close, however, the overwhelming bulk of the region's cattle was being sold for cash to men who promptly conveyed them to distant markets. Huge amounts of barley, in the form of whisky, were being exported in much the same way. It was inevitable in these circumstances – a money-based agriculture being an entirely different proposition from one dealing in foodstuffs for local consumption – that there would be changes in the way Highlands and Islands farming was organised.

Promoting just such changes, in fact, was accorded the highest possible priority by improving landlords of the sort mentioned earlier. Not least because they spent a good deal of time in the south, such men were well aware of the way the entire fabric of the Lowland and English countryside was unpicked and remade, in the course of the eighteenth century, as a result of developments which, in due course, were collectively entitled an agricultural revolution. As that revolution's highly positive impact on southern farmland's productivity became steadily more apparent, landowners in the Highlands and Islands were naturally seized with an ambition to have their estates subjected to a similar makeover.

This was most feasible in those districts possessing comparatively generous acreages, by Highlands and Islands standards, of arable land. Among such districts were and are: Bute; parts of Arran; much of Kintyre; parts of mid-Argyll; parts of Islay; the Moray coastal plain; Easter Ross; the south-easterly corner of Sutherland; the north-easterly corner of Caithness; much of Orkney. As continues to be evident from their differing appearances, not all those areas were to evolve agriculturally in the same direction. Nor were their older farming systems to pass away at anything like the same rate – Orkney's agricultural revolution, for example, being delayed until the later nineteenth century. But it is nevertheless the case that all the localities listed above were sooner or later equipped with 'improved' farming systems which resulted in the localities in question taking on some of the attributes of more southerly, or more easterly, country-sides – Highlands and Islands improvement being modelled on Low-land experience. Thus Bute, the southern segment of Arran, Kintyre, much of mid-Argyll and a fair slice of Islay have today a little of the look of Ayrshire. As for the lower-lying parts of Caithness and the rest of the easterly coastal zone stretching south through Sutherland to Inverness and beyond, this extensive tract of relatively fertile territory, as far as its modern land use is concerned, has more in common with Aberdeenshire, Angus and the Lothians than it has with the hillier and harder terrain which commences on its western borders and which stretches all the way to the Atlantic. It is on the Atlantic littoral, of course, as well as in the Hebrides and in Shetland, that there is most readily to be encountered the one type of agricul-ture, namely crofting, which is unique to the modern Highlands and Islands. But it might be as well, for the moment, to put crofting aside and to highlight, by way of illustrating how the non-crofting areas of the Highlands and Islands acquired their present-day appearance, the remarkable changes which occurred during the second half of the eighteenth century in Easter Ross – defined here as the part of the mainland Highlands (including the Black Isle) bounded on the north by the Dornoch Firth, on the east by the North Sea, in the south by the Beauly Firth and on the west by mountains like Ben Wyvis.

Like the rest of the Highlands and Islands, Easter Ross, during the seventeenth century, had been minutely divided into thousands of rigs of the sort described earlier – such rigs being worked by tenants residing in traditionally laid-out townships and owing allegiance to tacksmen who, in turn, were answerable to the several notables from whom such tacksmen received their tacks. The higher than average quality of its soils, admittedly, had long made Easter Ross a little bit exceptional. Hence the district's attractiveness to fifteenth-century Lords of the Isles. Hence, too, its ability, even in the pre-improvement era, to export considerable quantities of grain. But Easter Ross's pre-improvement yields of cereals, although substantial by contemporary criteria, were as nothing to the yields obtained as a result of what was accomplished here in the course of the eighteenth century. Prior to that century's end, tacksmen, townships and virtually every other attribute of the previous tenurial system – including Easter Ross's innumerable rigs – had been removed as totally as if they had never been. Dominating the new landscape which had thus been conjured into existence were features of the sort one still sees on driving from Fortrose, say, by way of Dingwall, to Invergordon and points north: wide, carefully planned and tidily enclosed fields; commodious, stone-built, comfortable-looking farmhouses. Presiding over those fields and occupying those farmhouses, as the eighteenth century moved towards its close, were men who had worked miracles: men who had supervised the levelling of countless rigs; men who had organised the planting of enormous lengths of hedge, the building of mile after mile of boundary wall, the installation of entire drainage networks; men who, in lots of instances, had made crops grow where neither crops, nor anything else of consequence, had ever grown before.

To glimpse something of the sheer scale of what was undertaken in eighteenth-century Easter Ross, it is necessary only to inspect the unusually flat – though nowadays silo-studded – area immediately to the north of the Bay of Nigg. This area is overlooked by a hill which rises behind Pitcalnie. If you were to climb that hill in summer, as I have done, and if – gazing across the prairie-like expanse of barley growing down below – you were to reflect on the effort required to carve such highly productive farmland out of what was earlier thought 'a morass', then you would begin to understand why I have nothing but admiration for the almost incredible achievements of Easter Ross's eighteenth-century agriculturalists.[16]

If, as has been implied, so much that was estimable was accomplished in Easter Ross and in the rest of the Highlands and Islands during the eighteenth century's closing decades, then why, to return to an issue raised on this chapter's opening page, was the same period characterised by an unprecedented outpouring of emigrants from the region? A part of the answer to that question, as it happens, is to be found in comments made, in the eighteenth century and in the nineteenth, about the homes in which Easter Ross people were then living. Those homes included the farmhouses which have already been mentioned. But they included, too, a wholly different set of dwellings: dwellings occupied by the men and women Easter Ross farmers employed to cultivate their land; dwellings which were 'pictures', as one shocked observer put it, 'of damp, filth, stench and putridity'.[17]

As such remarks serve to underline, improvement, despite the many material gains made by its beneficiaries, was not without its downside. While there were some folk – the residents of newly constructed Easter Ross farmhouses prominent among them – who profited hugely from the agrarian reforms which Highlands and Islands landlords implemented so extensively in the eighteenth century's second half, there were others whose position, as a result of exactly the same reforms, was made worse instead of better.

When Easter Ross agriculture had been organised on a runrig basis, its output may not have been nearly so high as that output afterwards became. But runrig had given thousands of families a permanent stake, as it seemed, in the land. It had enabled those families to provide for themselves from their own resources. And it had underpinned a society which, for all its material inequalities, was united, cohesive, at one with itself.

The social order which took shape in eighteenth-century Easter Ross lacked all such characteristics. In part, this was a consequence of the district's farmers having ceased to be drawn, in the previously standard manner, from within its boundaries. Some of Easter Ross's new-style agriculturalists, to be sure, had been born and bred there. But many had not – Easter Ross landlords, with a view to fostering the southern land management methods they so much favoured, having persuaded Lowland farmers to migrate to the area in much the same way as the Campbells had earlier persuaded other Lowland farmers to move into Kintyre. All such influxes of population produce tensions. In the Easter Ross case, those tensions were aggravated by the fact that farm tenancies of the improved type were necessarily far fewer in number than tenancies of the runrig sort – dozens of runrig tenants having been able to make some sort of living from lands which, with the beginning of improvement, became a single holding. Improvement, therefore, quickly resulted in hundreds, indeed thousands, of men – together with their families – finding themselves, as it were, cast adrift. Some of those former tenants, abandoning hope of ever again being farmers in their own right, became the poorly paid – and inevitably resentful – employees of the men who had taken their place. Others decided to try their luck in faraway localities like North Carolina where, it was widely reported, there was land to be got, more or less, for the asking. And in view of how little was on offer, either by way of a home or a wage, to the folk expected to provide Easter Ross's new farming class with its workforce, one can readily understand the attraction, to these folk, of the North Carolina option.

Nor was emigration something that appealed only in the particular circumstances produced by Easter Ross's agricultural revolution. Similar upheavals, as already indicated, were occurring, or were shortly to occur, in many other parts of the Highlands and Islands – in Moray and in Caithness, for example. And even in areas where there was little or no chance of establishing a high-yielding arable agriculture of the Easter Ross type, lots of stresses and strains were being produced as a result of landlord after landlord adopting estate management techniques of the sort pioneered by the dukes of Argyll. In hill and upland localities which were given over mostly to stock-rearing, the consequences of this development were less immediately obvious than they were in Easter Ross and other lower-lying districts. But for all that much of the eighteenth-century Highlands and Islands looked to be sticking with age-old farming practices, such as those involving township residents in regular treks to and from their shielings, the tenurial frameworks within which such farming was conducted were being altered markedly. As commercialised estate management took hold across the region, tacksmen were everywhere obliged to pay far more than formerly for their tacks. Sometimes, in fact, they were removed entirely – either to make way for new men from the south or because landlords now found it expedient, tacksmen's military functions having been made redundant by clanship's demise, to deal directly with folk who had previously been tacksmen subtenants. All such developments were unsettling. They were made more unsettling by their resulting in money rents – whether payable directly to the landlord or to a superior tenant – replacing the food renders which tacksmen had once collected on behalf of clan chiefs.

In the decades following the Battle of Culloden, therefore, more and more cash had to be found by the occupants of the typical Highlands and Islands township. And while that cash was fairly readily available in the form of revenues generated by the expanding trade in cattle and the equally buoyant market in whisky, township residents nevertheless resented what was happening to them. They blamed, naturally enough, the people to whom they were obliged to hand over an ever expanding slice of their agricultural, and other, earnings.

In those circumstances, the respect, even affection, which the Gaelic-speaking folk of the Highlands and Islands had previously felt for their social superiors ceased rapidly to count for a great deal. The English author, Samuel Johnson, who famously journeyed to the Hebrides in 1773, noted as much. 'Their chiefs,' Johnson wrote at the conclusion of his extensive travels in the Highlands and Islands, 'have already lost much of their influence; and as they gradually degenerate from patriarchal rulers to rapacious landlords, they will divest themselves of the little that remains.'[18]

To read the Gaelic poetry of this same period is to discover sentiments which accord exactly with Samuel Johnson's verdict. The average clan chieftain, whatever his faults and foibles, had been his clansfolk's protector. In his new role of landlord, however, such a man seemed simply parasitic: extracting higher and higher rents; providing, or so his tenants reckoned, nothing in return.

'The warrior chiefs are gone . . . who had regard for their faithful followers,' an eighteenth-century bard observed:

> Look around you and see the nobility without pity for poor folk, without kindness to friends; they are of the opinion that you do not belong to the soil and, though they have left you destitute, they cannot see it as a loss.[19]

That poet, for one, was in no doubt as to how the people of the Highlands and Islands should respond to their new situation:

> Depart now, my lads, to a country without want . . . to the country of milk, to the country of honey, to a country where you may buy land to your will.[20]

The country in question, of course, was North America, a place which another bard – a man who was to settle in North Carolina's Cape Fear River country – envisaged in even more glowing terms:

> Let us go and may God's blessing be with us. Let us go and charter a vessel. Better that than to remain under landlords who . . . would prefer gold to a brave man . . . We shall all go together . . . to where we shall find game of every kind, the most beautiful game to be seen. We shall get deer, buck and doe, and the right to take as many as we wish. We shall get

> woodcock and woodhen, teals, duck and wild geese. We shall get salmon . . . and white fish if it pleases us better. Imagine how prosperous they are over yonder; even every herdsman has his horse.[21]

More frequently than might be imagined, eighteenth-century emigrants from the Highlands and Islands were able to make such American dreams come true. North Carolina was 'the best poor man's country I have heard in this age', according to one such emigrant – who, despite arriving in the vicinity of the Cape Fear River with almost no capital to his name, quickly became a businessman on a substantial scale. 'You would do well to advise . . . people . . . to take courage and come to this country,' that same emigrant, Neil MacArthur, informed a kinsman still in Scotland. Were his relatives to remain in the Highlands and Islands, MacArthur asserted, they would be forever trapped in a place where 'the landlord will sure be master' and where 'the face of the poor is kept to the grinding stone'.[22]

Thus there was fuelled the 'epidemical fury of emigration' witnessed by Samuel Johnson in the course of his 1773 excursion to the Highlands and Islands. On occasion, such emigration was organised by displaced and disenchanted tacksmen who, drawing on longstanding leadership skills, chartered ships and organised the exodus of entire communities. But whether particular departures were of this wholesale nature or whether they involved no more than one or two family groups, there could be no doubting North America's growing allure. 'The idea of going to that country is at present a sort of madness among the common people,' one estate manager reported from Sutherland in 1772. And though accurate statistics are lacking, it is clear that, both from Sutherland and from much of the rest of the Highlands and Islands, thousands of folk were then leaving annually for this fabled continent whose inhabitants 'were not troubled with landlords' and where 'there was no rent paid'.[23]

There were few if any Shetlanders among the many people who left the eighteenth-century Highlands and Islands with a view to getting away, as one set of emigrants commented, from 'high rents and oppression'. But it is to Shetland that one needs to look, all the same, to see something of eighteenth-century Highlands and Islands landlordism at its most manipulative – the manipulation in question being all the more significant, in an overall Highlands and Islands context, because of the manner in which it gave an early indication of how the inhabitants of much of the rest of the Highlands and Islands were to be treated in the period ahead.[24]

On the Highland mainland and in the Hebrides, as already indicated, eighteenth-century landlords derived rental incomes from agricultural tenants whose own incomes depended – whether by way of improved farming or the cattle trade – on the crops they grew and the livestock they reared. Shetland's eighteenth-century landlords, however, confronted an entirely different situation. Since it was then impossible to ship live cattle from Shetland to the Scottish mainland, and since Shetland had little land of the type needed to sustain improved farming of the Easter Ross variety, eighteenth-century Shetland's landowners could not obtain worthwhile revenues from their estates if those estates were left in the occupation of tenants relying entirely on the land for their livelihoods. Hence the adoption by Shetland landlords of estate management practices intended to turn Shetlanders, whether willingly or not, into fishermen.

As modern archaeological excavations have demonstrated, and as might anyway have been expected, Shetland's earliest inhabitants, like most subsequent Shetlanders, depended on the sea for some part of their diet. But the export of fish from Shetland to other places – something which requires more organisation than taking fish for consumption in Shetland itself – began comparatively recently. The island group's fishing industry, in this more specialised and more modern sense, originated in the fifteenth and sixteenth centuries. The industry's founders, it appears, were seaborne merchants sailing out of German towns like Bremen and Hamburg.

The Bremeners and Hamburgers who came each year to Shetland in the 1400s and subsequently were Shetland people's principal source of such goods as they could not produce locally. In order to obtain such goods, Shetlanders had to supply their German visitors with commodities the latter could afterwards sell at a profit back in Germany. Looming large among the commodities in question were the hides or skins of cattle, sheep and seals. But also playing a part – a part which grew gradually larger – were quantities of dried fish.

German dominance of the continental market for Shetland fish – a market of growing significance by the end of the sixteenth century – was eventually challenged by the Dutch who succeeded in gaining more direct access to Shetland fish stocks than Bremeners and Hamburgers had managed. This access was obtained by way of factory ships known as *busses* – large vessels whose crews could both net substantial catches and preserve those catches by means of on-board curing. Although the Dutch, by virtue of their being their own catchers, did little to encourage the active involvement of Shetlanders in Shetland's fishing industry, they helped – because of the number of busses sailing north each year – to foster the emergence of a money-based economy in an island group which, like the Highlands and Islands more generally, had not previously possessed much in the way of cash. Among the more immediate consequences of this development was the appearance, at the beginning of the seventeenth century, of a whole new trading centre.

In Norse times and later, Shetland's administrative capital was Scalloway – its medieval prominence still signalled by its massive, if now ruined, castle. Scalloway, as might be expected of a formerly Viking settlement, possesses a good harbour. But that harbour is on Shetland's Atlantic coast. And because they fished mostly on the other side of the islands, Dutch skippers were in the habit, by 1600, of rendezvousing each spring in Bressay Sound – the North Sea inlet where, in 1263, Norway's King Hakon moored his fleet before sailing on to Orkney, the Hebrides and Largs.

The regular presence of hundreds, even thousands, of Dutch fishermen in Bressay Sound created all sorts of commercial opportunities. Those resulted in an array of temporary huts or booths springing up along the sound's western shore. Permanent buildings followed. And by 1615 – when it was reported to have become a notorious haunt of 'villanie, fornicatioun and adulterie' – Lerwick, as this new community became known, was securely launched on its long career of servicing the innumerable mariners who have found themselves, as the crews of oil-industry supply boats still find themselves, idly perambulating the town's narrow and winding streets.[25]

At an early point in its development, Lerwick's expansion, together with the growth of the wider Shetland economy, was endangered by fiscal and other changes associated with the Anglo-Scottish union of 1707. Those changes had the effect of making it harder and harder for continental fishermen and merchants – from Holland, Germany and elsewhere – to maintain links with Shetland. Something of an economic vacuum consequently ensued. Into this vacuum, in the eighteenth century, there stepped Shetland's lairds. In contrast to their counterparts in Gaelic-speaking parts of the Highlands and Islands, those lairds, as indicated earlier, were in no way a product of clanship. Indeed they were the inheritors, though not necessarily the direct descendants, of the immigrant Lowlanders who, by engineering the overthrow of Earl Patrick Stewart, played a prominent part in ridding both Shetland and Orkney of the second of the only two individuals (the other being Earl Patrick's father) among the post-Norse rulers of the Northern Isles who came close to assuming roles of the kind occupied elsewhere in the Highlands and Islands by clan chiefs. But for all that the pedigrees of the two groups were thus as divergent as they could be, Shetland's lairds had much in common, by the eighteenth century, with the landlords then emerging in mainland localities such as Argyll and Easter Ross. Like those landlords, Shetland lairds were motivated primarily by a wish to add to their incomes. And in continental Europe's continuing desire to have regular supplies of Shetland fish, the island group's landed proprietors scented an opportunity to access revenues of a kind they never could have accessed had they not thus begun to take an interest in Shetland's marine resources.

Although Shetlanders nowadays own some of the world's most expensive and sophisticated fishing craft, eighteenth-century Shetland, as its lairds were well aware, possessed neither the capital nor the technical skills which had enabled Holland to deploy its fleets of busses. If a locally-based fishing industry was to be developed in eighteenth-century Shetland, therefore, that industry, island lairds reckoned, would have to rely on cheaply constructed boats and on inexpensive equipment. Both those requirements were readily met: boats in the shape of undecked craft called fourerns and sixerns; gear in the form of multi-hooked long lines.

Fourerns and sixerns, as their names suggest, were powered by oars – four in the case of the former, six for the latter. The fourern, being smaller, was strictly an inshore vessel. The bigger sixern, however, could be taken much further out to sea. By the middle years of the eighteenth century, in fact, it was common for sixern crews to venture thirty, forty or fifty miles into the Atlantic. There, on the edge of the continental shelf, those crews – shooting lines which were hundreds of fathoms in length – could, and did, take substantial catches of the ling on which, by this stage, Shetland's fishing industry was largely reliant.

This ling-based fishery was known, in Shetland's Scots-derived but Norse-influenced dialect, as the *haaf* – a term denoting the open ocean. And to be involved in the haaf, for reasons implicit in the previous paragraph's account of it, was to be involved in a necessarily arduous and dangerous activity.

Haaf fishermen faced regular round trips of up to one hundred miles in seas which are as hazardous as any on earth. Since those trips were made in open boats, and since waterproof oilskins and seaboots were not easily to be got until the later nineteenth century, haaf fishermen were frequently wet, cold and uncomfortable. Navigating, as their Viking forebears had done, by sun, by star and by the 'feel' of the ocean itself, a haaf crew, once Shetland's hills had dropped below the eastern horizon, ran a very real risk – especially when a deterioration in the weather was accompanied by mist and fog – of never finding their way back to land. They ran the further risk of falling victim to the swamping effect of a sudden gale and a steeply rising sea. Despite the haaf being confined to summer months, when hours of daylight were long and when storms were less frequent than at other times of year, deaths and disasters were unavoidable – whole communities sometimes losing the bulk of their menfolk.

Nor were conditions at the haaf's shore bases markedly superior to those at sea. Because it made sense to minimise the time it took to get a sixern to the fishing grounds, the fishing stations established in association with the haaf were often located far from fishermen's homes – on shores that might, in fact, be several miles from permanent habitation of any kind. What such a station ideally required was a steeply shelving gravel beach on to which an inbound sixern could easily be run and on which that sixern's catch of ling – once each fish had been split and gutted – could be laid out to dry during the bright and breezy days which constitute the better sort of Shetland summer. What such a station did not require – and what it was consequently not provided with – were living quarters that were anything other than rudimentary.

In an attempt to get some small insight into the life of a haaf fisherman, I have taken time – in the course of visits to Shetland – to drive north out of Lerwick on the road that leads either to Northmavine, the north-western corner of Shetland's Mainland, or to the North Isles of Yell and Unst. Once in those places – around Gloup, South Ladie or Hamnavoe, perhaps – I have walked on ocean shores and tried to imagine such shores as they would have looked in the time of the haaf: the long, low sixerns pulled beyond the waves in the manner of the Viking longships which were those same sixerns' forerunners; the stinking heaps of fishguts being ravaged constantly by screaming, screeching gulls; the rows and rows of regularly turned ling destined, courtesy of cargo vessels sailing out of Lerwick, for distant dinner tables; the cluttered huts, hovels really, standing on each beach's landward fringe and accommodating, as well as sixern crews, the children, women and old folk whose job it was to clean such a fishing station's catch.

Why did eighteenth-century Shetlanders, without whom there would have been no haaf fishery, do what they did? Why did they undertake their annual migrations – often from comparatively comfortable homesteads – to those miserable encampments on the edge of the sea? Why did they repeatedly put themselves in such jeopardy by taking to that same sea in the flimsiest of craft?

The answers to such questions are most emphatically not to be found in fishermen's earnings. Those were extremely meagre. And such financial returns as accrued to the haaf's onshore workforce were, if anything, more slender still.

What actually underpinned the haaf, transforming it eventually into the mainstay of the entire Shetland economy, was a rigorously enforced and cleverly contrived system of compulsion devised by the lairds who were the haaf's real beneficiaries. Families who were their tenants, those lairds decreed, would have their tenancies terminated if they did not agree, first, to participate in the haaf and, second, to sell their catches exclusively to their landlords. By those means, Shetland lairds simultaneously made themselves the monopoly suppliers of a valuable commodity and secured the labour required to get that commodity into a marketable shape.

Eighteenth-century Shetlanders might have indulged, as contemporaries reported, in 'vast grumblings' about their having been transformed into 'the greatest slaves in nature'. They might, in their more defiant moments, have sold a few ling to the *yaugers*, or pedlars, whose free-marketeering activities Shetland lairds never quite managed to suppress. They might even have carried this carefully calculated rebelliousness to the length of deliberately damaging boats or otherwise engaging in the sabotage, go-slows and obstructionism which, as was acknowledged at the time, occasionally got in the way of an effective haaf fishery. But the haaf, all the same, had Shetlanders in its grip. And with Shetland lairds making refinement after refinement to the coercive techniques at their disposal, that grip grew more and more inescapable.[26]

It was important not to confuse 'the value of the estates in this country' with 'the rents payable to landlords', commented one shrewd observer of the eighteenth-century Shetland scene. What mattered was 'the fishing' which those same landlords 'obliged' their tenants 'to carry on for them'.[27]

Because his value to his laird lay in his role as a supplier of ling, the typical Shetland tenant's rent was usually low. But the extent of the land at his family's disposal, which may not have been very great to start with, was tending to become ever smaller. This was because of the haaf's impact on a tenurial system which had once featured a mix of collectively organised townships and more substantial farms – but which was increasingly characterised, as the eighteenth century wore on, by smallholdings or crofts established, in many instances, on hillsides which had previously been part of some nearby township's common pasture. From a purely agricultural point of view, those newly created crofts were hopelessly restrictive, the people occupying them finding it quite impossible to live on the produce of their tiny, and frequently infertile, fields. To feed himself and his family, therefore, a croft's tenant had to buy additional foodstuffs. To buy those foodstuffs, he needed money. This he could only obtain, in the circumstances of his place and time, by becoming a fisherman – which, of course, was what his landlord wanted and what the terms of his tenancy, in any case, insisted on.

Nor did this most ingenious double bind constitute the only source of the almost unimaginable burdens which their lairds loaded on to eighteenth-century Shetland's gradually emerging class of crofter-fishermen. Since his laird – other than when an itinerant *yauger* chanced along – constituted the only outlet for a haaf fisherman's ling, the laird could, and did, determine the price paid for fish. This price, predictably, was a small fraction of the true market value. And it was, to make matters still worse, made over to the fisherman in a manner which provided landlords with yet another source of profit. Because the crofter-fisherman, for reasons previously stated, had to purchase a range of foodstuffs, and because landlords were as quick to become monopolist storekeepers as they had been to become monopolist fish-buyers, the value which his landlord placed on his annual catch never took the shape, as far as the haaf fisherman was concerned, of hard cash. Instead this value was entered against the fisherman's name in the ledger which every Shetland estate kept for such purposes. From what the laird was thus shown to owe the fisherman, there was then deducted what the fisherman ostensibly owed the laird. This latter sum consisted, in part, of the fisherman's croft rent. But it consisted, too, of the expenditure which the fisherman had incurred on the foodstuffs and other supplies, such as fishing gear, which he could get only from the landlord's warehouse. When, at the end of all those complicated exercises in bookkeeping, the estate ledger's columns were tallied up, the result invariably demonstrated that each crofter-fisherman was due a larger sum to his landlord than his landlord was due to him. To all the other means by which Shetland's crofter-fishermen were deprived of anything approximating to freedom, there was thus added the bond of perpetual, and always increasing, indebtedness.

Towards the nineteenth century's close, British governments began belatedly to enquire into the repression and exploitation which had underpinned the haaf since its commencement. From a crofter-fisherman in Whalsay, Thomas Hutchison by name, an officially constituted tribunal was told of an occasion when, his landlord having declined to buy a consignment of fish, Hutchison decided to sell those fish elsewhere. On word of this plan reaching Whalsay's laird, the tribunal heard, one of the laird's employees was ordered to seize Hutchison's catch and to cut each fish in two – thus rendering the catch worthless. Had he or his crew received any payment in respect of their despoiled fish, Thomas Hutchison was asked. 'Not one farthing,' he replied. 'Not one mite; and we went home with tears in our eyes to think we were such servants, and could not help ourselves.'[28]

CHAPTER SEVEN

I never did witness such wretchedness

1792–1856

Prior to a more direct alternative becoming available with the 1991 opening of the Dornoch Bridge, the main route from the south to Sutherland and Caithness climbed steeply out of the Easter Ross village of Evanton, swung across the gorge of the Alness River and headed north, over the hill pass called the Struie, in the direction of Ardgay. Take a left turn off this road, some four or five miles north of Evanton, and you come, by way of Ardross, to Strathrusdale. This is a placid enough spot today. But for two or three feverish weeks in 1792, Strathrusdale's inhabitants were the organising spirits behind a protest movement which, or so it was feared by the authorities of the time, showed signs of developing into a Highlands and Islands revolution.

Near Ardross, anyone approaching Strathrusdale crosses the readily visible divide between Easter Ross's intensively cultivated fields – fields dating, as mentioned earlier, from the eighteenth century – and a more intractable, more mountainous, countryside. Despite its being located in this tougher terrain, Strathrusdale possesses – as all such settlements originally had to possess – a small tract of potentially arable land. But that land, mostly in permanent pasture nowadays, is unlikely ever to have yielded an abundance of crops. On looking into the basin-like valley of Strathrusdale from the east, it is easy to see, therefore, why the families living here in the 1790s were among the many Highlands and Islands folk then relying on cattle to provide them with incomes sufficient to meet the period's ever-higher rent demands.

Each May and June, Strathrusdale's cattle were driven, in the standard Highlands and Islands manner, into the hills which enclose the strath to the south, west and north. Westwards and northwards – along the line of a broiling stream named Abhainn Glac an t-Seilich – the Strathrusdale people, in the summer of 1792 as in hundreds of previous summers, could move their herds as they saw fit. Southwards, however, matters had been difficult for some months and, that summer, were becoming more difficult still. But it was southwards – or so it seems to me when I walk in this direction – that Strathrusdale's residents would most have wanted to drive their beasts. Here a gently rising pass leads to Loch Bad a' Bhathaich, a smallish body of water which is partly enclosed today by forestry plantations but which, a couple of hundred years ago, would have been encircled by reasonable grazings. Beyond Loch Bad a' Bhathaich, moreover, is a further expanse of grass which would have tended to draw Strathrusdale's cattle onwards until, somewhere on the slopes of a hill called Leathad Riabhach, those cattle moved beyond their owners' ill-defined boundaries.

From high on Leathad Riabhach's western flank, a walker – following in the footsteps, as it were, of Strathrusdale's herds – is presented with a panoramic view of the surprisingly large, but little visited, loch constituting the headwaters of the Alness River. At that loch's western extremity is a wide expanse of flat and cultivable land. Here are the ruins of an ancient church which, before the reformation, was dedicated to the Virgin Mary and which was consequently known in Gaelic as *Cille Mhuire.** Around that church there once clustered a township of the same name – a name which, by the eighteenth century, had begun to be anglicised to Kildermorie. Not much trace of this township can be found today. That is because it ceased to exist in 1791 when Kildermorie's landlord, Sir Hector Munro of Novar, having first ejected most of Kildermorie's previous tenants from a place their ancestors may have occupied since Cille Mhuire was built, rented both the township and its hill grazings to two sheep-farmer brothers, Allan and Alexander Cameron.

Between the Camerons and Strathrusdale's occupants there was bad blood from the outset. The Strathrusdale folk, fearing they might soon suffer the same fate as Kildermorie's people, naturally viewed their new neighbours with some animosity. That animosity was intensified by the Cameron brothers' habit of having their shepherds impound such Strathrusdale cattle as were judged to have strayed into Kildermorie territory. This, from a Strathrusdale standpoint, was bad enough. What made the Camerons' conduct still harder to bear, however, was their insistence on holding impounded animals until the Strathrusdale tenantry handed over cash payments or 'fines' – those being intended, the Camerons said, to compensate them for damage done by Strathrusdale's cattle to their grazings.

---

* Meaning Mary's church.

There were several such incidents in the course of 1791. But in June 1792, when a Strathrusdale herd – no doubt searching out the first flush of summer green on Leathad Riabhach – was again seized by the Camerons, the men of Strathrusdale declared their patience at an end. They would pay no more fines, they insisted. Instead they would go *en masse* to Kildermorie to repossess their cattle – forcibly if necessary.

To this pronouncement, Allan Cameron responded in kind. According to the legal documentation which the Kildermorie dispute was shortly to generate, he armed himself with a dagger and a gun and let it be known that, should the Strathrusdale folk actually descend on his farm, 'he would shoot them like birds'. Any survivors, Cameron added, would doubtless be transported 'to Botany Bay' – the Australian penal colony which Britain had established four years before.[1]

Those threats backfired badly when the Strathrusdale people, having recruited some additional manpower in Ardross, and having come as promised to Kildermorie, disarmed and beat up Allan Cameron – prior to triumphantly taking charge of their impounded cattle.

The law, at this point, intervened on the side of Kildermorie's sheep-farmers and their landlord. But the authorities – predictably – found it impossible to obtain the evidence needed for a formal prosecution of the individuals responsible for the assault on Allan Cameron. On a date being fixed for witnesses to make statements about what they knew of that assault and the events surrounding it, the witnesses in question simply failed to put in an appearance.

That was on Wednesday, 25 July. On the following Friday, as it happened, there was a wedding in Strathrusdale. To that wedding people came, as was the custom, from a wide area. Much of their conversation, over food and drink, was – naturally enough – of recent events. In the course of this conversation, it was afterwards reported, there was broached the possibility of broadening the campaign which had been launched so successfully at Kildermorie.

Allan and Alexander Cameron had been taught a lesson, it was believed by Strathrusdale's wedding guests. But what of the other sheep-farmers who had recently been acquiring land elsewhere in Easter Ross as well as in Strathoykel – the immediately adjacent part of Sutherland? And what of the further sheep-farmers who were doubtless contemplating a move north? The time had come, it was concluded, for the people of Easter Ross and Sutherland to eradicate sheep-farming from their area. There could be no more effective way of attaining this objective, it was agreed at Strathrusdale's 25 July wedding, than to get rid of the animals on which such sheep-farming ultimately depended.

On Sunday, 29 July, in a move which testifies to a good deal of organising ability on the part of the Strathrusdale people and their growing band of supporters, a proclamation was accordingly read – in Gaelic, of course – outside every parish church in a district stretching from Alness, just east of Strathrusdale, to Lairg, more than thirty miles away in the central part of Sutherland. All available and able-bodied men, that proclamation urged, were to assemble on the ensuing Tuesday at Brae in Strathoykel. There they were to round up all the sheep belonging to that locality's sheep-farmers. Then they were to drive those sheep southwards – linking up, all the while, with other parties who would be conducting similar round-ups in their own vicinities – until every sheep-farmer in both Sutherland and Easter Ross had been deprived of his stock. This task would be reckoned complete, it was stated, when there were no sheep left on the northern side of the Beauly River – marking, more or less, the boundary between Ross-shire and Inverness-shire. 'The curse of the children not yet born,' it was added, 'would follow such as would not cheerfully go and banish the sheep out of the country.'[2]

On the stipulated date, 31 July, some two hundred men turned up at Brae where they promptly set to work as instructed. Soon as many as ten thousand sheep were reported to be moving out of Strathoykel, passing through Ardgay and heading for the Struie.

Also on 31 July, Easter Ross's landlords met, in a mood of some alarm, in Dingwall. Those landlords – MacKenzies, Munroes, Rosses and the like – were men whose families had been resident in the district since it had been ruled by Lords of the Isles. Indeed their grandfathers, by the grandfathers of the men gathering that same day at Brae, would have been thought to occupy leadership roles of the sort which had long enabled the Highlands and Islands aristocracy to command substantial popular followings. But social solidarity of this traditional sort had all but vanished from Easter Ross by 1792. The locality's lairds were cordially disliked by their tenants – all of whom had been subjected to repeated rent increases and many of whom had been affected adversely, even before the introduction of sheep-farming, by the various upheavals associated with improved agriculture of the type to which Easter Ross's proprietorial class had so committed itself. Members of this class, for their part, were impatient with anything that smacked of opposition to improvement. And so the Dingwall meeting of 31 July was as dismissive of Easter Ross's wider population as that population was showing itself to be of its landlords.

But there was also fear on display in Dingwall – fear discernible in a letter drafted at this get-together and afterwards despatched to government ministers in Edinburgh. All across Easter Ross, those ministers were informed by the area's landowners, 'a great number of disorderly people', by engaging in 'outrage' and 'sedition', were 'setting the laws . . . of the kingdom at defiance'. And unless troops were speedily sent north, Easter Ross's landlords warned, worse might follow: 'We are at present so completely under the heel of the populace that, should they come to burn our houses, or destroy our property . . . we are incapable of resistance.'[3]

In retrospect, such anxieties may seem wildly overstated. But the Easter Ross gentry's talk of 'revolt' and 'insurrection' appeared a lot less far-fetched in 1792 than it appears today. In France, after all, the equivalents of Highlands and Islands landlords were – that very year – being expropriated, even killed, by peasants acting with the tacit approval of the democrats who had seized power in Paris and who, in the summer of 1792, were preparing to arrest, try and ultimately execute France's king. All over Scotland, too, a similar 'spirit of revolution', as one Easter Ross landowner afterwards observed, was 'fast gaining ground' in the months preceding the Strathrusdale outbreak. An 'almost universal spirit of . . . opposition to the established government' was reported to have gripped entire communities. Effigies of leading politicians had been burned 'in almost every village in the north of Scotland' by men and women who, following French precedent, also planted so-called 'liberty trees' by way of demonstrating their conviction that they – as well as the lairds and substantial farmers then constituting the Highlands and Islands electorate – should have some say in the United Kingdom's governance.[4]

The extent to which the Strathrusdale tenantry and their allies were inspired by democratic sentiment is impossible now to gauge. That they were aware of such sentiment is highly probable, however. Among the places where liberty trees were planted at this time was Cromarty, not many miles distant from Strathrusdale. And since some of the pro-democracy publications circulating widely in Scotland during 1792 are believed to have been translated into Gaelic, at that time most Strathrusdale folk's only language, it is by no means impossible that the contents of such publications had come to local people's attention.

But the Strathrusdale episode, for all that, probably owed a good deal more to purely local concerns than it did to the Scottish people's wider – and long to be frustrated – desire for political reform. In the opinion of Lord Adam Gordon, the man responsible in 1792 for army operations in northern Scotland, this was certainly the case. The Sutherland and Easter Ross 'tumults', Gordon commented, had 'solely originated' in what he called 'a too well founded apprehension' that a growing number of landlords 'were about to let their estates to sheep-farmers'. Any such development, Gordon pointed out, was bound to result in 'the former tenantry' being 'ousted and turned adrift'. It was with a view to forestalling this eventuality, rather than out of any inherent 'disloyalty' to the British state, that the folk of Easter Ross and Sutherland, or so Lord Adam Gordon believed, acted in the way they did.[5]

Those were perceptive, almost kindly, comments. But the sympathy which Lord Adam Gordon evidently felt for the Strathrusdale protestors was wholly at odds with the inclinations of Henry Dundas, the government minister responsible for the maintenance of law and order in Scotland. Dundas, an arch-conservative, was instinctively on the side of Easter Ross's landlords and absolutely at one with their conviction that the military should at once be despatched to deal with an uprising whose leaders, it had begun to be rumoured, were buying gunpowder and arming themselves. The 'alarming outrages in Ross-shire', Dundas made clear, were to be met with 'the most vigorous and effectual measures . . . for bringing those daring offenders to punishment'. The measures in question were to include the instant deployment of troops – for it was only by such means, Dundas went on, that government could 'convince the lower class of people that they will not be suffered to continue . . . acts of violence with impunity'.[6]

On Saturday, 4 August, the promised soldiers – three companies strong – reached Dingwall. There they were met with the news that, four days after its departure from Strathoykel, the southward-moving sheep flock at the centre of the Easter Ross troubles had reached Boath, a settlement just south of Strathrusdale. An immediate descent on Boath was sanctioned by Ross-shire's sheriff who also issued an appeal to Easter Ross's property-owners to arm themselves and to join the Boath-bound military. 'It does much honour to the gentlemen of the country with what alacrity the greatest part of them within reach turned up,' the sheriff observed in the course of the report he submitted subsequently to Edinburgh. As for Strathrusdale's people and their allies, the sheriff noted, they had readily been put to flight. No effective resistance had been offered to the military. Several prisoners had been taken. Easter Ross's summer uprising had been crushed.[7]

There had been sheep in the Highlands and Islands for thousands of years before 1792. But those sheep – being of the wiry and diminutive variety which survive today mainly on St Kilda – were judged by southern buyers to be hopelessly inferior to the much larger animals, known as blackfaces and cheviots, which had been reared, for several centuries, in the England–Scotland border country. There was thus no trade in Highlands and Islands sheep to match the trade in Highlands and Islands cattle. And it was only when it was discovered, some ten or twenty years after the Battle of Culloden, that breeds of the southern sort could survive a northern winter – something previously thought unlikely – that Highlands and Islands sheep-farming began to take off commercially. This happened initially in Perthshire and Argyll where blackface flocks were introduced around 1760 – and where it first became apparent that, if sheep were to play a big part in the Highlands and Islands economy, the consequences were bound to be disruptive.

Comparatively little such disruption had been caused by the growth in demand for cattle. Those were animals which the generality of Highlands and Islands tenants had long known how to handle. And because the necessary breeding stock was already to hand, they could expand their herds without incurring much of a financial outlay.

Nothing of this applied to the rearing of blackface and cheviot sheep. This was an enterprise demanding management skills which Highlands and Islands agriculturalists did not possess. It was also an enterprise which made sense economically only if sheep were managed in batches, or hirsels, several hundred-strong. Since such hirsels had to be established from scratch, individuals wishing to get into Highlands and Islands sheep-farming – for all that it proved a highly profitable venture – had to have a great deal of capital at their disposal. Very few people in the average Highlands and Islands township were in this affluent category.

Irrespective of who took charge of a newly established sheep-farm, moreover, that farm's presence tended to spell the end of alternative forms of agriculture in its neighbourhood. This was because sheep production, as it began to be practised in the Highlands and Islands during the 1760s, was incompatible with land-use patterns of the sort characteristic of the cereals-cattle mix on which the region's rural economy had traditionally depended. In summer, to be sure, a blackface or cheviot flock could be kept on hills where cattle had formerly grazed. In autumn, winter and spring, however, that same flock – especially the younger, more vulnerable, portion of it – needed access to more sheltered, low-level pastures. These could be made available only if rigs which had hitherto been given over to grain were put permanently under grass. This is what happened at Kildermorie when Allan and Alexander Cameron moved there. It happened in hundreds of other places as well.

From the standpoint of an overwhelming majority of the Highlands and Islands population, then, there was not the slightest reason to welcome the appearance in the region of *na caoraich mora* – the phrase, meaning simply 'big sheep', which eighteenth-century Gaelic-speakers applied to the blackface and the cheviot. These were species offering most folk absolutely nothing in the way of an agricultural opportunity. What the big sheep's coming signalled, in fact, was disaster: the rapid eviction and removal of family after family; the equally rapid installation, in ejected families' place, of men who, unlike the people whose townships were thus taken over, possessed both the cash and the expertise required to make a go of sheep-farming.

Those processes became known, in time, as the Highland Clearances. Their beginnings, as already indicated, can be discerned in Argyll and Perthshire in the middle decades of the eighteenth century. Thereafter, sheep-farming's spread was general and rapid. In the course of the 1780s, when localities like Glen Moriston, Glengarry and Knoydart were first affected, clearances commenced in Inverness-shire. By 1792, as shown by the extent of that year's protests, sheep-farming was advancing across Easter Ross into Sutherland. And during the nineteenth century's opening decades, the production of blackface and cheviot sheep became the territorially dominant type of agriculture in practically every part of the Highlands and Islands – with the number of sheep in Inverness-shire, to take one example, going up from around 50,000 in 1800 to nearly 600,000 fifty years later. This was the most dramatic – and by far the most sudden – change in land use to have occurred in the Highlands and Islands since the introduction of farming some five thousand years before.

'The lairds have transferred their affections from the people to flocks of sheep,' government ministers were told in 1802 by Thomas Telford, a civil engineer who had been asked to report on developmental prospects in the Highlands and Islands. This was primarily a consequence of sheep paying far better than any alternative. 'Under sheep,' it was remarked in 1795, 'the Highlands would be six, if not ten, times more valuable than under cattle.' An exaggeration when first made, that claim was soon a statement of the obvious.[8]

In contrast to their twenty-first-century successors, who depend on the sale of lambs for an income, Highlands and Islands sheep-farmers of the eighteenth and nineteenth centuries looked to wool for the bulk of their revenues. They did not look in vain. Today, because of its having lost out to synthetic fibres, wool is of little value. But in the years around 1800, when it constituted the British clothing industry's main raw material, wool was in huge, and steeply rising, demand – both because of new manufacturing techniques developed in the course of southern industrialisation and because of the population growth which such industrialisation helped to promote.

In those circumstances, it suited both textile producers and United Kingdom politicians – most of whom wished to enhance British industry's competitiveness and few of whom, in that pre-democratic era, were troubled by their policies' human consequences – to back Highlands and Islands land-use changes which were helping to provide the clothing trade with the wool it so urgently required. Among clearing landlords, textile manufacturers and the United Kingdom's government, then, there was a community of interest which made clearance inevitable and which ensured that the victims of such clearance failed to get a sympathetic hearing from their country's rulers. The overall outcome was neatly summarised by James Loch, a leading land manager:

> In this, as in every other instance of political economy, the interests of the individual and the prosperity of the state went hand in hand. The demand for the raw material of wool by the English manufacturers enabled the Highland proprietor to let his lands for quadruple the amount they ever before produced to him.[9]

Nor did the attractions of Highlands and Islands sheep-farming, from a landowner's point of view, end with the fact that sheep-farmers paid much higher rents than the cattle producers who were removed to make way for them. Since one sheep-farmer typically displaced dozens of tenants of the former sort, an estate which was let to such sheep-farmers could be managed more economically than one arranged in the older manner. A pre-clearance landlord dealt with several hundred tenants – many of whom took a perverse delight in making rent-collection as difficult and time-consuming as possible. A post-clearance landlord, on the other hand, had no more than a handful of tenants – most of them businesslike individuals whose rents were paid with the minimum of fuss.

Some sheep-farmers were of Highlands and Islands extraction. Kildermorie's Cameron brothers, who came from Lochaber, were in this category. So was Alexander MacDonald of Glencoe, a descendant of the chieftain killed in the 1692 massacre and a man who was described, shortly after his death in 1814, as 'perhaps the greatest and most extensive sheep-farmer in the Highlands'.[10]

But most Highlands and Islands sheep-farmers, and certainly most of those operating on the largest scale, were immigrants. Often they were the sons of men whose families had been rearing sheep for generations in counties like Selkirk and Dumfries-shire – the homelands of the blackfaces and cheviots which incoming sheep-farmers brought with them from the south.

Among the first generation of Highlands and Islands sheep producers, one man stands out. This was Thomas Gillespie who, after serving an apprenticeship on his father's farm near Moffat, came north in 1782, when just twenty-two years old, to lease lands in Glen Quoich – on the borders of Knoydart. A physically tough and commercially shrewd individual, Gillespie managed, in time, to make himself the sole tenant of an expanse of territory which had formerly been occupied by hundreds of people. To the Glen Quoich sheep-farmer, it appears, those people meant no more than the Indians or Aborigines whose dispossession he would just as energetically have arranged had circumstance brought him – as it brought others of identical background – to the North American or Australian frontiers rather than to the West Highlands. As Thomas Gillespie's appetite for land grew, so family after family was ejected, at Gillespie's instigation, by his various landlords: from Glen Quoich, in the first instance; then from a string of neighbouring localities. 'He is now the greatest farmer in all that country,' it was observed of Gillespie in 1803, 'and possesses a tract of land extending from the banks of Loch Garry to the shores of the Western Ocean, upwards of twenty miles.'[11]

With them from their places of origin, farmers like Thomas Gillespie brought shepherds: men with whom they could readily communicate in their own Broad Scots; men with sheep-handling skills of a sort which Gaelic-speaking Highlanders – to whom *na caoraich mora* seemed almost an alien species – did not then possess.

Among those shepherds was one of my great-great-grandfathers, David Dempster, a Dumfries-shire man who was born towards the end of the eighteenth century and who, in the 1830s, left his previous post, around Cumnock in Ayrshire, for a job in Gleann na h-Iubraich, deep in the hills between Strontian and Loch Shiel. Today Gleann na h-Iubraich is completely deserted – having been given over, like much of Strathrusdale, to plantation forestry. But even when my great-great-grandfather got here with his wife, Elizabeth, and with their several children, Gleann na h-Iubraich must have been a lonely place. Its former inhabitants, of whom I have been able to discover nothing, had been removed from their homes before my great-great-grandfather's arrival. And though the locality also contained another two south-country shepherds, whose names are given as Brown and Todd in the 1841 census, there could have been little in Gleann na h-Iubraich of the comparatively hectic community life which the Dempsters would have known in the vicinity of Cumnock. Nor was there much by way of compensation to be derived from David Dempster's wages and conditions. The annual income of the average nineteenth-century shepherd consisted largely of the few pounds he got from the sale of wool taken from the handful of sheep which his employer permitted him to run alongside that employer's own flock. In David Dempster's case, the greater part of this income had to be expended on the oatmeal which was his family's staple fare and which, according to my grandparents, he carried by the sackload to Gleann na h-Iubraich from Strontian – each such load, the story goes, weighing well over a hundredweight.

Several of David Dempster's grandchildren, my maternal grandmother among them, married into families whose roots ran deeply into the Gaelic-speaking population of the Strontian area. Some of those grandchildren, my grandmother included, were Gaelic-speaking themselves – as were, incidentally, some of the younger Gillespies who eventually took over from the founder of what had become, by the early nineteenth century, something of a sheep-farming dynasty. But this level of integration – as between newly arrived sheep-farmers and shepherds on the one side, and the native inhabitants of the Highlands and Islands on the other – was a long time coming. To begin with, it is clear, folk of Thomas Gillespie's and David Dempster's background were widely, and understandably, detested. Sometimes that detestation erupted into organised protest of the Strathrusdale type. More often it took the form of clandestine assaults on the flocks which men like Dempster managed on behalf of men like Gillespie. 'Numbers were shot,' runs a contemporary account of such activities, 'and droves were collected, surrounded, forced into lakes and drowned.'[12]

In 1796 alone, Thomas Gillespie lost 140 animals in this way. And despite my sympathies being with the people responsible for the thefts and killings which regularly thinned his flocks, there was, I feel, something verging on the heroic about Gillespie's stubborn perseverance in the face of all such reverses. Go to Glen Quoich and make the onward journey into the wild country to the west – country which, in the years around 1800, constituted Thomas Gillespie's sheep-farm. Think of him spending countless days and nights out here: sleeping rough, as he reportedly did, in abandoned shieling huts; struggling week after week, month after month, to get his blackfaces hefted* to hills where no blackfaces had ever been before; having to confront, day in, day out, the loathing with which he was inevitably regarded by the folk whose rigs had become his winter grazings. There have long been memorials in the Highlands and Islands commemorating lairds of the sort from whom Thomas Gillespie rented so much land. There are beginning to be memorials to the people such lairds evicted. But there are no memorials to Gillespie. Almost nobody now knows his name. These few paragraphs, I hope, will help to remedy that deficiency.

The events of 1792 – events which entered Gaelic tradition as *bliadhna nan caoraich*, the year of the sheep – constituted the only attempt made by the population of the Highlands and Islands to mount an organised challenge to the sheep-farming economy which, following that attempt's collapse, was established right across the region. 'In Ross and northwards,' one observer commented in 1802, 'all parts capable of [supporting] sheep are, or will be soon, occupied. I have not a doubt . . . that the whole race of Highlanders will, in a very few years, be extinguished.' This, however, was to misconstrue the policies both of Highlands and Islands landlords and of the British government. While most landed proprietors in the Highlands and Islands were undoubtedly anxious to foster sheep-farming, and while United Kingdom politicians had no intention of doing anything to frustrate that ambition, neither the region's landlords nor their political backers wished, at the start of the nineteenth century, to empty the Highlands and Islands of people.[13]

The British government's interest in the maintenance of a substantial population in the Highlands and Islands stemmed from that population's role as a reservoir of military manpower – manpower which was badly needed during the years on either side of 1800 as a

* Sheep are territorial animals. Once established on a hill farm, a flock is said, in Scotland, to be hefted to that farm and will not, on the whole, stray far beyond its boundaries. That is why, when sheep-farms change hands, the stock stays always with the farm. But getting stocks hefted in the first place, which is what Thomas Gillespie had to accomplish, was very difficult.

result of the United Kingdom's wars with revolutionary and Napoleonic France.

Extraordinarily high numbers of men from the Highlands and Islands were involved in those wars. So extensive were the operations of naval pressgangs in Shetland, for instance, that between a third and a half of that island group's adult male population served, during the opening years of the nineteenth century, with the Royal Navy. The haaf fishery, a naval officer observed, had resulted in 'every Shetland man and boy' knowing exactly 'how to handle an oar and manage a boat'. That could be said of virtually no other population in the British Isles. So pressgangs came again and again to Shetland: storming through settlement after settlement; taking away every able-bodied male they captured; resorting sometimes to the simpler, if even crueller, expedient of hijacking the crews of sixerns bound for Shetland's deep-water fishing grounds.[14]

Elsewhere in the Highlands and Islands, meanwhile, males were being drafted into the British army. This had begun to happen in a small way in the early eighteenth century. It occurred on a larger scale in the 1750s when, as already mentioned, men from the Highlands and Islands – serving both with Fraser's Highlanders and with several other regiments – saw a great deal of action in North America. The further American war which broke out in the 1770s, as a result of Britain's transatlantic colonies making their ultimately successful bid for independence, led to still more men from the Highlands and Islands – possibly as many as 25,000 in total – becoming British soldiers. But in none of those earlier conflicts had Britain been obliged to mobilise its resources so comprehensively as the country was forced to do when, between 1793 and 1815, the United Kingdom was interminably locked, as it appeared to contemporaries, in a life-and-death struggle with France.

'I sought for merit wherever it was to be found,' Britain's parliamentarians were told by William Pitt, prime minister when regiments like Fraser's Highlanders took shape:

> It is my boast that I was one of the first ministers who looked for it and found it in the mountains of the north. I called it forth and drew into your service a hardy and intrepid race of men. Those men . . . served with fidelity, as they fought with valour, and conquered for you in every part of the world.[15]

Despite Pitt having implied that men from the Highlands and Islands rallied freely to the British Empire's colours, Highlands and Islands military recruitment was generally coercive in character. Outside Shetland and the Orcadian and Hebridean localities where naval pressgangs were also given free rein, compulsion was exercised primarily by the landlords to whom ministers, in effect, contracted out the business of finding soldiers. Britain being in desperate need of troops, and British ministers being willing to reward anyone able to supply them, the business in question was highly profitable. It was also, from a landowning perspective, attractively uncomplicated. Getting young men to enlist, as was remarked at the time, could be achieved simply by insisting that any tenant wishing to retain his holding had better supply the army with a son:

> The tenant who . . . refused to comply with the wishes of his landlord was sensible that he could expect no further favour and would be turned out of his farm. The more considerable the possession he held, the more was it his interest . . . to exert himself. The most respectable of the tenantry would, therefore, be among the first to bring forward their sons; and the landlord might, upon an authority almost despotic, select from among the youth upon his estate all who appeared most suitable for recruits.[16]

Officered by men drawn from what remained of the tacksman class and consisting of private soldiers who had commonly known each other from childhood, regiments recruited on this basis often performed very well – in Egypt with Abercromby, in Spain with Moore, at Waterloo with Wellington. But for all that their commanders drew on a military tradition deriving ultimately from the era of clanship, the existence of such regiments – contrary to what was frequently said about them then and later – by no means proved that the Highlands and Islands remained an area where folk unquestioningly did their social superiors' bidding. Tenurial manipulation of the sort underpinning military recruitment was bitterly resented. Such manipulation was resented even more when it was undertaken – as was starting to be the case by about 1800 – with a view to creating smallholdings, or crofts, of the type pioneered in connection with Shetland's haaf fishery.

From the perspective of the landlords who ordered their creation, crofts served a range of useful purposes. In Easter Ross, a croft usually consisted of a patch of previously uncultivated moor or hillside which its occupant – often a refugee from clearances of the Kildermorie variety – was obliged to drain, plough and otherwise improve. Crofts of this kind were also common in Moray, eastern Inverness-shire and Caithness where, as in Easter Ross, crofters frequently had the job of breaking in ground which, on its being got into a productive condition, was usually added to some more substantial farm – the crofters whose labours had brought that farm into existence having meanwhile been removed to some other piece of wasteland where they had no option but to embark on the same grim cycle all over again.

Because crofts of the Easter Ross and Caithness kind were seldom large enough to sustain a family on a year-round basis, crofters in those localities doubled, very often, as part-time farm labourers. Their counterparts in other parts of the Highlands and Islands were equally, indeed much more, reliant on off-croft employment. Other than in parts of mainland Argyll, in Strathspey and along the eastern coastal fringe, however, that employment rarely had anything to do with agriculture. In Orkney, the Hebrides and along the Highland mainland's Atlantic seaboard, for example, crofting's expansion was entirely a consequence of those localities' landlords wishing to cash in on a singularly profitable commodity called kelp.

Kelp is made by incinerating seaweed. An alkaline substance, it was, during the eighteenth and early nineteenth centuries, an essential ingredient in several manufacturing processes – especially those associated with the making of soap and glass. First produced on the Firth of Forth coastline around 1720, kelp was soon being made in the Highlands and Islands – in Orkney to start with, then in the Hebrides. And because of the huge quantities of seaweed to be got – then as now – in those places, the Highlands and Islands gradually became by far the most important source of the kelp which Britain's emerging industrial economy needed just as badly as it needed wool.

The seaweed which went into the crudely built kelp kilns constructed at this time on many Highlands and Islands coastlines was not the sort of seaweed one finds cast up on beaches by the tide. The source of the purest kelp was weed cut from the underwater rocks where such weed grew. Kelpers – the name given to the kelp industry's workforce – were consequently obliged to wade into the sea at low tide and, with the help of saw-toothed sickles, harvest ton after ton of weed. This weed had then to be dragged ashore and dried before being incinerated. And since the most productive shorelines were often a long way from habitation, kelpers, like haaf fishermen, regularly spent the summer months in very rough-and-ready accommodation. To be a kelper, then, was anything but pleasant:

> If one figures to himself a man, and one or more of his children, engaged from morning to night in cutting, drying and otherwise preparing the seaweeds, at a distance of many miles from his home . . . often for hours together wet to his knees and elbows . . . living upon oatmeal and water with occasionally fish, limpets and crabs . . . sleeping on the damp floor of a wretched hut, and with no other fuel than twigs or heath, he will perceive that this manufacture is none of the most agreeable.[17]

Conditions of that sort might have been rendered more tolerable if kelpers had profited adequately from their labour. And in principle, this should have been possible. Kelp-making required no complex tools, no sophisticated technology. Its end product – the bluish, brittle substance taken from the base of a kelp kiln after each firing – was easily transportable and extremely valuable. Had kelpers been the ultimate beneficiaries of what they were doing, therefore, they would have been able – without having to make any initial investment of the sort that debarred this same population from engaging in sheep production – to derive worthwhile incomes from an abundant natural resource. But kelpers, like Shetland fishermen, were denied access to the buyers of their industry's output. Whenever it became apparent that there was money to be made from kelp, Orcadian, Hebridean and other landlords moved rapidly to acquire the same sort of mastery over the industry that those landlords' Shetland counterparts had already established over the haaf fishery. Seaweed, it was declared by landed proprietors and agreed by government, belonged to the owners of the coastlines off which that seaweed grew. Kelpers, it was simultaneously made clear, were legally obliged to surrender their kelp to the landlords whose property it was. The overwhelming bulk of the immense revenues generated by the kelp industry thus went to landowners, not kelpers. Even when, in the opening years of the nineteenth century, kelp was selling for as much as £20 a ton, its Hebridean producers were receiving no more than two or three pounds per ton from the landlords to whom they were compelled to sell their kelp. Another pound or so per ton was expended on shipping the finished product to southern ports like Glasgow and Liverpool. But the £16 or £17 per ton remaining to kelping proprietors at the end of those transactions represented a clear profit.

By a further sleight of hand, moreover, even that profit could be readily enhanced. A kelper, by definition, was also a crofter. As such, he owed an annual rent to the landlord who paid his wages. Once that particular outgoing had been deducted from the typical kelper's earnings, those earnings, all too often, shrank almost to vanishing point. It was little wonder, then, that landlord after landlord was prepared to subordinate all other land-management considerations to the almost unbelievably lucrative business of making and marketing kelp.

In Orkney, where the average property was far from large and where lairds had formerly lived modestly, the kelp boom enabled landed proprietors to take on all the trappings of wealth. Servants were hired. New and more commodious residences began to go up on many estates. Prestigious townhouses were built in Kirkwall where landowning families like the Traills, who had first come to Orkney in the wake of Earl Patrick Stewart, increasingly eclipsed the merchants and traders who had been Kirkwall's dominant group ever since the town began to take shape around Rognvald Kali Kolsson's cathedral:

> Traills up the toon,
> Traills doon the toon,
> Traills in the middle.
> De'il tak the Traills' guts
> For strings to his fiddle.[18]

In the Hebrides, too, kelp made it possible for landowners to realise social aspirations which – such landowners, as successors to clan chiefs, thinking themselves an especially consequential group – were even more ambitious than those of Orkney's lairds. Skye's Armadale Castle, built by the Macdonalds of Sleat at the start of the nineteenth century, is in ruins today. But when I wander round what remains of this enormous mansion – where even the stables were on a scale that completely dwarfed every other building in their vicinity – and when I think about the truly appalling circumstances of the kelpers whose toils financed this grandiose pile, I begin to understand how Armadale Castle's residents came to be so despised by people those same residents still liked to consider their clansfolk.

In 1799, Lord Macdonald of Sleat, inheritor of the peerage granted to his father and possessor of extensive properties in Skye and North Uist, had his estates surveyed as a prelude to their being reorganised. Runrig – 'a careless and slovenly' mode of management, in the surveyor's opinion – was to be swept away. Several large farms were to be established in inland localities. And some of those farms were to be stocked with sheep – Lord Macdonald, it was noted, having 'no objection . . . to try one or two sheep-farms on a proper scale'.[19]

The changes thus envisaged, it was acknowledged, were bound to result in many people being removed from their homes. But being well aware of the extent to which his employer relied on revenues from kelp, Lord Macdonald's surveyor was anxious to prevent such people leaving the Macdonald estate:

> The soil is not only to be tilled, but from the surrounding ocean and its rocky shore immense sums may be drawn, equal at least, if not passing, the produce of the soil. As these funds are inexhaustible, the greater number of hands employed, so much more will be the amount of produce arising from their labour.[20]

Displaced families, therefore, were to be settled on crofts, to be created for this purpose, by the seashore.

But how to be certain that newly installed crofters, instead of turning out the kelp needed to finance Armadale Castle's construction, did not simply devote themselves to cultivating their fields, growing crops and raising cattle? The solution lay in the design of the coastal crofts to which evicted families were to be despatched. Those crofts, it was commented in 1799, would be small. And in order to ensure that they did not 'interfere with, or mar, the laying out of better farms', crofts would be located on rocky and boggy land in 'the least profitable parts of the [Macdonald] estate'. A man provided with one of those crofts, if he and his family were to live at all adequately, would have to find some source of income to supplement the necessarily meagre output of his holding. Such a man, in other words, would be compelled – there being no alternative employment available – to become a kelper.[21]

As is demonstrated by the alacrity with which he adopted it, this strategy made sense to Lord Macdonald. It made equal sense to the proprietors of other estates with kelping potential. As the eighteenth century gave way to the nineteenth, therefore, crofts – already a familiar part of the Shetland scene and starting, as mentioned earlier, to appear in places like Easter Ross – began to be established everywhere that kelp was produced. Hence the beginnings of crofting in Orkney. Hence also crofting's emergence as the dominant form of settlement in the Hebrides and along the Highland mainland's west coast.

Crofting of the Hebridean and West Highland type constituted a marked, and tremendously sudden, break with the past. Shetland's adoption of a similar land-use pattern had been relatively gradual. And in Easter Ross or Caithness, crofts could be seen as an evolutionary modification of past practice – if only by virtue of the fact that their occupants, in endeavouring to extend the bounds of cultivation and in doubling as farm labourers, continued to be engaged in essentially agricultural pursuits. Along the mainland's Atlantic coast and on islands such as Lewis, Harris, the Uists, Barra, Skye, Tiree, Mull and Iona, however, entire populations were forced, in the space of a few years around 1800, to adopt a wholly new mode of existence – in which farming, the major economic activity in this and in other parts of the Highlands and Islands for thousands of years, played very little part.

Both on the western mainland and on larger islands like Mull, Skye and Lewis, inland districts were generally cleared – in the manner suggested to Lord Macdonald in 1799 – and made over to sheep producers. At the same time, and again with sheepmen's requirements in view, communities which escaped clearance had their hill pastures truncated. Those same communities almost everywhere ceased to be organised, as they had been for ages, on a runrig basis – not with a view to creating arable farms of the Easter Ross variety, but with the aim, instead, of providing landlords with the crofts they needed to accommodate their kelpers.

Where once there had been runrig settlements, with their intricately organised and carefully distributed rigs, their infields, their outfields and their clusters of homes, there were now crofting townships. Such hill grazings as were left with those townships continued to be held – and, as mentioned previously, are still so held today – in common. Their cultivable land, however, was permanently partitioned into blocks which were usually no more than four, five or six acres in extent and which – as if by way of emphasising the artificiality of such proceedings – were laid out, with a total disregard for natural features, by surveyors who simply ruled off croft after croft on estate maps or plans. This resulted in townships being divided into long, straight strips of land which tended – most such townships, because of kelp's role in their formation, occupying coastal locations – to be at right angles to a nearby shoreline. Somewhere on their elongated strip of earth, the family to whom each such scrap of territory was allocated had to build a house – nucleated villages of the former type having no place in the crofting scheme of things. Most croft houses, in the early nineteenth century, were by the sea. More recently they have been built beside the roads which nowadays link townships with their neighbours. But for all that housing patterns have altered in this way, crofting townships – of which dozens are to be seen in the more north-westerly parts of the Highlands and Islands – retain the shape they were given some two hundred years ago. The typical township's fields remain long and narrow. Its field boundaries, all of them exactly paralleling each other, are as unnatural in appearance as the day those boundaries were first delineated.

Because they were intended to provide their landlords with a kelping workforce, and because that workforce consisted partly of refugees from inland clearances, the crofting townships carved out of runrig communities always contained more people than their predecessor settlements. So insatiable was demand for kelpers, however, that landlords, in addition to piling more and more families into established places of habitation, also took to creating entirely new townships in spots which had never before been cultivated. Such townships – their crofts, to start with, consisting mainly of heather and rock – were extremely unpopular. But that is not to imply that other, slightly more favoured, crofts were well regarded. By their original occupants at any rate, few crofts were viewed with enthusiasm. Nor is this surprising. The average crofter knew very well that the croft to which he had been directed by his landlord was simply a means of compelling him to become one of the kelpers whose plight an early-nineteenth-century visitor to the Hebrides compared adversely with that of slaves on West Indian sugar plantations. It was little wonder, in such circumstances, that many prospective crofters, rather than tamely fall in with their landlords' plans, took themselves off to North America.

From Orkney, throughout the kelping period, North America was generally accessed by way of the Hudson's Bay Company. Founded in the seventeenth century with a view to exploiting North America's fur resources, this London-based concern began, during the early eighteenth century, to have its outward-bound ships – which left the Thames each May or June – provisioned at Stromness in Orkney prior to commencing the Atlantic crossing. Stromness – said to consist of no more than 'half a dozen houses . . . and a few scattered huts' in the early 1700s – began, as a result, to acquire the solidly constructed warehouses and other business premises which survive, here and there, on its modern waterfront. But Orkney's dealings with the Hudson's Bay Company, it soon became apparent, were not to be limited to supplying the fur-trading corporation's ships with salted beef and other commodities of that kind. Bay Company skippers were as keen to take on men as to take on stores at Stromness. And since the fur trade – despite its many hazards and hardships – seemed to offer better prospects than kelping, several hundred Orcadians were soon helping to man York Factory on Hudson Bay, then the Bay Company's principal North American base.[22]

Among York Factory's Orcadians was the Arctic explorer, John Rae. Also of Orkney extraction were the individuals – their names long forgotten – who first provided the Hudson's Bay Company with the so-called York boats which, for many years, were the Bay Company's principal mode of transport on North America's rivers and lakes. Clearly modelled on Orkney fishing craft, themselves the recognisable descendants of Viking longships, those York boats, or so I reckoned when inspecting recreated versions of them at a restored fur-trading post in Manitoba, constitute a tangible link between the Norse Earldom of Orkney and a continent which other Norse adventurers – some of them, as noted earlier, with Highlands and Islands connections – had tried, and failed, to settle.

They were 'a close, prudent, quiet people' who spent 'their time in endeavouring to enrich themselves', a Hudson's Bay Company representative remarked of York Factory's 'Orkneymen'. And since even the most unskilled Bay Company employee could easily clear more in one year than a kelper could in twenty, such enrichment was perfectly possible. A number of Orcadians were to become substantial farmers back in Orkney with the help of money earned in the fur trade.[23]

As that fact suggests, the Bay Company's Orkney recruits were single men who mostly came home at the end of their engagements. Beyond their shared aversion to being croft-bound kelpers, then, there was little similarity between such Orcadians and the people who set out for North America from the Hebrides and the West Highlands during the years when crofting was being imposed on those localities. Unlike their Orkney counterparts, West Highland and Hebridean emigrants left in family groups. Profoundly disapproving of what was being done to their communities by their landlords, and convinced that North America offered them opportunities which would never come their way at home, they had no intention of ever returning.

Among the many areas affected by emigration of this type were the parts of Lochaber occupied by the children or grandchildren of the clansmen whom Donald Cameron of Lochiel led to Glenfinnan, Derby and Culloden in 1745 and 1746. When the nineteenth century opened, this leading Jacobite's grandson – a less attractive personage than his grandfather – was embarking on a major building programme at Achnacarry, the narrow neck of thickly wooded land between Loch Arkaig and Loch Lochy where Donald Cameron's fine home once stood. That home had been destroyed by the Duke of Cumberland's troops in the months following Culloden. In its place there went up, during the nineteenth century's first two or three years, an approximate equivalent of Lord Macdonald's Armadale Castle. 'The whole scene is romantic beyond conception,' a visitor remarked of Achnacarry as construction was getting under way. He had 'spent the middle of the day viewing the new castle of Lochiel, the building of which was . . . going briskly on,' this visitor continued. 'The castle is on an extensive scale and promises to be a stately structure.'[24]

The people living on Cameron land were less impressed by those developments. 'The grand castle at Achnacarry is going on with great speed,' one Cameron tenant wrote. There was little doubt, the same man added, as to how it would be funded. 'Lochiel's lands are in the paper to be let at Whitsuntide first . . . and I am afraid the tenantry have no chance. The highest bidder of rent will be preferred.'[25]

So it proved. That was why, rather than fall victim to the evictions which duly ensued, several hundred Cameron tenants took themselves off in 1802 to Glengarry County – the part of Canada, just west of Montreal, then becoming home to thousands of people from Lochaber, from the original Glengarry, from Knoydart and from several other localities in that vicinity. Writing from the new Glengarry to a friend still in Scotland, one of this 1802 emigration's organisers, Archibald MacMillan, reflected on the mixed emotions generated by all such departures:

> We cannot help looking at our native spot with sympathy and [with] feelings which cannot be described. Yet I have no hesitation in saying that, considering the arrangements that daily take place and the total extinction of the ties betwixt chief and clan, we are surely better off to be out of the reach of such unnatural tyranny.[26]

From Archibald MacMillan's standpoint, then, North America offered the inhabitants of the Highlands and Islands their one chance of escape from their landlords. Much the same opinion is evident in many of the songs and poems composed by North America's Gaelic-speaking settlers. 'This is a free land for people who suffered extortion in the country they left,' runs one such composition. And because such sentiments quickly filtered back to those of the emigrant population's friends and relatives who were still resident in the Highlands and Islands, it was inevitable – particularly in the context of the disruption caused by the introduction of crofting – that more and more Highlands and Islands families should have begun to contemplate a move to North America. So extensive had been eighteenth-century contacts between that continent and the Highlands and Islands, after all, that, despite its geographical remoteness, it seemed familiar and accessible. 'We begin to look upon America as but one of our islands,' a Hebridean clergyman observed in 1801, 'and on the sea that intervenes as but a little brook that divides us.'[27]

Much the same point was made that same year by one of Lord Macdonald's estate managers or factors – as such managers were called in the nineteenth-century Highlands and Islands. Referring to the numerous Macdonald tenants who were turning down the crofts then on offer to them, this factor observed of such tenants that they would 'much rather try their chance in other countries'. Soon identical reports were being submitted to other landlords who – with a view to similarly boosting their revenues from kelp – were following Lord Macdonald's lead in the matter of dividing runrig townships into crofts. Among those landlords was MacDonald of Clanranald. Since his properties included South Uist, perhaps the premier kelping area, Clanranald's financial prospects were particularly at risk from any exodus to North America. 'If emigration from Uist took place to a great extent,' it was noted by this island landlord's advisers, 'it would prove most hurtful to the interest of Clanranald as . . . the kelp would remain unmanufactured from which Clanranald at present draws his principal revenue.' Hence the prominent role of Clanranald's factor, Robert Brown, in the campaign launched during 1802 to have emigration from the Highlands and Islands halted by Act of Parliament.[28]

That campaign was co-ordinated by the Highland Society of Edinburgh. Among the society's leading members were most of the more important kelping landlords – together with the Edinburgh lawyers who acted as those landlords' commercial agents. Working closely with this powerful grouping was Charles Hope, the British government's chief law officer in Scotland and a close friend and colleague of several kelping lobbyists.

Because the Highland Society's landlord members were naturally reluctant to acknowledge the extent to which the society's anti-emigration crusade was a product of their own self-interest, this crusade was cloaked, from the first, in strongly humanitarian rhetoric. Families leaving the Highlands and Islands for North America, it was insisted by Robert Brown and by his Highland Society allies, were not free agents but victims. They were victims, first, of shippers who were packing America-bound vessels with more emigrants than those vessels could safely carry; they were victims, second, of their own 'false hopes' of a continent where, or so Brown and the Highland Society asserted, only disappointment awaited the average settler.[29]

With intending emigrants having no access to anyone who counted politically, and with government ministers concerned that the Highlands and Islands might be drained of prospective soldiers and sailors, the anti-emigration case carried the day. In May 1803, at the start of a summer expected to witness the departure of some 20,000 people from the Highlands and Islands, a Passenger Vessels Act became law. By sharply reducing the number of people emigrant ships could take on board, this 1803 measure, which the United Kingdom parliament found scarcely any time to debate, had the effect of so raising the cost of a passage from Scotland to North America as to put such a passage beyond the means of most Highlands and Islands families. Emigration from the region was thus effectively curtailed.

This curtailment, it was contended publicly by Charles Hope, resulted from the 'common principles of humanity' which, he maintained, had actuated the 1803 legislation's promoters. In private, Hope was more forthcoming. Remarking in a letter of 1804 that his had been the 'chief hand in preparing and carrying through parliament' the Passenger Vessels Act, Hope readily admitted that, although the Act had been 'professedly calculated merely to regulate . . . ships carrying passengers to America', it had also been 'intended . . . to prevent the effects of that pernicious spirit of discontent against their own country, and rage for emigrating to America, which had been raised among the people [of the Highlands and Islands]'.[30]

The nineteenth century's first decade was as good a time as there has ever been to own a Highlands and Islands estate. That much is evident from the construction, during those years, of Achnacarry Castle, Armadale Castle and several other residences of that sort. It is evident, too, from the prosperity, at this point, of Inverness – a centre which served the landed gentry of the mainland Highlands and the Inner Hebrides in much the same way as Kirkwall, then almost equally prosperous, served Orkney's proprietorial class. Inverness, it was claimed in 1807, could 'vie with London in the assortment of rich goods displayed for sale'; its inns were 'of the first style'; its 'females' were 'luxurious in their attire'. The town, in short, had acquired such 'a degree of elegance' as to have been totally transformed: 'in every corner the bustle of trade is to be met and few idlers . . . are to be seen in the streets'.[31]

The affluence from which Inverness thus benefited, however, was the affluence of a tiny élite. By cashing in on the high price of wool and the even higher price of kelp, a small number of landlords, factors, sheep-farmers and the like were flourishing financially. But they were doing so largely as a result of their willingness to engage in the manipulation and exploitation of the wider population of the Highlands and Islands – a population which, during this same period, was subjected to clearance on an unprecedented scale.

The Passenger Vessels Act, its impact aggravated by their own growing poverty, was meanwhile making it harder for victims of clearance to seek refuge in emigration. 'These poor people, unable to go to America, are glad to get any sort of plot and hut,' a contemporary observer commented of the Highlands and Islands families turned out of their homes at this point. As sheep-farms became more numerous, therefore, so did crofts – their occupants, as this same observer noted, invariably 'tied . . . down to perform services' and 'to work at fixed prices when called upon'. In most of the more northerly and westerly parts of the Highlands and Islands, the services in question consisted of making kelp. There were exceptions to this rule, however. Shetland, where crofters were invariably intended for the haaf, was one. Sutherland was another. There, as in Shetland, crofting was intended – neither Shetland nor Sutherland possessing many seaweed-rich shores – to facilitate fishing rather than kelping.[32]

The bulk of Sutherland constituted, in the early nineteenth century, a single estate of more than a million acres. In the thirteenth century, those acres had been controlled by William de Moravia. In the sixteenth century, they were acquired by a cadet branch of the Gordons of Huntly. At the start of the nineteenth century, this family was headed by Elizabeth, Countess of Sutherland, who, some years previously, had married George Granville Leveson-Gower, Marquess of Stafford. Countess and marquess alike were committed – in the terminology of the time – to the improvement of their Sutherland property. The ensuing transformation was summarised thus by Patrick Sellar, a Sutherland estate factor:

> Lord and Lady Stafford were pleased humanely to order a new arrangement of this country: that the interior should be possessed by cheviot shepherds and the people brought down to the coast and placed there in lotts [or crofts] under the size of three arable acres, sufficient for the maintenance of an industrious family, but pinched enough to cause them to turn their attention to the fishing. I presume to say that the proprietors humanely ordered this arrangement, because it surely was a most benevolent action to put those barbarous hordes into a position where they could better associate together, apply to industry, educate their children and advance in civilisation.[33]

As that passage amply indicates, Patrick Sellar, an Edinburgh-trained lawyer, held attitudes which were fully in accord with the well-established Lowland tradition – one that can be traced all the way back to the middle ages – of regarding inhabitants of the Highlands and Islands with profound contempt. To Sellar, Sutherland's 'aborigines', as he habitually called the folk whom he encountered in the course of his estate-management duties, were characterised mainly by 'sloth, poverty and filth'. They were a 'parcel of beggars' whose 'obstinate adherence' to Gaelic – a 'barbarous jargon', in Sellar's opinion – had, by depriving Sutherland people of 'knowledge and cultivation', turned them into 'savages'.[34]

From Patrick Sellar's perspective, then, the relationship between men like himself on the one hand, and Sutherland people on the other, was 'not very different from that betwixt the American colonists and the aborigines of that country'. On some Sutherland families having the temerity actually to resist their eviction, an outraged Sellar accordingly had those 'insurgents' treated in precisely the same way as white Americans treated Indians who refused to move on to reservations. Although resistance to clearance in Sutherland was less well organised than had been the case in Easter Ross in 1792, troops – as requested by Sellar and by his aristocratic employers – were again sent north. And again there was ended such small prospect as there might have been of Highlands and Islands landlords failing to get their way.[35]

Sutherland's equivalent of Strathrusdale was the Strath of Kildonan where, in January 1813, a number of Patrick Sellar's subordinates, when engaged in mapping a sheep-farm, were physically assaulted by people whose removal was then being arranged. Within weeks, Kildonan's incipient revolt had been crushed every bit as absolutely as

Strathrusdale's. Here, as in so much of the rest of Sutherland, family after family was evicted; homes were demolished or burned to prevent their reoccupation; community after community was obliterated.

In 1825, some miles south of the Strath of Kildonan, a traveller chanced to come upon a settlement whose occupants, a few days before, had been provided with the opportunity, as Patrick Sellar would doubtless have asserted, to 'advance in civilisation':

> All was silence and desolation. Blackened and roofless huts, still enveloped in smoke; articles of furniture cast away as of no value to the homeless; and a few domestic fowls scraping for food among hills of ashes: [these] were the only objects that told us of man. A few days had sufficed to change a country-side, teeming with the cheeriest sounds of rural life, into a desert.[36]

Much of Sutherland is a desert still. The district's interior, so comprehensively depopulated during the nineteenth century's first quarter, when at least eight thousand people were turned out of their homes, has remained depopulated ever since. And such folk as hang on in Sutherland – nowadays one of the most thinly peopled parts of Europe – mostly live, as Sellar and his colleagues intended should be the case, on coastal crofts which continue to be every bit as 'pinched', to use Sellar's own term, as when they were initially laid out. This settlement pattern, of course, was dictated by the demands of the sheep-farming system to which Patrick Sellar was wedded and from which Sellar – a sheep producer as well as an estate factor – profited enormously. But it is a settlement pattern which makes no sense on any other basis.

To grasp this point, one need only drive along the single-track road which, starting from Helmsdale on Sutherland's east coast, traverses both the Strath of Kildonan and Strathnaver – a further valley opening on to Sutherland's north coast at Bettyhill. In a way that no words can, this journey underlines the huge contrast between the places from which so many people were ejected in the early nineteenth century and those other places to which the same people were directed by the estate managers responsible for their dispossession. By Highlands and Islands standards, the Strath of Kildonan and Strathnaver are sheltered, fertile and potentially productive. One can readily understand, driving through them, why they were thickly settled in neolithic times and why they continued to be thickly settled for several thousand years thereafter. One can equally well understand, on getting to the north-coast settlements which were nineteenth-century Sutherland's equivalent of Indian reservations, why so few folk from the interior straths were willing to accept the diminutive patches of land allocated to them here. Townships like Melness, Strathy and Bettyhill – where today's crofters have shown me heaps of stones removed from the earth in the course of their forebears' back-breaking attempts to make fields where no fields were meant to be – are, in comparison with Strathnaver and the Strath of Kildonan, desperately exposed, bleak and inhospitable spots.

'I don't feel bitter about it,' a Bettyhill crofter once told me when I asked him about his folk's compulsory removal and resettlement. 'There is no point in bitterness. But the clearances should never be forgotten.'

The Sutherland clearances, according to their originators, enabled entire communities to move from the county's interior, where living conditions were allegedly poor, to seaside locations offering more in the way of opportunity. Those clearances, in consequence, continue to be defended on the grounds that they constituted a vast and ultimately well-meant experiment in social engineering – one akin, it has been suggested, to the later removal of folk from city-centre slums to the housing estates which, during the 1950s and 1960s, began to appear on the peripheries of Glasgow, Edinburgh and other Scottish cities. Like most such housing estates, it is admitted, nineteenth-century Sutherland's crofting townships never quite performed as they were supposed to do: suburban housing schemes all too often turning into sinks of social deprivation; Sutherland crofting townships being characterised, throughout the nineteenth century and into the twentieth, by their own, even more extreme, brand of poverty. But the fact that the Sutherland experiment ended the way it did, or so that experiment's defenders maintain, does not, of itself, detract from the essentially beneficent intentions of its originators. It is as unfair to blame the Sutherland clearances' planners for what went wrong in Sutherland, this argument continues, as it would be to blame a housing scheme's designers for problems they could not reasonably have foreseen in advance of its construction.

I have difficulty with this contention. Patrick Sellar's letters, one of which has already been quoted, do not strike me as having been penned by a man who had the wellbeing of Sutherland's population at heart. But Sellar, it can be interjected at this stage, was merely the agent of the landowning couple who, towards the end of their lives, became the Duke and Duchess of Sutherland. Yes, it is agreed by that couple's apologists, Sellar was a most unappealing character. Yes, he was driven by a desire to get as much land as possible under sheep. But one should carefully distinguish – or so I am told by people who find it easier than I do to forgive clearing landlords – between a hired servant's motives and those of his hirers. The duke, the duchess and their more senior advisers – who included, incidentally, the previously mentioned James Loch – should not, on this argument, be bracketed with Patrick Sellar.

Subtleties of this kind, however, cannot survive a trip of the sort outlined a page or so back. Nobody acquainted with Sutherland geography – and both the duke and duchess were certainly acquainted with it – could ever have believed that a family's material prospects would be enhanced by removing them from Strathnaver or from the Strath of Kildonan, depositing them on an exceptionally stormy coastline, providing them with just three or four acres of rock-spattered wasteland and telling them that, once they had built a new home, they should acquire a boat in order to get urgently to grips with fishing.

The fish the former residents of Strathnaver and the Strath of Kildonan were meant to catch were herring. This made the development of a north-coast fishery a still more remote possibility than it might otherwise have been. Men who had no previous experience of seafaring, and who possessed little capital, were supposed to provide themselves with the expensive boats and gear required – even in the early nineteenth century – by anyone looking to take herring. And had the necessary boats and equipment been obtained, which they were not, a worthwhile north-coast fishery would have remained, in any case, elusive – places like Bettyhill and Strathy being bereft of the sheltered inlets or harbours which any such fishery has always required.

There were a few localities on Sutherland's east coast – the neat little village of Helmsdale is one – which possess reasonable harbours and which, as a result, became modestly flourishing herring centres. But there never was the slightest chance of herring becoming the economic mainstay of north-coast townships. Those townships' crofters, as a result, were forced to rely for a livelihood on their crofts. And so small were those crofts that their occupants became more and more pauperised with every year that passed.

By the 1820s, to be sure, that was very much the fate of crofters everywhere. It was especially the fate of the west-coast and Hebridean crofters whose entire *raison d'être*, as far as their landlords were concerned, was bound up with the making and selling of kelp.

The end of the French wars in 1815 enabled southern purchasers of kelp to obtain alternative, and cheaper, sources of alkali from continental Europe. The resulting inflow was stemmed, for a time, because Highlands and Islands landlords managed to persuade politicians to maintain high import duties on kelp substitutes. But on this front, as on many others, Britain's industrial interest eventually prevailed over its landed one. The relevant duties were slashed during the 1820s. At the same time, new – and still more competitive – forms of alkali began to be manufactured chemically from salt. The price of kelp duly plummeted.

With the returns on kelp collapsing, the proprietors of many Highlands and Islands estates found themselves deprived of revenues on which they had come to rely and against which, in numerous instances, they had borrowed recklessly. In the Hebrides especially, landed family after landed family went to the wall. Among the more notable casualties, all of them obliged to part completely with their island estates, were the MacKenzies of Seaforth who had acquired Lewis in the early seventeenth century; the Clanranald MacDonalds who had dominated South Uist and several other islands since the demise of the Lordship of the Isles; the MacLeods of Harris and the MacNeills of Barra whose pedigrees, like that of the Clanranald family, reached back into, or even antedated, the era of the lordship; the Campbells of Shawfield who, though comparative newcomers, had owned Islay since 1726. Other landlords survived only by shedding significant proportions of their properties. The Macdonalds of Sleat, the MacLeods of Dunvegan and even the Campbell dukes of Argyll were in this category – the latter family, for example, reluctantly parting with much of Mull and all of Morvern.

Crofters, meanwhile, were facing problems of a more basic nature. The incomes which they had derived from their work as kelpers might have been the merest pittances. But those incomes had nevertheless enabled them to pay their rents and to purchase the foodstuffs – oatmeal particularly – which they could not obtain from their crofts in quantities matching those which had been available in the runrig townships of the past. As kelp gradually ceased to be made, therefore, rent arrears accumulated and crofting families – seldom well off to start with – began to go short of the barest necessities. Increasingly, in fact, they went hungry.

Hunger was no new phenomenon in the Highlands and Islands, a region which had long been characterised by the precariousness of its agriculture. Prior to the nineteenth century, however, poor harvests and the difficulties to which they gave rise were episodic in nature. They followed on abnormally wet or stormy summers, on inter-clan feuding, on the ravages caused by some passing army. The crises produced by such eventualities, then, were essentially transient. Better times could be anticipated. And better times always arrived.

That was what differentiated previous periods of scarcity from the ever more parlous and destitute state in which many Highlands and Islands communities found themselves during the 1820s, 1830s and 1840s. There could no longer be any very plausible possibility of escape from hunger and want – because such hunger and want had ceased to be the accidental consequence of some chance sequence of events and had become, instead, inseparable from the way in which the crofting population, or a large proportion of it, was obliged to live.

In order to boost their revenues from activities such as kelp-making and fishing, the landed proprietors responsible for the introduction of crofting had created circumstances in which people who had traditionally looked to the land for a living could no longer do so. Appearances notwithstanding, crofters were not small-scale farmers. They were folk who, despite their being agricultural tenants, had been made dependent on non-agricultural earnings. In the absence of such earnings, it followed, the domestic economy of the typical crofting family was bound to fall apart. This was exactly what occurred across much of the Highlands and Islands in the course of the nineteenth century's second quarter. The eventual outcome, in 1846, was famine.

With that famine's commencement, the population of a large part of the Highlands and Islands touched rock bottom. Their conditions could scarcely have been worse. Their prospects could hardly have been bleaker. This makes it all the more tragically ironic that the catastrophe which thus enveloped the Highlands and Islands was both the consequence and the culmination of policies framed by folk who believed themselves – if their public statements are taken at face value – to be bringing betterment to the region.

Over a long period and as a result of developments which have already been explored, responsibility for what went on in the Highlands and Islands had inexorably been assumed by external agencies. The first of those agencies was the Scottish state which, from the eleventh century onwards, had sought to incorporate the Highlands and Islands into its sphere of influence: conquering the Kingdom of Moray; annexing the Hebrides; taking over the Earldom of Orkney; obliterating the Lordship of the Isles. The few semi-autonomous institutions which survived those various onslaughts were next destroyed – this process reaching its culmination in the eighteenth century when the United Kingdom, the Scottish state's better-resourced successor, eradicated clanship. And by the people who thus took control of the region, their every action was unfailingly described as constituting an advance on what had gone before. King James VI, when planning the colonisation of Lewis or sanctioning the Statutes of Iona, said he was civilising barbarians. The Duke of Cumberland, when authorising the burnings and hangings which followed Culloden, said much the same thing. And so, when he was organising the clearance of Sutherland, did Patrick Sellar.

From a Highlands and Islands perspective, however, matters looked – and still look – very different. What King James, Cumberland, Sellar and their numerous associates had ultimately succeeded in creating was a society whose component families were routinely turned out of their homes and regularly subjected to forms of oppression that stopped just short of slavery. Already racked by the pervasive and debilitating insecurity produced by repeated clearances and evictions, this society had been brought, by the early nineteenth century, to the edge of mass starvation. And for all that it is self-evidently impossible to know how the Highlands and Islands would have fared had the area's people been left to make their own history in their own way, it is hard not to suspect that, however things might have turned out in that eventuality, the region, if its inhabitants had remained in charge of their own destinies, would have entered the nineteenth century in better shape than it did.

Both as a part of Scotland and as a part of the United Kingdom, the Highlands and Islands were treated, in the period prior to the 1846 famine, in a manner which gave a far higher priority to southern interests than to the interests of the area's own population. To start with, admittedly, the external dominance which was gradually established over the region had been relatively limited in scope. Thus the medieval Scottish monarchy, while wishing to ensure that the Highlands and Islands ceased to contain worthwhile centres of governance, had not attempted to extend its influence – other than by founding one or two burghs – into the sphere of economic life. By the eighteenth century's end, however, the Highlands and Islands economy, too, was being managed in such a way as to serve extraneous objectives. And the region's landlords – those former clan chiefs who had preserved their own status by allying themselves as closely as possible with the folk who then mattered in the south – had gone along, in most instances, with this process. Here and there, particularly in more favourably endowed localities like Easter Ross, Kintyre or the more low-lying parts of Caithness, the proprietorial class had gone some way to creating diversified and self-sustaining economies – economies based on arable farming and on the various services which this type of farming demanded. But the overall tendency, as urban-centred industrialisation gathered pace both in the Scottish Lowlands and in much of England, had been for landlords to accept that Highlands and Islands estates should be geared to the production of such raw materials as southern factory-owners and southern townsfolk saw fit to demand. Shetland fish aside, the two most important such materials were wool and kelp. Production of the first of these had entailed the eviction of enormous numbers of people. Production of the second had made it necessary for the people thus evicted to be transformed – with others – into a croft-based workforce which, the moment cheaper supplies of alkali became available, was automatically rendered surplus to requirements.

Was this last sequence of events, in the conditions then prevailing, unavoidable? Or might landlords, had they taken a wider view of their responsibilities, have steered a more constructive course? Analysts – particularly academic analysts – of Highlands and Islands history have mostly responded to such questions in a manner which, while acknowledging the landowning class's central role in the clearances and in related developments, exculpates that class from any responsibility for what occurred. Landlords, such analysts suggest, were prisoners of circumstance; the choices open to them, it is asserted, were extremely limited; rather like dispossessed crofters, it is stated, they were merely the playthings of forces beyond their control. But this notion of the landlord as victim is one that fails totally to ring true. The individuals who lived in Inveraray Castle, Armadale Castle, Achnacarry Castle or Dunrobin Castle – the last being the extraordinarily splendid residence built to accommodate the Duke and Duchess of Sutherland – were manifestly not victims in the sense that their dispossessed and impoverished tenantries were victims. While those tenantries had certainly been deprived of virtually all capacity to influence events, this was never true of Highlands and Islands landlords. Such landlords, for example, could readily have diverted some proportion of the profits generated by wool and kelp into economic development of a type which would have provided both themselves and crofters with alternative sources of income. This was not done.

'The solid advantages which the new tide in their affairs had opened up to them,' as one nineteenth-century commentator remarked caustically of the kelping proprietors of the Highlands and Islands, 'were bartered for the merest baubles':

> In residences, dress, furniture, equipages, pleasures and style of living, the Highland chiefs copied the English model; and . . . resources, by which their rugged country . . . could have been brought into a cultivated and civilised condition, were wasted in the vain attempt to rival the magnificence of an aristocracy who possessed much richer domains and larger revenues. The decay of the kelp manufacture completed the ruin which personal extravagance had begun; and the men who had long reaped the profits of this lucrative trade passed from the scene, leaving their estates as unimproved as they had found them [and] a numerous population starving.[37]

There is just one respect in which the difficulties affecting the nineteenth-century Highlands and Islands can be convincingly attributed to anything other than the results of human action. Towards the end of the middle ages, the region began to be affected by a climatic downturn – involving lower temperatures and shorter growing seasons – which lasted into the nineteenth century. Might there have been some connection between this deterioration in the region's climate and its inhabitants' eventual inability to feed themselves? The answer, obviously, is yes. But the climatic downturn in question was very general in its impact. It affected Norway, for instance, every bit as severely as the Highlands and Islands. There is something suggestive, therefore, in the fact that nineteenth-century Norway did not experience any equivalent of the crisis which overtook the Highlands and Islands in the 1840s. This fact can reasonably be interpreted as indicating that the crisis in question was no simple product of worsening weather.

Nor was it brought about, as it continues occasionally to be claimed, by population growth. Admittedly, the number of people in the Highlands and Islands had been rising for some time. And in the course of the eighteenth century, for reasons which have still to be satisfactorily elucidated, the rate of population expansion, in the Highlands and Islands as in much of the rest of the British Isles, undoubtedly accelerated. During the four decades preceding the famine which began in 1846, however, the Highlands and Islands were not gaining population any faster than were England and Wales. Nor was population then increasing anywhere in the Highlands and Islands at anything like the rate that it grew in some parts of the region, most notably Skye, during the 1980s. But late-twentieth-century Skye, like early-nineteenth-century England and Wales, possessed an economy which was perfectly capable of providing for more and more people. Much of the pre-famine Highlands and Islands possessed, in contrast, no such economy. The region's landlords – by appropriating most of its available wealth and by squandering the bulk of that wealth in ways already described – had seen to that. They had done much additional damage also.

If there were more people occupying crofting townships in the 1820s and 1830s than was prudent, then that was largely the responsibility of the landlords who had brought those townships into existence. By promoting sheep-farming, landlords had deprived crofters of access to much of the land on which those crofters' ancestors had so productively grazed their cattle. By subdividing runrig settlements in such a way as to provide the maximum number of potential kelpers or fishermen, landlords had similarly deprived crofters of the chance to raise worthwhile crops of grain. And by pressing for legislation of the sort represented by the Passenger Vessels Act of 1803, landlords had done their best to seal the one escape route crofting families had left to them.

All of this, of course, was conveniently forgotten when the tumbling price of kelp rendered much of the crofting population, as contemporaries so chillingly put it, 'redundant'. Men who had previously done everything in their power to prevent emigration, now tried equally hard to foster it: pressing successfully for the removal of those restrictions on transatlantic travel which they had previously helped to impose; finding the money needed, in some instances, to have their tenants transported *en bloc* to North America.

Subsidised emigration of this type was no charitable gesture. When, in 1826, MacLean of Coll, who then owned Rum, had the bulk of that island's crofters shipped to Canada, the total cost of the exercise, though certainly considerable, was recouped in under two years – from the rent paid to MacLean by the single sheep-farmer to whom all of Rum was let in the wake of the island's clearance.

What was true of Rum, as an 1839 report on Lord Macdonald's North Uist estate serves to demonstrate, was true of other places:

> The fall in the value of kelp renders . . . a change in the management of the North Uist estate necessary. The tenants have hitherto been accustomed to pay for the greater part of their rents by their labour as kelpers. Kelp is not now a productive manufacture. The population of the estate is greater than the land, the kelp being abandoned, can maintain. The allotments

> of land held by the small tenants are so small that they cannot maintain their families and pay the proprietor the rents which the lands are worth if let in larger tenements [or farms]. It becomes necessary, therefore, that a number of small tenants be removed [and] that that part of the estate calculated for grazings be let as grazings.[38]

From a proprietorial standpoint, this was a compelling argument. Over the next four or five years, therefore, Lord Macdonald helped finance the emigration of some 1,300 people from North Uist – their departure being accompanied by the clearance of a number of crofting townships and by the appearance, in those townships' place, of several sheep-farms.

Clearances of this sort were by no means confined to Rum and the Uists. They occurred, during the 1820s and 1830s, on Arran, Islay, Mull, Skye, Harris and Lewis – as well as in numerous mainland parishes. And everywhere they produced results of the sort described, at this time, by John MacLachlan, a Gaelic poet from Morvern:

> As I climb up towards Ben Shiant,
> my thoughts are filled with sadness,
>
> seeing the mountain as a wilderness,
> with no cultivation on its surface.
>
> As I look down over the pass,
> what a chilling view I have!
>
> So many cottages in disarray,
> in green ruins on each side,
>
> and houses without a roof,
> in heaps by the water spring!
>
> Where the fire and children once were,
> that's where the rushes have grown tallest.[39]

Sometimes, as had occurred in the Strath of Kildonan, clearance was resisted. In 1820, when some six hundred people living around Culrain on the upper reaches of the Dornoch Firth were served with eviction orders, the outcome was summarised by a visiting journalist:

> On notice being given to these poor creatures to remove, they remonstrated and stated unequivocally that, as they neither had money to transport them to America nor the prospect of another situation to retire to, they neither could nor would remove and that, if force was to be used, they would rather die on the spot that gave them birth than elsewhere.[40]

On that occasion, as on several others, troops were made available – just as they had earlier been made available in the Strath of Kildonan – to enforce evictions. Those evictions duly took place as planned. But what happened to their victims will forever be uncertain. So commonplace were such events in the nineteenth-century Highlands and Islands that, both in the case of the Culrain episode and in the case of lots of other clearances, the fate of dispossessed families went unrecorded.

The human misery engendered by such happenings can barely be imagined today. But from even the most prosaic and laconic accounts of particular clearances, there can emerge – if one reflects a little on what is actually being described – some small inkling of the horror experienced by men, women and children caught up in such events. Here, for example, is one brief extract from the hundreds of pages of similar evidence laid before a royal commission which, in 1883, was given the job of enquiring into crofting grievances. The extract in question is taken from testimony supplied to the commission, in the course of its visit to Dunvegan in Skye, by a local crofter named Malcolm McCaskill:

> I am 36 years of age, and was born in Kilmuir, parish of Duirinish. My father was born at Ramasaig and is about 75 years of age. He was evicted from there to Idrigill, from Idrigill to Forse, and from Forse back to Idrigill, where he was only one year. Then he was removed or evicted to Kilmuir where he was only for a few years when he was removed to his present croft . . . He was removed from the first four places for no other reason than to make way for sheep. He was not in arrears of rent. He has seen all the following townships laid waste or depopulated: Lowergill, Ramasaig, Ollasdale, Dibidale, Idrigill, Forse, Varkasaig.[41]

The sites of five of the seven townships thus said to have been 'laid waste or depopulated' lie within the boundaries of the modern Orbost Estate. In November 1997 this estate – extending to several thousand acres – was bought by Skye and Lochalsh Enterprise (SALE) which, as it happened, I then chaired. SALE is a government-financed development agency. Its interest in Orbost was consequently forward-looking – SALE's purchase of the estate, which cost in excess of £500,000, having been undertaken with a view to finding new ways of accommodating, in a wholly rural setting, a part of Skye's expanding population. Being well aware of this perfectly proper emphasis on present needs and future possibilities, I had not made much – at the occasionally heated public meetings surrounding the estate's acquisition – of Orbost's past. On SALE's bid for Orbost being declared successful, however, I took time to re-read Malcolm McCaskill's 1883 account of his father's treatment by Orbost's earlier owners. I took time, too, to walk the estate.

My explorations of Orbost were conducted at the time of year when the sun is at its lowest and when the remnants both of former buildings and of former cultivation are, because of the lengthy shadows they then cast, relatively easy to spot. Although I knew that Orbost had been thickly settled prior to its clearance, I was surprised by just how much evidence there was – in an area given over to sheep for more than 150 years – of humanity's impact. In fact, as a SALE-sponsored archaeological survey has since revealed, traces of hundreds of buildings can be found on Orbost. Not all those buildings, to be sure, were permanent structures. Nor were all of them occupied at the same time. Orbost, like most such places, contained lots of relatively transient shieling huts, and some of the estate's more substantial dwellings were probably abandoned centuries prior to the evictions which Malcolm McCaskill described. But Orbost's numerous ruins nevertheless seem to me to demonstrate how evolutionary development of a type which had gone on over millennia could so readily be terminated by a few strokes of some nineteenth-century landlord's pen. Generation followed generation here from neolithic times. Generation would doubtless have continued to follow generation into the present had not this been made impossible by the emptying of Bharcasaig, Idrigill and all the other townships Malcolm McCaskill so evocatively listed.

On the shortest day of 1997, I sat on a hillside above Idrigill – the stone walls of its former homes catching the light of a curiously springlike morning – and thought about this community's end. That end is nowhere recounted in detail – Malcolm McCaskill's brief reference to his father's dual eviction from the place being Idrigill's sole published epitaph. The feelings of Idrigill's people at the point they left their houses for the last time, therefore, can only be surmised. But something of those feelings, I guess, is discernible on faces of the sort all too often seen on television news programmes: those faces that we glimpse, decade after decade, among the individuals constituting some new batch of displaced people; those faces which, whether they are Asian or African or European, are always so peculiarly blank, lifeless, traumatised. I do not, and cannot, know exactly how it felt to be so precariously situated as to be liable – in the way Malcolm McCaskill's father was liable – to ejection from one home, one locality, after another. But it seems to me that anyone endeavouring to understand the Highland Clearances should focus, now and then, on the distress and suffering they so patently occasioned. This I tried to do that day at Idrigill.

Some of the people removed by their landlords from settlements such as Idrigill made their way to the Lowlands where they gravitated to towns and cities like Greenock, Paisley, Glasgow, Edinburgh and Dundee. Some of those migrants prospered. A larger proportion did not. Many folk from the Highlands and Islands were to be found among families inhabiting the one-room slums which were all too prevalent in nineteenth-century Scotland's emerging industrial centres. The economic and other difficulties confronting such families were often insurmountable. The results are all too plain to see in studies of Botany Bay's convict population. Among that population's female component, prostitutes loomed large. And a lot of the prostitutes transported to Australia at the instigation of Scottish courts were women and girls who, despite their working Lowland streets, had been born in the Highlands and Islands.

Partly because they were well aware that North America was likely to offer better prospects than Scotland's urban areas, many victims of clearance continued to be attracted by the notion of emigration. So acute was their poverty, however, that – even after the removal of the controls imposed by the Passenger Vessels Act – intending emigrants from the Highlands and Islands had to settle for the cheapest of transatlantic passages. The typical such passage consisted of a place in the hold of one of the hulks engaged in the import to Britain of North American timber – a commodity invariably consigned to craft so run-down and rickety that the only westward-bound cargo they could attract consisted of the most impoverished emigrants.

'The accommodation on board was very rough,' it was reported from Skye of a vessel of this sort. 'The whole lower decks were cleared and two rows of sleeping berths were erected on each side of the ship . . . Into this den – for it could not be called anything else – were huddled some 200 or 300 men, women and children.'[42]

Food was frequently scarce on emigrant ships. Water was often bad. Privacy was always at a premium – males and females being obliged to 'relieve nature', as contemporaries put it, in full view of one another. Since such sanitary facilities as existed were rudimentary, the lower deck, in heavy seas, was invariably awash with urine, faeces and, of course, vomit – seasickness being the emigrant's constant companion. Even for the occupant of a private cabin on the better class of passenger ship, remarked the American novelist Herman Melville, whose knowledge of these matters derived from his own years as a sailor, seasickness was a dreadful scourge:

> How, then, with the friendless emigrants, stowed away like bales of cotton and packed like slaves in a slave ship; confined in a place that, during storm time, must be closed against both light and air; who can do no cooking, nor warm so much as a cup of water, for the drenching seas would instantly flood the fire in their exposed galley on deck? We had not been at sea one week, when to hold your head down the hatchway was like holding it down a suddenly opened cesspool.[43]

Both in city slums and in emigrant ships, thousands of the people who fled the Highlands and Islands as a result of their eviction were to die of typhoid, cholera and the various other diseases to which their conditions made them vulnerable. Nor was the situation of such folk as remained in the crofting districts of the Highlands and Islands significantly better than the situation of those who had left. As more and more land was lost to the crofting population, townships which escaped clearance became seriously overcrowded as crofts were subdivided in order to accommodate some at least of the people left homeless by their removal from other townships. Because crofts thus tended to become steadily smaller and because – with the kelp industry's demise – there was frequently no local means of obtaining off-croft earnings, both male and female members of crofting families took to travelling south, in large numbers, each August and September to assist with the Lowland harvest. But for all that the money generated by such activities made a valuable contribution to household economies right across the crofting area, crofters were obliged, just as their pre-crofting forebears had been, to look to their landholdings for much of their food. So tiny were those landholdings, however, that there was only one foodstuff they could produce in the quantities needed to meet the average crofting family's nutritional requirements. This foodstuff was the potato. In the crofting population's growing reliance on this single crop there is to be found the immediate cause of the greatest of all the many catastrophes to affect the Highlands and Islands in the course of the clearance era.

Potatoes were introduced to Europe from South America in the sixteenth century. They were first grown in the Highlands and Islands towards the close of the seventeenth century. They became common in the eighteenth. And by the start of the nineteenth century, as a Morvern minister observed, they constituted, over a large part of the Highlands and Islands, by far the most important item in people's diet:

> Indeed there are many . . . in the predicament of a little boy of the parish who, on being asked on a certain occasion of what his three daily meals consisted, gave the same unvarying answer, 'Mashed potatoes.' And on being further asked by his too inquisitive inquirer, 'What else?', [he] replied, with great artlessness but with evident surprise, 'A spoon!'[44]

Being less prone to storm damage and being more tolerant of damp soils than the oats and barley which they inexorably displaced, potatoes grew – and grow – very well in the Highlands and Islands. Acre for acre, it was calculated in the early nineteenth century, this new crop could easily support four times more people than any then available cereal. And especially if they were supplemented with a little milk and fish, as was the case in most Highlands and Islands localities, potatoes – of which the typical Highlands and Islands adult was soon consuming several pounds a day – could readily sustain health. By the 1820s and 1830s, therefore, virtually every scrap of the relatively restricted area left in crofting occupation was devoted to potato production.

Nor were potatoes confined to the fields immediately adjacent to croft houses. The frontier of cultivation was everywhere extended by means of that most ingenious Highlands and Islands device, the lazybed. This strangely misnamed (because it was extremely laborious) method of cultivation involved, as runrig had done earlier, the heaping of earth into ridges. But lazybeds or *feannagan*, being much narrower than rigs and being worked entirely by hand, could be established on terrain so intractable as to have never previously been cropped.

The ground markings left by nineteenth-century lazybeds are to be seen today in the most improbable spots: on the steepest of hillsides and even, as I have noted when flying across the Hebrides, on scarcely accessible offshore islets. Most such lazybeds have long been out of use. But when, in 1972, I first visited the eastern part of Harris, crops were still being grown there on *feannagan* dating from 150 years before.

This particular locality – known, in English, as the Bays – is so rocky and so bereft of vegetation as to be almost lunar in appearance. It came to be inhabited only because it was one of the few spots left to a population which, as a result of yet another military-enforced clearance, had been expelled, in the 1820s, from the infinitely more fertile *machair* land on Harris's Atlantic coast. On arriving in the Bays, these people had set about creating lazybeds of the sort I saw in 1972 – gathering together such small quantities of soil as were available and supplementing this soil with rotted and composted seaweed.

Some twenty years before I got to Harris, the island's *feannagan* had attracted the attention of the pioneer ecologist, Frank Fraser Darling:

> Nothing can be more moving to the sensitive observer of Hebridean life than these lazybeds of the Bays district of Harris. Some are no bigger than a dining table, and possibly the same height from the rock, carefully built up with turves carried there in creels by the women and girls. One of these tiny lazybeds will yield . . . a bucket of potatoes, a harvest no man should despise.[45]

But if one's entire harvest consists of potatoes and if this harvest fails, then famine inevitably results. So it was in the Highlands and Islands of 1846, *a' bhliadhna a dh'fhalbh am buntata*, the year the potato went away. What took the potato away was blight, a newly arrived fungal disease to which potatoes of that time had no natural resistance and from which, in the absence of modern fungicidal sprays, they could not be protected.

In June 1846, the all-important potato crop had everywhere been well advanced. In July and August, that crop was devastated. 'In course of a week,' it was reported, 'frequently in course of a single night or day, fields and patches of this vegetable, looking fair and flourishing, were blasted and withered and found to be unfit for human food.'[46]

Towards the end of August, an Inverness newspaper sent a reporter to Skye, Lochalsh, Kintail and Knoydart. 'In all that extensive district,' runs an article based on this reporter's despatches, 'he had scarcely seen one field which was not affected.' Potato plots and lazybeds alike were 'enveloped in one mass of decay'. And everywhere a 'foetid and offensive smell . . . poisoned the air' – that smell being the obnoxious, inescapable stench of rotting potatoes.[47]

As summer gave way to autumn and as autumn gave way, in turn, to a cold and snowy winter, both hunger and hunger-related illness became widespread. The outcome is most effectively described in the words of contemporaries. Here, for example, is part of a letter sent south by a member of a fact-finding delegation of Lowland clerics who, on Christmas Day 1846, visited families living in the Broadford area of Skye:

> We found the condition of very many of them miserable in the extreme, and every day, as they said, getting worse – their houses, or rather their hovels, and persons the very pictures of destitution and hopeless suffering. A low typhus fever prevails here . . . In one most deplorable case, the whole of the family of seven persons had been laid down, not quite at the same time, in this fever. The eldest of the children, a son about nineteen years of age, had died just when his mother was beginning to get on foot. No one [because of fear of infection] would enter the house with the coffin for the son's remains. It was left at the outside of the door, and the enfeebled parent and a little girl, the only other member of the family on foot, were obliged to drag the body to the door and put it in the coffin there, whence it was carried by the neighbours, with fear and alarm, to its last resting place.
>
> When I entered the wretched house . . . I found the father lying on the floor on a wisp of dirty straw, his bedclothes, or rather rags of blanket, as black nearly as soot, his face and hands of the same colour, never having been washed since he was laid down; and the whole aspect of the man, with his hollow features and sunken eyes, and his situation altogether, was such as I had never beheld before. In a miserable closet, beyond the kitchen where the father lay, I found the rest of the family, four daughters from about eleven years of age to seventeen, all crammed into one small bed, two at one end and two at the other; the rags of blanket covering them worse, if possible, than those on the father; their faces and persons equally dirty, the two youngest having no night clothes of any kind. One of these poor girls was very ill and was not likely to

> recover. The others had the fever more mildly, but had not yet been so long in it.
>
> The effluvia and stench in this place, and indeed in every part of the miserable dwelling, were such that I felt I could not remain long without great risk of infection, as there was no means of ventilation whatever, and not even of light. The poor woman said she had got a stone or two of meal, she said she did not know from whom, which had barely served to make gruel for the unfortunate patients. The family had no means whatever of their own.[48]

Equally harrowing accounts were given, at this time, of conditions in many other parts of the Highlands and Islands, not least Benbecula. From North Uist, in the 1840s, that island was accessed by way of a tidal ford which, in the 1960s, was replaced by a causeway. At this causeway's Benbecula terminus is Gramisdale where, in the middle years of the nineteenth century, Lachlan MacDonald, the brother of one of my great-great-grandmothers, kept an inn. Partly because of this, partly because of my fondness for the characteristically Hebridean scene produced by Gramisdale's mix of sea, sand, *machair* and sky, I have paused there, from time to time, when my work has taken me that way. Gramisdale's shores have always been deserted when I have strolled across them. But in my mind I have once or twice tried to populate those shores with figures of the sort seen here, in 1847, by Norman MacLeod, a Church of Scotland minister.

MacLeod was looking into the effects of famine on the Western Isles when, after spending a day or two in North Uist, he picked his way across the ford to Gramisdale. From Gramisdale southwards, the minister knew, his route would lie through lands which had been acquired, some years previously, by Colonel John Gordon of Cluny, an Aberdeenshire laird and businessman who, despite his being one of the wealthiest individuals in Victorian Scotland, was notoriously given to treating his Hebridean tenants with extraordinary harshness. MacLeod, being aware of this and knowing that the potato failure had impacted with particular severity on Gordon's properties, was not surprised to find Benbecula's people going hungry. He was surprised, however, to find many folk close to death:

> The scene of wretchedness which we witnessed as we entered on the estate of Col. Gordon was deplorable, nay heart-rending. On the beach the whole population of the country seemed to be met, gathering the precious cockles . . . I never witnessed

> such countenances: starvation on many faces; the children with their melancholy looks, big-looking knees, shrivelled legs, hollow eyes, swollen-like bellies; God help them, I never did witness such wretchedness.[49]

Our television sets, sadly, have accustomed us to images of famine-stricken African children with 'melancholy looks', 'hollow eyes' and 'swollen-like bellies'. Like other people of his place and time, however, Norman MacLeod had not previously been exposed – even in the second-hand way we have been exposed – to the consequences of advanced malnutrition and vitamin deficiency. Maybe that was why those consequences affected him so strongly.

But people do not need to see a famine's victims in order to be moved. The British public's remarkably generous reaction to African famines of the 1980s proved as much. So did the equally generous public response to the Highlands and Islands famine of the 1840s. On news of what was happening in places like Benbecula and Skye reaching the Scottish Lowlands, England, the United States and Canada, appeals for contributions to famine relief funds quickly began to yield enormous sums – sums equivalent to many millions of pounds at today's values. The spending of the cash thus generated was to go a long way to ensuring that the mid-nineteenth-century Highlands and Islands did not experience a holocaust of the type then occurring in Ireland.

Because the Irish famine – which arose out of circumstances similar to those prevailing in the Highlands and Islands – started in 1845, the British government, still ruling all of Ireland at this point, was able, when the Highlands and Islands potato harvest failed in 1846, to divert to the region some of the personnel whose task it had been, during the preceding twelve months, to cope with the Irish calamity. The officials in question were under the command of a Devon-born military man, Sir Edward Pine Coffin, who, despite his somewhat inauspicious name, ought to be remembered with gratitude in the Highlands and Islands. There was a period at the beginning of 1847 when the region stood on the brink of disaster – with dysentery, scurvy and typhus beginning to get a grip of famished communities and with death rates consequently rising fast among the most immediately vulnerable groups, the very old and the very young. By employing naval craft to distribute oatmeal and other supplies from storage depots he established at Tobermory and Portree, however, Coffin managed to retrieve the situation. Conditions remained bad. But they were a good deal less dreadful than they might so easily have been.

Despite Coffin's herculean efforts, the winter of 1846–47 was as miserable a one as the Highlands and Islands have ever experienced. Practically all of the region's rural communities were affected to some extent by the loss of their potato crops. And so general were fears of imminent starvation that even the inhabitants of towns like Wick, Cromarty and Invergordon turned out in the hope of forcibly preventing the export of grain from local harbours. As always in the nineteenth-century Highlands and Islands, popular protest was suppressed with the help of troops. But the fact that it took place so widely is indicative of the extent of food shortages.

Both during this terrible winter and subsequently, however, the Hebrides and the Highland mainland's west coast – where crofters were most numerous and where dependence on potatoes was greatest – were particularly hard hit. And with blight returning annually into the early 1850s, famine relief operations in this area gradually took on a semi-permanent character. Being reluctant to assume long-term responsibility for these operations, but being well aware of the need for their continuance, government ministers, although they withdrew Sir Edward Pine Coffin's team, did so on the understanding that Coffin's remit would at once be taken up by the charitable agencies – based in Edinburgh and Glasgow – which had been formed to take charge of funds donated in response to continuing public appeals.

The 'destitution meal' purchased by those agencies reached hungry families by way of open-air distributions:

> At the appointed time and place, the poor creatures troop down in hundreds, wretched and thin, starved and wan. Some have clothing, some almost none, and some are a mass of rags. Old and young, feeble and infirm, they take their stations and await their turn. Not a murmur, not a clamour, not a word – but they wept aloud as they told of their miseries.[50]

The basic ration in the Highlands and Islands during the famine years was one and a half pounds of meal per adult male per day – with women receiving three-quarters of a pound and children half a pound. Those amounts, roughly equivalent to the quantities doled out to the victims of late-twentieth-century famines in Africa, were reckoned to be just sufficient to sustain life. And they were not given freely. Sir Charles Trevelyan, a senior civil servant who had a hand in shaping government thinking on famine relief, summed up a key tenet of that thinking in these words:

> Next to allowing the people to die of hunger, the greatest evil that could happen would be their being habituated to depend upon public charity. The object to be arrived at, therefore, is to prevent the assistance given from being productive of idleness and, if possible, to make it conducive to increased exertion.[51]

Because of his insistence that it should be, Trevelyan's approach was quickly adopted by relief-agency staff in the Highlands and Islands. To earn their allowances of meal, therefore, crofters were expected to labour – for eight hours a day, six days a week – on some approved project. Among such projects were the 'destitution roads' constructed at this point in several parts of the Highlands and Islands. But among them, too, were a whole host of make-work schemes of very dubious value. This caused resentment. So did the administrative costs which relief agencies necessarily incurred in checking that meal was being distributed in accordance with their ever more complex rules. Famine relief in the Highlands and Islands, one critic complained, consisted increasingly of 'a huge staff of stipendiaries on liberal pay, and multitudes of starving supplicants receiving a modicum of meal'.[52]

Underpinning Sir Charles Trevelyan's approach to those matters was a profound conviction – which also went a long way to shape British policy in Ireland – that neither government nor charitable bodies should do anything to interfere with the workings of the free market by which economists, both then and afterwards, set such store. If crofters could not afford to pay for meal, as they manifestly could not, then they would have to work hard to obtain it. And if Easter Ross's farmers and landlords wished to export grain from Invergordon or Cromarty, then troops, if necessary, would be provided to enable them to do so – irrespective of the fact that, as rioters in those towns noisily pointed out, it seemed odd, to put it mildly, to be shipping foodstuffs out of a region where people were going hungry.

Even in the 1840s, however, there was some common ground between government representatives and the population of the Highlands and Islands. Both were of the view, for instance, that Highlands and Islands landlords could have responded more positively and more energetically to the crisis engulfing their tenantries. Admittedly, there were landlords, of whom Norman MacLeod of Dunvegan was the outstanding example, who did a great deal to mitigate the famine's impact on families living on their estates. But there were plenty of other landlords, as Sir Edward Pine Coffin never tired of complaining, who did little or nothing.

What the proprietorial class in the Highlands and Islands really wanted to achieve, Coffin commented in one of his more exasperated moments, was 'the extermination of the population'. This may have been to exaggerate. It is unarguable, however, that landlords, having been tending in this direction since kelping's collapse, were firmly and unanimously of the view, by the 1840s and 1850s, that it could only be of benefit to them to rid their properties of people. This they attempted to do, in the famine period, by evicting thousands of families and, in some instances, by contributing to the cost of shipping those families to Canada and Australia. More than 16,000 people were helped to emigrate from the Highlands and Islands between 1847 and 1857. Their departure was frequently facilitated by clearances of the type which, in 1853, completed the depopulation of Knoydart. Starting in Thomas Gillespie's time, Knoydart's townships had been emptied one by one. Now the last of them were so comprehensively eradicated that in this extensive peninsula – which once contained dozens of separate communities – there is to be found today not one single person who can claim Knoydart ancestry.[53]

Knoydart's 1853 evictions took several days to accomplish. They were witnessed by a reporter from *The Scotsman*, an Edinburgh newspaper which normally took a pro-landlord line but which felt itself unable, on this occasion, to defend the indefensible:

> On the third evening, when returning to Inverie, the factor's party came upon a small boathouse, erected on the shore at Doune, which they had overlooked. In this . . . ejected families had huddled at night for two nights . . . Fire was immediately applied to the roof, and the structure burned down. This completed the work of destruction, and eleven families were left absolutely without shelter – for, unfortunately for them, the coast of Knoydart has no caves in which protection from at least the rain might be found.[54]

Among the many other clearances of the famine period, perhaps the most far-reaching occurred on Barra, South Uist and Benbecula. Those islands belonged to John Gordon of Cluny and were inhabited, of course, by people of the sort Norman MacLeod glimpsed at Gramisdale. So self-evidently bleak were such people's prospects that, at the start of 1847, Sir Edward Pine Coffin felt obliged to raise their condition with their landlord.

Coffin's concerns stemmed from one of his subordinates having reported directly to him on the plight of Gordon's tenants:

> Every week for the last two months they have been expecting a supply of food from Colonel Gordon, but they have been disappointed. The very poor must live as they can, and die as they can, unless speedily relieved . . . No idea can be formed of the wretched state of the poor in these islands, as respects food, clothing and accommodation. It is quite heart-rending. They are nevertheless very patient.[55]

Coffin was less patient. He wrote as follows to Gordon:

> I cannot suppose that you intend deliberately to abandon to such a condition a large population whose fate is in a great measure dependent on your proceedings; but I am, nevertheless, bound to forewarn you that, if such a determination were possible, it would become my duty to interpose in favour of the sufferers, and to take those measures on your behalf which are at present neglected by you, leaving to parliament to decide whether or not you should be legally, as well as morally, responsible for the pecuniary consequences of this just and necessary interference.[56]

Gordon responded by embarking on a massive programme of evictions. Many of the families he dispossessed made their way, in due course, to mainland towns. There, as reported from Inverness, they lived on the streets:

> The sight of these creatures, men hugging their children to their bosoms to protect them from the weather, and women sitting on the cold wet stones on a winter night suckling their infants with perhaps little nourishment to give them, and all without a morsel of food, was sufficient to raise the sympathies of the most hardened.[57]

Episodes of the Inverness type having exposed him to further criticism, this time from the Scottish press, Gordon, who was meanwhile forging ahead with still more evictions, chartered a fleet of five ships in order to transport 1,700 people from his Hebridean properties to Canada. Among this group were folk who left their island homes so unwillingly that some of them hid themselves away rather than embark on Gordon's transatlantic convoy. Dogs were employed to hunt such individuals from their places of concealment. Several, on being found, were bound, hand and foot, in order to forestall renewed escape attempts.

After several weeks at sea in the late summer of 1851, John Gordon's former tenants came ashore at Grosse Ile, the quarantine station which the Canadian colonial authorities had established in the St Lawrence River with a view to stopping emigrant-borne diseases from reaching cities like Quebec and Montreal. Despite his having dealt with innumerable refugees from the Irish famine, Grosse Ile's medical officer, George Douglas, was shocked by the state of the Benbecula, South Uist and Barra families who became his responsibility. 'I never during my long experience at the station saw a body of emigrants so destitute of clothing and bedding,' Douglas reported. The wife of the captain of one of John Gordon's chartered ships, Douglas added, had chanced to make the ocean crossing from Scotland with her husband. She 'was busily employed all the voyage' in 'converting empty bread bags, old canvas and blankets' into 'coverings' for people who, prior to their being thus provided with makeshift garments, were practically naked.[58]

The considerable costs of caring for this refugee party from the Hebrides had to be met by Canadians. To George Douglas's superior, Alexander Buchanan, there fell the thankless task of attempting to obtain a contribution to those costs from John Gordon – a man revealed, following his death in 1858, to have been that rarest of nineteenth-century creatures, a sterling millionaire. The sum which Buchanan tried to get from Gordon was by no means excessive. But Gordon, Alexander Buchanan noted tiredly, 'refused to pay this charge'.[59]

It remained only for Buchanan, a most punctilious civil servant, to inform Highlands and Islands landlords more generally why emigration to North America – contrary to what was claimed, both then and later, by its promoters – did not always result in emigrants' immediate betterment. 'The mere transfer of an indigent tenantry, without an alteration in any respect in their condition, gives no reasonable ground for expecting their subsequent successful progress,' Alexander Buchanan commented. It was as good a verdict as any on the circumstances surrounding the removal to Canada of so many impoverished families from the Highlands and Islands. But it was a verdict to which landlords like John Gordon paid not the slightest heed.[60]

CHAPTER EIGHT

Is treasa tuath na tighearna

1857–1928

From Duror, in the early 1960s, I travelled daily to secondary school in Oban. Those journeys were made on trains pulled by the steam locomotives then serving the branch line between Oban and Ballachulish. Completed in 1903, that line was the last railway to be built in the Highlands and Islands.* The first, which opened in 1855, connected Inverness with nearby Nairn and, rather like the Ballachulish Branch, was thus of purely local significance. By 1858, however, the Inverness–Nairn line had been extended, via Forres and Elgin, to Aberdeen. Five years later, with the completion of a line through Strathspey and across Drumochter, direct rail links were established between Inverness and a range of southern centres. Additional construction followed. From Inverness, during the 1860s and 1870s, railway tracks were laid, stage by stage, to Dingwall, Invergordon, Lairg, Golspie, Brora, Helmsdale, Wick and Thurso. Next a branch of this north line was extended westwards to Strome Ferry on Loch Carron. From Stirling and Glasgow, meanwhile, further lines were pushed through the hills to Oban and Fort William.

Those railways constituted the culmination of a transport revolution which had been gathering pace since the appearance, in the nineteenth century's second decade, of steamships capable of connecting Glasgow with destinations in Argyll and the Hebrides. In the 1820s and 1830s, steamship operators dealt mainly in freight. But their vessels, by the 1850s, were carrying more and more passengers. In summer especially, such passengers consisted mainly of folk engaged in mid-nineteenth-century Britain's newest, and most fashionable, pursuit: they were taking a holiday. The Highlands and Islands had thus become, as the area has since remained, a tourist destination. Many of its communities were, as a result, to be altered fundamentally.

---

* It closed in 1966.

Among those communities was Oban. A place of no significance in 1800, it had grown, eighty or ninety years later, into the self-proclaimed 'Charing Cross of the North' – a title intended to convey something of the hectic activity generated by this Argyll town's stake in the holiday business. Even by the nineteenth century's end, of course, the tourism industry lacked the economic clout which has since enabled it completely to refashion localities like Spain's Mediterranean coast. But what tourism did, in the 1960s and 1970s, to Spanish fishing villages like Malaga and Benidorm was, all the same, no more than a larger-scale repetition of what it had earlier done to Oban. There, starting in the 1850s, scores of hotels – many of them fronting a purpose-built 'esplanade' – were constructed along a mile-long stretch of shoreline where previously there had been merely a beach. To those hotels came thousands of tourists. And as the town expanded, its harbour grew as busy as its streets. From June until September, Oban Bay and the adjacent Sound of Kerrera – where a shipboard Alexander II had died in 1249 – were filled with yachts and pleasure craft of every sort. Not every visitor's means stretched to the chartering of such vessels, but practically anyone could afford a trip to Iona on the Oban-based *Columba*, a steamer capable of accommodating around two thousand passengers and containing a hair-dressing salon, a bookstall, a fruitstall and a post-office – the latter handling, it was claimed, more than quarter of a million items of mail every month.

Its rail connection with the south – a connection completed in 1880 – was to Oban what the aircraft-based package tour is to many present-day resorts. Respectable Oban opinion, admittedly, was scandalised by the behaviour of the men whose job it was to get the Callander and Oban Railway Company's tracks into a terminus situated just a few yards short of Oban Bay. 'We cannot ignore the fact,' the *Oban Telegraph* editorialised in August 1878, 'that a navvy, with his pay in his pocket, ten-pounder brogues on his feet, his hair cut close to the scalp, and several inches of Highland whisky in his stomach, is . . . not the most amiable of men.' But two years later, the navvies in question having meantime done their work and departed, the *Telegraph* was in no doubt as to the significance of what their labours had accomplished:

> The advent of the Callander and Oban Railway has been the forerunner of a season of unparalleled prosperity and financial sunshine. The opening of the railway has developed an increase of trade in the burgh and caused a briskness in every depart-

> ment of our local business, particularly among our hotels and lodging houses . . . There has been no halt in the pressure of visitors and the cry is 'still they come'.[1]

In the eighteenth century, it took weeks for a traveller – or a letter for that matter – to reach the Highlands and Islands from London. Even getting from Edinburgh to Inverness might occupy several days. The improved roads and relatively speedy stagecoach services of the early nineteenth century, to be sure, had begun to shorten journey times by the 1820s. But it was the coming of the railways, followed by the arrival of the electric telegraph, which changed the previous position out of all recognition. When, as was the case by the 1880s, news of distant events could be transmitted instantly to most Highlands and Islands locations, or when, as was also the case by the later nineteenth century, people could reach the Highlands and Islands from England in no more than a few hours, then the region had ceased to be remote in the sense that it had earlier been remote. To begin with, understandably, that was a cause of considerable amazement.

Today we take rapid travel for granted. But our nineteenth-century predecessors, to whom it was a wholly novel phenomenon, treated such travel – and the means which made it possible – with something approaching reverence. That becomes immediately apparent to anyone visiting Aviemore Railway Station. Most such facilities are nowadays decrepit shadows of their former selves. This Strathspey station, in contrast, has been restored to a condition approaching its original splendour. Stand on the cast-iron bridge connecting Aviemore Station's twin platforms and spend a moment or two reflecting on the ornate and richly painted columns which support the station's highly decorated roof. This building – all the more remarkable in view of the fact that Aviemore, when the railway reached here, consisted of a mere handful of homes – was meant, in its heyday, to honour trains in much the same way that medieval churches were intended to honour God.

Alongside more opulent stations, there went up equally opulent hotels. The best known of the surviving examples in the Highlands and Islands is a lot less luxurious than it once was. But enough of its Victorian interior has survived – if in a rather faded state – to give some credence to the nineteenth-century advertisement proclaiming Inverness's station hotel to be one of the 'best appointed . . . in the kingdom'. Breakfast here no longer consists, as it did in the 1880s, of 'salmon, steak, or ham and eggs, or chicken with ham and tongue'. And pianos are no longer 'at the free disposal of the occupants in every private sitting-room'. But the hotel's 'elegant coffee-room, drawing-room, smoking and billiard rooms, lavatories and bath-rooms', for all that several of them have nowadays been put to alternative purposes, can still be inspected by guests who, as I have done when overnighting there, take the chance to poke around a little.[2]

There had long been inns in the Highlands and Islands. Such inns – most of them very basic – catered largely for drovers and the like. Hotels, in contrast, were built to serve tourists. And since nineteenth-century working folk had neither the means nor the opportunity to take holidays, the typical Highlands and Islands hotel of that era looked mainly to Victorian Britain's burgeoning middle-class for its customers. Those customers were attracted to the Highlands and Islands, as many people still are, by the region's scenery. But they were attracted, too, by the way in which that scenery had been woven into the literary productions of James MacPherson, Walter Scott and the various other poets and novelists who, in the later eighteenth and early nineteenth centuries, succeeded in countering earlier – mostly negative – perceptions of the Highlands and Islands. There continues to be argument about the merits and demerits of the manner in which the Highlands and Islands were depicted by MacPherson, Scott and their numerous emulators.* But there is no doubt as to such writers' key contribution to the process of turning the region into one which countless Victorians automatically associated with romance and adventure.

Queen Victoria herself contributed greatly to the region's appeal when, having first travelled the Highlands and Islands with Walter Scott's verses in hand, she acquired a summer retreat at Balmoral on Deeside. Soon plenty of other members of the United Kingdom's upper class, following where the queen had led, had also taken to pitching up, each August, in the Highlands and Islands. Unlike more modestly placed trippers, visitors of this type were not content to stay in hotels – however well appointed. What they wanted were holiday homes of the sort Victoria had pioneered: lavishly constructed mansions surrounded, ideally, by good deerstalking country.

Deer had been hunted in the Highlands and Islands from meso-lithic times. But stalking of the nineteenth-century variety – made possible by the invention of high-powered and accurate firearms – was as much a creation of the Victorian era as were the railways which

* This theme is explored in the same author's book, *On the Other Side of Sorrow: Nature and People in the Scottish Highlands*.

brought stalkers north. Quite why the cult of stalking acquired so passionate a following has never really been explained. But among the wealthier and more influential sections of British society its appeal, for a time, was virtually irresistible. 'As soon as a man has amassed a fortune in any way,' it was noted in 1892, 'his first desire seems to be to buy, or hire, a deer forest in Scotland.' Thus there emerged the sporting estates which continue, at the start of the twenty-first century, to be a feature of the Highlands and Islands scene and which, when the deerstalking craze was at its height in the decades immediately prior to the First World War, accounted, in total, for several million acres.[3]

Like many other Highlanders of his generation, my maternal grandfather, John Cameron, worked for a time as a ghillie – the Gaelic-derived term applied to an assistant stalker – on a sporting estate. The estate in question was Ardtornish in Morvern which also employed James Dempster, son of Gleann na h-Iubraich's David Dempster and father of Catherine who, in 1904, became John Cameron's wife.

In 1844, Ardtornish had been bought by Patrick Sellar whose principal concern, inevitably, was to realise its sheep-farming potential. But the estate – named after the nearby and long ruinous castle where a Lord of the Isles once negotiated with the representatives of an English king – was subsequently purchased by Octavius Smith, a Londoner who had made a fortune in the wholesale grocery business. Sheep mattered little to Octavius Smith. They mattered still less to his son, Valentine. Their Ardtornish has been well described as 'a machine for sport'. It was, in other words, a shooting and stalking establishment of the sort described so well, and so enticingly, in the early-twentieth-century novels of John Buchan – a regular visitor to Morvern.[4]

All sporting estates demanded – as some still demand – a forelock-tugging deference on the part of their employees. Unsurprisingly, therefore, my grandfather's descriptions of Ardtornish and places like it were less flattering than Buchan's. But John Cameron, even in old age, remained a little awestruck, as anyone perusing the surviving accounts of such properties also tends to be awestruck, by the sums – equivalent to millions of pounds at today's values – so casually sunk in estates of the Ardtornish type. Much of this money went into so-called shooting lodges, usually grandiose in conception and characteristically baronial in style, which continue to litter our glens in sufficient quantity to make the point – much the same point as is made by Aviemore's railway station and Inverness's station hotel –

that substantial amounts of cash washed through the Highlands and Islands in the later nineteenth century.

In 1800, Highlands and Islands estates were mostly managed by their owners, the kelping and clearing landlords of that time, in ways intended to provide the money those men needed to finance their extravagant lifestyles. But by 1900, as a result of the appearance in the Highlands and Islands of people like Octavius and Valentine Smith, this pattern had largely been reversed. To the area's new type of landlord, a Highlands and Islands property was a means of enjoying and flaunting wealth earned elsewhere. Cash had flowed out of a kelping estate. It flowed into Ardtornish and dozens of similar establishments – many of which became available to newly monied purchasers when earlier lairds were compelled, by mounting debts, to offer their lands, or large parts of them, for sale. A sporting estate's value, then, had next to nothing to do with its capacity to grow crops or carry livestock. It was determined – as the value of a great deal of landed property in the Highlands and Islands is still determined – by the extent to which its acquisition might enhance its purchaser's social standing.

From a landowning perspective, turning Highlands and Islands estates over to sport made more and more sense economically as the nineteenth century wore towards its close. This was because of the increasingly adverse impact on the area's agriculture, as on agriculture elsewhere in Britain, of overseas competition – with wool imports from Australia, to give one example, causing United Kingdom wool prices to fall alarmingly in the 1880s. Just prior to this late-Victorian slump, however, Highlands and Islands farming was as profitable as it had ever been. So high were wool prices in the 1860s and 1870s that both landowners and their farming tenants in upland parts of the Highlands and Islands showed signs of falling victim, it was said, to 'a sort of sheep mania'. With other agricultural sectors performing almost as well, the nineteenth century's third quarter was equally kind to low-ground farmers of the Easter Ross type – a group then being joined, incidentally, by growing numbers of Orcadians.[5]

Although it led, around 1800, to the appearance of crofts akin to those proliferating, at that time, in other parts of the Highlands and Islands, Orkney's kelp boom had not been accompanied by further fundamental changes in the island group's agrarian structure. Since the relatively small-scale nature of their estates made it hard for

Orkney landlords to devote large acreages to sheep-farming, kelping in Orkney was unaccompanied by clearances of the sort which led to much of the early-nineteenth-century Highlands and Islands being parcelled out among sheep-farmers on one side, crofters on the other. In Orkney, as a result, runrig lasted longer than elsewhere. In some localities, in fact, it persisted into the 1840s and 1850s – when the island group's rigs were replaced by field systems geared to the requirements of the highly commercialised agriculture in which Orcadians were then beginning to engage.

This development could not have occurred but for the fact that Orkney – in contrast to the Hebrides and Shetland – possesses a lot of very good land. It occurred when it did because of the inauguration, in the 1830s, of reliable steamship links between Orkney and mainland centres like Aberdeen. Those links created a rapidly expanding market for Orcadian farm products. Soon Orkney's agricultural exports to the rest of Britain were growing at the remarkable rate of 20 per cent annually. The island group's lairds – who had been casting about for an alternative to the kelp which had earlier provided the bulk of their incomes – were thus given powerful reasons to reshape Orcadian agriculture.

This reshaping was as rapid as it was comprehensive. Not much more than thirty years before, it was observed in 1883, Orkney farmers had endlessly cropped barley from higgledy-piggledy rigs of the kind worked by their great-great-grandfathers:

> Now rotation of crops on the five-shift course is the usual thing, the fields are squared off with almost painful regularity, and well dyked in, and the voice of the steam threshing machine is heard in the land . . . Altogether the Orkneys have passed out of the picturesque stage of history and are, at the present time, probably as thriving as any part of her majesty's dominions.[6]

Not every Orcadian agriculturalist was able to obtain the tenancy of one of the large farms which, during the nineteenth century's middle decades, became increasingly characteristic of the Orkney scene. Many of the folk uprooted in the course of runrig's abolition had no choice but to settle, as many similarly situated people in Easter Ross had done eighty or ninety years before, for crofts consisting of previously uncultivated ground – ground which its occupants were expected to improve by their own efforts and at their own expense.

Typical of such crofters was John Grieve who, in 1847, was granted the tenancy of eighteen acres of hill land on the island of Sanday. Grieve's reclamation of that land took him most of the rest of the nineteenth century and involved year after year of hard, backbreaking work. He began by dyking his croft, draining it and clearing it of stones. Then, in an attempt to deepen its naturally shallow soil, this Sanday crofter brought on to his holding no fewer than three thousand cartloads of earth. In 1889, towards the end of John Grieve's life, his stock consisted of four cows, two calves, a horse and three sheep. It was not a great deal to show for so much labour. But Grieve had at least managed to retain his croft. Others were less fortunate. Many Orkney crofters had to undergo the soul-destroying experience of seeing the plots they had so painstakingly brought into cultivation added to adjacent farms by lairds whose idea of recompense for such losses was to offer dispossessed crofters the chance to start afresh on some new hillside.

Evictions of this Orkney sort, which continued into the 1880s, usually involved no more than one or two families at a time. That did not mitigate the distress caused to the families concerned. But it does suggest that such ejections ought to be distinguished, both in origin and effect, from the more far-reaching removals which began to occur in Shetland during the 1850s and which were similar in intention, if not quite in scope, to the clearances which had already occurred on the Highland mainland and in the Hebrides.

Like Orkney, Shetland had no dependable, year-round shipping connections with other parts of Britain until the nineteenth century was fairly well advanced. The establishing of such connections during the 1840s and 1850s, therefore, presented Shetland lairds – just as they had already presented Orkney lairds – with new opportunities. Shetland's comparatively unproductive terrain ruled out an agricultural improvement programme of the Orcadian type. But with wool prices still rising at that period, sheep offered good prospects. And just as had happened elsewhere in the Highlands and Islands, the introduction of large-scale sheep-farming to Shetland, a development concentrated in the years around 1860, was accompanied by the destruction of entire communities – the most notorious such episode, which took place at Weisdale on Shetland's Mainland, resulting in some three hundred people losing their homes.

***

Shetland, during the 1860s and 1870s, was the only part of the Highlands and Islands enduring clearances of the sort which had previously been so common. This was not because of any marked change of heart on the part of the landlords responsible for the mass evictions of earlier decades. It was a function, rather, of the fact that clearance, if pushed beyond a certain point, ceased to make sense financially. By the mid-1850s, as far as the mainland Highlands and the Hebrides were concerned, practically all the land which lent itself to sheep production had been incorporated into sheep-farms. The comparatively small proportion of the total land area remaining in crofting occupation was, for the most part, of such indifferent quality that further clearance, from the landowning fraternity's perspective, would not have justified the expense and trouble which all such clearance necessarily entailed. Those crofting townships which were still in existence at the end of the famine period, it followed, were almost all permitted to survive thereafter. The same townships' occupants, moreover, were beginning to experience, by 1860, a modest upturn in their fortunes.

That upturn had several causes. Like other agriculturalists, crofters benefited, during the nineteenth century's third quarter, from rising product prices – especially, in the crofting case, from improved returns on cattle. But crofters, as has already been stressed, were mostly part-time farmers whose overall wellbeing depended largely on the extent to which they could obtain non-agricultural earnings. Kelping's demise had left many crofting families without any such earnings – a development which, as also stressed previously, had made lots of crofting localities dependent on the unreliable potato. This situation, however, was eased, from the 1850s onwards, as both crofters and their families began, once again, to acquire off-croft jobs.

Some such jobs were to be got in crofting localities themselves. Crofters and their sons worked on the railways, on steamships serving the various island groups and – as in the case of my grandfather, John Cameron, whose father, Alan, was a crofter at Ariundle, near Strontian – on sporting estates. But of even more importance to the late-nineteenth-century crofting economy were sources of income which could be accessed only by people prepared to travel considerable distances and to spend lengthy periods away from home. Crofters from many parts of the Highlands and Islands were commonly to be found among the navvies whose hikes between one construction project and another took them constantly to and fro across Scotland. From Shetland, crofters went off regularly as crewmen on the whalers which sailed each summer from ports like Dundee and Aberdeen – by way of Lerwick – to Arctic whaling grounds. From Lewis, Harris, the Uists, Skye and adjacent mainland districts, meanwhile, other crofters were hired to help man the large numbers of boats then engaged in the herring fishery.

Herring had been caught around the coasts of the Highlands and Islands for many hundreds of years. On the whole, however, the quantities landed had been small. This longstanding position was transformed, in the course of the nineteenth century, by the development of new catching and preserving techniques as well as by the emergence – first in the West Indies, then in Germany, Russia and the Baltic countries – of a seemingly insatiable demand for cured herring. In the nineteenth century's opening years, the total Scottish output of such herring stood at about 50,000 barrels annually. By the early 1880s, the corresponding figure was in excess of a million barrels. And at the herring boom's peak, a decade or so later, around two million barrels of cured, or salted, herring were produced each year.

In Shetland, one of its leading centres by the nineteenth century's end, the herring fishery was totally to eclipse the old-style haaf. But herring's impact on the Shetland economy, which it dominated in the years around 1900, had been foreshadowed by the same fishery's earlier role in Caithness, especially Wick. Over just three or four decades, starting about 1800, this previously insignificant settlement on the estuary of the Wick River grew into a sizeable town which, for two or three months every summer, became the herring capital of Europe. Where once a handful of fishing cobles had put to sea from the rivermouth, there were, by the 1840s, well over a thousand herring boats operating out of a purpose-built harbour around which there had developed – as well as scores of curing businesses – street after street of homes, shops, lodging houses and pubs. The last, according to a Wick clergyman, were 'seminaries of Satan and Belial'. 'It may seem incredible,' the same clergyman noted despairingly of nineteenth-century Wick's fondness for whisky, 'but it has been ascertained that, during the six weeks of a successful fishing, not less than 500 gallons a day [are] consumed.'[7]

Much of that vast quantity of spirits went down the throats of the many men of crofting background – some five thousand from Lewis alone – who were in the habit, by the 1860s and 1870s, of travelling to Wick each June and July to take advantage of the plentiful work to be got both in the town's harbour area and on its fishing fleet.

When, in the later nineteenth century, other North Sea ports began to rival Wick as herring centres, those ports attracted their own version of this seasonal migration – a migration by no means exclusively male. Gutting and packing herring was women's business.

And a high proportion of the herring industry's huge female workforce came from the Highlands and Islands – where, even towards the twentieth century's close, it was still possible to hear the first-hand recollections of old women who, as young girls, accompanied Scotland's herring fleet as it moved southwards, in the summers prior to the First World War, from Lerwick, by way of Wick and Peterhead, to Lowestoft and Yarmouth. What she most vividly remembered about her time as a herring gutter, one such woman once told me, was the sheer agony she experienced each morning as her hands – all cut and hacked after weeks of such activity – had yet again to be immersed in the icy brine which was central to the herring-packing process. 'I used to cry with the pain of it,' this woman said. 'But after half an hour or so, my hands seemed to turn numb and then it wasn't quite so bad.'

Conditions at sea were equally unpleasant. They were also dangerous. In the course of a single gale off Wick, in August 1848, no fewer than thirty-seven fishermen drowned. More such disasters would follow. But the risks run by the herring fleet's crewmen, like the discomforts endured by the industry's gutters and packers, were compensated for – to some extent at least – by money wages which, if not exactly generous, made it possible, in combination with the other income sources gradually becoming available, for crofting families to begin, at last, to better their situation.

In 1857, potatoes throughout the Highlands and Islands were free of blight for the first time in more than a decade. That helped the crofting population to feed itself adequately – something which, just four or five years earlier, had seemed an unattainable ambition. But of much more importance than improved potato yields was the growing ability of crofting households – for reasons just touched on – to access hard cash. Such cash enabled family after family to escape from the absolute poverty in which they had previously been trapped. And soon living standards were rising noticeably. Tea, an almost unknown luxury in the 1850s, had become a crofting staple by the 1870s. Many Highlands and Islands households, by that latter period, were also reasonably well supplied with sugar, wheat flour and tobacco – items which had earlier been confined to the homes of the well-to-do.

Most people, to be sure, were still far from affluent. John Cameron, born in 1872 and tramping daily in the later 1870s from his parents' croft house at Ariundle to school in Strontian, was typical of his generation in frequently being without boots or shoes. His coat, when he had one at all, consisted of an adult's worn-out jacket with its sleeves cut short. And eighty years after the event, as I remember well, John Cameron still spoke of his astonishment on seeing an orange –

the first he had ever tasted – which, in 1878 or thereabouts, constituted an unforgettable Christmas treat.

When young, I never could imagine one's Christmas presents being so paltry as to consist of a single orange. But when Alan Cameron, John's father and my great-grandfather, was growing up in Strontian during the 1820s and 1830s, there had been, whether at Christmas or at any other time, no oranges – just as there had been no tea to drink, no wheaten flour scones to eat, no school to attend. The crofting population, therefore, was making some degree of progress.

Despite that progress, however, the average crofter's position, as was observed in 1884, remained inherently precarious:

> A good harvest or a good haul may make him comfortable for a season. A blight, an early frost, a wet autumn, a long winter, a gale of wind, a wayward movement of the herring, may deprive him of food for his family, funds for his rent and seed for his ground.[8]

The consequences of bad weather, an immutable fact of life in the Highlands and Islands, a crofter could tolerate. What was less acceptable – what became, in fact, a source of steadily mounting discontent – was the extent to which the typical crofter's continuing difficulties could be traced to the hold exercised over him by others.

Crofting, as noted in earlier chapters, had been created in order to provide landlords with a convenient means of exploiting crofters – whose hold on the land was made conditional on their becoming haaf fishermen, kelpers and the like. Changes in the wider economic circumstances of the Highlands and Islands had made this type of exploitation virtually obsolescent by the 1860s and 1870s. But it was replaced, in all too many instances, by new impositions and exactions. In Shetland, for example, crofting families, though the haaf no longer had them quite so firmly in its grip, were very much at the mercy of the Lerwick-based merchants and shopkeepers who, during the nineteenth century, gradually assumed control of Shetland's economic life. 'The [Shetland] merchant,' it was observed in 1872, 'buys all that leaves the country, from a whale to an egg, and sells everything that the country people want, from a boll of meal, or a suit of clothes, to a darning needle.' By selling dear and buying cheap, such a merchant could readily ensure – and, in most cases, did so ensure – that his customers became as hopelessly in hock to him as previous generations of Shetlanders were to their lairds. Shetland crofters, as a result, remained unable to access wider markets – each crofter's produce, together with his fish catch, having to be handed over to a merchant in part-settlement of that same crofter's always escalating debts.[9]

Much the same situation existed in parts of the Hebrides. But there, as on the Highland mainland, landlords or their factors, rather than merchants, continued to be seen by most crofters as the principal cause of crofting troubles. Such troubles, inevitably, took many forms. But by far the most widespread, and easily the most intractable, were those arising from the appalling housing conditions to be found, even in the later nineteenth century, in crofting communities right across the Highlands and Islands.

The bulk of the nineteenth-century crofting population lived in so-called black houses.* Surviving, or recreated, examples can be seen today in a number of crofting localities. Those modern black houses, however, are carefully sanitised versions – as they have to be if they are to attract visitors – of a reality that was altogether less appealing.

The nineteenth-century black house was invariably grim and unprepossessing. Its stone-and-rubble walls were perpetually damp. It had neither windows nor a chimney; its floor was trampled mud; its furnishings were few and rudimentary. In such houses, a crofter, his family and their cattle all lived under the same straw-thatched and frequently leaking roof. Beasts and humans entered by a single door. Between the cattle's quarters and those of the cattle's owners there was often no partition. Particularly in winter, when cows had to be kept inside for weeks at a stretch, dung and filth penetrated from such a building's byre or cowshed to practically every corner of its living quarters.

In dark, dank, insanitary and foul-smelling homes of this sort, typhoid and cholera persisted long after they had been eradicated from most other parts of Britain. So did tuberculosis. And from all such illnesses, unsurprisingly, the crofting population's youngest members suffered most severely.

In 1877, a visitor to Torrin in Skye set down his impressions of this crofting township. The writer in question came from Edinburgh. That city then contained some notorious slums. But Torrin clearly bore comparison with the very worst of these:

> At the top of the village, gathered in a listless way on a bit of moss land before an almost ruinous cottage, were a dozen

* There are various theories as to the origins of this term. None is particularly convincing.

> children – as squalid and as miserable as any that could be produced from the innermost dens of the Cowgate . . . What I saw in Torrin, I have seen in many places since: children, not the bronzed, healthy urchins such as one meets in Lowland country districts, but puny, uncombed, blear-eyed, shivering little objects . . . This sorrowful index to the condition of the crofter forces itself very strongly on a stranger's notice as he passes through this island.[10]

As is suggested by their design and construction, black houses were lineal descendants of the type of dwelling – described in an earlier chapter – characteristic of the nucleated townships which had been standard in the Highlands and Islands prior to the clearances. But to inspect the remnants of a pre-clearance township such as Rossal in Strathnaver, cleared by Patrick Sellar in 1814, is instantly to suspect that the nineteenth-century black house was inferior, in practically every respect, to what had gone before. As is evident from the surviving foundations of Rossal's homes, those homes were comparatively spacious: much more spacious than the Ariundle croft house (now also a ruin) where my grandfather grew up; more spacious, too, than the houses erected, in 1814 and afterwards, on the coastal crofts which Sellar allocated to the families turned out of Rossal and so many other places.

When laying out sheep-farms, nineteenth-century landlords – being anxious to attract sheep-farming tenants of some substance – equipped such holdings, at their own expense, with solidly built farmhouses. Crofters, in contrast, were everywhere left to provide themselves with their own homes. The elementary nature of most such homes was a consequence, in part, of the crofting population's chronic lack of capital. But it was also the inevitable outcome of a tenurial system which precluded – even when, as in the 1860s and 1870s, capital became available – any worthwhile prospect of crofters investing in new houses.

Crofters tenanted their holdings on a year-to-year basis. They possessed no equivalent of the twenty-one-year leases commonly granted to nineteenth-century farmers. Despite wholesale clearances having largely ceased – outside Shetland – by the 1860s, individual crofters continued, therefore, to be vulnerable to eviction. In such circumstances, it made little sense to sink hard-earned cash in home improvements. This was because the crofter who built himself a good house necessarily ran a very real risk either of his having his rent increased (on the grounds that his holding had become more valuable) or of being deprived completely both of his home and his land (because factors were constantly looking for better-than-average crofts to allocate to estate functionaries).

When, as happened during the 1880s, crofters at last set out to challenge, and to change, the way they were treated, demands for an end both to evictions and to arbitrarily imposed rent hikes were, not unnaturally, to feature prominently on their agenda. But looming even larger on that agenda was a still more pressing crofting grievance. This grievance – destined to fuel decade after decade of crofting protest – stemmed from the way in which, as a result of earlier clearances, the crofting population had been left with far less land than the sheep-farmers who were among those same clearances' more obvious beneficiaries. By the nineteenth century's midpoint, of course, there were plenty of Highlands and Islands districts where crofting had more or less ceased to exist. But even in places where large numbers of crofters had contrived to hang on – in the Hebrides and on the west and north coasts of the Highland mainland, for instance – an extraordinarily small proportion of the total land area was left in crofting occupation. When land-use patterns in four crofting districts were scrutinised systematically in the early 1880s, less than 1 per cent of those districts' agricultural tenants – in other words, their sheep-farmers – were discovered to be occupying nearly two-thirds of the available land.

As crofters were painfully aware, moreover, practically all the land given over to sheep-farming – or to the sporting preserves which, by the 1880s, were taking sheep-farms' place – had formerly been tenanted by folk like themselves. This, inevitably, was a source of constantly rehearsed complaint. Into the 1880s and 1890s, many victims of clearance were still alive. Their sense of having suffered a huge injustice was acute. And even if younger generations of crofters had not had this living tradition of dispossession on which to draw, the record of such dispossession, as commented in 1883, was 'written in indelible characters on the surface of the soil'. That record took the shape of the ruined settlements which, even today, are capable of generating – among those of us, in particular, who have some family link with them – a deep anger. Such anger must have been a good deal more intense in the circumstances of the later nineteenth century when, from the desperately overcrowded and comfortless crofting townships of that period, people looked out, day after day, on enormous, and effectively uninhabited, sheep-farms from which they, their parents or their grandparents had been evicted.[11]

In the famine year of 1846, as starvation began to take hold of many crofting communities, Hugh Miller, the Cromarty stonemason who became one of nineteenth-century Scotland's best-known authors, contrasted what was happening then in the Highlands and Islands with what was going on, that same year, in Ireland:

> They [the Irish] are buying guns and will be by-and-by shooting magistrates and clergymen by the score; and parliament will, in consequence, do a great deal for them. But the poor Highlanders will shoot no one . . . and so they will be left to perish unregarded in their hovels.[12]

The passivity to which Miller thus drew attention can be exaggerated. As has already been underlined, clearing landlords and their factors often encountered considerable resistance. Almost invariably, however, such resistance was sporadic, unco-ordinated and, ultimately, futile. A particular set of removals might be delayed by attacks on the estate employees given the task of carrying them out. But this accomplished little more than a postponement of the inevitable. The ease with which Highlands and Islands landlords could obtain backing from the state – in the form, if necessary, of substantial bodies of troops – guaranteed that, in any localised confrontation with crofters, landowning interests rapidly prevailed. Matters might have been different if crofters had managed to organise on a wider front. But other than briefly in the summer of 1792, no attempt was made by the victims of the Highland Clearances to mount anything approximating to a generalised assault on their oppressors. Nor, after 1792, was there any sense among members of the landed establishment in the Highlands and Islands that their conduct might expose them to violent reprisal.

Why was this? The population of the Highlands and Islands, after all, was renowned for its martial traditions. A part of this population had taken up arms against the British state as recently as 1745. A further part – often a very large part – of the same population served subsequently in the United Kingdom's armed forces. Throughout the clearance period, therefore, the Highlands and Islands contained plenty of men who knew how to use guns. But with occasional early exceptions – such as the one leading to the execution of the Acharn tacksman, James Stewart – the inhabitants of the Highlands and Islands did not respond to clearance and eviction by engaging in death-dealing protest of the type which, as Hugh Miller observed, their Irish equivalents organised regularly.

Irish circumstances were by no means identical to those in the Highlands and Islands, however. The two areas, as earlier chapters made clear, were certainly linked historically. This was to be of some significance in relation to later-nineteenth-century developments in the Highlands and Islands. But of much more significance during immediately preceding decades, and especially during the opening stages of the Highland Clearances, was the extent to which the social composition of Ireland on the one hand, and the Highlands and Islands on the other, had diverged in the course of the three or four hundred years prior to 1800.

Nineteenth-century Ireland's landowners were the family successors, in many instances, of men who – in ways touched on previously – had obtained Irish estates in Elizabethan and Cromwellian times. Being British by extraction, English in speech and Protestant in religion, such landowners were regarded, by their mostly Catholic and mostly Gaelic-speaking tenantries, with an all-embracing detestation – a detestation commonly given popular expression in songs which, even into the Victorian period, hankered after the native Irish chieftains whose death or exile those same songs continued to lament.

Given the nature of the political attitudes built into this popular outlook, it was inevitable that Irish families, when evicted, considered their ejection the work of foreign conquerors whose agents, such families believed, they were morally entitled to resist with all the means – not excluding assassination – at their disposal. But evicted families in the Highlands and Islands, although they might seem to us to have been in exactly the same position as their Irish counterparts, confronted, in fact, a situation calculated to produce an entirely different response.

In contrast to Irish landlords, whose forebears had helped to expel or kill Gaelic Ireland's chieftains, Highlands and Islands landlords were frequently descended from men who themselves were chieftains. That explains the terrible sense of betrayal felt by folk turned out of their homes at the instigation of Highlands and Islands landowners whose ancestors had been the warmly regarded protectors of the communities thus destroyed. But if victims of the Highland Clearances were aware – as was the case – that clearing landlords were disregarding virtually all the ethical and cultural assumptions on which clanship had depended, it did not automatically follow that such victims were in a position to devise an appropriate response. Clan chieftains became landlords, as stressed in a previous chapter, by virtue of their having completed a lengthy process of adjustment to radically altered social and economic realities – a process involving, among other things, the abandonment of a chief's traditional obligations to his clansfolk. But most other people in the Highlands and Islands – especially the Gaelic-speaking Highlands and Islands – had scarcely begun to embark, when the clearances commenced, on their reciprocal versions of that same process. An evicting landlord, from such people's standpoint, was also a man to whom there was owed the loyalty which clansfolk had so unquestioningly given to their chiefs. This loyalty was eventually set aside. Clanship's ideological underpinnings were eventually exchanged for alternative perspectives on the world. New types of leadership eventually emerged from within the Highlands and Islands population. But these and related developments – as is demonstrated by the fact that Highlands and Islands landlordism did not come under effective attack until the 1880s – were to be a long, long time in reaching fruition.

As early as the mid-eighteenth century, admittedly, one segment of the older, clan-based society of the Highlands and Islands had proved capable of successfully countering landlord-inspired upheaval. Tacksmen – the group who had provided clan armies with their officer class – responded to the eighteenth-century commercialisation of land management, as noted a couple of chapters back, by helping lots of Highlands and Islands families to make new homes for themselves in places like the Cape Fear River country. But if emigration of this sort benefited – as it undoubtedly did – many of the folk who participated in it, such emigration, by taking tacksmen themselves to North America, also deprived the Highlands and Islands of the one group who were arguably capable of providing the region with a coherent alternative to the developmental strategy, if that is what it was, pursued by its landlords. Much was to be achieved by the numerous Highlands and Islands tacksmen who crossed the Atlantic in the decades following Culloden. Among their successful ventures, for example, was the North West Company, a fur-trading concern which, around 1800, controlled territories extending all the way from Montreal to the Pacific.* But to be aware of the North West Company's accomplishments is simultaneously to wonder, particularly if one lives in the present-day Highlands and Islands, what might have been done here by its tacksmen founders had they been able to operate in a Highlands and Islands setting rather than a North American one. As it was, the remarkably complete exodus of the tacksman class from the Highlands and Islands served only to add, as far as most of the area's Gaelic-speaking people were concerned, to

---

* The North West Company's story is told in *A Dance Called America*.

the sense that their world – a world which had its cultural roots in Dalriada – was inexorably disintegrating all around them.

Some seventy or eighty years into the nineteenth century, Peggy MacCormack from Lochboisdale, then an old woman, recalled her South Uist childhood in these words:

> How we enjoyed ourselves in those faraway days – the old as much as the young. I often saw three, and sometimes four, generations dancing together on the green grass in the golden summer sunset: men and women of fourscore or more – for they lived long in those days – dancing with boys and girls of five on the green grass. Those were happy days and happy nights, and there was neither sin nor sorrow in the world for us . . . But the clearances came upon us, destroying all, turning our small crofts into big farms for the stranger, and turning our joy into misery, our gladness into bitterness, our blessing into blasphemy, and our Christianity into mockery. *O a dhuine ghaolaich, thig na deoir air mo shuilean le linn smaoininn air na dh'fhuilig sinn agus na duirb thainig sinn `roimhe!* Oh dear man, the tears come on my eyes when I think of all we suffered and of the sorrows, hardships, oppressions we came through![13]

It is easy to respond to such sentiments by observing, quite correctly, that South Uist never was the earthly paradise Peggy MacCormack believed it to have been, but that is wholly to miss the point she so eloquently made. During Peggy MacCormack's lifetime there had been deliberately destroyed, both in South Uist and in much of the rest of the Highlands and Islands, socially cohesive and generally self-assured communities of the type she had been born into. In place of those communities, by the 1860s and 1870s, were congested collectives consisting, for the most part, of crofting families who, despite their having survived famine and clearance, had been so marginalised and so demoralised as to make it perfectly understandable that, for the greater part of the nineteenth century, no thought of taking on their landlords appears to have entered their heads.

Not far from the young Peggy MacCormack there lived Lachlan MacMhuirich. The names of his MacMhuirich ancestors, through eighteen generations, were known to him. Also known to him was the fact that many of his forebears had been bards: to the chiefs of the Clanranald MacDonalds in comparatively recent times; to the Lords of the Isles before that. This latest MacMhuirich, however, crafted no poetry. When, in 1800, enquirers came from the south in search of bardic verse, Lachlan MacMhuirich told them he was illiterate – something that had been true of no former male member of his family for more than five hundred years. Asked by the same enquirers what had happened to the bulky volumes in which earlier MacMhuirichs had inscribed their poems, Lachlan said the last such volumes known to him had been cut up in order to provide a Uist tailor with paper patterns.

The tragedy of the MacMhuirichs – becoming, despite their previous possession of so much learning, a bookless family who could not read – was symptomatic of the much larger tragedy which, by the nineteenth century's commencement, had overtaken the Gaelic-speaking Highlands and Islands as a whole. The language spoken by Colum Cille and by the monks of his Iona monastery; the language of Dalriada's kings; the language of the Lords of the Isles and of innumerable clan chiefs: this language was considered, by the people in charge of nineteenth-century Scotland, to be little more than an emblem of Highlands and Islands benightedness. To one Lowland commentator, writing in 1847, it seemed axiomatic that English was 'the language of civilisation'. From the fact that so many people in the Highlands and Islands could not speak this language, there was thus only one conclusion to be drawn: 'Morally and intellectually, the Highlanders are an inferior race.'[14]

There was nothing unusual about those remarks. Both the editorial columns and the letter pages of the period's newspapers amply attest to the way in which the Gaelic-speaking people of the nineteenth-century Highlands and Islands, together with their language, their culture and traditions, were routinely denigrated, mocked and ridiculed by Lowlanders. As was recognised by John Murdoch, a Gaelic revivalist and land reformer of whom more will shortly be said, such treatment had the inevitable effect of still further disheartening the folk against whom it was directed:

> The language and lore of the Highlanders being treated with despite has tended to crush their self-respect and to repress that self-reliance without which no people can advance. When a man was convinced that his language was a barbarism, his lore as filthy rags, and that the only good thing about him – his land – was, because of his general worthlessness, to go to a man of another race and another tongue, what remained . . . that he should fight for?[15]

Just how hard it is to energise a society consisting of folk who have been comprehensively stripped of land, language and dignity became apparent to me, during 1996, when I spent some time on the Flathead Indian Reservation in Montana. My hosts were an Indian family who owe their surname, McDonald, to their descent from a Highland-born fur trader.* From the McDonalds and from other Indian people I met on the Flathead Reservation, as well as from the evidence of my own eyes, I derived some impression of the long-run consequences of what was done to Native Americans in the course of the nineteenth century. Those consequences are invariably negative. They include, as far as the Flathead Reservation's Indian inhabitants are concerned, alcoholism, drug-dependence and, in many quarters, an all-pervasive hopelessness. Meaningfully to tackle such problems is necessarily to embark on a desperately difficult task. That task, however, is one with which several members of the McDonald family have chosen to engage. What motivates those Indian men and women is not, perhaps, for an outsider to say. But when they spoke about their ambitions, it seemed to me that they were driven primarily by a desire to provide their people with the self-confidence and with the self-esteem which those people, because of the way they have been treated, very generally lack.

Those same qualities, for similar reasons, were equally lacking in the early-nineteenth-century Highlands and Islands. Here, as also happened to Montana's Indians, whole communities had been peremptorily uprooted – while, at the same time, entire value systems, together with a whole mass of traditional beliefs and practices, had been labelled useless, ignorant, backward and outmoded. In such circumstances, it is perfectly understandable that external observers of the nineteenth-century Highlands and Islands should have characterised the region's crofting population as one that was almost invariably sunk in a despairing apathy. It is equally understandable that the same population – like others which have been so situated – should have sought some collective relief from its everyday frustrations and sufferings in the sphere of religious experience.

In earlier periods, the Highlands and Islands, as noted in a previous chapter, had been distinguished by their inhabitants' overall lack of enthusiasm for presbyterianism of the type established in the Lowlands in the sixteenth century. Following the Highland Clearances, however, a passionately evangelical variant of this presbyterianism began to win convert after convert in virtually all the non-Catholic

* The McDonald family feature in the same author's book, *Glencoe and the Indians*.

parts of the region. And to acquire the new faith, as is evident from a contemporary account of its beginnings in Skye, was to acquire much else besides:

> In the year 1812 . . . an uncommon awakening took place among the people, which was attended with distress and trembling of the body . . . These were days of power and of sweetness to as many as had spiritual taste and discernment; so that frequently when they met they were reluctant to part.[16]

When institutionalised – from the 1840s onwards – in Scotland's Free Church and its various offshoots, Highlands and Islands evangelicalism of the type thus described was quickly drained of a good deal of its initial fervour. But it has ever since remained a distinctive feature of the Highlands and Islands scene. And even today, despite the Free Church having lost much of its numerical strength and even more of its influence, there continues to be debate as to the nature of evangelicalism's impact on the area. My contributions to this debate can be read elsewhere.* Here I content myself with observing that, while it is certainly hard to warm to the narrowly sabbatarian, bitterly sectarian, faction-ridden and frequently reactionary Free Church of modern times, it is a mistake to assume that Highlands and Islands evangelicalism always exhibited only those traits. By providing its adherents with a deeply felt sense of personal purpose, early-nineteenth-century evangelicalism helped to counter some at least of the psychological dislocation produced by clanship's collapse and by the various catastrophes which followed that collapse. Equally important was the contribution made by early-nineteenth-century evangelicalism to supplying the Highlands and Islands population with leadership of a sort that had been missing since the tacksmen-led emigrations of the later eighteenth century. At the centre of much religious revivalism were immensely articulate and hugely charismatic lay preachers – usually of crofting background – who regularly attracted entire communities to the enormous, open-air gatherings which constituted the main means of spreading the evangelical message. It is no coincidence that, at a local level, the crofting protest movement of the 1880s was organised in much the same way and relied, very often, on much the same brand of leadership.

But if the grassroots crofting activists of the 1880s drew on the crofting population's widely shared experience of evangelicalism,

---

* In, for instance, *The Making of the Crofting Community.*

such activists drew, too, on the ideas of a number of individuals who made it their business to give an explicitly political – and determinedly radical – dimension to crofting discontents. Much the most influential such individual, to start with at any rate, was John Murdoch. Born at Lynemore, fifteen miles east of Inverness, in 1818, Murdoch grew up on Islay where his father – a crofting tenant of the island's owner – managed to provide the young John with a schooling sufficient to enable him, in 1838, to join the British government's excise service. In his excise capacity, John Murdoch was constantly on the move – serving successively in Kilsyth, Armagh, Lancashire, Islay, Kintyre, Dublin, Waterford, Guildford, Clonmel, Shetland and Inverness. Of those postings, the Irish ones were of particular significance in shaping Murdoch's outlook. While stationed in Dublin, for instance, he spent a lot of time in the company of Irish nationalists of the type who, as well as wishing to restore self-government to Ireland, wanted both to revive their country's Gaelic culture and to rid rural Ireland of its landlords. Those latter aims, Murdoch concluded, were as relevant to the Highlands and Islands as they were to the nation where they had originated. When, in 1873, he retired from the excise in order to found, in Inverness, a weekly newspaper entitled *The Highlander*, he consequently did so with a view to promoting, in a Highlands and Islands context, ideas which, as he acknowledged, were substantially of Irish provenance.

Having been obliged, as a British civil servant, to conceal his identity when contributing in the 1850s to Dublin's nationalist press, Murdoch adopted, as his journalistic pseudonym, the name of the part of Islay which, some four or five hundred years earlier, was home to successive Lords of the Isles. By thus entitling himself Finlagan, John Murdoch was making a point. The achievements of the lordship, together with the achievements of their ancestors more generally, Murdoch felt, were scarcely known to the inhabitants of the nineteenth-century Highlands and Islands. This, Murdoch was convinced, went some way to explain why the region's population had long been quiescent in the face of so much injustice. People taught and encouraged – as so many people in the Highlands and Islands had been taught and encouraged – to ignore, undervalue, even deprecate, their own heritage, were bound, or so John Murdoch thought, to have very little faith in their capacity to change things for the better. Murdoch's identification with attempts to engineer a Gaelic renaissance – attempts which attracted growing support in later-nineteenth-century Scotland – was thus bound up with his belief that the key to advancing crofting interests lay in persuading crofters to take concerted action on their own account. To convince crofters that they were the inheritors of a worthwhile culture was necessarily, in John Murdoch's opinion, to enhance their self-respect. And to enhance crofters' self-respect was to make it more likely that they would ultimately stand up to their landlords.

None of this, as John Murdoch had found by 1875, was easy:

> We have to record the terrible fact that, from some cause or other, a cowed, snivelling population has taken the place of the men of former days. In Lewis, in the Uists, in Barra, in Skye, in Islay, in Applecross and so forth, the great body of the people seem to be penetrated by fear. There is one great, dark cloud hanging over them in which there seem to be the terrible forms of devouring landlords [and] tormenting factors . . . People complain; but it is under their breaths and under such a feeling of depression that the complaint is never meant to reach the ear of landlord or factor. We ask for particulars, we take out a notebook to record the facts; but this strikes a deeper terror. 'For any sake do not mention what I say to you,' says the complainer. 'Why?' we naturally ask. 'Because the factor might blame me for it.'[17]

With a view to countering – and to altering – attitudes of this sort, Murdoch took to spending more and more time among crofters themselves: travelling huge distances on foot; tramping twenty or more miles daily from township to township; endeavouring everywhere to get crofters to speak up in defence of their interests; repeatedly stressing that it was only by embarking on such a course that the people of the Highlands and Islands could connect with potential allies elsewhere. 'They were in no doubt, as they confessed, afraid of the landlord,' Murdoch told an audience in Lochboisdale, 'but they were not more so than landlords and factors were of public opinion.'[18]

What was wanted, John Murdoch commented in his capacity as editor of *The Highlander*, was that crofters 'should hold up their heads, speak forth their minds like men and let each understand that the other feels like he does':

> Our Highland friends must depend on themselves and they should remember that union is strength . . . We do not advocate that they should fight or use violent means, for there is a better way of defending themselves than that. Why do they not form

> societies for self-improvement and self-defence? Why do we not have one such in every parish, if not in every village? Did they become thus united, they would become conscious that they possess more strength than they are aware of.[19]

This, more or less, was eventually to occur. Its occurrence owed a lot to John Murdoch. It owed a lot also to developments in Ireland – developments which Murdoch, because of his Irish connections, was uniquely well placed to capitalise on and to publicise.

In Ireland, towards the end of the 1870s, there was formed the organisation which became known as the Irish Land League. Founded by Michael Davitt, a man who was later to tour the Highlands and Islands in John Murdoch's company, the League rapidly acquired a mass following among farmers and smallholders whose situation – as Murdoch had seen at first hand – was closely akin to that of crofters. Despite the hostility its members encountered on the part both of their landlords and of Ireland's British rulers, the Land League – by virtue of sheer force of numbers and by virtue, too, of the skill with which it deployed rent-strikes and other tactics of that sort – proved politically irresistible. In the spring of 1881, the United Kingdom parliament began debating an Irish Land Bill which, it soon became clear, conceded to Irish tenants many of the rights, including security of tenure, which Land League members were demanding. The moral, from a Highlands and Islands perspective, was obvious. 'The Land Bill for Ireland,' John Murdoch's newspaper editorialised on 4 May 1881, 'is suggestive of many practical thoughts to every Highlander.'[20]

A week later, that same newspaper – burdened by debts and hounded by creditors – ceased publication. Its editor and owner was left to wonder if *The Highlander*, in which he had sunk all his savings, to say nothing of quite staggering amounts of time and energy, had accomplished anything of consequence:

> Judged by a banker's balance, which is the world's criterion of success, it has not. But if our eight years' work has resulted in one, only one, of our readers being assisted to raise himself out of do-nothingism, to realise the fact that he is a MAN, born with a purpose in life, then all our eight years' struggles, our eight years' sacrifices, have not been in vain and the paper has been a success.[21]

Murdoch need not have had any doubts. That month, as it happened, crofters in Kilmuir on Skye employed Irish Land League methods – in the shape of a rent-strike – so skilfully as to compel their landlord, William Fraser, to reduce their rents by a quarter. Not long afterwards, other Skye crofters, this time resident in the district of Braes, embarked on the further rent-strike which, from the standpoint of Britain as a whole, was to turn crofting grievances into matters of national importance. John Murdoch's long, and sometimes lonely, crusade had succeeded.

The little town of Kinsale – the place on the country's south coast where, in 1601, the military forces of Gaelic Ireland were overwhelmed by an English army – is today a holiday resort. In the nineteenth century, however, Kinsale's harbour, given over nowadays to yachts and cruisers, was a leading centre of Ireland's fishing industry. By the 1880s, moreover, it was a centre which, in much the same manner as Wick, had started to attract migrant labour from the Highlands and Islands – migrant labour consisting mostly of crofters who journeyed each year to Kinsale in search of the employment they could not obtain at home. Among the crofting contingent who thus made their way to this County Cork town in the early summer of 1881 was a group from Braes. Their work took the Braes men regularly to sea. But their leisure time they spent ashore: possibly venturing, on occasion, into the West Cork countryside; becoming aware, very definitely, of the techniques which the Irish Land League was employing, in that same summer of 1881, to bring West Cork to the verge of revolution. The precise extent of the Braes party's contact with Land League members is unknown. That such contact occurred is certain, though. Within weeks of the Braes men's return from Kinsale, it resulted in Skye being plunged into its own version of the crisis then gripping Ireland.

Behind Braes, which lies to the south of Portree, is a hill called Ben Lee. Grazings on Ben Lee, like grazings on most comparable hills in the Highlands and Islands, were traditionally reserved for the townships at its foot: Peinchorran, Balmeanach and Gedintailor. When – as happened very widely in the course of the Highland Clearances – Ben Lee's grazings were transferred from crofters to a sheep-farmer, this doubtless caused much grumbling in Braes. Until their 1881 trip to Kinsale suggested otherwise, however, it had seemed to the crofting occupants of Peinchorran, Balmeanach and Gedintailor that there was nothing they could do to make their landlord, Lord Macdonald, restore the use of Ben Lee to them. Similarly situated crofters elsewhere had long made the same assumption. Hence the enduring significance of the actions taken by the Braes men on their getting back to Skye from Ireland.

A petition was drawn up. That petition requested Lord Macdonald to reinstate his Braes tenantry's age-old right to pasture stock on Ben Lee. This request was rejected. That was predictable. What was less predictable – given the crofting population's longstanding reluctance to take such a step – was the nature of the Braes people's next move. In November 1881, on the day their rents were due, the Braes men marched into Portree, halted outside the office of Lord Macdonald's factor and announced, as a bemused estate employee recorded, 'that their rents would not be paid that day, or any other day, until Ben Lee was returned to them'.[22]

To this insubordination, as they saw it, Lord Macdonald and his estate managers responded in the manner that had always previously enabled Highlands and Islands landlordism to enforce its will on the region. They decided to evict a number of Braes rent-strikers on the grounds – perfectly acceptable, of course, to nineteenth-century Scotland's courts – that such rent-strikers were, by definition, in breach of the obligations on which their croft tenancies rested.

On 7 April 1882, a sheriff-officer was despatched from Portree to serve eviction orders on a dozen Braes families. At Braes, however, the sheriff-officer was met by a crowd of about 150 people who, forcibly seizing the orders in question, promptly burned them.

This was to commit the crime of deforcement – the name given in law to an attack made upon sheriff-officers, or other court officials, in the course of their duties. And since the names of five of the crofters who had taken a prominent part in the proceedings of 7 April were known to the authorities, warrants were immediately issued for their arrest.

The responsibility for enforcing those warrants rested ultimately with William Ivory, Sheriff of Inverness-shire, a county which included Skye. This responsibility was one which Ivory welcomed. Convinced that it was his duty to prevent the Highlands and Islands turning into another Ireland, Ivory resolved to teach the Braes crofters a lesson which, he hoped, would dissuade others from following their example. Because Inverness-shire's own police force was not numerous enough for his purposes, the sheriff obtained from Glasgow a detachment of some fifty constables who were speedily conveyed to Skye by steamer. Before dawn on 19 April, a day of cold, incessant rain, those Glasgow policemen – who must have been heartily wishing themselves back in Sauchiehall Street – left Portree, which they had made their base, to march the seven or eight miles to Braes.

Bringing up the rear of the police column, and comfortably ensconced in a coach, was Sheriff William Ivory whose day, from his perspective, started well – in that the five wanted men were easily apprehended. From that point forward, however, Ivory's expedition got into deeper and deeper trouble as a result of some Braes crofters' spontaneous decision to organise an immediate counter-attack both on the sheriff and on his accompanying constables.

In 1882, the townships of Gedintailor, Balmeanach and Peinchorran – as is still the case today – were connected with the rest of Skye by the narrow road linking them to Portree, the island's administrative capital. On the northern outskirts of Gedintailor, the first of the three townships to be reached by anyone approaching from the Portree direction, that road threads its way through a narrow defile flanked, on one side, by a sheer drop into the sea and, on the other, by Ben Lee's steeply rising slopes. As a result of their occupying this strategically located spot, at a stage in the proceedings when William Ivory and his police brigade were still a mile or two to the south of them in Peinchorran and Balmeanach, a large group of Braes residents succeeded in bottling the sheriff and his men into a locality where – with practically every crofting household in the vicinity mobilising against them – Ivory and his party were badly outnumbered.

On realising just how hazardous his position had become, Ivory first instructed his constables to draw their batons. Next he told them to charge the folk occupying the Portree road. The immediate outcome of this latter command was a pitched battle – each repeated police baton charge floundering in the face of a hail of stones and other missiles thrown by the men, women and children holding the high ground to Ivory's left. With rain still lashing down, with yells and screams echoing all around, and with blood pouring from broken heads on both sides, the scene – as afterwards described – quickly took on the character of one of those conflicts in which the clans of three or four centuries earlier had so often engaged. For a time, as fighting swayed back and forth, it seemed that the Braes people might actually force Ivory – who personally slipped and fell twice at the mêlée's height – to give up the five men he had earlier arrested and whose release was the Braes folk's key objective. But by means of a final, desperate charge, the sheriff's constables managed to break through the encircling crowd, regain control of the disputed road and – albeit in a state of some disorder – push on towards Portree with their captives.

A stone monument has been erected in modern times on the site of William Ivory's Gedintailor encounter with the community he had so confidently – and so mistakenly – expected to intimidate. 'Near this cairn on the 19th of April, 1882,' that monument's inscription reads, 'ended the battle fought by the people of Braes on behalf of the crofters of Gaeldom.'

Despite my long familiarity with the monument on which they are inscribed, those words – when I pause, as I habitually do on entering Braes, to read them – can move me still. It is an arguable proposition, admittedly, that Gedintailor's memorial cairn inflates the significance of what occurred here in 1882 while detracting, even if unintentionally, from the efforts made by other crofters who – prior to the Braes episode – had equally raised the standard of revolt. Prominent among such crofters were the Kilmuir people whose rent-strike, as already mentioned, antedated the one in Braes. Also deserving mention, in this context, are the folk of Bernera, Lewis, who, as far back as 1874, staged their own violent confrontation with representatives of a particularly repressive estate management. Events in Kilmuir and Bernera, however, produced only local consequences. The happenings commemorated by the Gedintailor cairn, as the inscription implies, were to have much more far-reaching effects. At Braes in 1882 there began to be created circumstances which, in the period since then, have resulted in the Highlands and Islands regaining at least some part of the autonomy which, between the eleventh century and the eighteenth, the region so comprehensively lost.

Some indication of the magnitude of what occurred at Braes is evident in the extent to which Highlands and Islands landlords – because of the manner in which the April 1882 clash interacted with wider developments – now found themselves forced, for the first time, on to the defensive. Improved communications, in the shape of the railway and the telegraph, had put Britain's newspaper readers – of whom there were rapidly growing numbers by 1882 – in close touch with events in the Highlands and Islands. The nature of those events, as reported by the journalists who flocked to Skye in Sheriff Ivory's wake, was such as to cause widespread outrage. And in a way that it would not have done fifty or sixty years earlier, when the United Kingdom parliament represented only Britain's ruling class, this outrage mattered a great deal.

As more and more of its people obtained the right to vote, late-nineteenth-century Britain was being inexorably transformed into a democracy. Its government, as a result, was increasingly responsive to public opinion. Much of that opinion, in the spring of 1882, was plainly shocked by the notion that, with a view to facilitating a wealthy landlord's eviction of his crofting tenants, baton-wielding policemen had been so readily unleashed against a Skye community. Government ministers consequently came under pressure to intervene actively in Highlands and Islands affairs: to extend to crofters, perhaps, rights of the sort so recently granted to agricultural tenants in Ireland; to initiate, at the minimum, a wide-ranging enquiry into the underlying causes of crofting discontents.

At the forefront of this pro-crofter campaign were people whose family origins could be traced to the Highlands and Islands but who – because their parents or grandparents had been obliged to move south at the time of the clearances – were themselves resident in urban areas. Many of those people were upwardly mobile and highly articulate professionals – businessmen, lawyers, teachers and the like. Members of this group had been among the more avid readers of John Murdoch's *Highlander*. They shared Murdoch's conviction that what the Highlands and Islands required, above all else, was land reform. Their distinctive contribution to the attainment of this objective – a contribution which they were uniquely well placed to make – lay in the extent to which, throughout the 1880s, they provided the population of the Highlands and Islands with effective political guidance.

Such guidance, however, would have counted for little had the rebellion which began at Braes remained confined to that single locality. It did not. During the summer of 1882, protest of the Braes type began to spread to other crofting areas. Such protest spread, in the first instance, to Glendale in Skye's north-western corner.

The Glendale equivalent of Ben Lee was the sheep-farm of Waterstein – a farm created, like all such holdings, in the course of the Highland Clearances. Waterstein's lease, as it happened, expired in the spring of 1882. But on a group of Glendale crofters asking the Glendale estate's owners if they might be permitted to have the farm, for which the crofters in question were willing to pay a reasonable rent, their request – just like the Braes people's request for the restoration to them of Ben Lee – was rejected. Instead, Waterstein was let to an estate employee.

On this becoming known, and on various Glendale crofters threatening simply to take over the disputed farm, Glendale's proprietors – in the shape of the executors, or trustees, of the estate's recently deceased landlord – came to Skye, at the beginning of May, to meet the Glendale people. Urged by their visitors to be patient, the latter responded in a manner which neatly encapsulated their growing determination to take matters into their own hands:

> We told them that our forefathers had died in good patience, and that we ourselves had been waiting in patience until now, and that we could not wait any longer – that they never got anything by their patience, but constantly getting worse.[23]

By the end of May, cattle belonging to Glendale crofters were being pastured on Waterstein. This, it was agreed by the courts to which Glendale's owners turned for help, was illegal. But the court order which the estate's proprietors obtained, and which instructed the offending crofters to remove their animals from Waterstein, was ignored. Waterstein remained in crofting occupation. And when, in November, one of the Glendale estate management's shepherds tried to clear the farm of crofters' livestock, he was promptly beaten up by the livestock's owners.

Shortly before Christmas, warrants were issued for the arrest of more than twenty Glendale men who had allegedly been implicated in the November assault. And on 16 January 1883, with a view both to enforcing those warrants and to ending the occupation of Waterstein, an attempt was made to station a police sergeant and three constables at Hamara, one of Glendale's several crofting townships. Alerted to the approach of this police detachment by sentries they had placed on the hills overlooking the road which leads westwards into Glendale from nearby Dunvegan, a large crowd mustered to await the detachment's arrival. The unfortunate constables and sergeant, together with an inspector who was accompanying them, were knocked down and beaten as a prelude to their being herded back the way they had come.

As such happenings indicate, Glendale, during the opening weeks of 1883, was passing – in a manner not seen in the Highlands and Islands since the 1740s – out of the United Kingdom's jurisdiction. This was dramatically underlined, on 20 January, when Glendale crofters inflicted a further humiliation on Inverness-shire's police force – a force whose members were widely considered, by Skye crofters, to act, for the most part, as the uniformed agents of the island's landlords. On hearing that morning of the approach of a well-drilled column of Glendale crofters, the several constables then based in Dunvegan – rather than confront men armed, it was reported, with clubs, scythes, graips and other makeshift weapons – took themselves off, as hurriedly as possible, in the direction of Portree.

Throughout 1882, the British government, struggling all the while to cope with Ireland's agrarian troubles, had resisted calls for government intervention in the Highlands and Islands. Events in Glendale, however, made such intervention unavoidable. In an unprecedented development, an official emissary was sent to Skye – aboard a naval gunboat – to commence negotiations with Glendale's crofters. At the close of those negotiations, a token five crofters agreed to stand trial in Edinburgh.* But this crofting concession was more than matched by ground given on the government side – ministers announcing that a royal commission would shortly commence inquiries into crofting conditions. On 8 May, this commission, chaired by Francis Napier, a Borders peer, began taking evidence from crofters at Braes.

The first witness to appear before Napier and his colleagues was Angus Stewart whose Peinchorran croft, when I went to live in Skye in 1986, was occupied by Stewart's great-great-nephew, Sorley MacLean, easily the most eminent Gaelic poet of recent times. His great-great-uncle, Sorley told me, planted the hawthorn trees which stand beside the gate where Sorley met me on my first visit to his Peinchorran home. His great-great-uncle, Sorley also told me, was a man of immense moral courage. Angus Stewart's testimony of 8 May 1883 confirms as much.

Asked by Lord Napier to list such 'hardships or grievances' as seemed to him important, Angus Stewart made this reply:

> I would wish that I should have an opportunity of saying a few words before I tell that, and that is that I should have the assurance that I will not be evicted from my holding by the landlord or factor as I have seen done already . . . I want the assurance that I will not be evicted, for I cannot bear evidence to the distress of my people without bearing evidence to the oppression and high-handedness of the landlord and his factor.[24]

On being pressed repeatedly by Lord Napier, the factor to whom Angus Stewart alluded – his name was Alexander MacDonald – grudgingly agreed that the Peinchorran crofter should consider himself free to speak his mind. This Stewart duly did.

Both he and his neighbours, Angus Stewart said, were poor. They were poor because they did not have enough land. And they did not

* Where they were afterwards sentenced to two months in jail.

have enough land because, in the course of the Highland Clearances, family after family – having been forcibly deprived of holdings elsewhere – had been crammed into places like Braes.

'I remember the factor clearing a township,' Stewart went on, 'and devoting the township's land to the purpose of [a] deer forest.' The township in question, Torramhichaig,* had been cleared in the 1850s, Angus Stewart explained. He had been a boy then, and he recalled how one of Torramhichaig's dispossessed tenants, a widow as it happened, had been settled by Lord Macdonald's factor on his father's holding – 'with the intention,' as Stewart put it, 'that my father would share with her . . . the half of the croft.' His father, Angus Stewart added, had been reluctant to part with so much land. However, 'when he [Stewart senior] went to the factor to complain of this proceeding, the factor told him that if he would not give her [the widow] room, he would not have a sod on Lord Macdonald's property'.[25]

So commonplace had been occurrences of this sort, Stewart claimed, that the number of tenants in Peinchorran had increased more than fivefold in the space of two generations – from five to twenty-seven.

His own corner of Peinchorran, Angus Stewart continued, consisted of the half-croft left to his father following the Torramhichaig widow's resettlement in the township. For this little piece of land, much of it 'rocky' and 'mossy', he paid an annual rent of £5 9s. – the equivalent, at that time, of more than two months' average wages. Because his croft was so small, Stewart said, he had no alternative but to crop it continually. Its fertility, not very great to begin with, had consequently declined to such an extent that his crop yields barely exceeded, in quantity, the seed he sowed each spring.[26]

'Can you suggest,' Lord Napier interjected, 'any measure which the landlord or other parties could take in order to improve your situation?' Referring, in part, to Ben Lee, Angus Stewart replied: 'It is easy to answer that. Give us land, out of the plenty that is about . . . That is the principal remedy I see. Give us land at a suitable rent.'[27]

From the hundreds of other crofters whom they interviewed right across the Highlands and Islands, Napier Commission members heard lots more to the same effect. Unsurprisingly, then, their report, published in April 1884, recommended reform. The particular reform package suggested to the British government by the Napier Commission, however, was not far-reaching enough to be acceptable in the Highlands and Islands. Commission members, for example, refused

---

* This township was located on the sourthern shore of Loch Sligachan, not far from Braes.

to endorse the notion – put repeatedly to them by crofters – that the land taken from crofting communities by clearing landlords should be compulsorily restored to those communities. Equally disappointing, from a crofting standpoint, were the commission's suggestions with regard to security of tenure. Such security, commission members felt, should be confined to the tiny minority of crofters whose livelihoods depended completely on agriculture. It should not be extended, the report stated, to the generality of the crofting population.

Far from solving what was starting to be known as the crofting problem, therefore, the report had the effect of stimulating renewed unrest of the sort which had resulted in the commission being established. This time, however, such unrest was not confined to Skye. Throughout the Hebrides, that most pro-landlord of newspapers, *The Scotsman*, commented in October 1884:

> Men are taking what does not belong to them, are setting all law at defiance, and are instituting a terrorism which the poor people are unable to resist . . . Rents are unpaid, not because the tenants cannot pay them, but because in some cases they will not, and in some cases they dare not.[28]

Intimidation was undoubtedly employed to enforce rent-strikes – some strike-breakers having their cornstacks burned and their cattle mutilated. But such tactics, despite endless claims to the contrary from landlord sources, were not used widely – the overwhelming majority of crofters needing very little encouragement to take part in a campaign intended to make government ministers concede, in a Highlands and Islands context, what had already been conceded in Ireland.

This campaign was given political focus and direction by an organisation which had been formed by the crofting population's urban allies but which acquired, during 1883 and 1884, many thousands of members in the Highlands and Islands. Originally called the Highland Land Law Reform Association, this organisation became known eventually as the Highland Land League. As is suggested by that latter title, this new Land League was explicitly modelled on its Irish precursor. It was also influenced – ideologically and in other ways – by a number of the socialist groupings then taking shape in Britain's industrial centres. But for all that it suited the Highland Land League's pro-landlord critics to portray the organisation as a front for people those same critics invariably dismissed as city-based 'agitators', the league – as is demonstrated by the proceedings of its dozens of local branches – was rooted very deeply in the population of the Highlands and Islands.

Consider, in this connection, the best known of the many slogans emblazoned on banners of the kind displayed at the numerous meetings and demonstrations which the Land League staged, in the mid-1880s, throughout the Highlands and Islands. *Is treasa tuath na tighearna*, that slogan proclaimed. In its standard English translation, 'The people are mightier than a lord', this Gaelic proverb seems aggressively modernist in concept. But the word *tuath* – though it can certainly be understood to mean 'people' in the democratic sense of that term – had originally been applied, as mentioned earlier, to a tribe or kin-group of the sort characteristic of sixth-century Dalriada. That is a most suggestive fact. It hints, in particular, at the extent to which the aspirations of Highland Land League members were derived from beliefs of great antiquity.

'The fish that was yesterday miles away from the land was claimed by the landlord the moment it reached the shore,' a crofter declared at a Land League meeting held in Skye during 1884:

> And so also were the birds of the air as soon as they flew over his land. The law made it so, because landlords were themselves the lawmakers, and it was a wonder that the poor man was allowed to breathe the air of heaven and drink from the mountain stream without having . . . the whole of the county police pursuing him as a thief.[29]

Underlying such comments was the notion – one set out clearly in the thousand-year-old law tracts mentioned in a previous chapter – that a locality's fish or game cannot reasonably be appropriated by any single individual. This notion, of course, counted for nothing in nineteenth-century Scotland's courts. But it survived, as it still survives, in the Gaelic-speaking Highlands and Islands where proverbs and sayings – asserting, for instance, everyone's right to a deer from the hill, a tree from the wood and a fish from the river – commonly embody ancient Celtic doctrine to the effect that a neighbourhood's natural resources should be managed and exploited in the interest of the neighbourhood as a whole.

Of even greater significance, in a Highland Land League context, were equally longstanding convictions relating to the occupancy of land. Of these, the most important concerned the entitlement, as it was thought, of all groups within any given *tuath*, or clan, to reside permanently on the territories of the *tuath* in question. This entitlement, as noted earlier, was referred to, throughout the Gaelic-speaking Highlands, as *duthchas* – by which was meant clansfolk's right, as long as such clansfolk did what clan chiefs required of them, to be left in undisturbed occupation of their rigs, their homes, their townships. Hence the widespread feeling in the Highlands and Islands that clearing landlords were in flagrant breach of an age-old social compact which, had it been honoured, would have made clearances impossible. Feeling of exactly this sort emerges clearly from a report of how her tenants reacted to evictions ordered, at the start of the nineteenth century, by the Countess of Sutherland:

> They argued that they had a prescriptive claim to the soil: that they did their lady justice if they farmed it as their fathers had done; and that, chieftainess though she were, she had no better title to eject them from their humble tenements than they had to drive her from her castle.[30]

From crofting delegate after crofting delegate, the Napier Commission heard identically phrased arguments. Crofters were universally of the opinion, the commission reported, 'that the small tenantry of the Highlands have an inalienable title to security in their possessions'. Although 'long . . . repudiated by the actions of the proprietors', the commission added, this opinion was 'indigenous to the country'.[31]

When the Highland Land League demanded that the United Kingdom parliament grant crofters security of tenure, therefore, the league was not requesting, as far as its members were concerned, something new. Parliament was simply being asked to restore a time-honoured right of which the inhabitants of the Highlands and Islands, or so the Land League asserted, had been unjustly deprived. From the perspective of the region's landed proprietors, needless to say, this was a wholly unpersuasive contention. But it depended on a reading of history which, as well as making sense to the population of the Highlands and Islands, also appealed to the one man who, by virtue of his being the United Kingdom's prime minister, was in a position to give crofters what they wanted. This man was William Gladstone.

Passionately committed to his own particular brand of justice and inclined always to suspect the worst of any aristocracy, Gladstone tended instinctively to take the crofting population's side. While it was certainly the case, the prime minister told his Liberal Party colleagues, that the property rights of landlords ought to be respected, it was equally the case that no such respect should be extended to landed property founded – as Gladstone, like the Highland Land League, believed much landed property in the Highlands and Islands to be – on the unilateral appropriation by landlords of clan territories to which the landlords in question had arguably possessed no exclusive claim. It was because their stake in the land had effectively been stolen from them, William Gladstone commented in a letter of 1885, that the people of the Highlands and Islands were entitled to expect some assistance both from him and from his government:

> It is . . . this historical fact that constitutes the crofters' title to demand the interference of parliament. It is not because they are poor, or because there are too many of them, or because they want more land to support their families, but because those whom they represent had rights of which they have been surreptitiously deprived to the injury of the community.[32]

With William Gladstone in power in London, it required less pressure than it might otherwise have done to obtain the reforms which the Highland Land League wanted. But it took a good deal of pressure all the same: in the shape of still more land seizures and rent-strikes; in the shape, too, of the electoral successes made possible by franchise reforms which gave crofters – male crofters, anyway – votes for the first time. The landowners, factors and sheep-farmers who had formerly constituted almost the entire – and, by definition, extremely small – electorate in the Highlands and Islands had been in the habit, naturally enough, of sending men of their own class to Westminster. That cosy arrangement was ended when, in the run-up to the British general election of December 1885, the Highland Land League announced its decision to contest every Highlands and Islands constituency. Reporting on the several Land League victories which followed, the *Oban Times*, then the leading Land League newspaper, was understandably ecstatic: 'The enemy have left the spoils and fled before the conquering hosts of land reform. From the Mull of Kintyre to the Butt of Lewis, the land is before us.'[33]

With a bloc of Highland Land League MPs in the House of Commons, with much of the Highlands and Islands in the grip of the most effective protest movement the region had witnessed since the demise of Jacobitism, and with William Gladstone warming perceptibly to the Land League case, parliament, it was evident at the start of 1886, was going to have to devote a lot of attention to the Highlands and Islands. By the summer, as a result, a Crofters Act had been passed.

This Act of 1886, a hugely more radical measure than the Napier Commission had advised, provided each and every crofter with the security of tenure the Highland Land League had demanded. A modernised and legally enforcible equivalent of the *duthchas* of earlier times, this security was of a peculiarly all-encompassing and never-ending kind – the 1886 Act, as well as rendering crofters immune from eviction, permitting them to transfer croft tenancies to their heirs. The Crofters Act thus guaranteed the continuation of crofting. And the benefits of its security-of-tenure provisions were at once apparent in a marked improvement in housing conditions – as thousands of crofters, freed at last from the threat of ejection and removal, began to equip their holdings with the slated and white-painted cottages which everywhere replaced black houses and which, for much of the twentieth century, were to be characteristic of crofting areas.

Reflecting on the implications of what had been accomplished in the year just ended, a Glendale crofter remarked at the beginning of 1887:

> If a crofter formerly built a house, it belonged [in effect] to the laird – as well as other improvements effected by the crofter. Now the crofter could call the house and croft his own, along with any improvements which he made. Fifty years ago, could their fathers have believed that such a change could be effected?[34]

Soon there were further gains to celebrate. The Crofters Act had established a judicial tribunal, the Crofters Commission,* to fix the level of croft rents and to determine what proportion landlords should receive of the arrears resulting from the rent-strikes in which, by 1886, crofters everywhere were engaging. Lambasted by landlords as 'autocratic' and 'despotic', the commission proved impervious to all such attacks. Croft rents were generally reduced by between 20 and 30 per cent. Half, or more than half, of outstanding arrears were cancelled.[35]

That was important. But what gives the Crofters Act still greater

* The rent-fixing powers of this first Crofters Commission were transferred in 1912 to the then newly established Scottish Land Court. The present-day Crofters Commission, which dates from 1955, has different responsibilities.

significance, in relation to this book's central theme at any rate, is the manner in which it represented a decisive reversal, by a British government, of a Highlands and Islands policy initiated by the medieval Scottish state and inherited, in the eighteenth century, by the United Kingdom in its role as that state's successor. This policy's key characteristic, as has been emphasised repeatedly, is to be found in its tendency to undermine, and eventually eradicate, all vestiges of Highlands and Islands autonomy – thus helping to make so prevalent, as argued previously, exactly those injustices which the Act of 1886 was intended to redress. During the later nineteenth century, admittedly, the negative consequences of the Highlands and Islands having been absorbed into the United Kingdom had begun to be countered by more positive developments deriving from Britain's gradual democratisation. Among such developments, for example, were schools of the sort John Cameron began attending in Strontian in 1877 – schools which followed on the British government's 1872 decision to make primary education available to every child in Scotland. But for all that schools like the Strontian one were an advance on the previous position, their curriculum – which, to the outrage of John Murdoch and many others, made absolutely no provision for teaching through the medium of Gaelic – was founded on the conviction that state-provided schooling must have as one of its major goals the inculcation of the English language. That was why John Cameron, knowing no English when he first went to school, so disliked, he said, the experience – an experience which was very much a product of the centralising and homogenising policies to which the Highlands and Islands had been subjected for so long and which were by no means confined, of course, to the sphere of speech and language.

Had there been no crofting revolt and no Highland Land League, policies of this type would doubtless have remained unquestioned in London. As it was, however, the Highlands and Islands began to be recognised, in 1886, as an area where conditions were such, after all, as to merit its being treated differently from the rest of Britain. Thus the region, from 1886 onwards, acquired, in the Crofters Act, its own land law. It also acquired, in the Crofters Commission, a body dedicated to the enforcement of this land law. The commission, to be sure, was scarcely on a par with the independent or quasi-independent principalities – such as the Earldom of Orkney or the Lordship of the Isles – which the medieval Highlands and Islands had possessed. But the formation of the Crofters Commission nevertheless represented a move – the first in several centuries – towards the formal recognition of the Highlands and Islands as a place requiring institutional structures of a wholly unique type. There would, in the years that followed, be several other such moves. Their eventual outcome, this book's concluding chapter contends, was the marked regeneration – economic, social and cultural – which the Highlands and Islands were to experience in the later part of the twentieth century.

The Crofters Act of 1886 applied to the then counties of Argyll, Inverness-shire, Ross and Cromarty, Sutherland, Caithness, Orkney and Shetland. In general terms, the Highlands and Islands, as thus defined, remain the Highlands and Islands – administratively at all events – today. In the later part of the twentieth century, when determining the responsibilities of the Highlands and Islands Development Board and its successor body, Highlands and Islands Enterprise (HIE), the United Kingdom parliament consented to some adjustment of the 1886 boundary – with the result that HIE deals today with localities, such as Arran, Bute and the more westerly part of Moray, which were excluded from the provisions of the Crofters Act. But this modest revision left outside the Highlands and Islands, as delimited legislatively, a number of districts – including the northern parts of Stirlingshire and Perthshire, as well as Deeside, Donside and upper Banffshire – which were once regarded as Highland and which some people, including residents of the districts in question, continue to regard as Highland still. From several such districts there had been appeals, in 1886, for a more generous view to be taken of the geographical extent of the Highlands and Islands. But those appeals – perhaps because of their being unsupported by direct action of the sort the Highland Land League had so successfully fomented – were ignored.

Nor was it only in respect of the area to which it applied that the Crofters Act of 1886 was judged insufficiently far-reaching by contemporaries. Much of the unrest preceding the Act's passage had been fuelled, as noted previously, by the crofting population's wish to regain access to land from which crofters had been expelled in preceding decades. The 1886 legislation contained no worthwhile provisions in this regard. That was a particular blow to the many folk, known as cottars or squatters rather than crofters, who – because of the sheer extent of earlier clearances – had been left without holdings of any kind and who mostly lived in makeshift huts erected on other people's crofts. Cottars and squatters had backed the Highland Land League in the expectation of obtaining crofts of their own. These, however, had not been forthcoming. During 1886, 1887 and 1888, as a result, cottars and squatters were at the forefront of renewed protest

– usually involving the seizure of sheep-farms – which, it was hoped, would have the effect of persuading the British government to offer further concessions of the sort William Gladstone had already made.

Within weeks of the Crofters Act reaching the statute book, however, Gladstone and his Liberal Party lost office. Their place was taken by a Conservative administration which initially adopted a much tougher line on Highlands and Islands issues. At the end of July 1886, hours after the installation of a Conservative minister, Arthur Balfour, at the recently created Scottish Office, some 250 troops were landed on Tiree with a view to terminating the occupation, by the Highland Land League's Tiree members, of one of the island's larger farms. This was not the first time the military had been deployed against the Land League – Balfour's Liberal predecessors having sent soldiers to Skye in 1884. But the new Scottish Secretary and his ministerial colleagues were much more willing than Gladstone's government had been to resort to force when confronted with Highlands and Islands unrest. During the winter of 1887–88, for instance, Land League members found themselves facing the military on three separate occasions – two of them in Lewis, the other in Sutherland. In the course of one of those episodes, sparked off by the occupation of Aignish Farm near Stornoway, marines and infantrymen fought hand-to-hand with an infuriated crowd. Elsewhere in the Hebrides, meanwhile, farm dykes were being demolished, telegraph lines cut and sheep-farmers' flocks mutilated by folk whose objective, as their representatives declared at a mass meeting in Stornoway in January 1888, was to force politicians 'to restore to the descendants of the clansmen . . . the whole of the lands . . . tilled by their ancestors for centuries'.[36]

Balfour and his Conservative successor as Scottish Secretary, Lord Lothian, refused to do this. But so fundamental was the policy readjustment which had commenced in 1886 – and so difficult had it become to take a purely coercive line in crofting localities – that the Conservatives, like their Liberal opponents before them, were increasingly obliged to adopt a more conciliatory stance with regard to the Highlands and Islands. Unwilling to engage at this point – although they were to do so later – in the redistribution of land, the Conservatives gradually began to make concessions of another sort. Declaring himself willing, for example, to invest public funds in the Highlands and Islands economy, Lothian embarked, in 1889, on measures – which, in a sense, are still ongoing – intended to expand and enhance the region's communications infrastructure. The immediate consequences included the construction of new railway lines from Fort William to Mallaig and from Strome Ferry to Kyle of Lochalsh. Among ensuing initiatives of the same sort was one which resulted in a programme of harbour upgradings. So successful was this overall approach judged by its Conservative promoters that they resolved, in 1897, to provide the Highlands and Islands with what amounted to the region's first development agency.

This agency was the Congested Districts Board. The board, as its name indicates, had the remit of enhancing living standards in overcrowded townships of the sort which, since the clearances, had been characteristic of most crofting areas. Despite its being hampered by the inadequacy of its budget, the board, which remained in being until 1912, achieved a great deal. By providing crofters with more expensive breeding stock than they would otherwise have been able to acquire, its staff were able to make significant improvements to the quality of crofting agriculture. Townships without access roads – of which there were many – began to be provided with such roads. Financial and other assistance was extended to the tweed industry which, around 1900, was just starting to get off the ground in Lewis and Harris. And in what amounted to a further concession of the 1886 sort, the Congested Districts Board, by purchasing land which had earlier been cleared and by re-establishing a crofting population on that land, launched the first serious attempt to undo the consequences of the Highland Clearances.

This programme of land settlement, as such activity became known, commenced with the acquisition, between 1900 and 1904, of two properties on Skye and one in Sutherland. The latter consisted of the sheep-farm of Syre in Strathnaver where the Congested Districts Board proceeded to provide some thirty crofts in a locality which, about eighty years before, had been cleared of its inhabitants by Patrick Sellar. Among the families whom the board helped to set up home at Syre was one whose oldest member, as a little girl, had been evicted, with her parents, from Strathnaver in 1814. This elderly woman's return to the strath where she had been born – symbolic, as it was, of the wider Highlands and Islands determination to win back what had been lost – was a victory of sorts. But the Congested Districts Board, being congenitally strapped for cash, was incapable of satisfying the widespread demand for further such initiatives. Additional financial resources would need to be found, it was evident, if land settlement was to have more than a purely local impact.

Although the Highland Land League fragmented during the 1890s, a good deal of its programme was taken over by the Liberal Party. In the Highlands and Islands, therefore, much was expected by many people of the Liberals when, after a lengthy period in the political wilderness, they were returned to power in the general election of 1906. Obstructionism by the House of Lords – its membership consisting disproportionately of landlords – delayed the land-reform legislation to which the Liberal Party, which had achieved sweeping electoral successes in the Highlands and Islands, was committed. By 1912, however, the Liberal government had replaced the Congested Districts Board with an entirely new organisation, the Board of Agriculture for Scotland. This board's principal task, ministers made clear, was to press ahead with as much land settlement as possible in the Highlands and Islands.

Board of Agriculture personnel were anxious to do what had been asked of them. But they were hamstrung by the complex and highly legalistic procedures governing their operations. On the ground, as a result, there was mounting frustration. This expressed itself in gestures of a sort which had first become common in crofting areas during the 1880s. The most common such gestures, increasingly known as land raids, typically involved the forcible takeover of the sheep-farms which, it was felt in many Highlands and Islands communities, the Board of Agriculture should immediately have made available for crofting settlement. By 1913, seizures of this type were occurring in several parts of the Highlands and Islands – especially in the Hebrides where the number of cottar or squatter families tended to be largest and where the demand for new holdings was correspondingly intense.

The thinking of 1913's numerous land raiders is illustrated by a letter sent to Scottish Office civil servants by men who took over, in December that year, the Lewis farm of Reef – on the island's Atlantic coast. This farm, those particular raiders explained, 'was for ages cultivated by smallholders before the clearances'. They felt themselves entitled to have crofts on it. They were looking both to the Liberal government and to the Board of Agriculture to make this possible:

> We were applying for land since the year 1908 . . . We were getting replies giving neither encouragement nor discouragement, as if the whole proceedings were in mockery. The only reply we now get is that our 'application is under consideration'. Anyhow, we were believing we would get land and that caused us to remain at home in anticipation of getting to work on the land, and that was not in our favour as we did not go elsewhere for work. If we won't have immediate possession, we

> shall be compelled to dispose of our stock which we were diligently gathering and keeping together in order to have some for the new land . . . As is well known, an Act of Parliament [the Act constituting the Board of Agriculture] was passed to give land to the landless and, as is equally well known, no land was received by anyone under the Act. Surely no one can blame us for the steps we have decided to take. But whether we get blamed or not is of no moment. We have suffered long enough.[37]

In fact, the Board of Agriculture did succeed in creating some new crofts in the first year or two of its existence. But its rate of progress, as the Reef raiders rightly pointed out, had been excruciatingly slow. Hence those raiders' decision to take the law into their own hands – a decision that would undoubtedly have been emulated right across the Highlands and Islands in ensuing months had not all such action been rendered redundant, in August 1914, by Britain's declaration of war on Germany.

The Great War, as contemporaries called the conflict which broke out in 1914 and which lasted for more than four years, affected the Highlands and Islands every bit as profoundly as it affected much of the rest of Europe. Other than in Orkney, where the sheltered waters of Scapa Flow were transformed into Britain's principal naval base, the war's impact was, admittedly, indirect. But to sense something of that impact's overwhelming scale, it is necessary only to glance, as I have done in dozens of Highlands and Islands localities, at the memorials which commemorate the young men from the Highlands and Islands – one of my great-uncles among them – who died on the Somme, in Passchendaele and on innumerable other battlefields. Just as they had been during the Napoleonic Wars, a hundred years earlier, the Highlands and Islands were, between 1914 and 1918, a principal recruiting area for the British military. And such was the Great War's nature that the death rate among Highlands and Islands recruits – as among recruits in general – was terrifyingly high.

The Caithness village of Reay, some ten miles west of Thurso, is not a large community. But its war memorial – in the shape of a Celtic cross of the sort first erected in the Highlands and Islands by monks of the Columban Church – lists no fewer than thirty-one men who, as the memorial's inscription puts it, 'fell in the Great War'. Among those men was David Sutherland. Probably below the minimum age when first recruited, he was still a teenager when, on 16 May 1916, he died in the course of a raid on German trenches somewhere in France. David's father, Sinclair Sutherland, was a crofter in Reay. And the young soldier's immediate superior, Lieutenant Ewart Alan Mackintosh of the 5th Battalion, Seaforth Highlanders, had been obliged – over a period – to read, and censor, the letters which David Sutherland sent back to the family smallholding from the Western Front. Following David's death, Mackintosh, who had himself been a university student when the war began, composed some verses in his memory. Those verses do not feature in anthologies of Great War poetry. But their possible lack of literary merit is countered by their feeling for a boy whose escape from the horrors around him consisted of sharing with his father, in faraway Reay, his thoughts of home and of all the routine duties attendant on the management of a Caithness croft. Mackintosh, recalling David's letters, addresses Sinclair Sutherland:

So you were David's father,
And he was your only son,
And the new-cut peats are rotting,
And the work is left undone,
Because of an old man weeping,
Just an old man in pain,
For David, his son David,
That will not come again.

Oh the letters he wrote you,
And I can see them still,
Not a word of the fighting,
But just the sheep on the hill.
And how you would get the crops in,
Ere the year got stormier.
And the Bosches have got his body,
And I was his officer.[38]

Towards the close of 1918, those servicemen who had been more fortunate than David Sutherland began to get back to the Highlands and Islands. Many lavish promises had been made to them in their absence. In Inverness in 1917, for example, a government minister stated that 'the land question in the Highlands' would, at the war's end, 'be settled once and for all'. 'Everyone is agreed,' this minister continued, 'that the people of the Highlands must be placed in possession of the soil.' Such pledges, inevitably, proved politically difficult to honour. But inhabitants of the Highlands and Islands, it soon became evident, were in no mood, in the Great War's aftermath, to forgive governmental dilatoriness. The period was one characterised internationally by a growing readiness – as was demonstrated, for instance, by events in Ireland and in Russia – to embrace revolutionary violence. And from this worldwide tendency, it appears, the Highlands and Islands were by no means immune. 'There has grown up with the war,' runs one of the police reports on which the Scottish Office relied for information as to what was happening in places like the Hebrides, 'a new feeling, a determination to cast aside legal methods and, by force of seizure, obtain what they deem their rights.' Soon this 'determination' manifested itself in a whole rash of land raids. It manifested itself, too, in the raiders' refusal to be intimidated by the authorities. Handed a sheriff court order instructing both him and his comrades – all newly out of the forces – to remove themselves from the sheep-farm they had invaded, one North Uist man, glancing at the document in question, gave it back with the words: 'We don't care a damn for the sheriff. We are soldiers!'[39]

With pressure of this sort mounting steadily, the post-war coalition government – dominated, incidentally, by Conservative ministers – had no alternative but to provide the Board of Agriculture both with increased funding and with powers of compulsory purchase. The board, in consequence, was soon establishing crofts in unprecedented numbers – in the Hebrides, for the most part, but in Shetland, Caithness, Sutherland and other localities as well. The overall effect, when this post-war effort is taken in conjunction with what had been accomplished before 1914, was to bring nearly 3,000 new crofts into existence. This was done by adding some 50,000 acres of arable land, together with some three quarters of a million acres of hill pasture, to the area in crofting occupation. Those gains were by no means sufficient, of course, to restore to twentieth-century crofters all the land affected by the preceding century's evictions. But there were many localities – including Tiree, Barra, the Uists, Harris, Lewis and much of Skye – where, as a result of land settlement, sheep-farming of the nineteenth-century sort had virtually ceased to exist by the later 1920s. In those localities, at least, the Highland Clearances – in a manner that would have seemed utterly improbable just half a century before – had been decisively reversed.

Land settlement was facilitated, in the 1920s, by the financial difficulties confronting the owners of many Highlands and Islands estates. For some decades past, the incomes such owners derived from their properties had been in decline: partly because of the work of the Crofters Commission; partly as a result of the fact that larger farms, ever since the price downturn of the 1880s, had been increasingly hard to let. Those lairds whose properties offered comparatively little in the way of stalking and shooting – still a fairly reliable source of earnings – were particularly hard hit. Hence the comparative willingness with which several Hebridean landlords – such as MacLeod of Dunvegan and Macdonald of Sleat – sold substantial acreages to the Board of Agriculture. Hence, too, the growing tendency – widely apparent by the mid-1920s – for landlords in other parts of the Highlands and Islands to dispose of their estates to their farming tenants.

Orkney provides the classic instance of this last phenomenon. For the better part of half a century, its lairds – in consequence of the generally depressed state of agriculture – had been badly overstretched financially. Often, in order to maintain their lifestyles, they had borrowed heavily. The inevitable reckoning came in the years after 1918 when landed family after landed family, right across Orkney, faced bankruptcy, and when estate after estate, as a result, came on the market. Given their inability to generate much in the way of revenue, those estates – all the more so in view of the fact that Orkney contained no deer forests – attracted little in the way of external interest. This left the way clear for Orkney's tenant farmers to buy their holdings from their former landlords for mutually agreed sums which were generally equivalent to twenty times such farmers' annual rents. So extensively did this happen that, by about 1928, the overwhelming bulk of Orkney – as has since remained the case – was in the possession of owner-occupying Orcadians.

In places like Caithness, Easter Ross and Kintyre, there were similar developments in the same period. The cumulative impact of such land transfers, in combination with the consequences of the Board of Agriculture's land settlement programme, was such as to ensure that a substantial proportion of the total land area of the Highlands and Islands changed hands in the course of the Great War's aftermath. When it was still possible to talk – as I did on a number of occasions in the 1970s and 1980s – to the immediate beneficiaries of this upheaval, whether the Board of Agriculture's crofters or owner-occupying farmers of the Orkney variety, it was obvious that they had no regrets about their having taken the opportunities which, so unexpectedly in many instances, had come their way. But it was obvious, too, that those crofters and farmers had found themselves confronting, throughout the 1920s and 1930s, economic conditions of an appallingly adverse kind. In that, they were not alone. Despite everything which had been accomplished in the Highlands and Islands during the forty or fifty years following the Braes confrontation of 1882, much more required to be done if the region was to be made capable of providing its inhabitants with prospects of the kind then beginning to be taken for granted elsewhere in the United Kingdom.

CHAPTER NINE

Wir ain aald language

1923–1999

Outside the Yell croft house to which I had been invited at the close of a meeting of the island's branch of the Scottish Crofters Union in June 1989, a drawn-out sunset was giving way to an elongated twilight of the sort that, towards midsummer, passes for night in Shetland. Inside, the talk was of the politics of crofting. Normally I would have been a keen participant, but the effects of a day spent travelling north were catching up on me. Gradually, therefore, I dropped out of a conversation which, in my drowsy state, I was in any case having difficulty following – this conversation being conducted, naturally enough, in Yell's variant of the dialect its speakers call Shetlandic. But I kept listening, if a trifle sleepily, to what was being said. As I did so, I began to feel that, somewhere else, I had heard voices and accents virtually identical to those of Yell. And so, in fact, I had. What I was hearing in Yell, I realised eventually, were speech rhythms, tones and inflections of much the same sort as those to which I had become accustomed when staying, several years before, in a family home on another North Atlantic island. That island is called Eysturoy. It is part of the Faroe group. Its people speak Faroese, not Shetlandic. But for all that the latter's vocabulary and structure are quite different from those of Faroese, the two languages sound very similar. Nor is that surprising. Both Faroe and Shetland were, for several centuries, part of the same Viking world. What I heard on Yell, as I had earlier heard on Eysturoy, were lingering echoes, I guess, of the way the Vikings spoke.

In one of his compositions, 'A Skyinbow o Tammy's', the mid-twentieth-century Shetland poet, T.A. Robertson, a man better known by his pen-name, Vagaland, both celebrated Shetlandic and demonstrated something of its potential:

Trowe wir minds wir ain aald language
still keeps rinnin laek a tön;
Laek da laverik ida hömin,
sheerlin whin da day is döne;
Laek da seich o wind trowe coarn
at da risin o da mön.

Hit's da skriechin o da swaabie,
an da kurrip o da craa,
An da bulder o da water
in aboot da brakkin baa;
Hit's da dunder o da Nort wind
whin he brings da moorin snaa.

Hit's da soond da sheep maks nyaarmin
whin you caa dem on afore,
An da noise o hens, aa claagin,
layin Paece-eggs ida Voar;
An da galder at da dug gies,
whin a pik comes ta da door . . .

Things at maks dis life wirt livin,
dey're jöst laek da strainin-post;
Whin he's brokken, hit's no aesy
gettin new eens – an da cost,
Hit'll shön owergeng da honour
if da aald true wyes is lost.[1]

In the importance he attached to 'da aald true wyes', Vagaland was wholly at one with the many other people who, from the later nineteenth century onwards, have sought to safeguard and preserve those cultural features which are central to the continuing distinctiveness of the Highlands and Islands. This preservationist endeavour today attracts growing financial assistance from public agencies. To start with, however, it was commonly regarded – by Scotland's administrators and by their political masters at any rate – as little short of subversive.

On the Highland mainland and in the Hebrides, for instance, the state apparatus, even in Victorian times, treated Gaelic with all the hostility which had been characteristic of governmental attitudes to the language for several hundred years – one senior official remarking, in 1878, that he 'should regard the teaching of Gaelic in schools . . . as a serious misfortune'. By that point, admittedly, such comments sounded a little more defensive, a little less assured, than once they had done. This was because anti-Gaelic postures of the traditional variety had begun to be countered by pro-Gaelic campaigning of the new and effective type fostered by organisations such as the Gaelic Society of Inverness. Formed in 1871 and very much a harbinger of the sort of thinking which was afterwards to underpin the Highland Land League, the Gaelic Society of Inverness, as one of its founding members wrote, adhered strongly to the notion that to make the people of the Highlands and Islands more aware of their 'glorious past' – a past in which Gaelic, of course, loomed large – would assist with 'the furtherance . . . of efforts for the amelioration of the present'. To take an interest and a pride in one's history and heritage, so this argument ran, was in no way to stand apart from efforts to provide one's contemporaries with better prospects. On the contrary, it was to foster such efforts by enhancing people's sense of their own worth.[2]

This, as noted earlier, was John Murdoch's view. It was a view which Murdoch developed primarily in relation to the Gaelic-speaking Highlands and Islands. But unlike most of his Gaelic-speaking contemporaries, Murdoch, as it happens, took an interest in developments in Shetland – where he had been stationed in the course of his excise service and where, as he was well aware, there were apparent, in the 1860s and 1870s, cultural and linguistic stirrings akin to those the Inverness Gaelic Society was trying to foment further south. 'We are often asked,' Murdoch observed in a newspaper article in which he reflected on his Shetland experiences, 'Do the people of Shetland speak Gaelic?':

> No, they do not . . . So far from being Highlanders, the Shetland people are far from being Scotch even. Whatever we may prove them to be historically, they . . . cherish as antagonistic a feeling towards Scotchmen as exists in any part of the Highlands . . . towards that class of Lowland Scotch who come in and take the land from under the feet of the natives. And we could give striking examples of the manner in which Lowland Scots' greed has contributed in latter years to keep up this feeling. Whole districts of Shetland have been swept of their peasant population . . . These cases go far to fan the flame of the desire for re-annexation to Denmark which has survived the centuries.[3]

The notion that Shetland might one day become again Scandinavian, instead of Scottish or British, failed to attract much serious backing in the nineteenth century. During the 1880s, however, a so-called Udal League, which advocated autonomy both for Shetlanders and Orcadians, flourished momentarily. At much the same time, and by no means coincidentally, Orcadians and Shetlanders, more particularly the latter, became increasingly caught up in a search for their historical origins. Such quests were much in fashion all over late-nineteenth-century Europe – not least, as is indicated by the activities of the Inverness Gaelic Society as well as by those of folklorists like John Francis Campbell and Alasdair Carmichael, among the Gaelic-speaking population of the Highlands and Islands. To look into this population's antecedents, for reasons already made clear, was to be led, as it were, to Ireland. In Shetland and Orkney, for reasons also touched on previously, to explore the past was similarly to be drawn overseas – not to Ireland, as in the case of the Gaelic-speaking Highlands and Islands, but to Faroe, Iceland and Norway.

Not least because those places were themselves affected by the period's overall fascination with earlier epochs, there were rediscovered and put into general circulation, in the later nineteenth century, the Viking sagas on which this book's third chapter drew heavily. Such sagas constituted powerful evidence that Norwegians, Icelanders and Faroese, despite all of them having been subject to external rule for centuries, were once independent peoples. For all their subordinate status, it consequently began to be contended in the three countries in question, Norway, Faroe and Iceland possessed their own unique, and historically documented, identities. Of crucial significance in relation to the maintenance of these identities, it equally began to be contended, were Norwegian, Faroese and Icelandic – languages which, prior to their becoming badges of nationhood, had been steadily losing ground to Swedish or Danish. And if, to start with, language revivalism in Norway, Faroe and Iceland was confined to a minority of intellectuals, antiquarians and the like, this was not long to remain the case. Just as much of Ireland was taken out of the United Kingdom in 1921 by a political movement committed to reasserting Gaelic at the expense of English, so Norway, Faroe and Iceland, in the course of the first half of the twentieth century, were swept by linguistically based nationalisms so powerful as to result in those nations regaining control of their own affairs – Norway (which had been transferred from Denmark to Sweden in 1814) becoming independent in 1905, Iceland and Faroe (controlled by Denmark since the fourteenth century) acquiring either independence (in

Iceland's case) or a large measure of home rule (in the case of Faroe) during the 1940s.

Twentieth-century Shetland was substantially affected by those events. As will be seen, Shetland was affected, in particular, by developments in Faroe – which, because of its having so much in common with their own island group, is a place of considerable fascination to modern Shetlanders. It is appropriate, then, that the first person seriously to study Shetlandic, Jakob Jakobsen, came from Faroe – where, in the 1880s and afterwards, he played a prominent part both in promoting the use of spoken Faroese and in providing the language with a written form. To Jakobsen and to other Faroese-speakers, Shetland, because of the way in which its original Norn had yielded to Scots, served as something of a warning as to the ease with which a language could be lost. And Norn's demise was given additional poignancy, as far as Jakob Jakobsen was concerned, by his suspicion that the Norn once spoken by Shetlanders had been closely related – as, indeed, it was – to Faroese. Hence Jakobsen's decision, given effect between 1893 and 1895, to spend some time in Shetland with a view to establishing what, if anything, could be learned of Norn's fate.

'The more I study this poor maltreated language and try to forge the fragments together,' Jakob Jakobsen wrote of Norn, 'the stronger I feel its . . . affinity to my own tongue, and the stronger [becomes my] bitterness towards the Scots and the English who have systematically hindered its growth and development.' But for all that Norn itself had gone beyond redemption, as Jakob Jakobsen soon recognised, it had bequeathed to Shetlandic, as this Faroese academic also recognised, a vast store of words and phrases – as well as speech patterns of the type I heard in the Yell croft house with which this chapter began. Although Shetlandic, technically considered, is simply a variant of the Broad Scots which first reached the Northern Isles in the middle ages, it embodies a good deal of material which is of Viking origin. The same is true – though to a lesser degree – of the dialects spoken in Orkney and in Caithness. When Shetlanders, Orcadians and Caithness people today stress the Scandinavian content of their everyday languages, therefore, they do so with some real justification. But they do so also because they, like their immediate predecessors, have consciously chosen to emphasise the Scandinavian, as opposed to the Scottish, component of their background. This choice, as preceding paragraphs have hinted, is one that first began to be made widely in the closing years of the nineteenth century.[4]

Right across the Highlands and Islands, then, the institutional gains made in the 1880s and 1890s – gains embodied in the Crofters Act, the Crofters Commission and the Congested Districts Board – were accompanied, and often bound up with, a marked reassertion of local and regional feeling. In areas that remained – or had recently been – Gaelic-speaking, this feeling was expressed in ways which emphasised the Celtic dimension of the wider Highlands and Islands experience. In such areas, Gaelic tradition began to be studied systematically by folklorists of the type already mentioned; pressure mounted for Gaelic to be treated more positively both by Highlands and Islands schools and by Lowland Scotland's universities; an annual Gaelic festival, or *Mod*, was launched; cultural and political links – including those which helped to give rise to the Highland Land League – were forged with Ireland. In Orkney and Shetland, meanwhile, there was corresponding enthusiasm for all things Nordic. Here Icelandic sagas – with *Orkneyinga Saga*, inevitably, to the fore – were suddenly all the rage; here, in the absence of Norn, Shetlandic and its Orcadian equivalent began to be vehicles of community feeling, community pride, community solidarity; here local festivals were given a Scandinavian gloss they had not previously possessed.

Of such festivals, by far the most influential, as the nineteenth century gave way to the twentieth, was Lerwick's *Up-Helly-Aa*. Until the 1870s, it had merely been the means by which the more riproaring elements in Lerwick greeted each new year. But during the 1880s and 1890s, the decades which also witnessed the emergence of Gaeldom's Mod, Up-Helly-Aa – as a result of its being equipped with a *Guizer Jarl*, with helmeted 'warriors' and with a carefully constructed longship which those warriors ceremonially set ablaze – was deliberately transformed into a spectacular annual commemoration of Shetland's Viking affiliations.

By 1933, it was possible for a local observer to write of Up-Helly-Aa:

> Norse blood tingles in the veins of the Shetlander as he takes part, even as a spectator, at Up-Helly-Aa. On such a night and with such a scene before him, Shetland seems to speak to him of its past and of the great, strong men who lived there in the ages that are gone. He sees the Viking galleys as they flash past like eagles of the sea and he . . . feels a thrill of pride that in his veins there still runs the fiery Northland blood.[5]

Up-Helly-Aa, of course, can readily be dismissed as romanticism run riot. For what is the festival, in its present shape at any rate, but a

Victorian invention? And what is modern Shetland's much-prized Norse heritage, when one gets down to it, but a set of placenames, a few fragments of udal law and a scattering of words in a dialect which, as Jakob Jakobsen himself admitted, owes far more to Broad Scots than to the Norn which such Scots long since superseded?

But to nit-pick thus is to miss the point. There may, indeed, be little in the way of a living link between Shetland's present and the island group's Viking past. There may similarly be no very strong connection between the Gaelic heritage the Mod aspires to keep alive and the choral and other competitions so popular with Mod-goers. But neither the Mod nor Up-Helly-Aa – however much their critics may wish this was the case – were conceived in a spirit of scientific scholarship. Their function is more basic. It is to give expression, in a manner simultaneously assertive and enjoyable, to a deep-seated conviction that Highlands and Islands communities possess, in relation to the rest of Scotland as well as to the rest of the United Kingdom, characteristics which make them unique. And since the governments of Scotland and of the United Kingdom tried hard over a lengthy period to eliminate just such characteristics, the emergence both of the Mod and of Up-Helly-Aa – together with the appearance of the wider movements which gave rise to them – are pointers to changes of the sort also signalled by the campaign which culminated in crofters gaining security of tenure. Culturally as well as politically, it was clear by the nineteenth century's end, inhabitants of the Highlands and Islands were once again having some success in setting their own agenda.

Nor was this to be a transient phenomenon. Commitment to the concept of a Highlands and Islands identity – or, to be more precise, a set of Highlands and Islands identities – remains a key element in Highlands and Islands affairs. That it does so is due, in no small part, to the manner in which late-Victorian interpretations of the region's history were taken up and elaborated by leading figures in the literary renaissance experienced by the Highlands and Islands in the course of the twentieth century. Vagaland's Shetlandic verse was one small component of that renaissance. Among larger components were the novels and poems of Neil Gunn (from Caithness), Sorley MacLean (from Raasay), George MacKay Brown (from Orkney) and Iain Crichton Smith (from Lewis). In those men's treatment of the Highlands and Islands, the past – whether Celtic, Nordic or a blend of the two – is a constant theme. Sometimes, as in Neil Gunn's reflections on a Sutherland township just prior to its obliteration by Patrick Sellar, that past is contemplated elegiacally:

> Here where they made their own clothing, their own shoes, built their houses, produced their food and drove a few cattle to market to get coin to pay rent, surely the forces that had so shut them in could do without them and forget them. It could hardly be within God's irony that a world which had forgotten their very tongue should be concentrating all its forces of destruction upon them. What could the pride and power of emperors have to do with this little pocket of self-sufficing earth lost in the hills, this retreat, this end of an age, this death of a culture which, a millennium before, had been no more offensive to the nations of the West than to set Christianity and learning amongst them?[6]

But not even the shattering events of the Highland Clearances, other twentieth-century writers countered, necessarily ended the possibility of building, purposefully and constructively, on what had gone before. Nowhere is this more positive note struck more forcefully than in the closing lines of Sorley MacLean's unfinished epic, *An Cuilithionn, The Cuillin*:

> Thar bochdainn, caithimh, fiabhrais, àmhghair,
> thar anacothrom, eucoir, ainneart, ànraidh,
> thar truaighe, eu-dòchas, gamhlas, cuilbheart,
> thar ciont is truaillidheachd; gu furachair,
> gu treunmhor chithear an Cuilithionn
> `s e `g éirigh air taobh eile duilghe.[7]

'Beyond poverty, consumption, fever, agony,' MacLean wrote, 'Beyond hardship, wrong, tyranny, distress; beyond misery, despair, hatred, treachery; beyond guilt and defilement: watchful, heroic, the Cuillin is seen rising on the other side of sorrow.' Despite all the numerous horrors inflicted on them over several centuries, in other words, the people of the Highlands and Islands retain the capacity, in the poet's opinion, to create a society which – as is suggested by MacLean making the Cuillin symbolic both of changelessness and of regeneration – carries forward into a better future much that derives from earlier epochs.

The transcendent optimism of *An Cuilithionn* is all the more remarkable in view of the time and place of its composition. Sorley MacLean began work on the poem in 1938. He had just accepted a teaching post on Mull – an island so scarred by 'the terrible imprint of the clearances', MacLean commented afterwards, as to be 'heartbreaking'. Nor was there any very visible indication, in the year *An Cuilithionn* was commenced, that Mull's forcibly emptied glens, together with their many equivalents elsewhere, might ever be repopulated. Much had certainly been accomplished, as the preceding chapter emphasised, in the Highlands and Islands during the 1880s and subsequently: evictions had ceased to occur; the amount of territory in crofting occupancy had expanded enormously; lots of farmers had managed to obtain ownership of their land; housing conditions had started to improve. And there had been other, equally encouraging, developments. When, at the start of the twentieth century's second decade, a Liberal government first provided Britain's elderly with old-age pensions, the Highlands and Islands – being a more than usually deprived area – benefited greatly. The region gained, too, from the establishment, by the same Liberal administration, of a Highlands and Islands Medical Fund which made it possible – the fund being used to underwrite the incomes of general practitioners – for every Highlands and Islands community, however remote, to call on the services of a doctor. But for all that such measures helped to make individuals within the Highlands and Islands a little less vulnerable to illness and to the adverse financial consequences of growing old, the region – as the 1920s and 1930s were amply to demonstrate – remained largely at the mercy of forces beyond its population's control.[8]

Because of the extent to which the early-twentieth-century Highlands and Islands depended on farming and crofting, the area was very hard hit, in the years around 1920, by dramatic falls in agricultural commodity prices. Wool lost three-quarters of its value between 1920 and 1921; prices for oats went down by two-thirds between 1919 and 1922; returns on sheep and cattle plunged almost as steeply. Especially vulnerable to the effects of the ensuing collapse in agricultural incomes were farmers who had swapped tenancy for ownership and crofters who had taken on holdings of the sort created by land settlement. Both groups incurred onerous financial obligations – in the way of loan charges and the like – through assuming new responsibilities. And both groups were to suffer severely as a result. Their troubles, however, were simply a more than usually extreme version of the hardship then being experienced by almost every crofter and farmer in the Highlands and Islands. Something of the nature of that hardship is evident in an account provided by

Ernest Marwick, afterwards a noted local historian, of the Orkney smallholding on which he grew up in the years immediately following the Great War:

> To save fodder, we kept only one horse. A relative with a croft of similar size kept another, and we used the two horses as a team on both crofts. We had three milk cows on our croft. If we were lucky, there would be three calves. If not, we might have to buy one. Thus we hoped to sell each year three two-year-olds. There were also a few sheep and 100 hens.[9]

In an average year, Ernest Marwick continued, his father might raise £54 from the sale of his cattle beasts, £12 from the sale of his lambs, £30 from the sale of some 600 dozen eggs and £10 or so from the sale of milk, oats and potatoes. A further £14 might come Marwick senior's way if he succeeded, as he usually did, in getting some part-time work. The Marwick household's total annual income, then, amounted to around £120. Against that figure, there had to be set the £50 expended on feeding-stuffs, fertilisers, seeds, horseshoes and other necessities. Some £70 remained on which to maintain the Marwick family. Even allowing for the fact that the family grew the bulk of its food requirements, this was not a sum – despite money values being a lot higher in the 1920s than they are today – on which a man, a woman and their children could live well.

To have £50 a year in the Highlands and Islands of the 1920s, however, was, as Ernest Marwick readily acknowledged, to be relatively affluent. The Marwick croft was comparatively sizeable and its fields, like most Orkney fields, were highly productive. Where crofts consisted of smaller acreages and poorer soils, as was the case in Shetland and in the Hebrides, for instance, crofting families were in a still worse plight than were the Marwicks. Their situation was rendered all the more problematic, as was the situation of the Highlands and Islands population generally, by a marked contraction in overall employment.

The herring fishery, once the mainstay of numerous Highlands and Islands communities, fared just as badly as agriculture in the 1920s. War and revolution led to the loss of the German and Russian markets on which Scottish curers had latterly been reliant. Crewmen, gutters and packers, it followed, were no longer in demand. And such Highlands and Islands fishermen as possessed their own boats – a group including the many Shetlanders who had earlier managed to exchange their sixerns for the sailing smacks on which the herring fishery depended in its heyday – were seldom able to afford steam-powered drifters and trawlers of the sort becoming standard in the post-1918 period.

Other, more localised, industries followed farming and fishing into crisis. Thus the quarrying of flagstones in Caithness, a business which employed over a thousand people at the start of the twentieth century, had closed down completely by 1925 – its markets, in southern cities, swamped by cheaply turned-out paving slabs made from concrete. It is little wonder, in such circumstances, that the thoughts of many people, not only in Caithness but right across the Highlands and Islands, turned once more to emigration. Families living in homes which were often as bereft of cash as they were bereft – the gradual betterment of housing standards notwithstanding – of the most basic amenities, had no great incentive, after all, to remain where they were. Often, as was afterwards recalled by Robert MacLeod, a Lewisman, it was the younger members of such families who were most anxious to be off:

> In the family in which I grew up, as each one came to the stage where criticism is voiced as well as complaint, we . . . asked our parents to get rid of the croft, house and all, and clear out. There was no special preference where to, except that it would undoubtedly have to be a place where neither children nor their mother carried creels of peat and pails of water, where sooty rain never dripped through the roof and where people had never heard of a manure heap.[10]

As the 1920s advanced, plenty of folk from Lewis were to act on this increasingly prevalent desire to get away. In 1918, the island had been bought by Lord Leverhulme, a self-made millionaire and a man who, by means of investment in fishing and fish-processing, aspired to turn both Lewis and Harris, which he also purchased, into veritable hives of industry. Leverhulme's plans, however, came to nothing: partly because of a breakdown in relations between Lewis's new proprietor and a number of the island's crofters; more fundamentally as a result of the fact that any commercial venture dependent on fish and fishing was, in the circumstances of the 1920s, practically guaranteed to fail. Hence the re-enactment in Stornoway, in April 1923, of scenes reminiscent of those of a century before – with several hundred people setting sail on a single ship, the *Metagama*, for North America. 'The element of compulsion is not entirely absent from this modern instance of mass emigration,' it was observed by a Scottish newspaper of the day. But the compulsion in question, the paper went on, owed nothing to evicting landlords of the nineteenth-century sort. It stemmed rather from adverse economic conditions.[11]

So widespread were such conditions in the Highlands and Islands of the 1920s that the region's total population fell more steeply in that decade than it had done even in the aftermath of the previous century's famine. The thousands of Hebrideans then emigrating to the United States and Canada had their counterparts in the hundreds of Shetlanders leaving for New Zealand. Remoter islands – of which St Kilda was the most publicised example – were abandoned altogether. The more isolated parts of the Highland mainland seemed set to experience a similar fate. And even relatively accessible localities – such as the Black Isle village of Cromarty which possessed nearly 2,000 inhabitants in 1914 and only 837 in 1931 – were affected by outward movement on an unprecedented scale.

Such movement, admittedly, slowed greatly in the 1930s. That it did so, however, was due largely to the global recession triggered by the American stockmarket crash of 1929 – a recession which closed off the prospect of men and women from the Highlands and Islands getting jobs in other parts of the world. The inevitable consequence was a steep rise in unemployment rates in every part of the Highlands and Islands – the increase being all the more pronounced as a result of Britain's merchant navy, in which many men from the Highlands and Islands had obtained work, being obliged to respond to the downturn in international trade by laying up ship after ship. In Wick, where more than a thousand men were unemployed by the end of 1929, soup kitchens were set up on street corners. And neither in Wick nor in the other parts of the Highlands and Islands where they appeared at this time were such soup kitchens to be rapidly dispensed with. By the later 1930s, when unemployment rates in some Highlands and Islands counties stood at over 40 per cent, they were needed more than ever. It is easy to understand, then, why there was felt to be a need for the Highland Development League – its name derived, of course, from the Land League of fifty years before – which was launched, amid considerable publicity, in the early months of 1936.

The Development League's key objective was to involve the British government much more directly in stimulating economic activity in the Highlands and Islands. Its emergence, as matters turned out, coincided with the formation of the Scottish Economic Committee (SEC) – an offshoot of an already existing and officially backed organisation known as the Scottish Development Council. The SEC operated principally in Lowland Scotland's hard-pressed industrial centres. But in the summer of 1937, with encouragement from the Scottish Office, the SEC set up a sub-committee whose members' task was to enquire into 'economic conditions' in the Highlands and Islands. 'The government,' the Secretary of State for Scotland, Walter Elliot, told the House of Commons in December, 'will not shrink from . . . drastic action . . . if it is so recommended in a well-thought-out plan by the Highlands Sub-Committee'. Days later the Scottish press began to carry informed speculation to the effect that it was 'not improbable' that the Highlands and Islands, following the appearance of the SEC grouping's report, would be granted a 'special development board . . . with wide powers to co-ordinate and give effect to schemes for the betterment of agriculture, fishing . . . and other industries'.[12]

Just such a development board would probably have been established in the Highlands and Islands during 1939 had not external events – in the shape of the security threat posed to Britain by Nazi Germany – made it impossible for the necessary funds to be found by a United Kingdom government increasingly obliged to devote all available cash to the country's rearmament. As it was, the best the Scottish Office could do was to set aside the modest sum of £65,000 with a view to acting on the recommendations of the SEC's sub-committee whose report, published in November 1938, contained a series of detailed suggestions as to how the Highlands and Islands economy might most effectively be expanded. None of this cash had been spent when, at the beginning of September 1939, Britain found itself embroiled in the conflict which rapidly escalated into the Second World War.

As had occurred during the First World War and during several earlier wars, the Highlands and Islands provided the United Kingdom military with many thousands of recruits in the course of the hostilities which commenced in 1939 and continued until 1945. Among those recruits was my father who, following his training at Fort George in the winter of 1939–40, served in Faroe, Egypt, Libya, Tunisia, Italy and Greece. Private Donald Hunter, having survived his involvement in some of the war's fiercest fighting, came home to marry Jean Cameron, my mother. But for all that casualty levels in Britain's armed forces were much lower between 1939 and 1945 than they had been between 1914 and 1918, plenty young men from the Highlands and Islands were less fortunate – another nine names having to be added, for example, to Reay's war memorial. Nor were Highlands and Islands deaths confined to those suffered on faraway battlefields. When a German plane bombed Wick on 1 July 1940, for instance, fifteen people – including seven children – lost their lives.

The nature of the Second World War was such as to make the Highlands and Islands strategically important. In the spring of 1940, Shetland became the base from which Norwegian resistance fighters – following, in reverse, routes pioneered by Viking marauders of a thousand years before – slipped regularly into their German-occupied homeland. And with German U-boats active throughout the North Atlantic, both the Northern Isles and the Hebrides became stepping-off points for the numerous British aircraft engaged in anti-submarine offensives. The military aerodromes established at this time – in localities like Islay, Tiree, Benbecula, Stornoway, Kirkwall and Sumburgh – are nowadays, in many instances, civilian airfields. Although Highlands and Islands families would doubtless have traded such gains for a peace sufficient to bring their boys home, the war of 1939–45, from a strictly economic standpoint if from no other, was thus of some long-run advantage to the region. It was of more immediate economic advantage as well – in that the demand for labour generated by military construction programmes had the effect of virtually eliminating, for a time, unemployment of the type which had persisted throughout the 1930s.

Among the more significant consequences of the Second World War – from a Highlands and Islands perspective – was the manner in which it led to the acquisition of immense executive authority by a man who, with the single exception of William Gladstone, contributed more than any other United Kingdom politician to the modern regeneration of the Highlands and Islands. This man was Tom Johnston – Secretary of State for Scotland in Winston Churchill's wartime coalition government. As a socialist activist and propagandist in Glasgow during the twentieth century's opening decades, Johnston – whose earliest claim to fame stemmed from his scorching attacks on Scotland's lairds – had taken a close interest in Highlands and Islands issues. This interest was one Johnston kept up on his becoming a Labour MP in the 1920s. And it was partly with an eye to clearing the way for new initiatives in the Highlands and Islands that Tom Johnston, when accepting Churchill's offer of the Scottish Secretaryship, insisted on his being given a far freer hand than previous Secretaries of State had possessed.

Of the several enquiry teams which Johnston quickly established with a view to seeing what could be done to improve Highlands and

Islands prospects, by far the most significant was one headed by the high court judge, Lord Cooper. Cooper's remit was to report on 'the practicability and desirability' of damming Highlands and Islands rivers with a view to utilising the water power resources thus tapped 'for the generation of electricity'. Highlands and Islands landlords, who predictably attached more weight to their angling interests than to such benefits as might flow from the region's electrification, were largely of the view that neither dams nor power stations should be allowed to impinge on the Highlands and Islands scene. Other sections of opinion – consisting, for the most part, of the type of Highlands and Islands visitor attracted by the region's allegedly 'unspoiled' character – were similarly hostile. But Cooper and his colleagues peremptorily brushed aside all such opposition:

> If it is desired to preserve the natural features of the Highlands unchanged in all times coming for the benefit of those holidaymakers who wish to contemplate them in their natural state during the comparatively brief season imposed by climatic conditions, then the logical outcome . . . would be to convert the greater part of the area into a national park and to sterilise it in perpetuity . . . But if, as we hope and believe, [national] policy, to which this report is a small contribution, is to give the Highlands and the Highlanders a future as well as a past and to provide opportunity in the Highlands for initiative, independence and industry, then we consider a few localised interferences with natural beauties would be an insignificant price to pay for the solid benefits which would be realised [by such interferences].[13]

Those were Tom Johnston's sentiments exactly. He hastened, therefore, to give effect to the conclusions of Lord Cooper's report. That report reached the Secretary of State in November 1942. A Hydro-Electric Development Bill received its second reading in the House of Commons just three months later. And by the summer of 1943, the North of Scotland Hydro-Electric Board – the body given the job of realising the energy-giving potential of Highlands and Islands rivers – was an accomplished fact.

It is indicative of Tom Johnston's commitment to the Hydro Board – as the new organisation became known – that, in 1946, he left politics to become its chairman. In this role, which he retained until 1959, Johnston did the Highlands and Islands one more great service. By government ministers in post-war London, it was felt that the

Hydro Board's priority should be to channel cheap energy in the direction of industry. Tom Johnston disagreed. The Hydro Board's first loyalty, he insisted, was to the population of the Highlands and Islands. Yes, Johnston assented, it would be hugely expensive, as ministers never tired of pointing out, to instal the power lines needed to provide each and every Highlands and Islands community with domestic electricity supplies. But that did not matter. The Hydro Board's founding Act – which Tom Johnston, of course, had piloted through parliament – obliged the board to devise 'measures for the economic development and social improvement of the North of Scotland district'. There could be no more effective such measure, he insisted, than making electricity available – at heavily subsidised connection rates – to Highlands and Islands households. Thus it came about that one of my earliest memories is of the evening, not far into the 1950s, when my sister and I were able to greet our father's homecoming from work by throwing the switch which miraculously, as it seemed to us, filled our Duror kitchen with what we called, for years afterwards, 'electric light'.[14]

The North of Scotland Hydro-Electric Board's achievements constitute an enduring testimony to what state power – so long exercised in a manner inimical to Highlands and Islands interests – was capable of accomplishing if applied to constructive purposes of the sort Tom Johnston sought so tirelessly to promote. Had the Highlands and Islands not secured the rural electrification programme over which Johnston presided as Hydro Board chairman, the post-war decades, which were to be difficult enough for the region, would have been disastrous. In the absence of an electricity supply and of the ever-widening range of domestic appliances such a supply made possible, the depopulation of the Highlands and Islands – which, as will shortly be emphasised, was hard to halt anyway – would have become unstoppable.

But if the Hydro-Electric Development Act of 1943 made a particularly critical contribution to laying the groundwork for the economic and demographic turnaround which was eventually to occur in the Highlands and Islands, other initiatives taken in the same decade were also to be of assistance in this regard. The Rural Water Supplies and Sewerage Act of 1944 may not have been the most exciting piece of legislation ever passed by the United Kingdom's House of Commons, but its impact on the Highlands and Islands – where the Act's provisions helped ensure that piped water reached thousands of homes in the course of the 1950s and 1960s – was immense. 'She had brought up a family in a croft house with no sanitation,' a post-war committee of inquiry into crofting conditions was informed by one of its female witnesses:

> If asked whether she would rather have electricity or water and sanitation, she would say you can keep your electricity if you give me water and sanitation. Electricity was good, but not nearly so important as water.[15]

Still more beneficial – despite their being designed to meet national, as opposed to Highlands and Islands, needs – were the social welfare measures put in place by the Labour government which swept to power in the general election of 1945. Like others of my background, I owe a lot to those measures. The National Health Service, which took effect within weeks of my birth in 1948, entitled me to unlimited medical care. I was provided, in addition, with free secondary schooling and grant-aided entrance to university. As my experience demonstrates, therefore, to grow up in the Highlands and Islands of the 1950s and 1960s was to have access to opportunities of a sort never before on offer to the area's population. Nor were those opportunities, it should possibly be mentioned, exclusively educational in nature. It may not have counted for much, in the overall scheme of things, that Duror, in the post-war years, acquired a publicly subsidised community hall in which there were regularly shown, by the publicly subsidised Highlands and Islands Film Guild, the latest productions from Ealing and Hollywood. But our hall and our film shows mattered greatly to me and to my friends. To this day, I am inclined to cite them – when in dispute with anyone who thinks free markets sacrosanct – as evidence of the good that can be done by governments prepared to intervene in the workings of regional economies.

In a Highlands and Islands context, interventionism of that type dates, as noted previously, from the 1880s. But it expanded massively in scope during the first half of the twentieth century. Prominent among its early products, and antedating even the Hydro Board, was the Forestry Commission, which took shape towards the close of the Great War. This state agency's task was to expand the United Kingdom's timber output, and the Highlands and Islands, because of the nature of their terrain and climate, figured largely in its thinking from the outset. One of the first tracts of land to be acquired by the Forestry Commission was Glen Duror – tenanted, in the mid-eighteenth century, by James Stewart and afterwards converted, like so many similar localities, into a sheep-farm. Tree-planting in Glen Duror began in 1919. Among the men who gained employment there during the next few years was my paternal grandfather, James Hunter, who became the Forestry Commission's Glen Duror trapper – what would nowadays be called a ranger – in 1929. My father eventually succeeded his father in that post. It was not, by present-day standards, well paid – as is underlined by the fact that I can recall the excitement with which my mother, at some point in the 1950s, greeted the news that, because of bonuses arising from his having shot rather more than the standard quota of deer, my father's weekly earnings had reached the magic figure of £10. But had such earnings – modest though they were – not been available to Donald Hunter and to the other forty or so people employed by the Forestry Commission in our vicinity in the years following the Second World War, the Duror I knew as a boy could hardly have existed.

But forestry was not the only economic sector of importance in the mid-twentieth-century Highlands and Islands. Even in the depressed conditions of the 1920s and 1930s, tourism – a feature of the Highlands and Islands scene since Victorian times – had proved remarkably resilient. It had, however, altered gradually in character – as first the bicycle and then the motor car made it possible for folk from the south to give up single-centre vacations of the older type in favour of touring holidays. The growing popularity of such holidays, although impacting adversely on some resort towns of the nineteenth-century variety, created a growing demand for accommodation in virtually every corner of the rural Highlands and Islands. That demand was met by families letting rooms to visitors on a nightly basis. On their setting up home in Duror in 1937, my maternal grandparents began to dabble in this bed-and-breakfast trade. My mother, in due course, followed suit. In the 1950s, therefore, our household was one of thousands, right across the Highlands and Islands, deriving a welcome additional income from the car-borne tourists who came north in growing numbers every summer.

If Highlands and Islands tourism was evolving in new directions in the post-war period, so was the region's farming. In 1953 or thereabouts, I spent an afternoon with my maternal grandfather – the John Cameron who featured in the previous chapter – at a Duror ploughing match. Insofar as I can recall, and I was only five or six at the time, horses were as plentiful at that ploughing match as tractors. But the latter were quickly to become universal in consequence of a post-war consensus to the effect that the United Kingdom's food output should be boosted by all conceivable means. With the help of the extraordinarily generous state aids and incentives made available to Britain's farming industry by politicians wedded to that consensus, the larger-scale end of Highlands and Islands agriculture, in particular, was revolutionised. As tractors replaced horses, as combine harvesters began to put in an appearance and as product prices soared, districts where the farming structure was such as to allow farmers to make the most of the opportunities on offer – districts like Orkney and Easter Ross, for instance – were transformed into places, as far as their agriculturalists were concerned, where it was almost impossible not to do well.

As agriculture became increasingly mechanised and more capital-intensive, however, farms tended both to grow in size – by means of a widespread process of amalgamation – and to shed the greater proportion of their workforces. With agricultural employment thus contracting, and with fishing showing few signs of emerging from its pre-war slump, there was, in much of the post-war Highlands and Islands, an acute shortage of jobs. That was bad enough. Making matters still worse was the fact that such jobs as were available – whether in forestry, in tourism or in the construction activity associated with the building of the Hydro Board's dams – tended to be relatively unremunerative, seasonal or temporary. Since the United Kingdom as a whole was then enjoying high rates of economic growth, together with unprecedented increases in living standards, it was obvious to people in the Highlands and Islands of the 1950s that such progress as was being made by their area was insufficient to prevent a further widening of disparities in the overall quality of life between the Highlands and Islands on the one hand, and more southerly regions of Britain on the other. Unsurprisingly, therefore, people continued to move out of the Highlands and Islands in substantial numbers. Just how large were the numbers in question was revealed by the United Kingdom census of 1951 – which showed that the worst affected areas, such as the western seaboard of the Highland mainland between Applecross and Cape Wrath, had lost some 25 per cent of their population in only two decades.

'A decrease of population, however small, is usually a matter for concern,' it was observed by the authors of one post-war study of the depopulation issue. But when the loss amounted to 'a quarter or a fifth in the space of twenty years', as it did in a good deal of the Highlands and Islands, then the situation could legitimately be reckoned 'grave indeed'. Still more alarming, it was remarked in Shetland, was the manner in which the contraction of Highlands and Islands communities had begun to take on a self-reinforcing character:

> If a district declines too much, it becomes a much less pleasant place to live in. Not only is there less company, but . . . the church and school may close, there may not be enough people to support a shop, and it may not be worthwhile to improve roads, build a new water scheme or lay on electricity. We can all think of some districts where some of these things are happening. Thus there is the danger that, when the population declines, life in the district may become unattractive for those remaining, and they may decide to leave too.[16]

In 1953, *Picture Post*, then the United Kingdom's most widely read magazine, turned its attention to the Highlands and Islands. The region's 'dwindling communities', *Picture Post* commented gloomily, were a symptom of the Highlands and Islands having become 'Britain's most gravely depressed area'. A confidential report prepared for Scottish Office ministers was equally pessimistic in tone:

> In brief, the Highland scene presents a picture of a drift of the younger population to the towns, leaving behind a diminished and ageing population which, in many of the remoter sectors of the area, is approaching a position at which it can no longer maintain itself.[17]

By the early 1950s, then, it was depressingly evident that the numerous policy initiatives taken in the Highlands and Islands during the preceding sixty or seventy years had, for all their beneficent effects, failed to halt demographic trends which seemed set to end in a complete cessation of community life over much of the region. From this failure, it was possible to conclude, or so some southern economists argued in the 1950s, that Britain should simply leave the Highlands and Islands to their own devices; that there was little merit in 'propping up, with increasing government expenditure, a decaying social order'; that it would make more sense simply to facilitate 'the movement of labour out of . . . the area'. This was not a verdict, needless to say, which attracted support from within the Highlands and Islands. Nor, fortunately for the region, was it one which United Kingdom politicians were disposed to accept. Increasingly, in fact, such politicians were persuaded that what was required in the Highlands and Islands was not less state action but more – with this latest bout of interventionism to have as its primary objective the creation of a more diversified regional economy.[18]

As indicated earlier, the need for such diversification, together with the closely related need for an agency capable of bringing it about, had first been identified in the 1930s by the Highland Development League and by the SEC's Highland sub-committee among others. The post-war Labour government – though its Scottish Office ministers seem initially to have thought that the Highlands and Islands required few, if any, policy measures over and above those being applied to Britain as a whole – was gradually to move towards a similar position. If what had become known as 'the Highland problem' were to be solved, the government acknowledged in its *Programme for Highland Development*, published in 1950, 'new economic activity' would have to be promoted. And such activity, or so the *Programme for Highland Development* maintained, could more readily be engendered in the Highlands and Islands of the 1950s than in the Highlands and Islands of previous decades:

> For a long time, the scope for any more constructive approach was limited. There was little prospect of introducing new economic activity and the agricultural and fishing industries passed through periods of depression which affected their vitality not only in the Highlands but in all parts of the country. In recent years, however, new factors have emerged which provide the basis for a more constructive approach to the Highland problem and for treating it effectively as one of economic development. These new factors are the increased importance of home food production, the necessity for a large-scale programme of afforestation, the development of hydro-electric power in the Highlands and the greatly increased importance of the tourist trade. The need now is to reassess the Highland problem in the light of these new factors and to frame plans for securing the full benefits which they make possible.[19]

Those were admirable sentiments. But what remained lacking was any very convincing means of translating policy prescriptions into action – Labour politicians being prepared to do no more in this regard than provide the Secretary of State for Scotland with an Advisory Panel on the Highlands and Islands. Consisting principally of the region's MPs and of senior members of relevant local authorities, this body was to make plenty of potentially far-reaching recommendations to government. But the Highland Panel, as its full title indicates, did not possess the executive authority needed to give effect to its own suggestions. And though demands for a Highlands and Islands development agency continued to be voiced throughout the 1950s, the Conservative administration which succeeded Labour in 1951 chose not to go down that road – Conservative ministers confining themselves to making further changes in the legislation governing crofting.

The security of tenure gained by crofters in 1886 had been understood originally to apply only to those crofters who resided on their holdings. In 1917, however, Scotland's senior judges ruled that a crofter's tenancy was to be regarded as inviolable even if he elected to abandon his croft. When combined with depopulation of the sort already mentioned, this decision created an expanding class of absentee crofters – people who, despite their having left the Highlands and Islands in search of employment, chose to hang on to their crofts in the hope, seldom realised, that they might one day return to them. The sheer scale of such absenteeism was revealed when, in the early 1950s, a Commission of Enquiry into Crofting Conditions was given the job of reporting on this and other aspects of the crofting situation:

> We give details of one . . . township. It consists of thirteen crofts, twelve of them equipped with reasonable houses. Seven of the crofts are occupied by absentee tenants whose homes are in Glasgow, Motherwell, the United States, Edinburgh, Conon Bridge, Greenock and Australia. They use the houses mainly for holiday purposes . . . This is an extreme case, but the same kind of thing is happening in many places.[20]

With a view to tackling absenteeism, Conservative ministers, in 1955, created an organisation entitled – a little confusingly in that its powers were quite different to those exercised by its nineteenth-century predecessor of the same name – the Crofters Commission.* Although its members and staff set to work with a will, the new commission's ability to bring about worthwhile change was soon shown to be extremely limited. Attempts to deal with absenteeism became hopelessly enmeshed in the terribly bureaucratic procedures which, because of the inadequacies of the commission's founding legislation, were the only tools at its disposal. And when, in 1960, the Crofters Commission, frustrated by so much failure, declared its intention to reorganise crofting entirely, the sole effect of its pro-

---

* This and other developments in twentieth-century crofting policy are explored in the same author's book, *The Claim of Crofting*.

posals – which, had they been implemented, would have involved the legally enforced amalgamation of crofts – was to precipitate a bitter confrontation between the Inverness-based commission and the crofting communities whose interests it was meant to be promoting.

At the heart of this confrontation was a dispute as to what crofting ought to be about in modern circumstances. To the Crofters Commission, as well as to that body's backers among the Scottish Office civil servants who were ultimately responsible for Highlands and Islands policy, the typical croft – invariably providing its occupant with an agricultural income so tiny as to be almost meaningless – was an anachronism. From this perspective, it seemed perfectly reasonable to advocate, as the Crofters Commission did in 1960, an approach predicated on the notion that a large number of small crofts should be replaced, as soon as feasible, by a much reduced number of more sizeable units. Crofters disagreed. For all its imperfections, they insisted, the crofting system ought to be kept in being because of its vital role in maintaining comparatively densely populated rural communities in localities where such communities would otherwise not exist. Absenteeism on the part of crofters certainly constituted a difficulty, it was conceded by defenders of the small croft. But to Charles MacLeod, the Lewis teacher who became the crofting population's most effective spokesman in the course of that population's 1960 conflict with the Crofters Commission, this difficulty demanded solutions very different from those the commission had put forward:

> The problems of whole communities whose croftlands are only partly used as a result of the able-bodied having to seek a living away from home cannot be solved by enlargement of holdings . . . Our principle is this, that the population of the Highlands and Islands is worth preserving within the Highlands and Islands and accordingly must be preserved there . . . The croft is ours by every right upon which a civilised nation bases its social values: by the right of having inherited it as the creation of our forefathers; by the right of having fought for it as our stake in the country at times of war; and by the right of having been born on it and having for it the attachment which everyone has for the spot on God's earth where he was reared. If the [Crofters] Commission can do no better than cast these bonds asunder, they had better realise, before they go further, that they will earn for themselves the everlasting hatred of crofting folk.[21]

In MacLeod's words, there is discernible something of the thinking which, centuries ago, underpinned clanship and which, more recently, served to fuel campaigning of the type organised by the Highland Land League. In stating his belief that 'the population of the Highlands and Islands is worth preserving within the Highlands and Islands and accordingly must be preserved there', Charles MacLeod was bringing up to date, as it were, the concept of *duthchas*. This ancient notion, as previous chapters stressed, was understood by the people of the Gaelic-speaking Highlands and Islands to mean that they possessed an enduring and inalienable right to reside in the localities their ancestors had inhabited. That right had been recognised by William Gladstone in 1886. And given the strength of the crofting population's attachment to the resulting Crofters Act, it was – at the minimum – unwise of the Crofters Commission to inform tenants of smaller crofts, as the commission did in 1960, that their cherished and hard-won security of tenure ought to be withdrawn in the interest of creating more substantial landholdings. To make such a pronouncement was simply to raise the spectre of a return to the bad old days of clearance and eviction. It is unsurprising, therefore, that Charles MacLeod and his crofting allies eventually forced the Crofters Commission to abandon its amalgamation plans. While there remained the prospect of action being taken (as, indeed, it has since been taken from time to time) against absentee crofters, all resident crofters were left in undisturbed occupancy of their crofts.

One outstanding issue remained, however. If, as Charles MacLeod argued, 'the population of the Highlands and Islands [was] worth preserving within the Highlands and Islands and accordingly [had to] be preserved there', it clearly would not suffice simply to guarantee the tenurial gains of 1886. The average crofter, if he or she were to enjoy anything approximating to a reasonable livelihood, needed to have some source of income over and above the earnings generated by his or her croft. And what was true of crofters was still truer of the many other people, in every part of the Highlands and Islands, who, not being crofters, were even more dependent, if their continued residency in the region was to be assured, on the ready availability of remunerative employment. Talk of 'preserving' the population of the Highlands and Islands was all very well. But no such goal was likely to be attained in the absence of measures to stimulate job creation. That, to be fair to Charles MacLeod and his colleagues, was well known to the leadership of the crofting movement which, in 1960, so triumphantly saw off the Crofters Commission. Much of that leadership, as it happens, was associated politically with the Labour Party. It was partly due to prompting from MacLeod and his associates, then, that Labour came round to the view, in the early 1960s, that one of its priorities, on regaining power, would be the establishment of a Highlands and Islands Development Board. When, in the general election of October 1964, Labour was returned to office, this was duly done.

The Bill which resulted in the formation of the Highlands and Islands Development Board (HIDB) was presented to the United Kingdom's House of Commons, at the start of 1965, by the new Labour government's Scottish Secretary, Willie Ross. In his introductory remarks to MPs, Ross commented:

> For two hundred years, the Highlander has been the man on Scotland's conscience . . . No part of Scotland has been given a shabbier deal by history . . . Too often there has only been one way out of his troubles for the person born in the Highlands and Islands: emigration.[22]

In relation to this book's central thesis, those remarks are of great interest. If, as earlier chapters contended, the Highlands and Islands were treated harshly and exploitatively by the Scottish state and if, as previous chapters also maintained, the United Kingdom, until the later nineteenth century at all events, simply conducted itself in the Highlands and Islands in much the same way as the Scottish state had formerly done, then it is an arguable proposition – to put the matter no higher – that twentieth-century Scotland owed it to the Highlands and Islands to make some restitution. This was certainly Willie Ross's view. And the restitution he proposed, in his role as the incoming Labour government's Scottish Secretary, was nothing if not far-reaching in its implications. 'We have to tackle the problem on a wide front,' Ross said of the all-too-evidently inadequate performance of the Highlands and Islands economy, 'and, for that reason, the new board will require wide powers.'[23]

The powers actually granted to the HIDB were fully in accord with this billing. By way of grant, loan or the taking of appropriate equity, the agency was able to give financial assistance to any enterprise or company which, in its view, might contribute to the expansion of the Highlands and Islands economy. The HIDB could also set up businesses on its own account, acquire land, build factories, equip and service those factories, produce promotional material, assist with the construction of community facilities and market the Highlands and Islands as a tourist destination. If the legislation which provided for all of this was not quite the 'Marxist enactment' which Willie Ross's Conservative shadow, Michael Noble, thought it to be, it was undeniably radical. The HIDB – all the more so as a result of its being funded on a reasonably generous basis – did not lack the means to bring about Highlands and Islands renewal.[24]

From the outset, the HIDB's leading personnel were convinced that no such renewal would be forthcoming until the Highlands and Islands economy contained a substantial industrial sector. And by 1965, as luck would have it, the bones of such a sector were beginning to be in evidence. During the first half of the twentieth century, large-scale industry in the Highlands and Islands had consisted mainly of aluminium smelting – an activity made possible by the region's hydro-electric potential and one which led, between the 1890s and the 1920s, to the establishment of smelter plants (each one of them equipped with its own hydro power station) at Foyers (beside Loch Ness), Kinlochleven (at the northern end of Argyll) and Fort William. In the years immediately prior to the HIDB's formation, however, the Foyers, Kinlochleven and Fort William smelters had been overshadowed by the launch of several new, and much bigger, industrial ventures in different parts of the Highlands and Islands. Among the more important such ventures were the United Kingdom Atomic Energy Authority's fast-breeder reactor centre at Dounreay in Caithness, a pulp and paper mill at Fort William, a gigantic grain distillery at Invergordon in Easter Ross and, also at Invergordon, a further aluminium smelter with a capacity far in excess of those which had preceded it.

Most of those plants were to have extremely chequered histories. Thus the Invergordon smelter, which went into full production in May 1971, lasted only ten years – its closure being announced by its owners, the British Aluminium Company, on 29 December 1981. At that time, as it happened, I was working for a Sunday newspaper whose editor detected the possibility of a human interest feature in a New Year's Day spent with the families of some of the eight hundred men whom British Aluminium had – forty-eight hours before – declared redundant. In Alness, the Easter Ross village transformed into a town in the wake of the Invergordon smelter's construction, I duly went from house to house on 1 January 1982 – witnessing, at first-hand, a little of what it means to be caught up in developmental planning of the sort that goes wrong. In Alness sitting-rooms festooned with Christmas cards and Christmas decorations, I talked with women who were frequently in tears. I talked, too, with men who were understandably bitter about the lies, as they saw it, which had been fed to them by the promoters of Highlands and Islands industrialisation. They had been promised, those men believed, work for life. Now their jobs had gone. So had, or so would, lots of other similar jobs. The pulp-making component of Fort William's pulp and paper mill shut down in 1980. The Dounreay reactor establishment was taken out of commission in the mid-1990s. And though Invergordon's distillery survives, the possibility – much canvassed in the 1960s – of its becoming the core of a much larger chemicals operation was one of numerous such possibilities which came, in the end, to nothing.

All the major projects mentioned in immediately preceding paragraphs resulted, as already indicated, from government initiatives which antedated, sometimes by several years, the formation of the HIDB. But the HIDB warmly identified itself with the projects in question; it repeatedly called for more of the same; and – from myself among others – it took a lot of criticism, therefore, when first the pulp mill, then the smelter, closed. Such criticism notwithstanding, there was, and is, a case to be made in defence of the HIDB's pro-industry stance. That case was stated by the HIDB itself in the organisation's first annual report:

> Manufacturing industry is very poorly represented in the Highlands and Islands. Without it, the region will continue to lack any real possibility of a substantial enough rise in numbers to give credibility to Highland regeneration.[25]

If the depopulation of the Highlands and Islands was to be decisively reversed, this argument ran, new and substantial enterprises would have to be attracted to the area. Only thus would it be possible, the HIDB maintained, to replicate the huge boost which Caithness, for example, received as a result of its becoming home, in the mid-1950s, to the Dounreay nuclear centre – a development which, as the HIDB pointed out, led to Thurso trebling in size and the population of Caithness as a whole more than doubling. What the HIDB wanted, then, was to attract heavy industry to the Highlands and Islands in sufficient quantities to ensure that what had been achieved in Caithness was repeated elsewhere. This was a reasonable ambition. But it quickly foundered on the fact that each of the HIDB's much-advertised 'growth centres' – in Lochaber, Easter Ross and Caithness – themselves ran into trouble of one sort or another. The HIDB's entire growth centre strategy, as a result, began to be condemned as totally misconceived. That – given the shattering impact of the pulp mill and smelter closures, together with the scarcely less debilitating effects produced, in the 1980s and early 1990s, by the gradual run-down of the Dounreay reactor programme – was inevitable. But if the HIDB's original expectations of incoming industry were exaggerated, so, events showed, were the more gloomy prognostications of the HIDB's critics – myself, I stress, included. There will, as things have turned out, be some two thousand people employed at Dounreay, on reactor decommissioning work, until the middle decades of the twenty-first century. And despite the smelter and pulp mill disasters, the economies of Easter Ross and Lochaber, by the later 1990s, were a lot larger, and a good deal more varied in their composition, than they had been ten, twenty or thirty years before.

Some part of the growth which has occurred in districts like Lochaber and Easter Ross is due to Highlands and Islands Enterprise, the HIDB's successor, having stuck stubbornly with its predecessor organisation's commitment to fostering inward investment in the Highlands and Islands economy. But the late-twentieth-century expansion of that economy – an expansion by no means limited to the places identified as growth centres by the HIDB – was not due solely to the arrival of businesses from outside the region. Much of what was achieved economically in the Highlands and Islands, during the thirty or so years following the HIDB's establishment, was achieved as a result of indigenous effort. And the first locality to be demonstrably revitalised by such effort was Shetland.

During the 1950s, Shetland was every bit as depressed economically as most of the rest of the Highlands and Islands. Unemployment was rife. Younger Shetlanders were heading elsewhere, it sometimes appeared, on virtually every southbound boat. And a remarkably high proportion of those Shetland families who had succeeded in hanging on in the islands were managing to do so only by virtue of the fact that their menfolk had gone far from home to get work: into the merchant navy, in some instances; into the Antarctic whaling industry, in others. Domestic and community life, in consequence, suffered perceptibly:

> The man needed to draw water from the well on a harsh winter's day was thousands of miles away. So, too, was he when there was a call for an additional couple on the dance floor. The sight of two girls dancing together was all too common.[26]

There were individuals in Shetland, however, who believed, despite so much evidence to the contrary, that the island group possessed the wherewithal to make a fresh start. Among them was Shetland County Council's part-time development officer, a young man called Bob Storey. In 1962, Storey, who was afterwards to be recruited by the HIDB, set out his personal vision of Shetland's future:

> The isolation that had so far bedevilled them in the twentieth century . . . could, perhaps, be a virtue and a strength. Isolation made for the integration of the community and a stronger identity. The fact that Shetland was so undeniably Shetland, and Shetlanders were so undeniably what they were, could . . . be their greatest strength in this matter of development.[27]

That Shetland people possessed, and possess, a sense of their own collective distinctiveness is undeniable. In its modern guise, as already noted, this Shetland consciousness, as it can be entitled, is rooted in the island group's Scandinavian links, in its dialect and in those other features thought, by Shetlanders anyway, to make Shetland unique. Such features might have been expected to become less significant as the twentieth century advanced and as Shetland – because of the growing exposure of everyone in the Highlands and Islands to radio, films and the like – became more susceptible to external influences. In fact, the opposite occurred. T.A. Robertson or Vagaland, with whose verse this chapter began, produced most of his Shetlandic poetry in the years after the Second World War. Several of Robertson's contemporaries started writing in Shetlandic in the same period. And the literary movement thus produced was given an organised focus when a number of the movement's adherents – headed, in this instance, by a further poet named Peter Jamieson – helped launch, in 1947, a periodical, *The New Shetlander,* which at once attracted, as it still attracts, a substantial readership. Nor was pro-Shetland feeling exclusively a matter of the written, or spoken, word. The Shetland Folk Society, another creation of the post-war era, was to do for Shetland music what *The New Shetlander* did for Shetlandic – by transforming Shetland's fiddle-playing tradition, in particular, into another source of local pride.

Fiddle music and Shetlandic poetry may appear unlikely foundations on which to build a productive economy of the type Shetland had so manifestly lacked since the collapse of its early-twentieth-century herring industry. But it does not do, as this book's closing pages have emphasised repeatedly, to underestimate the effects that can be produced by activity of the type represented by *The New Shetlander* and by the Shetland Folk Society. While it is hard to be definite as to the precise connection between manifestations of cultural reinvigoration on the one side, and engagement with economic development on the other, there is – as the modern history of the Highlands and Islands demonstrates over and over again – an undoubted tendency for there to be cross-over from the cultural sphere to the economic one. In the Shetland case, it is certainly no coincidence that an enhanced sense of Shetland identity – as expressed in the columns of *The New Shetlander* and in the work of the Shetland Folk Society – began to be paralleled by attempts, from within Shetland itself, to improve local job prospects. A Shetland Development Council was formed; a conference was organised on Yell with a view to exploring ways of halting that island's slide towards total depopulation; a fact-finding delegation was despatched to Faroe which, subsequent to its gaining home rule from Denmark in 1948, had experienced rates of economic and demographic growth that were, from a Shetland perspective, little short of phenomenal.

This Faroe trip took place in 1962. By its participants, a major factor in Faroe's success was reckoned to be 'the right and power of the Faroese to manage their own affairs'. Hence Shetland County Council's decision, in 1963, to ask the Conservative-controlled Scottish Office to grant a measure of Faroe-style independence to Shetland. No such independence, needless to say, was forthcoming. But even within the constraints imposed on them by their relatively subordinate constitutional position, it was apparent by that point, Shetlanders – their self-confidence, as is indicated by the county council's 1963 exchange with central government, growing markedly – could achieve a great deal. Incoming industry of the kind then being attracted to Fort William and Invergordon was not on offer, at this stage. What was available, however, was a dawning realisation – on the part both of the island group's county council and local business people – that it might be possible to update and to expand two industries which had been present in Shetland for centuries. One of those industries was knitwear – a business whose products had first been sold outside Shetland by the German merchants who began visiting the island group in the middle ages. The other such industry – its origins lying even further back in time – was fishing.[28]

The modernisation effort which followed in both the knitwear and fishing sectors of the Shetland economy, for all that it began in advance of the HIDB's creation, was greatly assisted by the agency's appearance. So overwhelming was the demand for HIDB aid from Shetland, in fact, that by 1969, a little to the HIDB's embarrassment, Shetlanders, despite their constituting only 6 per cent of the total Highlands and Islands population, were accounting for no less than 17 per cent of HIDB spending. With the help of this spending, Shetland's knitwear industry was overhauled, mechanised and put in touch with overseas buyers. At the same time, the island group's fishing industry was entirely restructured. Fishermen were given the assistance they needed to acquire larger boats and the latest fish-catching technologies; fish-processing and fish-freezing plants were established; markets for those plants' products were found in North America and elsewhere. This was impressive. More impressive still, as the HIDB commented in 1972, was the overall impact of these developments on life in Shetland:

> The high level of prosperity in Shetland, based on the fishing and knitwear industries, has become almost a byword; but to those who knew Shetland in the circumstances of a decade or more ago, the present situation contains something unreal and miraculous. In contrast to the former depression, unemployment and emigration, the two main industries are at full stretch, labour is not easy to get, and the drift of population arrested.[29]

In relation to what had gone before, both in Shetland and in the rest of the Highlands and Islands, this was an accomplishment, as the HIDB recognised, of huge significance. It was also of importance, from a purely Shetland perspective, that the island group's turning around of its economy had been completed, in effect, by the early 1970s. When, in 1971, massive reserves of oil were discovered below the waters separating Shetland from Norway, it immediately became apparent that Shetland was about to acquire a new, and potentially disruptive, industry. In their dealings with that industry's representatives, Shetlanders were greatly assisted by the fact that Shetland was a lot less badly in need of jobs than it had been just ten years before. A 'tiny group of homespun farmers', the United States consul general in Edinburgh was afterwards to remark of Shetland's negotiations with the oilmen who now began to show up in Lerwick, had 'hornswoggled' some of the world's biggest and most forceful corporations. That was maybe to exaggerate. But such benefits as Shetland managed to extract from the oil industry certainly owed a good deal to the island group's ability – an ability which would not have existed had the oil majors put in an earlier appearance – to negotiate from a position of some economic strength.[30]

At the start of the twentieth century's last quarter, offshore oil impacted on the Highlands and Islands in ways which, some thought, bore comparison with the effects produced, two hundred years before, by the upsurge in demand for kelp. Nor was this comparison necessarily far-fetched. As had been the case with kelp, oil lent itself to development of a type likely, or so it was feared by many people in the Highlands and Islands, to bring few, if any, long-term benefits to the communities closest to its places of origin. Suspicions of the oil industry's motives and intentions are at the heart of John McGrath's 1974 play, *The Cheviot, the Stag and the Black, Black Oil.* McGrath's musical drama – which attracted big audiences in village halls and community centres in every part of the Highlands and Islands – features an oilman, Texas Jim, who sings:

> Take your oilrigs by the score,
> Drill a little well just a little offshore,
> Pipe that oil in from the sea,
> Pipe those profits home to me . . .
>
> So leave your fishing, and leave your soil,
> Come work for me, I want your oil.
> Screw your landscape, screw your bays,
> I'll screw you in a hundred ways . . .
>
> All you folks are off your head,
> I'm getting rich from your seabed.
> I'll go home when I see fit,
> All I'll leave is a heap of shit.[31]

Particularly in its early stages, this seemed a reasonable analysis of the Highlands and Islands oil boom. As company after company tried to obtain the onshore sites required for a whole range of oil-related enterprises, and as speculative interests of one sort or another clambered on to the gravy train thus conjured so unexpectedly into existence, it was tempting to see offshore oil as just the latest phase in an exploitative continuum which – as the title of McGrath's play implies – had begun with the Highland Clearances and, by way of the Victorian rush to buy sporting estates, had lasted into modern times. But there was one big difference between the behaviour of nineteenth-century landlords and the conduct of the twentieth-century multinationals which dominated both the offshore oil business and the onshore activities so crucial to that business's success. Landlordism had unleashed processes which went a long way to ridding the Highlands and Islands of people. The oil majors, in contrast, were a vital factor – though not, as preceding pages have made clear, the only such factor – in bringing those processes to an end. This was especially evident, by the mid-1970s, in the two localities most dramatically altered by offshore oil. Those localities were Easter Ross and Shetland.

At Nigg, on the northern shore of the entrance to the Cromarty Firth, Easter Ross acquired, in 1972, one of the several Highlands and Islands fabrication yards where oil production platforms were built. Some six hundred people would be employed at Nigg, it was predicted initially. By the summer of 1974, however, the actual number of employees in the Nigg yard had passed five thousand. And with hundreds more at work in further oil-related businesses in the vicinity, Easter Ross – which had already been obliged to accommodate the Invergordon smelter workforce – seemed, when I spent some time there in 1975, to have been transformed into one vast construction camp. Homes, schools and other buildings were going up in village after village. And for all that such activity had its inevitable downsides, I was, I confess, tremendously taken by the spectacle of so much happening in a region which – despite, or possibly because of, my own Highlands and Islands upbringing – I had formerly thought incapable of providing career opportunities of any consequence.

Because of its proximity to the oilfields discovered in the early 1970s in the northern North Sea, Shetland, where I also spent several weeks in 1975, was, if anything, even more affected by the offshore bonanza than Easter Ross. At Sullom Voe, in the north-eastern corner of the Shetland mainland, a massive pipeline terminal and tanker-loading facility took shape with astonishing rapidity. Lerwick harbour, something of a backwater since the herring industry's collapse, became a leading centre of operations for the scores of ships involved in ferrying heavy equipment to the rigs, platforms and accommodation modules being installed a couple of hundred miles to the east. Sumburgh, Shetland's principal airport, began to handle an almost incredible 50,000 aircraft movements a year as huge numbers of exotically entitled oil-industry personnel – roughnecks, roustabouts, toolpushers and the rest – were transferred daily from incoming charter planes to outgoing helicopters.

Shetland might easily have been overwhelmed by the offshore oil industry. As already underlined, however, Shetlanders, during the 1950s and 1960s, had shown a striking capacity to shape the pattern of events. They had engineered their island group's economic recovery. They had simultaneously demonstrated an ability – of a sort last displayed, in a Highlands and Islands context, by the Highland Land League – to impose their collective will on British politicians.

When the United Kingdom government, in the later 1960s, set out to reform Scotland's local-authority structure, it was suggested that the entire Highlands and Islands be equipped with a single elected council operating out of Inverness. Because this proposal, if acted upon, would have drastically curtailed their freedom of action, Shetlanders resisted it vigorously. Shetland, they insisted, needed more autonomy, not less. And as had become something of a Shetland habit, the case for such autonomy was backed by repeated references to Scandinavian precedent and example:

> There is a very real fear that any weakening of the administration of local affairs here – in Shetland, by Shetland and for Shetland – will disastrously undermine the basic social and economic fabric of the islands . . . Indeed, one could argue that our unique position demands that [our] local authority's powers should be broadened rather than reduced . . . on the same basis and for the same reason as the *kommunes* [or rural councils] in Northern Norway are recognised as a basis for progress in each community and are empowered to play a vital part in the life of [that] region.[32]

Similar arguments were advanced by Orcadians. Soon they were taken up, in addition, by residents of the Western Isles – a locality which, unlike Shetland or Orkney, had never possessed its own local authority because of its having been divided, when county councils were first set up in Scotland towards the end of the nineteenth century, between Inverness-shire and Ross-shire. In the face of so much strong feeling, United Kingdom ministers abandoned their original blueprint and conceded the island case. Alongside a number of mainland-based authorities, of which the most important was Highland Regional Council, there consequently emerged, in 1975, three island councils serving, respectively, the Western Isles, Orkney and Shetland.

From a Shetland perspective, in particular, this represented a substantial victory. That victory was made all the more noteworthy because the formation of Shetland Islands Council (SIC) was preceded by a further campaign which led to the SIC gaining statutorily sanctioned powers – of a kind possessed by no other local authority in the United Kingdom – to control the development of, and to raise revenues from, the offshore oil industry. The manner in which the powers in question have since been exercised by Shetland's elected representatives has itself, perhaps inevitably, been a source of controversy – the SIC having come in for a good deal of criticism, during the 1980s, from Shetlanders who felt, rightly or wrongly, that the council was guilty of excessive secrecy in its dealings with oil companies. As even the SIC's critics acknowledge, however, the funds obtained from such dealings have been instrumental in effecting a marked improvement in the Shetland population's quality of life. And that improvement, it seems to me, would never have been forthcoming had Shetlanders not been sufficiently self-confident, in the course of their various negotiations with the oil industry and with the British government, to hold out for concessions of the remarkably far-reaching type that Shetland, in the event, obtained. Shetland's accomplishments, then, have been considerable. It is to those accomplishments that I owe, in part at least, my conviction – a conviction which underpins a good deal of this book – that there is a close correlation, in Highlands and Islands circumstance, between a particular locality's overall success and the extent to which that same locality is in a position to exercise a worthwhile degree of autonomy.

Nigg's platform yard, as already indicated, was not the only such facility acquired by the Highlands and Islands in the 1970s. Other such yards were created at Kishorn in Wester Ross, and at Ardersier, near Fort George. A further yard – though on a lesser scale and concentrating on smaller items of equipment – was established at Arnish near Stornoway. One of those facilities, the Kishorn yard, was in business for just a few years. The other three, despite occasional and sometimes drastic fluctuations in their labour requirements, remain in operation at the time of writing. Since oil-related activity also occurred in Orkney, where the island of Flotta in Scapa Flow became a pipeline terminal, it is evident – especially if Shetland's huge stake in the industry is kept in mind – that offshore oil made a key contribution, in the twentieth century's closing decades, to providing the Highlands and Islands with an expanding economy of the sort the region had so long lacked. Just how startling was the expansion in question can be seen from a single set of statistics. In 1961, the total number of people in employment in the Highlands and Islands was some 97,000. In 1991, this total had risen to 134,000 – an increase of almost 40 per cent.

Offshore oil, for all its importance, was not solely responsible for the economic upturn which began in the Highlands and Islands around 1970 and which – reverses like the pulp mill and smelter closures notwithstanding – was to be sustained into the 1990s. Of the many thousands of jobs created in the Highlands and Islands during those years, the bulk were in small businesses – most of them owned and managed by local people. Financial assistance to indigenous enterprises of this type had been available since the launch, in 1953, of the Highland Fund – a charitable organisation which made, and still makes, low-interest and unsecured loans for developmental purposes. With the formation of the HIDB, however, grants as well as loans became available to prospective entrepreneurs. Numerous ventures – ranging from single-person operations to companies which eventually took on substantial workforces – were accordingly helped to get off the ground. By no means all those ventures, in fields ranging from tourism to electronics, were successful in the longer term. But their overall effect was to boost substantially the prospects of lots of communities which would otherwise have been condemned to a further period of economic stagnation.

Of particular help in relation to some of the more disadvantaged parts of the Highlands and Islands was the development, in the 1970s and 1980s, of salmon-farming. Centred on the Highland mainland's west coast, in the Hebrides and in the Northern Isles, this new industry was employing, by the later 1980s, many hundreds of people – with hundreds of others working in associated processing plants.

Also of assistance to the Highlands and Islands was Britain's decision, given effect in 1973, to join the European Union (EU). At the time, admittedly, that decision was viewed with some suspicion in the Highlands and Islands. Such suspicion was most intense in localities with fishing interests – interests which it was believed, with some justification, would be put at risk by the EU practice of treating fisheries as European, not national, resources. In the 1975 referendum which ratified the United Kingdom's EU entry, therefore, the Western Isles and Shetland were the only areas, in the entire country, to record anti-EU majorities. Had there been further such referenda in the 1980s and 1990s, however, that result would not have been repeated

– EU development funds having been ploughed, during these decades, into a whole array of Highlands and Islands projects.

Right across the Highlands and Islands, meanwhile, major improvements were being made to the region's transport systems. Air services, which had commenced in the 1930s, expanded greatly in the post-war period. Steamers of the nineteenth-century type were replaced by car ferries. And although the railway network was tending to shrink by the 1960s, roads, in contrast, were widely upgraded. The consequent tendency for journey times to shorten was greatly assisted by a series of new, and often very large, bridges – spanning the Beauly Firth, the Cromarty Firth, the Dornoch Firth, Kylesku, Loch Leven and several other estuaries or narrows.

Better communications and the beginnings of economic revitalisation jointly helped produce, by the 1970s, a marked reversal in Highlands and Islands population trends. Starting with the famine decade of the 1840s, the region's overall population had fallen, decade by decade, for well over a hundred years – the lowest point being reached, at about the time of the HIDB's establishment, in the mid-1960s. Then the number of people resident in the Highlands and Islands was 312,000. Some thirty years later, however, the corresponding figure was 372,000. When set against the 120-year-long decline which preceded it, this increase of 20 per cent, while still leaving the region's total population a long way short of its early-nineteenth-century maximum, is a highly visible indicator of the extent to which, by the twentieth century's end, the Highlands and Islands had at last begun to make real, and measurable, progress. Striking in itself, the late-twentieth-century growth of population in the Highlands and Islands becomes all the more impressive when account is taken of the fact that the population of late-twentieth-century Scotland as a whole was, if anything, tending slightly downwards.

Partly because its longstanding role as a regional service centre has been massively enhanced by the ease with which – thanks to improved roads – it can be accessed today from other parts of the Highlands and Islands, Inverness, from the 1960s onwards, gained population at an especially rapid rate. As already mentioned, the town was, by the 1980s, one of the fastest growing urban centres in the United Kingdom – acquiring, in the process, new satellite communities, at Culloden and Balloch, as well as sprawling industrial estates and several out-of-town shopping malls. But the expansion of Inverness, it ought to be emphasised, in no way accounts by itself for the overall rise in Highlands and Islands population. In the 1980s, to stick with that decade, Inverness and Nairn – the wider area of which the town of Inverness is part – saw its population expand by 11 per cent. In the same decade, however, Ross and Cromarty's population grew by 7 per cent, north-west Sutherland's population by 5 per cent, Orkney's population by 4 per cent, Badenoch and Strathspey's population by 3 per cent, Skye and Lochalsh's population by 15 per cent. There were one or two Highlands and Islands localities, to be sure, where population was still falling in the 1980s – the most adversely affected being the Western Isles. But the unprecedented increase in the population of Skye and Lochalsh – an area where depopulation had formerly been acute – highlighted the extent to which even the more peripheral parts of the Highlands and Islands, during the twentieth century's last quarter, were undergoing positive changes of a kind which, just twenty or thirty years before, had been thought unlikely, even impossible.

Nor was population increase, in the Skye and Lochalsh case, confined to Portree – the little town which, because of its locally focal position, is the district's equivalent of Inverness. In the course of the 1980s, for example, the population of the Sleat peninsula, at the southern tip of Skye, rose by 18 per cent. That was partly because of developments at Sabhal Mor Ostaig where, in 1973, a set of ruined farm buildings became the nucleus of a college which, almost from the moment of its establishment, was to play a leading role in efforts to safeguard the future of Gaelic – a by-product of those efforts, as far as Sleat was concerned, being the sudden availability, in a place where no such opportunities had formerly been on offer, of high-quality jobs for teachers, lecturers, researchers and the like.

In much the same way as the beginnings of Highlands and Islands repopulation, the start of a recovery in Gaelic's social and cultural standing – a recovery of which Sabhal Mor Ostaig is one of the more evident symbols – signalled something of a turning point in Highlands and Islands affairs. Gaelic's medieval withdrawal from the Scottish Lowlands to the Highlands and Islands had been followed, in the nineteenth and early twentieth centuries, by a further retreat which resulted, by the 1970s and 1980s, in the language – as the everyday speech of families and communities – becoming confined, more or less, to the Hebrides. Had nothing been done at this critical stage to counter the causes of its seemingly inexorable contraction, Gaelic would almost certainly have become extinct – in much the same way as Pictish and Norn before it – by the middle years of the twenty-first century. Extinction, of course, may yet be Gaelic's ultimate fate. But its demise, at the minimum, has been substantially delayed by the various campaigns – some of them re-energised versions of campaigns first launched in the later nineteenth century – mounted on the language's behalf from the 1970s onwards. Among the more immediately obvious outcomes of this pro-Gaelic endeavour were: the introduction of Gaelic-language radio services; major public investment in Gaelic-language television programming; the formation of dozens of Gaelic-medium playgroups; the widespread provision of Gaelic-medium primary schooling; the beginnings of Gaelic-medium teaching in secondary schools; and the setting up, as already noted, of Sabhal Mor Ostaig which, by the later 1990s, was offering degree-level courses taught through the medium of Gaelic.

Underpinning Sabhal Mor Ostaig's commitment to Gaelic is an intense conviction, on the part of the college's staff, that social and economic regeneration can be stimulated by linguistic renewal. At Sabhal Mor Ostaig, then, a good deal of stress is laid on ideas of the sort advanced in the course of this book's attempts to make sense of the connection between the expansion of Shetland's economy in the 1960s and the marked quickening of interest, a decade or two previously, in that island group's cultural heritage. As observed in relation to Shetland occurrences, it is easier to state such notions than to prove them. But just as linkages between cultural revivalism and other types of regenerative effort can be discerned in mid-twentieth-century Shetland, so such linkages underlie a good deal of what took place, nearer the twentieth century's close, in those Highlands and Islands communities which feel themselves to be Gaelic or Celtic, as opposed to Nordic, in background.

In the 1970s, 1980s and 1990s, those communities, whether on the Highland mainland or in the Hebrides, were the source of artistic creativity on a scale not witnessed in this area since the collapse of the Lordship of the Isles. Some of that creativity involved the fostering of age-old literary and other forms. Much of it, however, was boldly experimental: in poetry; in the visual arts; in the founding of all sorts of local festivals; in the emergence of wildly popular bands capable of combining Gaelic lyrics with sounds derived from the world of American-inspired rock. And as had happened earlier in Shetland, those essentially cultural developments were accompanied by the emergence of more assertive, even aggressive, attitudes on the part of local authorities and others – with both the Western Isles Council and Highland Regional Council, for example, manifesting a sharply increased willingness to tangle with central government in pursuit of locally agreed objectives.

Increasingly, too, there was debate – some of it explicitly political in content – as to where the Highlands and Islands might, or should, be heading. This debate both fuelled, and was fuelled by, new explorations of the region's past. Highlands and Islands history, not least the history of the Land League period, began to be studied and written about by people, myself among them, who felt strongly that the earlier drive for land reform – something that had been virtually in abeyance since the 1920s – ought to be resumed. And when, in 1972, there was launched in Skye the *West Highland Free Press*, the Highlands and Islands were presented with a newspaper which – in a way no other paper had done since John Murdoch's *Highlander* ceased publication – took up causes like land reform, Gaelic revivalism and the wider right of Highlands and Islands communities to determine their own futures. To those of us who had grown up in the West Highlands and Islands at a time when political protest had been largely confined to Free Church demonstrations against Sunday ferries, the *West Highland Free Press* was as startlingly iconoclastic as it was liberating. Some of us might have heard over and over again, from our own families, that the Highlands and Islands would be better rid of the landlords who had controlled so much of the area's life for so long. But to see such views in print was tremendously exciting.

One of the relatively few organisations to be consistently backed and endorsed by the *Free Press* was the Scottish Crofters Union (SCU). Formed in the mid-1980s, the SCU, having recruited several thousand members, set about the task of making the case for crofting in a manner consistent with the wider spirit of the times.* Those times, as it happened, were particularly challenging because the United Kingdom was dominated politically, throughout the 1980s and into the 1990s, by Conservative governments which set immense store by free enterprise and which, as a result, were overtly hostile to, and critical of, most of the state agencies they had inherited from earlier administrations. Conservative thinking of this type, for reasons set out in preceding pages, posed obvious dangers from a Highlands and Islands perspective. Although the British state's impact on the region may originally have been entirely negative, United Kingdom governments, when they began at last to engage constructively with the region, had made – in the eighty-year period which commenced with the Crofters Act of 1886 and ended with the setting up of the HIDB – an immeasurable contribution to Highlands and Islands betterment. For a time in the 1980s, much of that contribution seemed at risk. State support for crofting – partly because of the SCU's success in

* The case in question is set out in the closing chapter of *The Claim of Crofting.*

developing pro-crofting arguments which took account of Conservative priorities – was, in the event, maintained. But there was widespread concern in the Highlands and Islands when the Hydro Board became one of the many publicly owned utilities to be privatised at the Conservative Party's insistence.* And there was still more concern on it becoming evident, towards the end of the 1980s, that the HIDB was to give way to several new bodies.

When there eventually emerged, in the HIDB's place, Highlands and Islands Enterprise (HIE) and its associated network of ten Local Enterprise Companies (LECs), it became apparent, however, that the HIDB's developmental mission had not been diluted. Having retained the HIDB's powers, having gained significant new powers in respect of training and of environmental renewal, and having acquired – through LECs like Argyll and the Isles Enterprise or Skye and Lochalsh Enterprise – a capacity both to shape and to execute policy at a local level, the HIE network, in fact, could convincingly be portrayed as an improvement on what had gone before. That was certainly the view taken, in 1992, by Iain Robertson, HIE's chief executive:

> The network's first twelve months have been a year of radical achievement, adding value to resources employed, aggressively building on experience, ensuring local motivation and control – and confounding the sceptics. We have set ourselves the task of being a model rural development agency in Europe by questioning past practice, seeking new opportunities and pressing the Highlands and Islands cause with deeds, not rhetoric.[33]

Not everyone agreed with that verdict, of course. But it was of some significance, perhaps, that the return of the Labour Party to power in May 1997 was not followed by any move to dismantle HIE. Nor was there any very credible body of Highlands and Islands opinion, by 1997, to the effect that such a move might be desirable.

Having been closely involved – as a journalist, as director of the Scottish Crofters Union, as chairman of Skye and Lochalsh Enterprise and, at the time of writing, as chairman of HIE – in what has been going on in the Highlands and Islands since the mid-1970s, I am inevitably open to the charge of having interpreted recent events in a

* The Hydro Board's private-sector successor is Scottish Hydro-Electric PLC.

manner that tends towards the self-serving. Partly for that reason, partly because the Highlands and Islands – unsurprisingly in view of what has been done to the region over the years – contain more than their fair share of pessimists, there will be no lack of folk wishing to take issue with this book's generally upbeat ending. It might be as well, therefore, if – prior to turning, in conclusion, to the future – I acknowledge the many problems and obstacles which the Highlands and Islands presently confront.

These paragraphs are being composed in April 1999, some two years after my going to Inchtuthil in search of the Roman remains with which my account of Highlands and Islands history began. I write at a point, therefore, when Highlands and Islands agriculture, as a result of financial and other forces operating at the United Kingdom and European level, is in a more depressed state than at any time since the Second World War; at a point when our salmon-farming industry is menaced both by disease at home and by intense competition from overseas; at a point when the Nigg, Ardersier and Arnish fabrication yards, because of a steep slide in the world price of oil, seem likely to run out of orders; at a point when several other sectors of the Highlands and Islands economy are, if not in crisis, then certainly in trouble.

There is much, in other words, for HIE, and for me as HIE's chairman, to be doing. We have urgently to enlarge a Highlands and Islands business base which, for all that has been accomplished in this direction, continues to be far too narrow. We have to find ways of putting upward pressure on Highlands and Islands wage levels – which, taken in the round, are unacceptably low. We have to ensure that repopulation extends from the parts of the Highlands and Islands where it is already occurring to those localities – Kintyre, a number of the Argyll islands, the Western Isles, the south-eastern corner of Sutherland, some parts of Caithness, the north isles of Orkney – where population loss has yet to be halted. We have to do our bit to eradicate poverty, poor housing, unemployment, homelessness; for, despite the gains of recent times, such things still exist in many parts of our area. And, as if all that were not enough, we have to grapple, as inhabitants of the Highlands and Islands have always had to grapple, with difficulties inherent in our geography and climate: with wet and stormy weather; with a lack of winter daylight; with inhospitable terrain; with the high transport costs which are an unavoidable concomitant of our distance from the United Kingdom's principal manufacturing centres.

Four months into the last year of the twentieth century, then, the debit side of the Highlands and Islands balance sheet has a distinctly forbidding look. But there are entries on that balance sheet's credit side as well. Several of those have already been mentioned: the enormous growth registered, since the 1960s, in the Highlands and Islands workforce; the scarcely less impressive increase in the region's total population; the burgeoning of our area's cultural life. Other positives include ongoing European Union contributions – worth several hundred million pounds in total – to the cost of infrastructural and other improvements in the Highlands and Islands; the fact that the Highlands and Islands possess, in part because of HIE spending, a telecommunications network of the most up-to-date type; the related fact that inward investment, much of it dependent on our telecommunications network, brought more than a thousand new jobs to the Highlands and Islands in the year to March 1999; the further fact that, in addition to making considerable advances in traditional sectors like food and drink, the Highlands and Islands have managed either to attract or to nurture businesses which today are turning out – and this list could readily be extended – pharmaceutical products (Lewis), menswear (Campbeltown), medical diagnostic equipment (Inverness), carbon fibres (Easter Ross), freezers (Caithness), lithium batteries (also Caithness) and jewellery (Orkney).

Even comparatively successful commercial concerns, I concede, do not last for ever. Several years on from April 1999, possibly even in advance of this book's publication, one or more of the enterprises I have just cited may have gone the way of the many other Highlands and Islands firms which, in the course of the last ten, twenty or thirty years, have been obliged to close their doors and to lay off their employees. But in that eventuality, I believe, there will be still-unborn companies on hand to take the place of those that die. And the Highlands and Islands in which those as-yet-uncreated enterprises take shape, I predict, will be more advantageously situated, in a number of vital respects, than the Highlands and Islands with which the region's late-twentieth-century inhabitants were familiar. Before the twenty-first century is very old, for example, the Highlands and Islands will acquire a university.

Referring in 1996 to the resources which HIE was then committing – and additional such resources have been committed since – to the University of the Highlands and Islands (UHI) project, Fraser Morrison, my predecessor as HIE chairman, commented:

> HIE has put considerable effort into steering this project forward as we believe there could be few developments more

> significant to this area's future status and economic and cultural wellbeing.[34]

UHI has been a long time in gestation – the notion of a Highlands and Islands university having first been canvassed seriously in the nineteenth century. But it was only in the 1990s that HIE, in collaboration with Highland Council (as the former Highland Regional Council had by then become) and other local authorities, managed to persuade a number of Highlands and Islands further education colleges – one of them, incidentally, being Sabhal Mor Ostaig – to combine with a number of Highlands and Islands research centres in order to create a multi-campus university of a sort without precedent in the United Kingdom. Making a reality of UHI has not been, and will not be, easy. But something of the university's ultimate potential is evident from UHI's first prospectus which was published – at a point when several thousand students had already embarked on higher education courses in the UHI project's component institutions – at the end of 1998:

> We are creating a unique federal university. Across the Highlands and Islands major new construction worth £55 million is under way, changing the appearance of many of our partner colleges. A £7 million deal with Scottish Telecom has led us to develop one of the most advanced telecommunications wide area networks in the world. UHI students will be able to transmit or receive high-quality pictures, text and sound at the touch of a button . . . UHI will be a university not only in, but of, the region. The courses in this prospectus reflect the economic, social and physical qualities of the people and landscape from which they arise. Many highlight issues faced by remote communities. Others celebrate the region's cultural and environmental richness. All are making history and, together with UHI, are attracting interest from all over the world.[35]

The twenty-first-century Highlands and Islands, then, will be a place where people make imaginative use of the latest technologies. The area will also consist increasingly, I believe, of communities which are in charge of their own destinies in a way they have not been for a long time. Something of the possibilities in this regard – possibilities which are starting to extend into the physically and psychologically crucial sphere of land ownership – are illustrated by occurrences in Assynt, a crofting locality in the north-western corner of the Highland mainland, on 8 December 1992.

Some months previous to that date, the North Assynt Estate, extending to 21,000 acres, had been placed on the market by the overseas property company that then owned it. The sale brochure, having described the estate as a 'wilderness', went on:

> One need only enter Assynt . . . to sense the atmosphere of unreality, almost fantasy, which permeates the character of the people who live there. Mountains such as Quinag, Canisp, Ben More Assynt, Cul Mor, Cul Beag, Stac Polly and Conival have immense power to impress and serve to emphasise that man himself is, perhaps, the alien in this landscape.[36]

In fact, families have lived in Assynt for some ten thousand years. And if, in 1992, Assynt folk harboured a fantasy, then it was of a singularly down-to-earth variety. What Assynt people had the courage to imagine, in the summer of 1992, was that they themselves – instead of yet another of the landlords who have been managing, or mismanaging, such localities since the eighteenth century – might become the proprietors of the North Assynt Estate. On 6 June 1992, at a meeting called by the Assynt branch of the Scottish Crofters Union, it was accordingly decided to do what had never been done before in the Highlands and Islands: to mount a bid, on behalf of a locally constituted crofters' trust, for the land on which the bidders resided but over which they had formerly exercised only tenants' rights.

Six months later, on 8 December, after several intervening upsets and disappointments, the Assynt bid was declared successful. That evening, a celebratory gathering in Stoer Primary School heard from, among others, Allan MacRae, one of the leaders of the Assynt Crofters' Trust and a man whose ancestors had been among the victims of the Highland Clearances:

> Well, ladies and gentlemen, it seems we have won the land. It certainly is a moment to savour. There is no doubt about that . . . My immediate thoughts are to wish that some of our forebears could be here to share this moment with us . . . Assynt crofters have struck a historic blow.[37]

Assynt's achievement – one every bit as historic as Allan MacRae claimed – was to show that Highlands and Islands communities could aspire to, indeed obtain, ownership of land that, for generations past, had been firmly under the jurisdiction of others. Soon Assynt's example was being followed by further localities: Borve and Annishadder in Skye; Melness in Sutherland; the island of Eigg; Valtos in Lewis; Knoydart. And when, in the British general election of May 1997, the Labour Party – several of whose leading members had taken a close interest in these developments – was returned to power, governmental backing for the community-ownership concept was assured. The Labour minister with responsibility for HIE and for Highlands and Islands affairs generally was, as it happened, Brian Wilson – a man whose public career in the Highlands and Islands had begun with his central role in founding the *West Highland Free Press*. Within weeks of taking office, Wilson asked HIE to set up a Community Land Unit (CLU) with a view to facilitating additional experiments in community ownership. Among the immediate consequences of the CLU's emergence was the previously mentioned purchase by Skye and Lochalsh Enterprise – acting with CLU backing – of the Orbost Estate. Other initiatives quickly followed. And by the start of 1999, the CLU had more than thirty cases on its books.

At the political level, meanwhile, further advances were being secured. Labour's May 1997 manifesto had stated that the party, if elected, would establish a devolved Scottish parliament which – while operating in a United Kingdom context – would be primarily responsible for the governance of Scotland. The same manifesto had promised that Labour, on assuming power, would 'initiate a study into the system of land ownership and management in Scotland'. This study, it soon emerged, was itself to be a part of the wider devolutionary processes in which the Labour government was engaged – with the Labour-controlled Scottish Office setting up, in October 1997, a Land Reform Policy Group whose remit was to prepare reform proposals for consideration by Scotland's new legislature.[38]

The proposals in question were unveiled by the Secretary of State for Scotland, Donald Dewar, at the beginning of 1999 – some five or six months in advance of the Scottish parliament coming into existence. Among the legislative changes he envisaged, the Secretary of State made clear, were measures intended to encourage more Highlands and Islands communities to do what had been done in Assynt. Donald Dewar added:

> Land reform, for so long an issue out of the spotlight, has now moved firmly centre stage. On all sides, it seems to be understood that it would be fitting for legislation on land reform to be amongst the first acts of our new Scottish parliament.[39]

The Highlands and Islands, as this book has stressed, had little cause to be grateful to the modern Scottish parliament's pre-1707 forerunner. But if that parliament's successor – to be formally installed in Edinburgh in July 1999 – helps more Highlands and Islands communities take control of the land around them, many people in the Highlands and Islands will be most appreciative.

Conclusion

During the 1880s, perhaps the most formative decade in the modern history of the Highlands and Islands, Mary MacPherson, the Skye poet whose compositions became the Highland Land League's battle songs, tried to visualise the Highlands and Islands as they might be at the end of the struggles in which the Land League was engaged. Although she did not expect to see the Highlands and Islands future she envisaged, MacPherson, who intended her words to be in the nature of prophecy, was in no doubt as to that future's key characteristics. The Highlands and Islands, as imagined by Mary MacPherson, contain no landlords. They also constitute a region made capable – its 'gentry' having at last been 'routed' – of attracting, and accommodating, large numbers of people:

> And there will return the stock of the tenantry
> who were driven over the sea . . .
> And the cold, ruined stances of houses
> will be built on by our kinsmen.[1]

Today a part at least of Mary MacPherson's vision – a vision which, for most of the hundred years following her death in 1898, seemed no more than wishful thinking – is starting to come true. In Assynt, Eigg, Knoydart and elsewhere, Highlands and Islands communities have assumed ownership of the land. And in much of the Highlands and Islands – in MacPherson's own Isle of Skye, for instance – people are beginning to be re-established.

Among the folk moving into the Highlands and Islands at the twentieth century's close, however, were just a handful who can be categorised as 'the stock of the tenantry who were driven over the sea'. Many such immigrants are of Scottish Lowland background; more still, in places like Skye, come from England. By bigots, of whom there is no scarcity in the Highlands and Islands, people of this type are commonly described – with all the verbal ingenuity which prejudice seems to foster – as 'sooth-moothers', 'ferry-loupers' or 'white settlers'. And in such immigrants' origins, or so it has been alleged in certain quarters, there can be detected a potent threat to what remains of the various Highlands and Islands identities which earlier pages charted and, to some degree, celebrated.

There is considerable irony implicit in the fact that the Gaelic and Nordic cultures said to be jeopardised by immigration into the Highlands and Islands are themselves products of previous immigration – the Gaels and the Vikings having been prominent among the 'white settlers' and 'ferry-loupers' of the Christian era's first millennium. But of more immediate relevance, in this context, is the contribution twentieth-century immigrants have made to the revitalisation of numerous Highlands and Islands communities – including some which, in their absence, would have become extinct. Hence my strong conviction that the numerous families and individuals who have set up home here in recent years ought to be welcomed – irrespective of who they are – by everyone committed to Highlands and Islands betterment. Whether in the Highlands and Islands or anywhere else, after all, there can be no cultural life – no society of any kind – in the absence of human beings. And it was towards such a people-less Highlands and Islands that we looked to be heading not so long ago.

The particular case of Knoydart is of significance in this regard. Because of what was done to that West Highland peninsula by its landlords, present-day Knoydart, as noted in a previous chapter, contains not one person descended from the folk – and there were many hundreds of them – who lived there in the eighteenth century. But that does not make any less meaningful the takeover by Knoydart residents, in March 1999, of the Knoydart Estate. What matters in relation to that takeover is the fact that Knoydart, despite landlordism's repeated attempts to depopulate the place, still contains people. What matters even more is the further fact that the people in question, as is stated on the plaque commemorating their acquisition of the Knoydart Estate's 17,500 acres, 'have custody of the land on which they live'.

Speaking on the occasion of that plaque's unveiling, Iain Wilson, a Knoydart farmer, said:

> Custody, as I understand it, means guardianship or protective care. We don't really own the land – nobody does. We are only stewards of it for as long as we are here. We, as a community,

> accept the challenge to take care of it and to try to pass it on to the next generation in a slightly better state than that in which we receive it.[2]

Those comments show how beliefs rooted in the Highland and Island past can readily surface in today's Highlands and Islands – despite the genetic composition of the region's population having altered in the interim. And there is plenty of other evidence to the same effect. To visit – in Skye or Ardnamurchan, for example – a Gaelic-medium primary-school class, and to find there Gaelic-speaking seven-year-olds whose parents are of English birth, is to be made aware, in a most graphic manner, that it is not necessary to be of Highlands and Islands extraction in order to empathise with, and carry into the future, vital aspects of our Highlands and Islands heritage.

'Just as human beings make their own history,' it has been observed by Edward Said, 'they make their own cultural and ethnic identities.' Said, whose career as an American-based Palestinian Arab academic gives substance to this contention, is surely right. If the collective outlook of Highlands and Islands communities should one day be unaffected by what has gone before in the Highlands and Islands, that will not be a consequence of such communities having ceased to consist of families possessing Highlands and Islands grandmothers. It will be a consequence, rather, of Highlands and Islands residents – whoever they may be – having judged the region's past incapable of offering them anything of consequence.[3]

At the time of writing, no such judgement appears imminent – the late-twentieth-century repopulation of the Highlands and Islands having been accompanied, as already emphasised, by a marked renaissance in cultural forms which, just decades before, were thought hopelessly imperilled.

On the day I began jotting down those words, something of this Highlands and Islands renaissance was captured in an article by the leading Scottish journalist and cultural commentator, Joyce MacMillan. Reporting on the Celtic Film and Television Festival held on Skye in March 1999, MacMillan told of a week spent debating – in the Sorley MacLean Theatre at Portree's Aros Centre or in Arainn Chaluim Chille, Sabhal Mor Ostaig's 'superb new building' – the myriad opportunities now opening up to the Highlands and Islands. MacMillan's article concluded:

> Then it's back to the hotel, through a radiant Skye sunset, and on to ceilidh through the night at a glittering festival banquet

> where I felt almost blown away by the sheer force of . . . energy and confidence coming from Europe's once-neglected western edge. For what have I learned . . .? That Skye is not the hard, bleak place of my imagination, but a fine, rich landscape, in which people might live a good life; that negative attributes of poverty and 'remoteness' have been imposed on it, and on many landscapes like it, by people and their power structures, and can be changed by them; and that the movement of which the Celtic Film and Television Festival is part is beginning to make that change happen, right in front of our eyes, with consequences we can barely begin to imagine.[4]

When writing thus about the Highlands and Islands of 1999, as I have acknowledged, one must take care not to overdo the positives. There is much about the region, as I have also acknowledged, which presently gives cause for concern. And should you be one of those Highlands and Islands residents obliged to work long hours for poor wages, or should you be forced to occupy (in the absence of any half-way affordable house) a cramped, cold, condensation-soaked caravan, then you are entitled, I concede, to be unimpressed by talk of the Highlands and Islands being on the up and up.

But such talk is true all the same. Despite its having faltered in the 1920s, the 1930s, the 1940s and the 1950s, the forward momentum which the Highlands and Islands began to gain in the 1880s – the years when Mary MacPherson dared to dream her magnificently optimistic dreams – has been renewed. Real headway is being made. And to grasp the nature of that headway, it is necessary only to hear of the exhilaration experienced by folk who, having taken their destinies into their own hands, begin to realise the scope of what may, in the end, be feasible. Something of this is evident in Joyce MacMillan's account of her visit to Skye. Something of it is evident, too, in an Eigg resident's description of the 'tremendous feeling of elation' she experienced on helping to initiate the campaign which culminated in this same woman and her neighbours – all of them sick to death of landlords – purchasing their island.[5]

But for all that there is plenty of success to celebrate in the modern Highlands and Islands, I am uneasily aware both of the fragility of the gains we have made and of the extent to which our further progress depends on the view taken of the Highlands and Islands by members of the devolved parliament which, by the time those words are in print, will be at work in Edinburgh. Hence my decision to start this book with a story featuring a certain scepticism – to put it mildly – about the merits, from a Highlands and Islands perspective, of Scottish devolution. Given the political circumstances prevailing currently in Scotland, that story – so bitterly condemnatory of Edinburgh attitudes and pretensions – might seem gratuitously provocative. But it is a story which serves, from my standpoint, two useful purposes. It constitutes, first, an appropriate beginning to a book which is intensely critical of the way Scotland dealt, in the past, with the Highlands and Islands. And, second, it may just conceivably have the effect of helping to stimulate debate about the proposition – a proposition which this book both advances and endorses – that the present-day Highlands and Islands need and deserve their own equivalent of the devolutionary bargain which Scotland as a whole has made with the United Kingdom.

As will be evident to anyone who has followed my narrative this far, I regret the loss to the Highlands and Islands of the regional independence which Calgacus was defending when, in 83AD, he addressed his followers as the 'last of the free'. As will equally be evident to readers of preceding chapters, I blame the destruction of this independence on rulers of Scotland. Almost from the moment of Scotland's emergence, its political class, often by very violent means, sought aggressively to expand the country's borders in order to bring the entire Highlands and Islands within those borders. This same political class then took steps to eliminate, inside the greater Scotland thus created, anything deemed to threaten Scottish unity. Thus it came about that the Kingdom of Moray, the Earldom of Orkney and the Lordship of the Isles were conquered, annexed and crushed. Thus it came about, too, that the people of the Highlands and Islands – an overwhelming majority of whom had the misfortune to speak Gaelic in an era when Scotland's business was conducted mainly in Broad Scots – came to be regarded, by almost everyone who mattered in Scotland's capital, as barbarians who needed civilising or, on occasion, as savages deserving of being killed.

Particularly if it is told – as this book tries to tell it – from the inside looking out, instead of from the outside looking in, much of the story of the Highlands and Islands, then, consists of the downside of a process of Scottish nation-building which most histories of Scotland tend to treat as if it amounted to the working out of some divine, and unfailingly beneficent, plan. Because I regard Scotland's growth and consolidation as having had – from a Highlands and Islands standpoint – calamitous and disastrous consequences, my interpretation of Scottish history is a trifle more jaundiced than the standard one. But that interpretation, I stress, attributes no peculiar malevolence or viciousness to the Scottish state. In relation to comparable territories, most other states – and England's behaviour in Ireland makes the point to perfection – have behaved in much the same imperialist fashion as Scotland habitually behaved in relation to the Highlands and Islands. It is no cause for surprise, therefore, that when, in 1707, the Highlands and Islands became a part of the United Kingdom, rather than a part of the formerly self-governing Scotland which then merged with England, the immediate outcome, as far as the Highlands and Islands were concerned, was a tightening, not a slackening, of external control.

As this book's last two chapters emphasise, however, the United Kingdom's attitude to the Highlands and Islands has become, of late, a good deal more enlightened. In response initially to protest from within the region, then because it was considered the most democratically responsible way forward, successive governments of the United Kingdom endeavoured, between the 1880s and the 1990s, to establish mechanisms of a kind which – whatever their deficiencies – have made it possible for people living in the Highlands and Islands to obtain some meaningful leverage, once again, over what happens here. That approach culminated in the formation, during 1994, of a Convention of the Highlands and Islands – at which representatives of a whole range of Highlands and Islands groupings have discussed regional policy with the Secretary of State for Scotland and with Scottish Office ministers. This convention or something like it, I hope, will be continued by Scotland's parliament and by the Scottish executive, or government, which the parliament will sustain. Indeed I see no reason, as already indicated, why there should not be devolved to the Convention of the Highlands and Islands, or to the organisations represented on it, a proportion at least of the powers which have already been devolved to Edinburgh from London.

I hold no brief for attempts to resuscitate long-dead institutions. Political entities like the Earldom of Orkney and the Lordship of the Isles were of their time. And that time will not come again. But if the Scotland presided over by the country's recreated parliament is to do better by the region than Scotland did when last in charge of the Highlands and Islands, it is essential that people living in the area are permitted, as far as practicable, to shape their own future. We have benefited greatly in the Highlands and Islands from such autonomy as we have regained in the course of the last hundred or so years. We would benefit still more if that autonomy were now to be expanded.

The first board meeting of Highlands and Islands Enterprise which I chaired was held on 16 November 1998 in Kirkwall. On the morning following that meeting, in the company of two or three colleagues, I took the inter-island flight from Kirkwall to Westray, one of Orkney's north isles and one of the Highlands and Islands localities selected, some months previously, to serve as an *Iomairt aig an Oir*, or Initiative at the Edge, pilot area. Another of the projects devised by Brian Wilson, following his arrival at the Scottish Office in May 1997, Initiative at the Edge is intended to give communities in places like Westray some grip on development strategy. And because people there had responded energetically to this opportunity, by organising a weekend-long conference on Westray's future as well as by coming up with a whole series of suggestions as to what they might do to improve their island's prospects, I was anxious to hear something, at first hand, of what Westray folk had on their minds.

The closing months of 1998, even by Highlands and Islands standards, were exceptionally wet and stormy. The day of our Westray trip, however, was strangely bright and cloudless. From the plane, as we flew over the cathedral of St Magnus and headed north, the view was as stunning as any I have seen in all my Highlands and Islands travels. Although there was no wind to speak of, an Atlantic swell was edging the west-facing coasts of Shapinsay, Stronsay, Egilsay and Eday with a white line of surf. Long, black shadows cast by the rising sun were pointing to each house, each dyke, each long-abandoned rig, each enduring mark, in short, that humanity has ever made on Orkney's landscape. And so clear was the air, I realised as we approached Westray, that it was possible to make out Fair Isle and Foula – Shetland outliers separated from Orkney by between fifty and seventy miles of open ocean.

Seeing me gazing at the spectacle spread out so amazingly below, Arlette Banister, an HIE board member, leaned across and raised her voice above the racket of our little aircraft's engine. 'If the job ever gets you down,' she said, 'remember that it brought you here this morning.'

That was good advice. I shall forever recall how Orkney looked on 17 November 1998. I shall always recollect, too, something of what I was told in the course of my meetings and conversations with Westray people. From those encounters, I took away – as I often take away from localities like Westray – a strong impression of the immense human potential to be found in the Highlands and Islands. Unleashing that potential, as the organisation's mission statement asserts, is HIE's long-term objective. I think myself lucky – at what I believe to be a decisive period in the history of the Highlands and Islands – to have been given a chance to contribute, even if marginally, to that objective's realisation.

In spite of all the difficulties I have dwelt on, much good has been achieved in the Highlands and Islands during the several thousand years surveyed by this book. Given the right circumstances, much more good will be accomplished, I am convinced, in the decades and the centuries that lie ahead.

Kiltarlity
April 1999

References

To have referenced every statement made in this book would have resulted in a proliferation of notes. References are consequently provided only for quotations.

Introduction

1 H. Mattingly (ed), *Tacitus: The Agricola and the Germania*, London, 1970, 80-81.
2 Mattingly, *Tacitus*, 80.
3 S. Schama, *Landscape and Memory*, London, 1996, 24.

Chapter 1: The most distant dwellers upon Earth

1 Mattingly, *Tacitus*, 80, 85.
2 Mattingly, *Tacitus*, 60-61, 74-77.
3 A. Mitchell (ed), *MacFarlane's Geographical Collections*, 3 vols, Edinburgh, 1906, II, 213.
4 Mattingly, *Tacitus*, 75-76.
5 Mattingly, *Tacitus*, 76-77.
6 Mattingly, *Tacitus*, 86.
7 Mattingly, *Tacitus*, 89-90.

Chapter 2: Born of a noble lineage

1 R. Sharpe (ed), *Adomnan of Iona: Life of St Columba*, London, 1995, 175-76.
2 Sharpe, *Adomnan of Iona*, 176.
3 Sharpe, *Adomnan of Iona*, 176.
4 Sharpe, *Adomnan of Iona*, 184.
5 J. McClure and R. Collins (eds), *Bede: The Ecclesiastical History of the English People*, Oxford, 1994, 27.
6 Mattingly, *Tacitus*, 75.
7 E. MacNeill, *Celtic Ireland*, Dublin, 1921, 167-69.
8 T. Kinsella, *The Tain*, Oxford, 1970, 153.
9 D. O'Croinin, *Early Medieval Ireland*, Harlow, 1995, 14.
10 Sharpe, *Adomnan of Iona*, 105.
11 Sharpe, *Adomnan of Iona*, 105.
12 A.O. Anderson, *Early Sources of Scottish History*, 2 vols, Edinburgh, 1922, I, 75.
13 Sharpe, *Adomnan of Iona*, 119.
14 T.O. Clancy and G. Markus, *Iona: The Earliest Poetry of a Celtic Monastery*, Edinburgh, 1995, 105.
15 B. Cunliffe, *The Celtic World*, London, 1992, 190.
16 Sharpe, *Adomnan of Iona*, 130, 133.
17 Sharpe, *Adomnan of Iona*, 225.
18 Sharpe, *Adomnan of Iona*, 226-27.
19 Sharpe, *Adomnan of Iona*, 228; Psalm 34, v. 10.
20 Sharpe, *Adomnan of Iona*, 228-29.
21 McClure and Collins, *Bede*, 115.
22 McClure and Collins, *Bede*, 113-14.
23 Sharpe, *Adomnan of Iona*, 228.
24 Sharpe, *Adomnan of Iona*, 234.
25 Sharpe, *Adomnan of Iona*, 103.
26 P. Brown, *The Book of Kells*, London, 1980, 83.
27 D. Greene and F. O'Connor (eds), *A Golden Treasury of Irish Poetry*, Dingle, 1990, 65.

Chapter 3: The broad loom of slaughter

1 M. Magnusson and H. Palsson (eds), *Njal's Saga*, London, 1960, 349.
2 Magnusson and Palsson, *Njal's Saga*, 349.
3 H. Palsson and P. Edwards (eds), *Orkneyinga Saga: The History of the Earls of Orkney*, London, 1978, 38.

4 Palsson and Edwards, *Orkneyinga Saga*, 38.
5 Magnusson and Palsson, *Njal's Saga*, 347.
6 Magnusson and Palsson, *Njal's Saga*, 347-48.
7 Magnusson and Palsson, *Njal's Saga*, 351-52.
8 A.O. Anderson (ed), *Early Sources of Scottish History*, 2 vols, Edinburgh, 1922, I, 255-58.
9 G. Jones, *A History of the Vikings*, Oxford, 1984, 215.
10 Anderson, *Early Sources*, I, 263-65.
11 M. Magnusson and H. Palsson (eds), *Laxdaela Saga*, London, 1969, 49.
12 Magnusson and Palsson, *Laxdaela Saga*, 51; H. Palsson and P. Edwards (eds), *The Book of Settlements*, Winnipeg, 1972, 51.
13 F.D. Logan, *The Vikings in History*, London, 1991, 62.
14 Palsson and Edwards, *Book of Settlements*, 55.
15 Magnusson and Palsson, *Laxdaela Saga*, 52.
16 M. Magnusson and H. Palsson (eds), *The Vinland Sagas*, London, 1965, 95.
17 Palsson and Edwards, *Orkneyinga Saga*, 30.
18 Palsson and Edwards, *Orkneyinga Saga*, 30-31.
19 Palsson and Edwards, *Orkneyinga Saga*, 38.
20 Palsson and Edwards, *Orkneyinga Saga*, 49-50.
21 Palsson and Edwards, *Orkneyinga Saga*, 190-91.
22 B. Fidjestol, 'Arnor Thordarsson, Skald of the Orkney Jarls', in A. Fenton and H. Palsson (eds), *The Northern and Western Isles in the Viking World: Survival, Continuity and Change*, Edinburgh, 1984, 243.
23 Palsson and Edwards, *Book of Settlements*, 97.
24 Palsson and Edwards, *Orkneyinga Saga*, 83.
25 Palsson and Edwards, *Orkneyinga Saga*, 87-88.
26 Palsson and Edwards, *Orkneyinga Saga*, 88.
27 Anderson, *Early Sources*, II, 471.
28 Palsson and Edwards, *Orkneyinga Saga*, 198.
29 Anderson, *Early Sources*, II, 451.
30 Anderson, *Early Sources*, II, 105-08; E. Monsen and A.H. Smith (eds), *Snorre Sturlason: Heimskringla*, New York, 1990, 592-93.
31 Monsen and Smith, *Heimskringla*, 594; Palsson and Edwards, *Orkneyinga Saga*, 81.
32 A. Cameron (ed), *Reliquiae Celticae*, 2 vols, Inverness, 1892-94, II, 155.
33 Anderson, *Early Sources*, II, 254-58.
34 Anderson, *Early Sources*, II, 555.
35 G.W.S. Barrow, *Kingship and Unity: Scotland, 1000-1306*, London, 1981, 105; Anderson, *Early Sources*, II, 557.
36 G.W. Dasent (ed), *Icelandic Sagas and Other Documents*, 4 vols, London, 1887-94, IV, 340.
37 Dasent, *Icelandic Sagas*, IV, 340.
38 Anderson, *Early Sources*, II, 609-10; Dasent, *Icelandic Sagas*, IV, 344.
39 Anderson, *Early Sources*, II, 625; Dasent, *Icelandic Sagas*, IV, 354-55.
40 Dasent, *Icelandic Sagas*, IV, 366.
41 G. Donaldson (ed), *Scottish Historical Documents*, Edinburgh, 1970, 35.

Chapter 4: Children of Conn

1 H.B. Mackintosh and J.S. Richardson, *Elgin Cathedral*, Edinburgh, 1980, 37.
2 A. Grant, 'The Wolf of Badenoch', in W.D.H. Sellar (ed), *Moray: Province and People*, Edinburgh, 1993, 143.
3 S. Boardman, *The Early Stewart Kings: Robert II and Robert III*, East Linton, 1996, 85.
4 A. Grant, 'National Consciousness in Medieval Scotland', in C. Bjorn, A. Grant and K. Stringer (eds), *Nations, Nationalism and Patriotism in the European Past*, Copenhagen, 1994, 76-77; R. Nicholson, *Scotland: The Later Middle Ages*, Edinburgh, 1974, 207.
5 J.R.N. MacPhail (ed), *Highland Papers*, 4 vols, Edinburgh, 1914–34, I, 24.
6 MacPhail, *Highland Papers*, I, 24; M. Martin, *A Description of the Western Islands of Scotland*, Edinburgh, 1994, 273.

7 MacPhail, *Highland Papers*, I, 24.
8 R.W. Munro (ed), *Munro's Western Isles of Scotland*, Edinburgh, 1961, 43.
9 W.J. Watson (ed), *Scottish Verse from the Book of the Dean of Lismore*, Edinburgh, 1937, 7.
10 D. Thomson, *An Introduction to Gaelic Poetry*, London, 1974, 30-31.
11 J.N. Alison (ed), *Poetry of Northeast Scotland*, London, 1976, 14.
12 Alison, *Poetry of Northeast Scotland*, 15.
13 MacPhail, *Highland Papers*, I, 24.

Chapter 5: No joy without Clan Donald

1 B. Bryson, *Notes from a Small Island*, London, 1996, 320.
2 E. Burt, *Letters from the North of Scotland*, 2 vols, Edinburgh, 1974, I, 35-36.
3 W. MacKay and H.C. Boyd (eds), *Records of Inverness*, 2 vols, Aberdeen, 1911-24, I, lxxiii.
4 W. MacKay (ed), *Chronicles of the Frasers: The Wardlaw Manuscript*, Edinburgh, 1905, 95.
5 E. Ewan, *Townlife in Fourteenth-Century Scotland*, Edinburgh, 1990, 23.
6 Burt, *Letters from the North of Scotland*, I, 45, 52, 74.
7 Burt, *Letters from the North of Scotland*, I, 4-5.
8 MacKay and Boyd, *Records of Inverness*, I, lxxxiv.
9 J. Hunter, *On the Other Side of Sorrow: Nature and People in the Scottish Highlands*, Edinburgh, 1995, 102; T.M. Devine, *Clanship to Crofters' War: The Social Transformation of the Scottish Highlands*, Manchester, 1994, 85.
10 Burt, *Letters from the North of Scotland*, I, 78.
11 I.D. Whye and K. Whyte, *The Changing Scottish Landscape, 1500-1800*, London, 1991, 30.
12 Munro, *Munro's Western Isles*, 43.
13 Munro, *Munro's Western Isles*, 42.
14 A. Gibson and T.C. Smout, 'Scottish Food and Scottish History, 1500-1800', in R.A. Houston and I.D. Whyte (eds), *Scottish Society, 1500-1800*, Cambridge, 1989, 65.
15 Burt, *Letters from the North of Scotland*, II, 130; F. J. Shaw, *The Northern and Western Islands of Scotland: Their Economy and Society in the Seventeenth Century*, Edinburgh, 1980, 80.
16 Shaw, *Northern and Western Islands*, 169.
17 P.D. Anderson, *Robert Stewart: Earl of Orkney, Lord of Shetland*, Edinburgh, 1982, 13.
18 W.P.L. Thomson, *History of Orkney*, Edinburgh, 1987, 174.
19 Cameron, *Reliquiae Celticae*, II, 167.
20 J. Bannerman, 'The Lordship of the Isles', in J.M Brown (ed), *Scottish Society in the Fifteenth Century*, London, 1977, 215.
21 Watson, *Verse from the Book of the Dean of Lismore*, 93.
22 P. Galliou and M. Jones, *The Bretons*, Oxford, 1991, 261; Munro, *Munro's Western Isles*, 57.
23 Thomson, *Introduction to Gaelic Poetry*, 68.
24 W. Matheson (ed), *The Blind Harper: The Songs of Roderick Morrison and his Music*, Edinburgh, 1970, liii.
25 J.C. Watson (ed), *Gaelic Songs of Mary MacLeod*, Edinburgh, 1965, 63-65.
26 Watson, *Songs of Mary MacLeod*, 33-35.
27 Martin, *Description of the Western Islands*, Edinburgh, 1994, 106-7.
28 L. Maclean (ed), *The Seventeenth Century in the Highlands*, Inverness, 1986, 13; I.F. Grant, *The MacLeods: The History of a Clan*, 2nd edition, Edinburgh, 1981, 179, 194.
29 Bannerman, 'The Lordship of the Isles', 215; V.E. Durkacz, *The Decline of the Celtic Languages*, Edinburgh, 1983, 5.
30 N.C. MacKenzie, *History of the Outer Hebrides*, Edinburgh, 1974, 230.
31 Mattingly, *Tacitus*, 72-73.
32 A.M. MacKenzie (ed), *Orain Iain Luim: Songs of John MacDonald*, Edinburgh, 1964, 143.
33 MacKenzie, *Orain Iain Luim*, 35; D. Stevenson, *Alasdair MacColla and the Highland Problem in the Seventeenth Century*, Edinburgh, 1980, 82.

34 Stevenson, *Alasdair MacColla*, 147; MacKenzie, *Orain Iain Luim*, 25, 35.
35 MacKenzie, *Orain Iain Luim*, 23-25.
36 MacKay, *Chronicles of the Frasers*, 353.
37 F.D. Dow, *Cromwellian Scotland*, Edinburgh, 1979, 67.

Chapter 6: Moments when nothing seemed impossible

1 J. Hunter, *Glencoe and the Indians*, Edinburgh, 1996, 60-63.
2 A.J. Youngson, *The Prince and the Pretender*, Beckenham, 1985, 71.
3 J.L. Campbell, *Highland Songs of the Forty-Five*, Edinburgh, 1984, 5-7; J. MacInnes, 'The Oral Tradition in Scottish Gaelic Poetry', *Scottish Studies*, 12, 1968, 30.
4 F.J. McLynn, *Charles Edward Stuart*, London, 1988, 191.
5 W.A. Speck, *The Butcher: The Duke of Cumberland and the Suppression of the Forty-Five*, Caernarfon, 1995, 112-13.
6 Speck, *The Butcher*, 147, 164-66; Youngson, *The Prince and the Pretender*, 259; J. Fergusson, *Argyll in the Forty-Five*, London, 1951, 120; Devine, *Clanship to Crofters' War*, 21; A.L. Carswell, 'The Most Despicable Enemy that Are', in R.C. Woosnam-Savage (ed), *1745: Charles Edward Stuart and the Jacobites*, Edinburgh, 1995, 29.
7 Speck, *The Butcher*, 89.
8 Devine, *Clanship to Crofters' War*, 86.
9 R.W. Munro, *Taming the Rough Bounds*, Isle of Coll, 1984.
10 J. Hunter, *A Dance Called America: The Scottish Highlands, the United States and Canada*, Edinburgh, 1994, 71.
11 MacKenzie, *Orain Iain Luim*, 124-25; Matheson, *Blind Harper*, 69.
12 E. Grant, *Memoirs of a Highland Lady*, 2 vols, Edinburgh, 1988, I, 329-30.
13 Grant, *Memoirs*, I, 24-26.
14 T. Pennant, *A Tour of Scotland in 1769*, Edinburgh, 1979, 160.
15 A.R.B. Haldane, *The Drove Roads of Scotland*, Edinburgh, 1971, 24.
16 M. Ash, *This Noble Harbour: A History of the Cromarty Firth*, Invergordon, 1991, 110.
17 I.R.M. Mowat, *Easter Ross, 1750-1850: The Double Frontier*, Edinburgh, 1981, 98, 102.
18 S. Johnson, *A Journey to the Western Islands of Scotland*, London, 1984, 97.
19 W. Matheson (ed), *The Songs of John MacCodrum*, Edinburgh, 1938, 199-203.
20 Matheson, *Songs of John MacCodrum*, 199-203.
21 M. MacDonnell, *The Emigrant Experience: Songs of Highland Emigrants in North America*, Toronto, 1982, 36-37.
22 Hunter, *Dance Called America*, 43.
23 Hunter, *Dance Called America*, 39-40; J.M. Bumsted, *The People's Clearance*, Edinburgh, 1982, 136.
24 Hunter, *Dance Called America*, 38.
25 A. Fenton, *The Northern Isles: Orkney and Shetland*, Edinburgh, 1978, 6.
26 B. Smith, 'Adam Smith's Rents from the Sea', in T.C. Smout (ed), *Scotland and the Sea*, Edinburgh, 1992, 104.
27 S.A. Knox, *The Making of the Shetland Landscape*, Edinburgh, 1985, 15.
28 B. Smith, 'Shetland and the Crofters Act', in L. Graham (ed), *Shetland Crofters: A Hundred Years of Shetland Crofting*, Lerwick, 1987, 4.

Chapter 7: I never did witness such wretchedness

1 E. Richards, *A History of the Highland Clearances*, 2 vols, London, 1982-85, I, 256.
2 K.J. Logue, *Popular Disturbances in Scotland*, 1780-1815, Edinburgh, 1979, 61.
3 Richards, *History of the Clearances*, I, 258; Logue, *Popular Disturbances*, 62.
4 Richards, *History of the Clearances*, I, 249-51; H.W. Meikle, *Scotland and the French Revolution*, Glasgow, 1912, 81-82.
5 Richards, *History of the Clearances*, I, 264.
6 Richards, *History of the Clearances*, I, 260-61.

7 Richards, *History of the Clearances*, I, 263.
8 A.R.B. Haldane, *New Ways Through the Glens*, Isle of Colonsay, 1995, 22; Richards, *History of the Clearances*, I, 190.
9 J. Hunter, *The Making of the Crofting Community*, Edinburgh, 1976, 15.
10 I.S. Macdonald, 'Alexander MacDonald of Glencoe: Insights into Early Highland Sheep Farming', *Review of Scottish Culture*, 10, 1996-97, 55.
11 W.F. Laughlan (ed), *James Hogg's Highland Tours*, Hawick, 1981, 69.
12 Richards, *History of the Clearances*, I, 250.
13 Richards, *History of the Clearances*, I, 202.
14 A.T. Cluness (ed), *The Shetland Book*, Lerwick, 1967, 81.
15 Hunter, *Dance Called America*, 53.
16 Hunter, *Dance Called America*, 57.
17 Hunter, *Crofting Community*, 17.
18 R.P. Fereday, 'The Lairds and Eighteenth-Century Orkney', in R.J. Berry and H. Firth (eds), *The People of Orkney*, Kirkwall, 1986, 231.
19 Hunter, *Crofting Community*, 19.
20 Hunter, *Crofting Community*, 19.
21 Hunter, *Crofting Community*, 19.
22 W.C. Wonders, 'Orkney and the "Nor-Waast"', *Alberta History*, Winter 1993, 9.
23 P.C. Newman, *Company of Adventurers: The Story of the Hudson's Bay Company*, London, 1987, 239.
24 Laughlan, *Hogg's Highland Tours*, 72.
25 Hunter, *Dance Called America*, 101.
26 Hunter, *Dance Called America*, 102.
27 MacDonnell, *The Emigrant Experience*, 145; Bumsted, *The People's Clearance*, 100.
28 Hunter, *Crofting Community*, 20; Hunter, *Dance Called America*, 103.
29 Hunter, *Dance Called America*, 104.
30 Hunter, *Dance Called America*, 104.
31 Richards, *History of the Clearances*, I, 134.
32 Hunter, *Crofting Community*, 26.
33 R.J. Adam (ed), *Papers on Sutherland Estate Management*, 2 vols, Edinburgh, 1972, I, 156.
34 Richards, *History of the Clearances*, II, 373-407.
35 Richards, *History of the Clearances*, II, 399; Hunter, *Dance Called America*, 176.
36 Richards, *History of the Clearances*, I, 349.
37 R. Somers, *Letters from the Highlands on the Famine of 1846*, Inverness, 1977, 103.
38 Hunter, *Crofting Community*, 46.
39 D.E. Meek (ed), *Tuath is Tighearna: Tenants and Landlords*, Edinburgh, 1995, 57-58.
40 Ash, *This Noble Harbour*, 117.
41 *Report of Commissioners of Inquiry into the Condition of the Crofters and Cottars in the Highlands and Islands of Scotland*, 5 vols, Edinburgh, 1884, II, 201-02.
42 Hunter, *Dance Called America*, 111.
43 T. Coleman, *Passage to America*, London, 1972, 86.
44 Hunter, *Crofting Community*, 48.
45 F. Fraser Darling (ed), *West Highland Survey: An Essay in Human Ecology*, Oxford, 1955, 44.
46 Hunter, *Crofting Community*, 53.
47 Hunter, *Crofting Community*, 53.
48 Hunter, *Crofting Community*, 54-55.
49 Hunter, *Crofting Community*, 65.
50 Hunter, *Crofting Community*, 64.
51 T.M. Devine, *The Great Highland Famine*, Edinburgh, 1988, 126.
52 Hunter, *Crofting Community*, 67.
53 Devine, *Highland Famine*, 60.
54 Richards, *History of the Clearances*, I, 454-55.
55 Richards, *History of the Clearances*, I, 406.
56 Richards, *History of the Clearances*, I, 407.
57 Richards, *History of the Clearances*, I, 412.
58 Hunter, *Dance Called America*, 120.
59 Hunter, *Dance Called America*, 121.
60 Hunter, *Dance Called America*, 121.

Chapter 8: Is treasa tuath na tighearna

1 J. Thomas and D. Turnock, *A Regional History of the Railways of Great Britain: North of Scotland*, Newton Abbot, 1989, 267; J. Thomas, *The Callander and Oban Railway*, Newton Abbot, 1966, 79.
2 Thomas and Turnock, *Regional*

History of Railways, 219.
3 Devine, *Clanship to Crofters' War*, 79-80.
4 P. Gaskell, *Morvern Transformed: A Highland Parish in the Nineteenth Century*, Cambridge, 1966, 81.
5 J. Hunter, 'Sheep and Deer: Highland Sheep Farming, 1850-1900', *Northern Scotland*, I, 1974, 200.
6 W.P.L. Thomson, *The Little General and the Rousay Crofters*, Edinburgh, 1981, 32.
7 F. Foden, *Wick of the North: The Story of a Scottish Royal Burgh*, Wick, 1996, 355.
8 *Commissioners of Inquiry into Condition of Crofters*, I, 110.
9 H.D. Smith, *The Making of Modern Shetland*, Lerwick, 1977, 50.
10 Hunter, *Crofting Community*, 113.
11 *Commissioners of Inquiry into Condition of Crofters*, I, 3.
12 Hunter, Crofting Community, 89.
13 A. Carmichael, *Carmina Gadelica*, 6 vols, Edinburgh, 1928-71, III, 328-29.
14 Devine, *Clanship to Crofters' War*, 169.
15 J. Hunter, 'The Gaelic Connection: The Highlands, Ireland and Nationalism', *Scottish Historical Review*, 54, 1975, 183.
16 Hunter, *Crofting Community*, 99.
17 Hunter, *For the People's Cause*, 29-30.
18 Hunter, *For the People's Cause*, 31.
19 Hunter, *For the People's Cause*, 29.
20 Hunter, *For the People's Cause*, 35.
21 Hunter, *For the People's Cause*, 35.
22 Hunter, *Crofting Community*, 134.
23 Hunter, *Crofting Community*, 138-39.
24 *Commissioners of Inquiry into Condition of Crofters*, II, 1.
25 *Commissioners of Inquiry into Condition of Crofters*, II, 4.
26 *Commissioners of Inquiry into Condition of Crofters*, II, 6.
27 *Commissioners of Inquiry into Condition of Crofters*, II, 4-5.
28 Hunter, *Crofting Community*, 149.
29 Hunter, *Crofting Community*, 156.
30 Richards, *History of the Clearances*, I, 349.
31 *Commissioners of Inquiry into Condition of Crofters*, I, 8.
32 E. Cameron, *Land for the People: The British Government and the Scottish Highlands, 1880-1925*, East Linton, 1996, 33.
33 J. Hunter, 'The Politics of Highland Land Reform, 1873-1895', *Scottish Historical Review*, 53, 1974, 54.
34 Hunter, *Crofting Community*, 179.
35 Cameron, *Land for the People*, 43.
36 Hunter, *Crofting Community*, 174-75.
37 Hunter, *Crofting Community*, 194.
38 A. Budge, *Voices in the Wind: Caithness and the First World War*, Wick, 1996, 123.
39 Hunter, *Crofting Community*, 195, 202.

Chapter 9: Wir ain aald language

1 T.A. Robertson, *The Collected Poems of Vagaland*, Lerwick, 1980, 2-3.
2 J.A. Smith, 'The Position of Gaelic in Scottish Education', in D.S. Thomson and I. Grimble (eds), *The Future of the Highlands*, London, 1968, 62; W. Gillies, 'A Century of Gaelic Scholarship', in W. Gillies (ed), *Gaelic and Scotland*, Edinburgh, 1989, 9.
3 Hunter, *For The People's Cause*, 25-26.
4 L.K. Schei, *The Shetland Story*, London, 1988, 89.
5 C.G. Brown, *Up-Helly-Aa: Custom, Culture and Community in Shetland*, Manchester, 1998, 158.
6 N.M. Gunn, *Butcher's Broom*, London, 1977, 21.
7 S. MacLean, *From Wood To Ridge: Collected Poems*, Manchester, 1989, 130-31.
8 J. Hendry, 'The Man and His Work', in R.J. Ross and J. Hendry (eds), *Sorley MacLean: Critical Essays*, Edinburgh, 1986, 20.
9 J.D.M. Robertson (ed), *An Orkney Anthology: Selected Works of Ernest Walker Marwick*, Edinburgh, 1991, 228.
10 J. Hunter, *The Claim of Crofting: The Scottish Highlands and Islands, 1930-1990*, Edinburgh, 1991, 33.
11 M. Harper, 'Crofter Colonists in Canada', *Northern Scotland*, 14, 1994, 69.
12 Hunter, *Claim of Crofting*, 42-44.
13 P.L. Payne, *The Hydro*, Aberdeen, 1988, 43.

14 Payne, *The Hydro*, 190.
15 Hunter, *Claim of Crofting*, 65.
16 Darling, *West Highland Survey*, 100; Cluness, *Shetland Book*, 23.
17 J. Hunter, *The Highland Fund*, Glasgow, 1991, 1; Hunter, *Claim of Crofting*, 59.
18 K. Alexander, 'The Highlands and Islands Development Board', in R. Saville (ed), *The Economic Development of Modern Scotland*, Edinburgh, 1985, 218.
19 Alexander, 'Highlands and Islands Development Board', 215.
20 *Report of the Commission of Enquiry into Crofting Conditions*, Edinburgh, 1954, 41.
21 Hunter, *Claim of Crofting*, 117-18.
22 Hunter, *Claim of Crofting*. 152.
23 Hunter, *Claim of Crofting*, 152.
24 A. Hetherington, 'Northern Scotland: Real Lives', in A. Hetherington (ed), *Highlands and Islands: A Generation of Progress*, Aberdeen, 1990, 2.
25 HIDB, *First Report*, Inverness, 1966, 4-5.
26 E. Thomason, 'Shetland in the Seventies', in J.R. Baldwin (ed), *Scandinavian Shetland: An Ongoing Tradition*, Edinburgh, 1978, 43.
27 E. Thomason, *Island Challenge*, Lerwick, 1997, 25.
28 R. Gronneberg, *Island Governments*, Sandwick, 1976, 4.
29 J. Grassie, *Highland Experiment: The Story of the Highlands and Islands Development Board*, Aberdeen, 1983, 4.
30 J. Wills, *A Place in the Sun: Shetland and Oil*, Edinburgh, 1991, 1.
31 J. McGrath, *The Cheviot, the Stag and the Black, Black Oil*, Isle of Skye, 1975, 27-28.
32 H.D. Smith, *The Making of Modern Shetland*, Lerwick, 1977, 74.
33 HIE, *First Report*, Inverness, 1992, 4-5.
34 HIE, *Fifth Report*, Inverness, 1996, iv.
35 University of the Highlands and Islands Project, *Prospectus 1999 Entry*, Inverness, 1998, 2.
36 J. Macaskill, *We Have Won the Land: The Story of the Assynt Crofters Trust*, Stornoway, 1999, 28-29.
37 Macaskill, *We Have Won the Land*, 2.
38 Land Reform Policy Group, *Identifying the Problems*, Edinburgh, 1998, 1.
39 Donald Dewar, speaking at the launch of the Land Reform Policy Group's final recommendations, Edinburgh, 5 January 1999.

Conclusion

1 S. MacLean, *Ris a' Bhruthaich: The Criticism and Prose Writings of Sorley MacLean*, Stornoway, 1985, 74.
2 J. Conway, 'Sun Shines for Knoydart Celebrations', *West Highland Free Press*, 2 April 1999.
3 E.W. Said, *Culture and Imperialism*, London, 1993, 408.
4 J. MacMillan, 'Portree Posts a Gael Force Warning', *The Scotsman*, 1 April 1999.
5 C. Dressler, *Eigg: The Story of an Island*, Edinburgh, 1998, 186.

Bibliography

Abbreviations: *NS*, *Northern Scotland; SHR, Scottish Historical Review; SS, Scottish Studies; TGSI, Transactions of the Gaelic Society of Inverness.*

Adam, R.J. (ed), *John Home's Survey of Assynt*, Edinburgh, 1960.

—, *Papers on Sutherland Estate Management*, 2 vols, Edinburgh, 1972.

Adams, Ian and Somerville, Meredyth, *Cargoes of Despair and Hope: Scottish Emigration to North America*, Edinburgh, 1993.

Adams, Ian H., *The Making of Urban Scotland*, London, 1978.

Aitken, Adam J., McDiarmid, Matthew P. and Thomson, Derick S. (eds), *Bards and Makars*, Glasgow, 1977.

Alcock, Leslie, *Arthur's Britain*, London, 1990.

—, *The Neighbours of the Picts: Angles, Britons and Scots at War and at Home*, Dornoch, 1993.

Alison, J.N. (ed), *Poetry of Northeast Scotland*, London, 1976.

Allan, John R., *North-East Lowlands of Scotland*, London, 1974.

Anderson, Alan O. (ed), *Early Sources of Scottish History*, 2 vols, Edinburgh, 1922.

Anderson, Marjorie O., *Kings and Kingship in Early Scotland*, Edinburgh, 1973.

Anderson, Peter D., *Robert Stewart: Earl of Orkney, Lord of Shetland*, Edinburgh, 1982.

Ansdell, Douglas, *The People of the Great Faith: The Highland Church, 1690-1900*, Stornoway, 1998.

Anson, Peter F., *Underground Catholicism in Scotland, 1622-1878*, Montrose, 1970.

Armit, Ian, *Beyond the Brochs: Changing Perspectives on the Later Iron Age in Atlantic Scotland*, Edinburgh, 1990.

—, *The Archaeology of Skye and the Western Isles*, Edinburgh, 1996.

—, *Celtic Scotland*, London, 1997.

Ash, Marinell, *This Noble Harbour: A History of the Cromarty Firth*, Invergordon, 1991.

Ashmore, Patrick J., *Calanais: The Standing Stones*, Stornoway, 1995.

—, *Neolithic and Bronze Age Scotland*, London, 1996.

—, *Maes Howe*, Edinburgh, 1997.

Baldwin, John R. (ed), *Scandinavian Shetland: An Ongoing Tradition*, Edinburgh, 1978.

— (ed), *Caithness: A Cultural Crossroads*, Edinburgh, 1982.

— (ed), *Firthlands of Ross and Sutherland*, Edinburgh, 1986.

— (ed), *Peoples and Settlement in North-West Ross*, Edinburgh, 1994.

Baldwin, Pamela L. and Baldwin, Malcolm F., *Onshore Planning for Offshore Oil: Lessons from Scotland*, Washington, 1975.

Ballantyne, John H. and Smith, Brian (eds), *Shetland Documents, 1580-1611*, Lerwick, 1994.

Bannerman, John, *Studies in the History of Dalriada*, Edinburgh, 1974.

—, *The Beatons: A Medical Kindred in the Classical Gaelic Tradition*, Edinburgh, 1986.

—, 'The King's Poet and the Inauguration of Alexander III', *SHR*, 68, 1989.
—, '*Comarba Coluim Cille* and the Relics of Columba', *Innes Review*, 44, 1993.
Barnes, Michael P., *The Norn Language of Orkney and Shetland*, Lerwick, 1998.
Barnes, Patricia M. and Barrow, G.W.S., 'The Movements of Robert Bruce between September 1307 and May 1308', *SHR*, 49, 1970.
Barron, Evan M., *Inverness in the Fifteenth Century*, Inverness, 1906.
—, *Inverness in the Middle Ages*, Inverness, 1907.
Barrow, G.W.S., *The Kingdom of the Scots*, London, 1973.
— (ed), *The Scottish Tradition*, Edinburgh, 1974.
—, *The Anglo-Norman Era in Scottish History*, Oxford, 1980.
—, *Kingship and Unity: Scotland, 1000-1306*, London, 1981.
—, *Robert Bruce and the Community of the Realm of Scotland*, Edinburgh, 1986.
—, 'Badenoch and Strathspey, 1130-1312: Secular and Political', *NS*, 8, 1988.
—, 'Badenoch and Strathspey, 1130-1312: The Church', *NS*, 9, 1989.
—, 'A Kingdom in Crisis: Scotland and the Maid of Norway', *SHR*, 69, 1990.
—, *Scotland and its Neighbours in the Middle Ages*, London, 1992.
Barrett, John C., Fitzpatrick, Andrew P. and Macinnes, Lesley (eds), *Barbarians and Romans in North-West Europe*, Oxford, 1989.
Batey, Colleen E., Jesch, Judith and Morris, Christopher D. (eds), *The Viking Age in Caithness, Orkney and the North Atlantic*, Edinburgh, 1993.
Beenhakker, Adrian J., *Hollanders in Shetland*, Lerwick, 1973.
Beith, Mary, *Healing Threads: Traditional Medicines of the Highlands and Islands*, Edinburgh, 1995.
Bennett, Margaret, *Scottish Customs from the Cradle to the Grave*, Edinburgh, 1992.
Berry, R.J. and Firth, Howie N. (eds), *The People of Orkney*, Kirkwall, 1986.
Bil, Albert, *The Shieling, 1600-1840: The Case of the Central Scottish Highlands*, Edinburgh, 1990.
Binchy, D.A., *Celtic and Anglo-Saxon Kingship*, Oxford, 1970.
Birks, Hilary H. (ed), *The Cultural Landscape: Past, Present and Future*, Cambridge, 1988.
Bitel, Lisa M., *Isle of Saints: Monastic Settlement and Christian Community in Early Ireland*, Cork, 1993.
Bjorn, Claus, Grant, Alexander and Stringer, Keith J. (eds), *Nations, Nationalism and Patriotism in the European Past*, Copenhagen, 1994.
Black, Jeremy, *Culloden and the Forty-Five*, London, 1990.
Black, Ronald, 'The Genius of Cathal MacMhuirich', *TGSI*, 50, 1977.
—, 'The Gaelic Academy: The Cultural Commitment of the Highland Society of Scotland', *Scottish Gaelic Studies*, 14, 1986.
—, *MacMhaighstir Alasdair: The Ardnamurchan Years*, Isle of Coll, 1986.
Blair, John and Sharpe, Richard (eds), *Pastoral Care Before the Parish*, Leicester, 1992.
Boardman, Stephen, *The Early Stewart Kings: Robert II and Robert III*, East Linton, 1996.
Bourke, Cormac (ed), *Studies in the Cult of St Columba*, Dublin, 1997.
Bossy, John and Jupp, Peter (eds), *Essays Presented to Michael Roberts*, Belfast, 1976.
Boswell, James, *The Journal of a Tour to the Hebrides*, London, 1984.
Boyd, J. Morton and Boyd, Ian L., *The Hebrides: A Natural History*, London, 1990.
Bradley, Ian, *The Celtic Way*, London, 1993.
—, *Columba: Pilgrim and Penitent*, Glasgow, 1996.
Bradley, Richard, *The Social Foundations of Prehistoric Britain*, London, 1984.
Bray, Elizabeth, *The Discovery of the Hebrides*, Edinburgh, 1996.
Broderick, George and Stowell, Brian (eds), *Chronicle of the Kings of Man and the Isles*, Edinburgh, 1973.
Broun, Dauvit, Finlay, R.J. and Lynch, Michael (eds), *Image and Identity: The*

Making and Remaking of Scotland through the Ages, Edinburgh, 1998.
Brown, Callum G., *Up-Helly-Aa: Custom, Culture and Community in Shetland*, Manchester, 1998.
Brown, George Mackay, *An Orkney Tapestry*, London, 1969.
Brown, Gordon (ed), *The Red Paper on Scotland*, Edinburgh, 1975.
Brown, Jennifer M. (ed), *Scottish Society in the Fifteenth Century*, London, 1977.
Brown, Keith M., *Bloodfeud in Scotland, 1573-1625*, Edinburgh, 1986.
—, *Kingdom or Province: Scotland and the Regal Union, 1603-1715*, London, 1992.
Brown, Michael, *James I*, Edinburgh, 1994.
Brown, Peter, *The Book of Kells*, London, 1980.
Breeze, David J., *The Northern Frontiers of Roman Britain*, London, 1982.
— (ed), *Studies in Scottish Antiquity*, Edinburgh, 1984.
—, *Roman Scotland*, London, 1996.
Bryant, G.J., 'The Scots in India in the Eighteenth Century', *SHR*, 64, 1985.
Bryden, John and Houston, George, *Agrarian Change in the Scottish Highlands*, London, 1976.
Bryson, Bill, *Notes from a Small Island*, London, 1996.
Buchanan, Joni, *The Lewis Land Struggle: Na Gaisgich*, Stornoway, 1996.
Budge, Ally, *Voices in the Wind: Caithness and the First World War*, Wick, 1996.
Bumsted, J.M., *The People's Clearance*, Edinburgh, 1982.
Burnett, Ray, *Benbecula*, Torlum, 1986.
Burt, Edmund, *Letters from the North of Scotland*, 2 vols, Edinburgh, 1974.
Button, John (ed), *The Shetland Way of Oil*, Sandwick, 1978.
Byrne, Francis J., *Irish Kings and High-Kings*, London, 1973.
Cahill, Thomas, *How the Irish Saved Civilization*, London, 1995.
Callander, Robin F., *A Pattern of Landownership in Scotland*, Finzean, 1987.
—, *How Scotland is Owned*, Edinburgh, 1998.
Cameron, A.D., *Go Listen to the Crofters*, Stornoway, 1986.
Cameron, Alexander (ed), *Reliquiae Celticae*, 2 vols, Inverness, 1892-94.
Cameron, David Kerr, *The Ballad and the Plough*, London, 1987.
Cameron, Ewen A., *Land for the People: The British Government and the Scottish Highlands, 1880-1925*, East Linton, 1996.
—, 'The Scottish Highlands as a Special Policy Area', *Rural History*, 8, 1997.
Campbell, John L. (ed), *Highland Songs of the Forty-Five*, Edinburgh, 1984.
—, *Canna: The Story of a Hebridean Island*, Edinburgh, 1994.
Campbell, Marion, *Argyll: The Enduring Heartland*, Bath, 1986.
Cannadine, David, *The Decline and Fall of the British Aristocracy*, London, 1990.
Cant, R.G., *Historic Elgin and its Cathedral*, Elgin, 1974.
Cargill, Kenneth (ed), *Scotland 2000: Eight Views on the State of the Nation*, Glasgow, 1987.
Carmichael, Alexander, *Carmina Gadelica*, 6 vols, Edinburgh, 1928-71.
Carney, Seamus, *The Killing of the Red Fox*, Moffat, 1989.
Carter, Ian, 'Economic Models and the Recent History of the Highlands', *SS*, 15, 1971.
—, *Farm Life in Northeast Scotland, 1840-1914: The Poor Man's Country*, Edinburgh, 1979.
Carty, Tony, and Smith, A. McCall (eds), *Power and Manoeuvrability*, Edinburgh, 1978.
Chadwick, Nora, *The Celts*, London, 1971.
Chapman, J.C. and Mytum, H.C. (eds), *Settlement in North Britain, 1000BC–AD1000*, Oxford, 1983.
Chapman, Malcolm, *The Gaelic Vision in Scottish Culture*, London, 1978.
Cheape, Hugh, 'A Song on the Lowland Shepherds: Popular Reaction to the Highland Clearances', *Scottish Economic and Social History*, 15, 1995.
Clancy, Thomas O. and Markus, Gilbert, *Iona: The Earliest Poetry of a Celtic*

Monastery, Edinburgh, 1995.
Clarke, David and Maguire, Patrick, *Skara Brae*, Edinburgh, 1995.
Cleary, A.S. Esmonde, *The Ending of Roman Britain*, London, 1989.
Cluness, A.T., *The Shetland Isles*, London, 1951.
— (ed), *The Shetland Book*, Lerwick, 1967.
Clyde, Robert, *From Rebel to Hero: The Image of the Highlander*, East Linton, 1995.
Coleman, Terry, *Passage to America*, London, 1972.
Colley, Linda, *Britons: Forging the Nation*, London, 1992.
Collier, Adam, *The Crofting Problem*, Cambridge, 1953.
Coull, James R., *The Sea Fisheries of Scotland: A Historical Geography*, Edinburgh, 1996.
Cowan, Edward J., 'Clanship, Kinship and the Campbell Acquisition of Islay', *SHR*, 58, 1979.
—, 'Myth and Identity in Early Medieval Scotland', *SHR*, 63, 1984.
—, *Montrose: For Covenant and King*, Edinburgh, 1995.
Cowan, Ian B., *The Medieval Church in Scotland*, Edinburgh, 1995.
Cowan, Ian B. and Easson, David E., *Medieval Religious Houses in Scotland*, London, 1976.
Cowan, Ian B. and Shaw, Duncan (eds), *The Renaissance and Reformation in Scotland*, Edinburgh, 1983.
Craig, Cairns (ed), *The History of Scottish Literature: Twentieth Century*, Aberdeen, 1987.
Craig, David, *On the Crofters' Trail: In Search of the Clearance Highlanders*, London, 1990.
Craig, Maggie, *Damn Rebel Bitches: The Women of the Forty-Five*, Edinburgh, 1997.
Crawford, Barbara E., 'The Pawning of Orkney and Shetland', *SHR*, 48, 1969.
—, 'The Earldom of Caithness and the Kingdom of Scotland', *NS*, 2, 1977.
— (ed), *Essays in Shetland History*, Lerwick, 1984.
—, *Scandinavian Scotland*, Leicester, 1987.
— (ed), *St Magnus Cathedral and Orkney's Twelfth-Century Renaissance*, Aberdeen, 1988.
—, 'North Sea Kingdoms, North Sea Bureaucrat', *SHR*, 69, 1990.
— (ed), *Scotland in Dark Age Europe*, St Andrews, 1994.
— (ed), *Northern Isles Connections: Essays from Orkney and Shetland*, Kirkwall, 1995.
—, *Earl and Mormaer: Norse-Pictish Relationships in Northern Scotland*, Rosemarkie, 1995.
— (ed), *Scandinavian Settlement in Northern Britain*, Leicester, 1995.
— (ed), *Scotland in Dark Age Britain*, Aberdeen, 1996.
Cregeen, Eric R. (ed), *Argyll Estate Instructions*, Edinburgh, 1964.
—, 'The Tacksmen and their Successors', *Scottish Studies*, 13, 1969.
Cregeen, Eric R. and MacKenzie, Donald W., *Tiree Bards and their Bardachd: The Poets in a Hebridean Community*, Isle of Coll, 1978.
Cullen, L.M. and Smout, T.C. (eds), *Comparative Aspects of Scottish and Irish Economic and Social History, 1600-1900*, Edinburgh, 1977.
Cummings, A.J.G. and Devine, T.M. (ed), *Industry, Business and Society in Scotland Since 1700*, Edinburgh, 1994.
Cummins, W.A., *The Age of the Picts*, Stroud, 1995.
Cunliffe, Barry, *Iron Age Communities in Britain*, London, 1974.
—, *The Celtic World*, London, 1992.
Daiches, David, *Charles Edward Stuart*, London, 1973.
D'Arcy, Julian, *Scottish Skalds and Sagamen: The Old Norse Influence on Modern Scottish Literature*, East Linton, 1996.
Darling, Frank Fraser, *West Highland Survey: An Essay in Human Ecology*, Oxford, 1955.

Dasent, George W. (ed), *Icelandic Sagas and Other Documents*, 4 vols, London, 1887-94.
Davidson, Hilda E., *The Lost Beliefs of Northern Europe*, London, 1993.
Davies, Norman, *Europe: A History*, Oxford, 1996.
Davies, R.R., *The British Isles, 1100-1500: Comparisons, Contrasts and Connections*, Edinburgh, 1988.
—, *Domination and Conquest: The Experience of Ireland, Scotland and Wales, 1100-1300*, Cambridge, 1990.
—, *The Revolt of Owain Glyn Dwr*, Oxford, 1995.
Dawson, Alastair G., *Ice Age Earth: Late Quaternary Geology and Climate*, London, 1992.
Day, John P., *Public Administration in the Highlands and Islands*, London, 1918.
Delaney, Frank, *The Celts*, London, 1986.
—, *Legends of the Celts*, London, 1991.
De Paor, Liam, *Saint Patrick's World: The Christian Culture of Ireland's Apostolic Age*, Dublin, 1993.
Derry, T.K., *A Short History of Norway*, London, 1968.
Devine, T.M., 'The Rise and Fall of Illicit Whisky-Making in Northern Scotland', *SHR*, 54, 1975.
—, 'Temporary Migration and the Scottish Highlands in the Nineteenth Century', *Economic History Review*, 32, 1979.
— (ed), *Lairds and Improvement in the Scotland of the Enlightenment*, Glasgow, 1980.
—, 'Highland Migration to Lowland Scotland, 1760-1860', *SHR*, 42, 1983.
—, *The Great Highland Famine*, Edinburgh, 1988.
—, *Clanship to Crofters' War: The Social Transformation of the Scottish Highlands*, Manchester, 1994.
— (ed), *Scottish Emigration and Scottish Society*, Edinburgh, 1992.
—, *Scottish Elites*, Edinburgh, 1994.
Devine, T.M. and Dickson, David (eds), *Ireland and Scotland, 1600-1850: Parallels and Contrasts in Economic and Social Development*, Edinburgh, 1983.
Devine, T.M. and Finlay, R.J. (eds), *Scotland in the Twentieth Century*, Edinburgh, 1996.
Devine, T.M. and Mitchison, Rosalind (eds), *People and Society in Scotland, 1760-1830*, Edinburgh, 1980.
Dewey, Clive, 'Celtic Agrarian Legislation and the Celtic Revival', *Past and Present*, 64, 1974.
Dickson, A. and Treble, J. (eds), *People and Society in Scotland, 1914-1990*, Edinburgh, 1992.
Dillon, Miles and Chadwick, Nora, *The Celtic Realms*, London, 1967.
Dodgshon, Robert A., *Land and Society in Early Scotland*, Oxford, 1981.
—, 'Farming Practice in the Western Highlands and Islands before Crofting', *Rural History*, 3, 1992.
—, 'Strategies of Farming in the Western Highlands and Islands of Scotland prior to Crofting and the Clearances', *Economic History Review*, 46, 1993.
—, 'West Highland and Hebridean Landscapes: Have they a History without Runrig?', *Journal of Historical Geography*, 19, 1993.
—, 'West Highland and Hebridean Settlement prior to Crofting and the Clearances', *Proceedings of the Society of Antiquaries of Scotland*, 123, 1993.
—, *From Chiefs to Landlords: Social and Economic Change in the Western Highlands and Islands, 1493-1820*, Edinburgh, 1998.
Donaldson, Gordon, *Shetland Life Under Earl Patrick*, Edinburgh, 1958.
— (ed), *Scottish Historical Documents*, Edinburgh, 1970.
—, *A Northern Commonwealth: Scotland and Norway*, Edinburgh, 1990.
Donaldson, John E., *Caithness in the Eighteenth Century*, Edinburgh, 1938.

Donaldson, William, *The Jacobite Song*, Aberdeen, 1988.
Donnachie, Ian and Whatley, Christopher (eds), *The Manufacture of Scottish History*, Edinburgh, 1992.
Dow, F.D., *Cromwellian Scotland*, Edinburgh, 1979.
Dowle, Martin, 'The Birth and Development of the Shetland Movement', *The Scottish Government Yearbook 1981*, Edinburgh, 1980.
Dressler, Camille, *Eigg: The Story of an Island*, Edinburgh, 1998.
Driscoll, Stephen T. and Nieke, Margaret R. (eds), *Power and Politics in Early Medieval Britain and Ireland*, Edinburgh, 1988.
Dunbar, John G. and Duncan, Archibald A.M., 'Tarbert Castle', *SHR*, 50, 1971.
Dunbar, John G. and Fisher, Ian, *Iona: A Guide to the Monuments*, Edinburgh, 1995.
Duncan, Archibald A.M. and Brown, A.L., 'Argyll and the Isles in the Earlier Middle Ages', *Proceedings of the Society of Antiquaries in Scotland*, 90, 1959.
Duncan, Archibald A.M., *The Nation of Scots and the Declaration of Arbroath*, London, 1970.
—, *Scotland: The Making of the Kingdom*, Edinburgh, 1975.
Dunlop, Jean, *The British Fisheries Society*, Edinburgh, 1978.
Durkacz, Victor E., *The Decline of the Celtic Languages*, Edinburgh, 1983.
Dwyer, John, Mason, Roger A. and Murdoch, Alexander (eds), *New Perspectives on the Politics and Culture of Early Modern Scotland*, Edinburgh, 1982.
Dyrvik, Stale, Mykland, Knut and Oldervoll, Jan (eds), *The Satellite State in the Seventeenth and Eighteenth Centuries*, Bergen, 1979.
Eluere, Christiane, *The Celts: First Masters of Europe*, London, 1993.
Etchingham, Colman, *Viking Raids on Irish Church Settlements*, Maynooth, 1996.
Ewan, Elizabeth, *Townlife in Fourteenth Century Scotland*, Edinburgh, 1990.
Farrell, R.T. (ed), *The Vikings*, London, 1982.
Fawcett, Richard, *Scottish Abbeys and Priories*, Edinburgh, 1994.
Fenton, Alexander, *The Northern Isles: Orkney and Shetland*, Edinburgh, 1978.
Fenton, Alexander and Palsson, Hermann (eds), *The Northern and Western Isles in the Viking World: Survival, Continuity and Change*, Edinburgh, 1984.
Ferguson, William, *The Identity of the Scottish Nation: An Historical Quest*, Edinburgh, 1998.
Fergusson, James, *Argyll in the Forty-Five*, London, 1951.
Finlay, Ian, *Columba*, 1979.
Flinn, Michael (ed), *Scottish Population History*, Cambridge, 1977.
Foden, Frank, *Wick of the North: The Story of a Scottish Royal Burgh*, Wick, 1996.
Fojut, Noel, *A Guide to Prehistoric and Viking Shetland*, Lerwick, 1993.
Foster, Sally M., *Picts, Gaels and Scots*, London, 1996.
Frame, Robin, *The Political Development of the British Isles, 1100-1400*, Oxford, 1995.
Fraser, Ian A., 'Gaelic and Norse Elements in Coastal Place Names in the Western Isles', *TGSI*, 50, 1978.
—, 'The Placenames of Argyll: An Historical Perspective', *TGSI*, 54, 1985.
Fraser, W. Hamish and Morris, R.J. (eds), *People and Society in Scotland: Two, 1830-1914*, Edinburgh, 1990.
Friell, J.G.P. and Watson, W.G. (eds), *Pictish Studies*, Oxford, 1984.
Fry, Michael, *The Dundas Despotism*, Edinburgh, 1992.
Galliou, Patrick and Jones, Michael, *The Bretons*, Oxford, 1991.
Gaskell, Philip, *Morvern Transformed*, Cambridge, 1996.
Giblin, Cathaldus, *The Irish Franciscan Mission to Scotland, 1619-46*, Dublin, 1964.
Gibson, John S., *Lochiel of the Forty-Five: The Jacobite Chief and the Prince*, Edinburgh, 1994.
Gifford, Douglas (ed), *The History of Scottish Literature: Nineteenth Century*, Aberdeen, 1988.

Gillies, William (ed), *Gaelic and Scotland*, Edinburgh, 1989.
Glashan, William, *Old Buildings of Inverness*, Inverness, 1978.
Glass, Norman M., *Caithness and the War, 1939-45*, Wick, 1994.
Gledhill, J., Bender, B. and Larsen, M.T. (eds), *State and Society: The Emergence and Development of Social Hierarchy and Political Centralization*, London, 1988.
Goodlad, C.A., *Shetland Fishing Saga*, Lerwick, 1971.
Goodlad, John, *Shaping the Future: A Shetland Perspective*, Stornoway, 1993.
Gordon, George and Dicks, Brian (eds), *Scottish Urban History*, Aberdeen, 1983.
Graham, Laurence (ed), *Shetland Crofters: A Hundred Years of Island Crofting*, Lerwick, 1987.
Graham-Campbell, James, *The Viking World*, London, 1980.
Grainger, John D., *Cromwell Against the Scots*, East Linton, 1997.
Grant, Alexander, 'The Revolt of the Lord of the Isles and the Death of the Earl of Douglas, 1451-1452', *Scottish Historical Review, 60, 1981.*
—, *Independence and Nationhood: Scotland, 1306-1469*, London, 1984.
Grant, Alexander and Stringer, Keith J. (eds), *Medieval Scotland: Crown, Lordship and Community*, Edinburgh, 1993.
Grant, I.F., *Highland Folk Ways*, London, 1961.
—, *Along a Highland Road*, London, 1980.
—, *The MacLeods: The History of a Clan*, Edinburgh, 1981.
—, *Everyday Life on an Old Highland Farm*, London, 1981.
—, *The Lordship of the Isles*, Edinburgh, 1982.
Grant, I.F. and Cheape, Hugh, *Periods in Highland History*, London, 1987.
Grant, James S. (ed), *Diary 1851: John Munro MacKenzie, Chamberlain of the Lews*, Stornoway, 1994.
Grassie, James, *Highland Experiment: The Story of the Highlands and Islands Development Board*, Aberdeen, 1983.
Gray, Malcolm, *The Highland Economy, 1750-1850*, London, 1957.
—, *The Fishing Industries of Scotland, 1790-1914*, Aberdeen, 1978.
—, *Scots on the Move: Scots Migrants, 1750-1914*, Edinburgh, 1990.
Greene, David and O'Connor, Frank, *A Golden Treasury of Irish Poetry*, Dingle, 1990.
Grigor, Iain F., *Mightier than a Lord*, Stornoway, 1979.
Grimble, Ian, *The Trial of Patrick Sellar*, London, 1962.
—, *Chief of Mackay*, London, 1965.
—, *The World of Rob Donn*, Edinburgh, 1979.
Gronneberg, Roy, *Island Governments*, Sandwick, 1976.
— (ed), *Island Futures*, Sandwick, 1978.
Guilbert, Graeme (ed), *Hill Fort Studies*, Leicester, 1981.
Gunn, Neil M., *Butcher's Broom*, London, 1977.
Haldane, A.R.B., *The Drove Roads of Scotland*, Edinburgh, 1971.
—, *New Ways Through the Glens*, Isle of Colonsay, 1995.
Hanson, William S., *Agricola and the Conquest of the North*, London, 1987.
Hanson, William S. and Maxwell, Gordon S., *Rome's North West Frontier: The Antonine Wall*, Edinburgh, 1983.
Hanson, William S. and Slater, E.A. (eds), *Scottish Archaeology: New Perspectives*, Aberdeen, 1991.
Harper, Marjory, 'Crofter Colonists in Canada', *NS*, 14, 1994.
Hart-Davis, Duff, *Monarchs of the Glen: A History of Deerstalking in the Scottish Highlands*, London, 1978.
Harvie, Christopher, *Fool's Gold: The Story of North Sea Oil*, London, 1994.
—, *The Rise of Regional Europe*, London, 1994.
Hayes-McCoy, Gerard A., *Scots Mercenary Forces in Ireland, 1565-1603*, Dublin, 1937.
Hechter, Michael, *Internal Colonialism: The Celtic Fringe in British National*

Development, London, 1975.
Hedeager, Lotte, *Iron Age Societies: From Tribe to State in Northern Europe*, Oxford, 1992.
Henderson, Diana M., *Highland Soldier: A Social Study of the Highland Regiments*, Edinburgh, 1989.
Henderson, George, *From Durrow to Kells: The Insular Gospel Books*, London, 1987.
Henderson, Isabel, *The Picts*, London, 1967.
Hedges, John W., *Tomb of the Eagles: A Window on Stone Age Tribal Britain*, London, 1984.
Herbert, Maire, *Iona, Kells and Derry: The History and Hagiography of the Monastic Familia of Columba*, Oxford, 1988.
Hetherington, Alastair (ed), *Highlands and Islands: A Generation of Progress*, Aberdeen, 1990.
Hewison, W.S., *Scapa Flow in War and Peace*, Kirkwall, 1995.
— (ed), *The Diary of Patrick Fea of Stove, Orkney*, East Linton, 1997.
Highlands and Islands Development Board, *Annual Reports*, Inverness, 1966-91.
Highlands and Islands Enterprise, *Annual Reports*, Inverness, 1992-98.
Hill, Michael J., *Celtic Warfare, 1595-1763*, Edinburgh, 1986.
—, *Fire and Sword: Sorley Boy MacDonnell and the Rise of Clan Iain Mor*, London, 1993.
Hingley, Richard (ed), *Medieval or Later Rural Settlement in Scotland*, Edinburgh, 1993.
Hodder, Ian, *The Domestication of Europe: Structure and Contingency in Neolithic Societies*, Oxford, 1990.
Hollander, Lee M., *The Skalds: A Selection of Their Poems*, New York, 1945.
Holliday, Fred, *Wildlife of Scotland*, London, 1979.
Hook, Andrew (ed), *The History of Scottish Literature: Volume 2, 1660-1800*, Aberdeen, 1989.
Hopkins, Paul, *Glencoe and the End of the Highland War*, Edinburgh, 1986.
Hossack, B.H., *Kirkwall in the Orkneys*, Kirkwall, 1900.
Houston, Anne L., *Lest We Forget: The Parish of Canisbay*, Wick, 1996.
Houston, Robert A., *The Population History of Britain and Ireland, 1550-1750*, Cambridge, 1992.
Houston, Robert A. and Whyte, Ian D. (eds), *Scottish Society, 1500-1800*, Cambridge, 1989.
Howarth, David, *The Shetland Bus*, London, 1951.
Hudson, Benjamin T., *Kings of Celtic Scotland*, Westport, 1994.
Hudson, Benjamin T. and Ziegler, Vickie (eds), *Crossed Paths: Methodological Approaches to the Celtic Aspect of the European Middle Ages*, New York, 1991.
Hughes, Kathleen, *Celtic Britain in the Early Middle Ages*, Woodbridge, 1980.
Hughes, Mike, *The Hebrides at War*, Edinburgh, 1998.
Hulbert, John (ed), *Gaelic: Looking to the Future*, Dundee, 1985.
— (ed), *Land: Ownership and Use*, Dundee, 1986.
Hunter, Charles K., *Oban, Kilmore and Kilbride*, Oban, 1984.
Hunter, James, 'Sheep and Deer: Highland Sheep Farming, 1850-1900', *NS*, I, 1974.
— , 'The Emergence of the Crofting Community: The Religious Contribution', *SS*, 18, 1974.
—, 'The Politics of Highland Land Reform, 1873-1895', *SHR*, 53, 1974.
—, 'The Gaelic Connection: The Highlands, Ireland and Nationalism, 1873-1922', *SHR*, 54, 1975.
—, *The Making of the Crofting Community*, Edinburgh, 1976.
—, *For the People's Cause: From the Writings of John Murdoch*, Edinburgh, 1986.
—, *Skye: The Island*, Edinburgh, 1986.
—, *Crofting Works, But It Should Work Better*, Isle of Skye, 1990.

—, *The Claim of Crofting: The Scottish Highlands and Islands, 1930-1990*, Edinburgh, 1991.
—, *The Highland Fund*, Glasgow, 1991.
—, *Scottish Highlanders: A People and their Place*, Edinburgh, 1992.
—, *A Dance Called America: The Scottish Highlands, the United States and Canada*, Edinburgh, 1994.
—, *Towards a Land Reform Agenda for a Scots Parliament: The John McEwen Memorial Lecture*, Perth, 1994.
—, *On the Other Side of Sorrow: Nature and People in the Scottish Highlands*, Edinburgh, 1995.
—, *Glencoe and the Indians*, Edinburgh, 1996.
—, *Scottish Highlanders, Indian Peoples*, Helena, 1998.
Hutton, Ronald, *The Pagan Religions of the British Isles*, Oxford, 1991.
Irvine, James W., *Lerwick: The Birth and Growth of an Island Town*, Lerwick, 1985.
Jack, R.D.S. (ed), *The History of Scottish Literature: Origins to 1660*, Aberdeen, 1988.
Jackson, Anthony, *The Symbol Stones of Scotland*, Stromness, 1984.
—, *The Pictish Trail: A Traveller's Guide to the Old Pictish Kingdoms*, Stromness, 1989.
Jackson, Kenneth H., *A Celtic Miscellany*, London, 1971.
—, *The Gaelic Notes in the Book of Deer*, Cambridge, 1972.
Johnson, Samuel, *A Journey to the Western Islands of Scotland*, London, 1984.
Jones, Gwyn, *A History of the Vikings*, Oxford, 1984.
Jupp, Clifford N., *The History of Islay*, Port Charlotte, 1994.
Kadt, Emanuel de and Williams, Gavin (eds), *Sociology and Development*, London, 1974.
Kay, Billy and Maclean, Cailean, *Knee Deep in Claret: A Celebration of Wine and Scotland*, Edinburgh, 1983.
Kelly, Fergus, *A Guide to Early Irish Law*, Dublin, 1988.
Kennedy, Duncan, *The Ballachulish Line: The Birth and Death of a Highland Railway*, Isle of Colonsay, 1996.
Keppie, Lawrence, *Scotland's Roman Remains*, Edinburgh, 1986.
Kermack, W.R., *The Scottish Highlands: A Short History*, Edinburgh, 1957.
Kinsella, Thomas, *The Tain*, Oxford, 1970.
Kinvig, R.H., *The Isle of Man: A Social, Cultural and Political History*, Liverpool, 1975.
Kirk, James, 'The Kirk and the Highlands at the Reformation', *NS*, 7, 1986.
Knox, Susan A., *The Making of the Shetland Landscape*, Edinburgh, 1985.
Ladurie, Emmanuel Le Roy, *Times of Feast, Times of Famine: A History of Climate Since the Year 1000*, London, 1972.
Laing, Lloyd, *Celtic Britain*, London, 1979.
Laing, Lloyd and Laing, Jenny, *The Picts and the Scots*, Stroud, 1993.
Lamb, Hubert H., *Climate, History and the Modern World*, London, 1982.
Lamont, W.D., 'Alexander of Islay, Son of Angus Mor', *SHR*, 60, 1981.
Land Reform Policy Group, *Identifying the Problems*, Edinburgh, 1998.
—, *Recommendations for Action*, Edinburgh, 1999.
Laughlan, W.F. (ed), *James Hogg's Highland Tours*, Hawick, 1981.
Lee, Maurice, *Government by Pen: Scotland under James VI and I*, Urbana, 1980.
Leneman, Leah, *Living in Atholl, 1685-1785: A Social History of the Estates*, Edinburgh, 1986.
— (ed), *Perspectives in Scottish Social History*, Aberdeen, 1988.
—, *Fit for Heroes: Land Settlement in Scotland after World War I*, Aberdeen, 1989.
Lenman, Bruce, *The Jacobite Risings in Britain, 1689-1746*, London, 1980.
—, *The Jacobite Clans of the Great Glen, 1650-1784*, London, 1984.
—, *The Jacobite Cause*, Glasgow, 1986.
Libaek, Ivar and Stenersen, Oivind, *History of Norway*, Oslo, 1991.

Lindsay, Ian G. and Cosh, Mary, *Inveraray and the Dukes of Argyll*, Edinburgh, 1973.
Lindsay, J.M., 'The Iron Industry in the Highlands', *SHR*, 56, 1977.
Linklater, Eric, *Orkney and Shetland*, London, 1990.
Linklater, Magnus and Denniston, Robin (eds), *Anatomy of Scotland*, Edinburgh, 1992.
Logan, F. Donald, *The Vikings in History*, London, 1991.
Logue, Kenneth J., *Popular Disturbances in Scotland, 1780-1815*, Edinburgh, 1979.
Low, Mary, *Celtic Christianity and Nature: Early Irish and Hebridean Traditions*, Edinburgh, 1996.
Lustig, Richard I., 'The Treaty of Perth: A Re-examination', *SHR*, 65, 1979.
Lynch, Michael, *Scotland: A New History*, London, 1991.
— (ed), *Jacobitism and the Forty-Five*, London, 1995.
Lynch, Michael, Spearman, Michael and Stell, Geoffrey (eds), *The Scottish Medieval Town*, Edinburgh, 1988.
MacArthur, E. Mairi, *Iona: The Living Memory of a Crofting Community*, Edinburgh, 1990.
—, *Columba's Island: Iona from Past to Present*, Edinburgh, 1995.
Macaskill, John, *We Have Won the Land: The Story of the Assynt Crofters' Trust*, Stornoway, 1999.
MacAulay, John, *Birlinn: Longships of the Hebrides*, Isle of Harris, 1996.
McClure, Judith and Collins, Roger (eds), *Bede: The Ecclesiastical History of the English People*, Oxford, 1994.
McConnell, David, *Rails to Kyle of Lochalsh*, Oxford, 1997.
McCrone, David, *Understanding Scotland: The Sociology of a Stateless Nation*, London, 1992.
McCrorie, Ian, *Steamers of the Highlands and Islands: An Illustrated History*, Greenock, 1987.
MacDonald, Donald, *Lewis: A History of the Island*, Edinburgh, 1978.
MacDonald, Fiona A., 'Irish Priests in the Highlands', *Innes Review*, 46, 1995.
Macdonald, Iain S., 'Alexander MacDonald of Glencoe: Insights into Early Highland Sheep Farming', *Review of Scottish Culture*, 10, 1996–97.
McDonald, Isobel, *A Family in Skye*, Stornoway, 1980.
McDonald, R. Andrew, *The Kingdom of the Isles: Scotland's Western Seaboard, 1100-1336*, East Linton, 1997.
MacDonald, Stuart, 'Crofter Colonisation in Canada', *NS*, 7, 1986.
MacDonell, Margaret, *The Emigrant Experience: Songs of Highland Emigrants in North America*, Toronto, 1982.
MacDougall, Norman, *James III: A Political Study*, Edinburgh, 1982.
—, *James IV*, Edinburgh, 1989.
McEwen, John, *Who Owns Scotland?*, Edinburgh, 1977.
Macfarlane, Leslie J., *William Elphinstone and the Kingdom of Scotland*, Aberdeen, 1985.
McGladdery, Christine, *James II*, Edinburgh, 1990.
McGrath, John, *The Cheviot, the Stag and the Black, Black Oil*, Isle of Skye, 1975.
MacGregor, Edith, *The Story of Fort William*, Inverness, 1954.
Macinnes, Alan I., 'Repression and Conciliation: The Highland Dimension, 1660-1688', *SHR*, 65, 1986.
—, 'Social Mobility in Late Medieval and Early Modern Gaeldom, *TGSI*, 48, 1994.
—, *Clanship, Commerce and the House of Stuart, 1603-1788*, East Linton, 1996.
MacInnes, John, 'The Oral Tradition in Scottish Gaelic Poetry', *SS*, 12, 1968.
—, 'Clan Unity and Individual Freedom', *TGSI*, 47, 1972.
—, 'West Highland Sea Power in the Middle Ages', *TGSI*, 48, 1974.
—, 'The Panegyric Code in Gaelic Poetry and its Historical Background', *TGSI*, 50, 1978.

MacKay, D.I. And Mackay, G.A., *The Political Economy of North Sea Oil*, London, 1975.
MacKay, M.I., *Sar Ghaidheal: Essays in Memory of Rory MacKay*, Inverness, n.d.
MacKay, Margaret M. (ed), *The Rev Dr John Walker's Report on the Hebrides*, Edinburgh, 1980.
MacKay, William (ed), *Chronicles of the Frasers: The Wardlaw Manuscript*, Edinburgh, 1905.
MacKay, William and Boyd, Herbert C. (eds), *Records of Inverness*, 2 vols, Aberdeen, 1911-24.
MacKenzie, Alexander, *History of the Highland Clearances*, Inverness, 1986.
MacKenzie, Annie M. (ed), *Orain Iain Luim: Songs of John MacDonald*, Edinburgh, 1964.
MacKenzie, N.C. *History of the Outer Hebrides*, Edinburgh, 1974.
MacKenzie, W.C., *The Highlands and Isles of Scotland: A Historical Survey*, Edinburgh, 1949.
McKerral, Andrew, *Kintyre in the Seventeenth Century*, Edinburgh, 1948.
Mackey, James P. (ed), *An Introduction to Celtic Christianity*, Edinburgh, 1989.
MacKinnon, Kenneth, *The Lion's Tongue*, Inverness, 1974.
—, *Gaelic: A Past and Future Prospect*, Edinburgh, 1991.
Mackintosh, H.B. and Richardson, J.S., *Elgin Cathedral*, Edinburgh, 1980.
Maclean, Alasdair, *A MacDonald for the Prince*, Stornoway, 1982.
Maclean, Calum I., *The Highlands*, Inverness, 1975.
Maclean, Allan (ed), *Elgin Cathedral and the Diocese of Moray*, Inverness, 1974.
Maclean, Lorraine (ed), *The Hub of the Highlands: The Book of Inverness and District*, Edinburgh, 1975.
— (ed), *The Middle Ages in the Highlands*, Inverness, 1981.
— (ed), *The Seventeenth Century in the Highlands*, Inverness, 1986.
— (ed), *An Inverness Miscellany*, Inverness, 1987.
MacLean, Malcolm and Carrell, Christopher (eds), *As an Fhearann: From the Land*, Edinburgh, 1986.
McLean, Marianne, *The People of Glengarry: Highlanders in Transition*, Montreal, 1991.
MacLean, Sorley, *From Wood To Ridge: Collected Poems*, Manchester, 1989.
—, *Ris a' Bhruthaich: The Criticism and Prose Writings of Sorley MacLean*, Stornoway, 1985.
Maclean-Bristol, Nicholas, *Warriors and Priests: The History of the Clan MacLean*, East Linton, 1995.
McLellan, Robert, *The Isle of Arran*, Newton Abbot, 1985.
MacLeod, Angus (ed), *The Songs of Duncan Ban MacIntyre*, Edinburgh, 1952.
MacLeod, John, *Highlanders: A History of the Gaels*, London, 1996.
McLynn, Frank J., *The Jacobite Army in England*, Edinburgh, 1983.
—, *The Jacobites*, London, 1985.
—, *Charles Edward Stuart*, London, 1988.
MacNeill, Eoin, *Celtic Ireland*, Dublin, 1921.
MacPhail, I.M.M., *The Crofters' War*, Stornoway, 1989.
MacPhail, J.R.N. (ed), *Highland Papers*, 4 vols, Edinburgh, 1914-34.
Macquarrie, Alan, *The Saints of Scotland: Essays in Scottish Church History*, Edinburgh, 1997.
Macquarrie, Alan and MacArthur, E. Mairi, *Iona through the Ages*, Isle of Coll, 1992.
MacRae, Norman, *The Romance of a Royal Burgh: Dingwall's Story of a Thousand Years*, Dingwall, 1923.
Magnusson, Magnus, *Viking Expansion Westwards*, London, 1973.
—, *Vikings*, London, 1980.
—, *Iceland Saga*, London, 1987.
Magnusson, Magnus and Palsson, Hermann (eds), *Njal's Saga*, London, 1960.

Magnusson, Magnus and Palsson, Hermann (eds), *The Vinland Sagas*, London, 1965.
Magnusson, Magnus and Palsson, Hermann (eds), *Laxdaela Saga*, London, 1969.
Magnusson, Magnus and White, Graham (eds), *The Nature of Scotland: Landscape, Wildlife and People*, Edinburgh, 1991.
Magnusson, Sigurdur A., *Northern Sphinx: Iceland and the Icelanders from the Settlement to the Present*, London, 1977.
Marsden, John, *The Illustrated Colum Cille*, London, 1991.
—, *Sea Road of the Saints: Celtic Holy Men in the Hebrides*, Edinburgh, 1995.
—, *The Fury of the Northmen: Saints, Shrines and Sea-Raiders in the Viking Age*, London, 1996.
—, *Alba of the Ravens: In Search of the Celtic Kingdom of the Scots*, London, 1997.
Marshall, Elizabeth (ed), *Shetland's Oil Era*, Lerwick, 1978.
Martin, Angus, *Kintyre: The Hidden Past*, Edinburgh, 1984.
—, *Kintyre Country Life*, Edinburgh, 1987.
Martin, Martin, *A Description of the Western Islands of Scotland*, Edinburgh, 1994.
Marwick, Hugh, *The Orkney Norn*, Oxford, 1929.
Mason, Roger and MacDougall, Norman (eds), *People and Power in Scotland*, Edinburgh, 1992.
Mather, Alexander S., *State-Aided Land Settlement in Scotland*, Aberdeen, 1978.
—, 'Government Agencies and Land Development in the Scottish Highlands', *NS*, 8, 1988.
Matheson, William (ed), *The Songs of John MacCodrum*, Edinburgh, 1938.
— (ed), *The Blind Harper: The Songs of Roderick Morrison and his Music*, Edinburgh, 1970.
—, 'The Morrisons of Ness', *TGSI*, 50, 1977.
—, 'The Ancestry of the MacLeods', *TGSI*, 51, 1977.
—, 'The MacLeods of Lewis', *TGSI*, 51, 1979.
Mattingly, Harold (ed), *Tacitus: The Agricola and the Germania*, London, 1970.
Maxwell, Gordon S., *The Romans in Scotland*, Edinburgh, 1989.
—, *A Battle Lost: Romans and Caledonians at Mons Graupius*, Edinburgh, 1990.
Meek, Donald E., 'The Role of Song in the Highland Land Agitation', *Scottish Gaelic Studies*, 16, 1990.
—, 'The Catholic Knight of Crofting: Sir Donald Horne MacFarlane MP', *TGSI*, 58, 1994.
— (ed), *Tuath is Tighearna: Tenants and Landlords*, Edinburgh, 1995.
Meikle, Henry W., *Scotland and the French Revolution*, Glasgow, 1912.
Meldrum, Edward (ed), *The Dark Ages in the Highlands*, Inverness, 1972.
Mellor, Ronald, *Tacitus*, London, 1993.
Menzies, Gordon (ed), *Who Are the Scots?*, London, 1971.
— (ed), *History is my Witness*, London, 1976.
Miket, Roger and Roberts, David L., *The Medieval Castles of Skye and Lochalsh*, Isle of Skye, 1990.
Mileham, Patrick, *The Scottish Regiments*, Staplehurst, 1996.
Milne, Alan P., *Arran: An Island's Story*, Kilbrannan, 1982.
Mitchell, Arthur (ed), *MacFarlane's Geographical Collections*, 3 vols, Edinburgh, 1906.
Mitchison, Rosalind, *Agricultural Sir John: The Life of Sir John Sinclair*, London, 1962.
— (ed), *The Roots of Nationalism: Studies in Northern Europe*, Edinburgh, 1980.
Mitchison, Rosalind and Roebuck, Peter (eds), *Economy and Society in Scotland and Ireland, 1500-1939*, Edinburgh, 1988.
Monsen, Erling and Smith, A.H. (eds), *Snorre Sturlason: Heimskringla*, New York, 1990.
Morris, John, *The Age of Arthur: A History of the British Isles from 350 to 650*, London, 1973.

Morrison, Ian, *The North Sea Earls*, London, 1973.
Moss, Michael S. and Hume, John R., *The Making of Scotch Whisky*, Edinburgh, 1981.
Mowat, Ian R.M., *Easter Ross, 1750-1850: The Double Frontier*, Edinburgh, 1981.
Munro, Jean and Munro, R.W. (eds), *Acts of the Lords of the Isles*, Edinburgh, 1986.
Munro, R.W. (ed), *Munro's Western Isles of Scotland*, Edinburgh, 1961.
—, *Taming the Rough Bounds*, Isle of Coll, 1984.
Murray, W.H., *Rob Roy MacGregor: His Life and Times*, Edinburgh, 1993.
Newman, Peter C., *Company of Adventurers: The Story of the Hudson's Bay Company*, London, 1987.
Newton, Norman, *The Life and Times of Inverness*, Edinburgh, 1996.
Nicholson, Ranald, *Scotland: The Later Middle Ages*, Edinburgh, 1974.
Nicoll, Eric H. (ed), *A Pictish Panorama: The Story of the Picts*, Balgavies, 1995.
Nicolson, Alexander, *History of Skye*, Isle of Skye, 1994.
Nicolson, James R., *Shetland and Oil*, London, 1975.
O'Baoill, Colm (ed), *Eachan Bacach and Other MacLean Poets*, Edinburgh, 1979.
O'Croinin, Daibhi, *Early Medieval Ireland*, Harlow, 1995.
O'Cuiv, Brian (ed), *The Impact of the Scandinavian Invasions on the Celtic-Speaking Peoples*, Dublin, 1975.
O'Dell, A.C. and Walton, K., *The Highlands and Islands of Scotland*, London, 1962.
Omand, Donald (ed), *The Caithness Book*, Inverness, 1972.
— (ed), *The Moray Book*, Edinburgh, 1976.
— (ed), *The Sutherland Book*, Golspie, 1982.
— (ed), *The Ross and Cromarty Book*, Golspie, 1984.
— (ed), *The New Caithness Book*, Wick, 1989.
Oram, Richard, *Scottish Prehistory*, Edinburgh, 1997.
Orr, Willie, *Deer Forests, Landlords and Crofters: The Western Highlands in Victorian and Edwardian Times*, Edinburgh, 1982.
—, *Discovering Argyll, Mull and Iona*, Edinburgh, 1990.
Palsson, Hermann and Edwards, Paul (eds), *The Book of Settlements*, Winnipeg, 1972.
Palsson, Hermann and Edwards, Paul (eds), *Orkneyinga Saga: The History of the Earls of Orkney*, London, 1978.
Parry, M.L. and Slater, T.R. (eds), *The Making of the Scottish Countryside*, London, 1980.
Paterson, Lindsay, *The Autonomy of Modern Scotland*, Edinburgh, 1994.
Payne, Peter L., *The Hydro*, Aberdeen, 1988.
Pennant, Thomas, *A Tour of Scotland in 1769*, Edinburgh, 1979.
Perceval-Maxwell, M., *The Scottish Migration to Ulster in the Reign of James I*, London, 1973.
Phillipson, Nicholas T. and Mitchison, Rosalind (eds), *Scotland in the Age of Improvement*, Edinburgh, 1970.
Pittock, Murray G.H., *The Invention of Scotland*, London, 1991.
—, *Poetry and Jacobite Politics in Eighteenth-Century Britain and Ireland*, Cambridge, 1994.
—, *The Myth of the Jacobite Clans*, Edinburgh, 1995.
Pitts, Lynn F. and St Joseph, J.K., *Inchtuthil: The Roman Legionary Fortress*, Gloucester, 1985.
Pollard, Tony and Morrison, Alex (eds), *The Early Prehistory of Scotland*, Edinburgh, 1996.
Pollitt, A. Gerard, *Historic Inverness*, Perth, 1981.
Power, Rosemary, 'Magnus Barlegs' Expeditions to the West', *SHR*, 65, 1986.
Purser, John, *Scotland's Music*, Edinburgh, 1992.
Prebble, John, *Culloden*, London, 1967.
—, *Glencoe: The Story of the Massacre*, London, 1968.

—, *The Highland Clearances*, London, 1969.
—, *Mutiny: Highland Regiments in Revolt*, London, 1977.
Prentis, Malcolm D., *The Scots in Australia*, Sydney, 1983.
Price, Robert, *Highland Landforms*, Aberdeen, 1991.
Pryde, George S., *The Burghs of Scotland*, Oxford, 1965.
Randall, Robert A. (ed), *Species History in Scotland*, Edinburgh, 1998.
Rankin, H.D., *Celts and the Classical World*, Beckenham, 1987.
Reid, Norman H. (ed), *Scotland in the Reign of Alexander III*, Edinburgh, 1990.
Renfrew, Colin (ed), *The Prehistory of Orkney*, Edinburgh, 1985.
—, *Archaeology and Language: The Puzzle of Indo-European Origins*, London, 1987.
Report of Commissioners of Inquiry into the Condition of the Crofters and Cottars in the Highlands and Islands of Scotland, 5 vols, Edinburgh, 1884.
Report of the Commission of Enquiry into Crofting Conditions, Edinburgh, 1954.
Richards, Eric, *The Leviathan of Wealth: The Sutherland Fortune in the Industrial Revolution*, London, 1973.
—, 'Highland Emigrants to South Australia in the 1850s', *NS*, 5, 1982.
—, *A History of the Highland Clearances*, 2 vols, London, 1982-85.
Richards, Eric and Clough, Monica, *Cromartie: Highland Life, 1650-1914*, Aberdeen, 1989.
Richmond, Ian A. (ed), *Roman and Native in North Britain*, London, 1958.
Ritchie, Anna, *Picts*, Edinburgh, 1989.
—, *Viking Scotland*, London, 1993.
—, *Prehistoric Orkney*, London, 1995.
—, *Iona*, London, 1997.
Ritchie, J.N. Graham, *Brochs of Scotland*, Aylesbury, 1988.
— (ed), *The Archaeology of Argyll*, Edinburgh, 1997.
Ritchie, J.N. Graham, and Ritchie, Anna, *Scotland: Archaeology and Early History*, Edinburgh, 1991.
Rixon, Denis, *The West Highland Galley*, Edinburgh, 1998.
Roberts, John L., *Lost Kingdoms: Celtic Scotland and the Middle Ages*, Edinburgh, 1997.
Roberts, Neil, *The Holocene: An Environmental History*, Oxford, 1989.
Robertson, Alan G.R., *The Lowland Highlanders: The Story of Tain and District*, Inverness, 1970.
Robertson, Iain, 'Governing the Highlands: The Place of Popular Protest in the Highlands of Scotland after 1918', *Rural History*, 8, 1997.
Robertson, John D.M. (ed), *An Orkney Anthology: Selected Works of Ernest Walker Marwick*, Edinburgh, 1991.
Robertson, T.A., *The Collected Poems of Vagaland*, Lerwick, 1980.
Roesdahl, Else, *The Vikings*, London, 1987.
Rosie, George, *Cromarty: The Scramble for Oil*, Edinburgh, 1974.
—, *The Ludwig Initiative: A Cautionary Tale of North Sea Oil*, Edinburgh, 1978.
Ross, Anne, *The Pagan Celts*, London, 1986.
Ross, Neil (ed), *Heroic Poetry from the Book of the Dean of Lismore*, Edinburgh, 1939.
Ross, Raymond J. and Hendry, Joy (eds), *Sorley MacLean: Critical Essays*, Edinburgh, 1986.
Rubinstein, W.D., 'New Men of Wealth and the Purchase of Land in Nineteenth-Century Britain', *Past and Present*, 92, 1981.
Said, Edward W., *Culture and Imperialism*, London, 1993.
Salway, Peter, *Roman Britain*, Oxford, 1981.
Sanderson, Margaret H.B., *Scottish Rural Society in the Sixteenth Century*, Edinburgh, 1982.
Saville, Richard (ed), *The Economic Development of Modern Scotland*, Edinburgh, 1985.

Schama, Simon, *Landscape and Memory*, London, 1996.
Schei, Liv K., *The Shetland Story*, London, 1988.
—, *The Faroe Islands*, London, 1991.
Scherman, Katharine, *Iceland: Daughter of Fire*, London, 1976.
Scott, William W., 'John of Fordun's Description of the Western Isles', *SS*, 23, 1979.
Scott-Moncrieff, Lesley (ed), *The Forty-Five: To Gather an Image Whole*, Edinburgh, 1988.
Sellar, W.D.H., 'The Origins and Ancestry of Somerled', *SHR*, 45, 1966.
—, 'Family Origins in Cowal and Knapdale', *SS*, 15, 1971.
—, 'Marriage, Divorce and Concubinage in Gaelic Scotland', *TGSI*, 51, 1978.
— (ed), *Moray: Province and People*, Edinburgh, 1993.
Sharpe, Richard, *Raasay: A Study in Island History*, 2 vols, London, 1977.
Sharpe, Richard (transl), *Adomnan of Iona: Life of St Columba*, London, 1995.
Shaw, Christina B., *Pigeon Holes of Memory: The Life and Times of Dr John MacKenzie*, London, 1988.
Shaw, Frances J., *The Northern and Western Islands of Scotland: Their Economy and Society in the Seventeenth Century*, Edinburgh, 1980.
Shearer, John, Groundwater, W. and MacKay, J.D. (eds), *The New Orkney Book*, London, 1966.
Simpson, Grant G. (ed), *Scotland and Scandinavia*, Edinburgh, 1990.
— (ed), *The Scottish Soldier Abroad*, Edinburgh, 1992.
— (ed), *Scotland and the Low Countries*, Aberdeen, 1996.
Simpson, James A., *Dornoch Cathedral*, Derby, 1989.
Simpson, W. Douglas, *Bishop's Palace and Earl's Palace*, Edinburgh, 1991.
Small, Alan (ed), *The Picts: A New Look at Old Problems*, Dundee, 1987.
Smith, Alan G.R. (ed), *The Reign of James VI and I*, London, 1973.
Smith, Annette M., *Jacobite Estates of the Forty-Five*, Edinburgh, 1982.
Smith, Brian (ed), *Shetland Archaeology*, Lerwick, 1985.
Smith, Hance D., *The Making of Modern Shetland*, Lerwick, 1977.
—, *Shetland Life and Trade, 1550-1914*, Edinburgh, 1984.
Smout, T. Christopher, *A History of the Scottish People, 1560-1830*, London, 1970.
—, 'Tours in the Highlands and Islands from the Eighteenth to the Twentieth Centuries', *NS*, 5, 1983.
—, *A Century of the Scottish People, 1830-1950*, London, 1986.
— (ed), *Scotland and the Sea*, Edinburgh, 1992.
—, *Scotland Since Prehistory: Natural Change and Human Impact*, Aberdeen, 1993.
— (ed), *Scottish Woodland History*, Edinburgh, 1997.
Smyth, Alfred P., *Warlords and Holy Men: Scotland, AD80-1000*, London, 1984.
Somers, Robert, *Letters from the Highlands on the Famine of 1846*, Inverness, 1977.
Spearman, Michael R. and Higgitt, John (eds), *The Age of Migrating Ideas: Early Medieval Art in Northern Britain and Ireland*, Edinburgh, 1993.
Speck, W.A., *The Butcher: The Duke of Cumberland and the Suppression of the Forty-Five*, Caernarfon, 1995.
Steer, K.A. and Bannerman, John, *Late Medieval Monumental Sculpture in the West Highlands*, Edinburgh, 1977.
Stevenson, David, *Alasdair MacColla and the Highland Problem in the Seventeenth Century*, Edinburgh, 1980.
Stewart, James A., 'The Clan Ranald and Catholic Missionary Successes, 1715-1745', *Innes Review*, 45, 1994.
Storrie, Margaret T., 'Landholdings and Population in Arran', *SS*, 11, 1967.
—, *Islay: Biography of an Island*, Isle of Islay, 1997.
Stringer, Keith J. (ed), *Essays on the Nobility of Medieval Scotland*, Edinburgh, 1985.
Sutherland, Iain, *Caithness*, Wick, 1995.
Symon, J.A., *Scottish Farming: Past and Present*, Edinburgh, 1959.

Szechi, Daniel, *The Jacobites: Britain and Europe, 1688-1788*, Manchester, 1994.
Tabraham, Chris and Grove, Doreen, *Fortress Scotland and the Jacobites*, London, 1995.
Taylor, William, *The Military Roads in Scotland*, Isle of Colonsay, 1996.
Thomas, Charles, *Celtic Britain*, London, 1986.
Thomas, John, *The Callander and Oban Railway*, Newton Abbot, 1966.
Thomas, John and Turnock, David, *A Regional History of the Railways of Great Britain: North of Scotland*, Newton Abbot, 1989.
Thomason, Edward, *Island Challenge*, Lerwick, 1997.
Thomson, Derick S., 'The MacMhuirich Bardic Family', *TGSI*, 43, 1963.
—, 'Gaelic Learned Orders and Literati in Medieval Scotland', *SS*, 12, 1968.
—, *An Introduction to Gaelic Poetry*, London, 1974.
— (ed), *The Companion to Gaelic Scotland*, Oxford, 1983.
— (ed), *Gaelic and Scots in Harmony*, Glasgow, 1990.
—, *Gaelic Poetry in the Eighteenth Century*, Aberdeen, 1993.
— (ed), *Alasdair MacMhaighstir Alasdair: Selected Poems*, Edinburgh, 1996.
Thomson, Derick S. and Grimble, I. (eds), *The Future of the Highlands*, London, 1968.
Thomson, William P. L., *The Little General and the Rousay Crofters: Crisis and Conflict on an Orkney Estate*, Edinburgh, 1981.
—, *Kelp-Making in Orkney*, Stromness, 1983.
—, *History of Orkney*, Edinburgh, 1987.
Todd, Malcolm, *Roman Britain*, London 1997.
Turner, Val, *Ancient Shetland*, London, 1988.
Turnock, David, *Patterns of Highland Development*, London, 1970.
University of the Highlands and Islands Project, *Prospectus 1999 Entry*, Inverness, 1998.
Wainwright, F.T. (ed), *The Problem of the Picts*, London, 1955.
— (ed), *The Northern Isles*, London, 1962.
Walker, David, *The Normans in Britain*, Oxford, 1995.
Walker, Graham, *Thomas Johnston*, Manchester, 1988.
Watson, Don, *Caledonia Australis: Scottish Highlanders on the Frontier of Australia*, Sydney, 1984.
Watson, J. Carmichael (ed), *Gaelic Songs of Mary MacLeod*, Edinburgh, 1965.
— (ed), *Scottish Verse from the Book of the Dean of Lismore*, Edinburgh, 1937.
Watt, D.E.R. (ed), *A History Book for Scots: Selections from the Scotichronicon*, Edinburgh, 1998.
Waugh, Doreen J. (ed), *Shetland's Northern Links: Language and History*, Edinburgh, 1996.
Wayne, Norton, 'Malcolm MacNeill and the Emigrationist Alternative to Highland Land Reform', *SHR*, 70, 1991.
Webster, Bruce, *Medieval Scotland: The Making of an Identity*, London, 1977.
West, John F., *Faroe: The Emergence of a Nation*, London, 1972.
Whitelock, D., McKitterick, R. and Dumville, D. (eds), *Ireland in Early Medieval Europe*, Cambridge, 1982.
Whittaker, C.R., *Frontiers of the Roman Empire*, London, 1994.
Whyte, Ian D., *Agriculture and Society in Seventeenth-Century Scotland*, Edinburgh, 1979.
—, *Scotland Before the Industrial Revolution: An Economic and Social History*, Harlow, 1995.
—, *Scotland's Society and Economy in Transition, 1500-1760*, London, 1997.
Whyte, Ian D. and Whyte, Kathleen, *The Changing Scottish Landscape*, London, 1991
Wickham-Jones, Caroline R., *Scotland's First Settlers*, London, 1994.
Wigan, Michael, *The Scottish Highland Estate: Preserving an Environment*, Shrewsbury, 1991.

Wightman, Andy, *Who Owns Scotland?*, Edinburgh, 1996.
Wilkie, Jim, *Metagama: A Journey from Lewis to the New World*, Edinburgh, 1987.
Williams, Ronald, *The Lords of the Isles*, London, 1984.
Williamson, Kenneth, *The Atlantic Islands: A Study of the Faroe Life and Scene*, London, 1948.
Willis, Douglas, *Discovering the Black Isle*, Edinburgh, 1989.
—, *The Story of Crofting in Scotland*, Edinburgh, 1991.
Wills, Jonathan, *A Place in the Sun: Shetland and Oil*, Edinburgh, 1991.
Willson, D. Harris, *King James VI and I*, London, 1956.
Wilson, Roger J.A., *A Guide to the Roman Remains in Britain*, London, 1980.
Withers, Charles W.J., *Gaelic in Scotland, 1698-1981: The Geographical History of a Language*, Edinburgh, 1984.
—, 'Kirk, Club and Culture Change: Gaelic Chapels, Highland Societies and the Urban Gaelic Subculture in Eighteenth-Century Scotland', *Social History*, 10, 1985.
—, 'Highland Clubs and Chapels: Glasgow's Gaelic Community in the Eighteenth Century', *Scottish Geographical Magazine*, 101, 1985.
—, *Highland Communities in Dundee and Perth, 1787-1891*, Dundee, 1986.
—, *Gaelic Scotland: The Transformation of a Culture Region*, London, 1988.
—, 'Highland Migration to Aberdeen, 1649-1891', *NS*, 9, 1989.
—, *Urban Highlanders: Highland-Lowland Migration and Urban Gaelic Culture*, East Linton, 1998.
Withrington, Donald J. (ed), *Shetland and the Outside World, 1469-1969*, Aberdeen, 1983.
Womack, Peter, *Improvement and Romance: Constructing the Myth of the Highlands*, London, 1989.
Wonders, William C., 'Orkney and the "Nor-Waast"', *Alberta History*, Winter, 1993.
Wood, Emma, *Notes from the North*, Edinburgh, 1998.
Wood, Ian and Lund, Niels (ed), *People and Places in Northern Europe, 500-600*, Woodbridge, 1991.
Wood, John D., 'Transatlantic Land Reform: America and the Crofters Revolt', *SHR*, 63, 1984.
Woosnam-Savage, Robert C. (ed), *1745: Charles Edward Stuart and the Jacobites*, Edinburgh, 1995.
Wormald, Jenny, *Court, Kirk and Community: Scotland, 1470-1625*, London, 1981.
—, *Scotland Revisited*, London, 1991.
Yeoman, Peter, *Medieval Scotland: An Archaeological Perspective*, London, 1995.
Young, Alan, *Robert the Bruce's Rivals: The Comyns*, East Linton, 1997.
Young, John R., *Celtic Dimensions of the British Civil Wars*, Edinburgh, 1997.
Youngson, A.J., *After the Forty-Five: The Economic Impact on the Scottish Highlands*, Edinburgh, 1973.
—, *The Prince and the Pretender*, Beckenham, 1985.

Index